SIXTH EDITION

the communication CIRCUIT

Reading and Writing Skills

June Baker
Confederation College

Prentice Hall Allyn and Bacon Canada
Scarborough, Ontario

To my husband, Fred, and children,
Susan, Allan, Dan, and Lindsay.

Canadian Cataloguing in Publication Data

Baker, June
  The communication circuit : reading and writing skills

6th ed.
Includes index.
ISBN 0-13-084180-3

1. English language — Composition and exercises. 2. English language
— Grammar — Problems, exercises, etc. 3. Reading comprehension
— Problems, exercises, etc. 4. Reading (Higher education) —
Problems, exercises, etc. 5. Study skills. I. Title.

PE1413.B34 2000   428.2'076   C99-930717-7

ISBN 0-13-084180-3

Vice President, Editorial Director: Laura Pearson
Acquisitions Editor: David Stover
Marketing Manager: Sophia Fortier
Developmental Editor: Susan Ratkaj
Production Editor: Cathy Zerbst
Copy Editor: Judith Turnbull
Production Coordinator: Wendy Moran
Art Director: Mary Opper
Cover Design: Sarah Battersby
Page Layout: Pixel Graphics Inc.

5 6 7 DPC 06 05 04 03

Printed and bound in Canada.

CONTENTS

UNIT SEVEN
WRITING MORE SKILLFULLY   267

PREFACE

Students at university, college, adult education centres, and high school have had various experiences with practical communication skills. This text reviews the reading, studying, and writing skills that they require to progress to the more complex skills of writing essays, reports, or creative works. *The Communication Circuit: Reading and Writing Skills, Sixth Edition* presents this review in a unique, practical, and self-motivating manner.

The text is divided into eight units, each with specific, measurable, student-centred learning objectives. The first three units present the foundation block of the program. In these sections, students are introduced to reading and study-skill techniques. First, students learn how to decode words by using word construction and context clues. Next, they learn how to comprehend what they read. They then apply these skills to reading materials, listening in lectures, and note-taking. Learning to identify a central theme, recognize patterns of development, and put this information in outline format — these skills not only are necessary for comprehension but also are effective ways for students to establish unity and coherence in their own writing projects. In these first three units, students also use freewriting assignments to get to know themselves as writers. This activity helps students to put their thoughts on paper — a task that many have not practised. These guided exercises are used in future assignments when students begin to take a more formal approach to writing.

The next five units present basic writing skills. Each contains an integration of spelling, grammar, punctuation, and composition. The combination of elements in each unit is designed to allow students to apply the new information immediately to their own writing needs. Variety and short-term goals keep them motivated; the immediate practical application helps them to develop good proofreading techniques. In the final section of Unit Eight, students apply their accumulated skills to study techniques in preparing for and writing essay examinations.

A guide to using the Internet as a resource (see pages 469–70) suggests online resources for those who may require additional research articles or practice in the grammar and writing objectives. Collaborative exercises are used throughout the text to encourage groups of students to work together on interesting and challenging exercises in which they apply the skills of the unit. All answers are contained within the text; included with many of these are explanations to reinforce the methods presented in the lesson. A Glossary of Terms is located at the back of the text, and a Quick Reference Guide and a Correction Symbols Guide are, respectively, on the inside front and back covers.

This self-evaluated, self-paced method encourages better use of students' time as it directs them to study just those skills that require upgrading and allows them to skip sections they already know. At the same time, however, they gain an understanding of the relevance of each skill in the total communication circuit. In this text, students are involved with acquiring communication skills that suit their personal needs.

Whenever possible, individual skills have been reinforced or related to those in other sections or units. Some examples of this kind of interrelationship are as follows:

- Vocabulary skills presented in the first unit are reinforced in the section on underlining and marginal notes.
- Comprehension skills, such as locating main ideas, understanding paragraph development, and outlining are reinforced in listening skills, note-taking techniques, and all the composition sections.
- Freewriting activities are used for proofreading exercises as well as for brainstorming information for formal compositions.
- Reading the newspaper is presented in Unit Two and reinforced in more detail in Units Three and Four.
- Directed use of the dictionary and thesaurus is reviewed in Unit Four and students are encouraged to use these reference books for all the spelling, grammar, and composition sections that follow.
- Diverse methods of sentence combining encourage students to create more effective sentence patterns in their writing assignments.
- Writing summaries, précis, and abstracts combines reading skills, use of the thesaurus, and sentence-combining skills.
- The review of plural forms of words in the spelling section of Unit Five is followed by a grammar lesson on subject-verb agreement.
- Composition lessons are reinforced and expanded in each of the successive units.
- In Unit Eight, grammar lessons on parallel structure are followed by composition lessons on writing a three-part thesis statement.
- The section in Unit Eight on studying and preparing for essay examinations requires students to use the skills from all eight units.

In fact, this text presents a picture of the complete communication circuit. The reading skills students learn in the first three units are the same skills they are taught to use in later units when they become the "authors" of what others will read.

Most sections end with a self-checking post-test on that particular section. Here, students apply the skills covered in the section to the type of integrated content they would meet in their everyday communication tasks. Each of the post-tests in the writing units includes an article for proofreading, which allows the students to develop the art of recognizing and correcting errors.

Units Six to Eight have formal writing assignments as well as integrated lessons and post-tests on the mechanics. Students are guided through practical composition lessons, which are reinforced and expanded in each of the successive units until students have mastered the skills of writing an expository essay of at least four paragraphs. In the collaborative exercises for these lessons, students are taught how to do peer marking and encouraged to discuss each other's writing plans and compositions.

The *Instructors' Manual* contains a test bank of questions that can be used for teacher-administered tests. Because of the number of questions, teachers can easily develop alternate test forms. In addition, the manual contains transparency masters and suggestions for program delivery.

NEW FEATURES OF THE SIXTH EDITION

- Quick Reference Guide to assist students in finding solutions for their immediate problems
- Revised exercises throughout
- Collaborative exercises in each unit
- Internet resource guide and instructions
- Tips for using the computer
- Correction Symbols Guide
- Instructions on peer marking

The learning objectives and materials in this text are all student-centred. *The Communication Circuit, Sixth Edition* presents in a logical order the essential communication skills that students require, illustrates the relevance of each skill to the others, and encourages students to make direct application of their accumulated learning. I hope you will find this program to be the "missing link" you have been searching for.

ACKNOWLEDGMENTS

I sincerely appreciate the guidance and assistance from all those who have contributed to creating this text. In particular I would like to thank the following reviewers: A.J. Sutherland, Cairine Wilson Secondary School; Nina Butska, Humber College; Joseph Lyons, St. Lawrence College; Marian Kowler, Grant McEwan Community College; John Pentick, Confederation College; Barbara Danbrook, Humber College; and Nancy Roby-Cassidy and Sandra Muir, the Institute for Early Childhood Education and Developmental Services. Their thorough reviews and expert opinions helped me to improve and expand my original ideas.

I also offer my sincere thanks to the students and to my former colleagues from Confederation College who, throughout the years, were great supporters and critics of my work and offered such positive suggestions. Most of all, I am grateful for the opportunity of working with the expert editorial staff at Prentice Hall, Allyn and Bacon Canada. Special thanks to Cliff Newman, Marta Tomins, Susan Ratkaj, Imogen Brian, Chelsea Donaldson, Cathy Zerbst, and Judith Turnbull for your thoroughness and care in the preparation and production of this sixth edition.

June Baker

DISCOVERING VOCABULARY SKILLS

There are many words in the English language that help to express our thoughts and actions. However, our ability to comprehend a writer's message depends on the level of vocabulary used and on the limits of our own vocabulary. Occasionally, these two levels do not match!

When you are reading a textbook, a novel, or an article, what do you do when you meet a word you do not understand? Some people skip the word and continue to read without understanding its meaning. This practice is acceptable *if* you understand the overall content and do not skip too many words. Other people stop reading and puzzle over the pronunciation and meaning of each word they do not know. A few others stop reading and look up each unknown word in a dictionary. If you use either of these last two approaches, you are not applying effective reading skills. If you focus on individual words and continually interrupt your concentration, you will reduce your overall understanding of the content.

In this unit, you will learn or review two main vocabulary skills—namely, "guessing" the definition of a word by knowing the meanings of its various parts and interpreting definitions from the clues given by all other words contained in the sentence or passage.

In addition, you will begin the first in a series of freewriting activities. These exercises will help you to know yourself as a communicator and to begin practising the art of transferring your thoughts to paper. The collection of your writings will serve as a basis for future lessons and exercises.

LEARNING OBJECTIVES FOR UNIT ONE

Upon completion of this unit, you should be able to:

1. Determine the definitions of words by their construction. Specifically,
   a) recall and apply the common Latin and Greek prefixes that are used in everyday language
   b) recall common root words and identify their meanings
   c) identify the meaning of words according to their suffixes, and apply this knowledge in your writing

2. Decide the meaning of unknown words by using the following context-clue methods:
   a) recalling and using clue words that suggest an explanation will follow
   b) using the action in the sentence as a clue to define a word
   c) analyzing the circumstances described in the sentence or paragraph
   d) using expressions of similarities and differences as guides

3. Communicate personal comments and attitudes in letter-writing style as a way of getting to know yourself as a writer.

PRETEST: WORD CONSTRUCTION

I. By using only the prefix (first portion of the word), try to determine the word or phrase that best defines each of the following words. This exercise tests your ability to use prefixes, root words, and suffixes in helping you determine the meaning of unknown words.

1. prepense
   a) monetary term used in England
   b) to be sorry for
   c) planned beforehand

2. circumflex
   a) flakes of dandruff on a collar
   b) muscular arms
   c) winding around

3. surplusage
   a) excess words; irrelevant material
   b) feathers of a bird
   c) very old

4. tripartite
   a) the stomach of an animal used as food
   b) divided into three parts
   c) stepping lightly

5. postprandial
   a) after dinner
   b) a part of an automatic telephone
   c) causing fright or horror

II. From the clue words given in each question, determine the correct meaning of the root word.

6. dis*tract*   The root *tract* means   a) possess
    re*tract*   (b) draw or pull
    ab*stract*   c) build

7. tran*sport*   The root *port* means   a) hold
    im*port*   b) say or speak
    re*port*   (c) carry

8. *dict*aphone   The root *dict* means   (a) say or speak
    pre*dict*   b) live
    contra*dict*   c) lie

9. pre*scribe*   The root *scribe* means   a) possess
    sub*scrip*tion   (b) write
    de*scribe*   c) hang

10. inter*ject*   The root *ject* means   a) say or speak
    re*ject*   b) guess
    con*ject*ure   (c) throw or hurl

III. By referring to the suffix (the last portion of a word) of each of the following word choices, choose the appropriate word to suit the meaning of the sentence. (Some choices may require an "s" to make their meaning suit the sentence.)

11. a) dermatology   Because she appeared to have a form of ___dermatitis___,
     b) dermatologist   she made an appointment to see a doctor.
     c) dermatitis

12. a) fearless   The courageous man was ___fearless___ in
     b) fearful   the face of danger.
     c) feared

13. a) employment   The applicant was interviewed and hired by the ___employer___ ;
     b) employee   she was asked to start work at the beginning of the week.
     c) employer

14. a) symbolist   Colour ___b___ differs from one culture to another; for example, in
     b) symbolism   Japan white, not black, is the symbol of mourning.
     c) symbolize

15. a) communicative   I suspected that John's ___communicative___ skills were weak
     b) communicable   because he began the semester by making excuses for not comple-
     c) communication   ting his reading and writing assignments.
     d) communicator

Check your answers with those in the Answer section at the end of the book.

If you were successful in every section of the test (I, II, and III), proceed to the Pretest for "Context Clues." If you had more than one error in any section, review the appropriate vocabulary skills on the following pages.

WORD CONSTRUCTION

Much of our vocabulary originated from ancient Latin and Greek. Many English words were created by combining prefixes, roots, and suffixes drawn from two or more of these languages. Your ability to recognize and define some of these common derivatives will help you to unlock the meanings of many words.

I. PREFIXES

A prefix is one or more letters (of Latin, Greek, or English origin) that can be attached to the beginning of a word to give it meaning; for example,

unicycle *bicycle* *tricycle*

Review the following lists of common prefixes, their meanings, and example words; then complete each exercise that follows.

COMMON PREFIXES DEALING WITH NUMBERS

Prefix	Meaning	Origin	Example Word
uni-	one	(Latin)	*uni*que—*one* of a kind
mono-		(Greek)	*mono*gamy—having only *one* husband or wife at a time
bi-	two	(Latin)	*bi*lingual—speaking *two* languages
tri-	three	(Latin)	*tri*angle—a figure having *three* straight sides and *three* angles
quad-	four	(Latin)	*quad*ruped—a *four*-footed animal
cent-	one hundred	(Latin)	*cent*ennial—*one hundred* years
milli-	one thousand	(Latin)	*milli*on—*one thousand* times *one thousand*
mille-			*mille*nnium—a *thousand* years
hemi-	half	(Greek)	*hemi*sphere—*half* a sphere
semi-	half, partly	(Latin)	*semi*circle—*half* a circle
			*semi*skilled—*partly* skilled

● EXERCISE 1.1

By referring to the list of common prefixes dealing with numbers, add the appropriate prefix to create the word that suits the given definition.

1.	_____ plane	an airplane with two sets of wings, one above the other
2.	_____ rilateral	a four-sided figure
3.	_____ son	together as one
4.	_____ ury	a period of one hundred years
5.	_____ pod	a three-legged stand for a camera
6.	_____ conscious	partly conscious
7.	_____ rail	a railroad whose train runs on a single rail
8.	_____ second	one thousandth of a second
9.	_____ tone	a single unvaried tone
10.	_____ focals	eyeglasses having two portions, one for near and one for far vision
11.	_____ foliate	having three leaves, leaflets, or leaflike parts
12.	_____ lateral	involving or done by only one person or group
13.	_____ sphere	half of the terrestrial globe or celestial sphere
14.	_____ nary	consisting of, indicating, or involving two
15.	_____ rant	a quarter of a circle

Check your answers with those in the Answer section at the end of the book.

COMMON PREFIXES DEALING WITH POSITION

Prefix	Meaning	Origin	Example Word
trans-	across	(Latin)	*trans*port—carry *across*
circum-	around	(Latin)	*circum*navigate—sail or fly *around*
inter-	between	(Latin)	*inter*rupt—break *between*
sub-	under, below	(Latin)	*sub*terranean—*under* the earth
sur-	over	(Latin)	*sur*pass—go *beyond* or *over*
contra- contro-	against	(Latin)	*contra*dict—speak *against* *contro*versy—an argument *against*
anti-	against	(Greek)	*anti*thesis—a *contrasting* statement
pre- ante-	before	(Latin) (Latin)	*pre*arrange—arrange *before*hand *ante*nuptial—*before* marriage
post-	after	(Latin)	*post*war—*after* the war
pro-	forward, in in favour of	(Latin)	*pro*duce—bring *forward* *pro*-American—*in favour of* Americans

● EXERCISE 1.2

By referring to the list of common prefixes dealing with position, add the appropriate prefix to create the word that suits the given definition.

1.	_____ marine	a warship designed to operate under the sea
2.	_____ vent	go around
3.	_____ vene	act against
4.	_____ cede	go before

5. _____ script   an addition to a letter written after the writer's name has been signed (usually referred to in abbreviated form as P.S.)

6. _____ scholastic between or among schools

7. _____ pathy   a feeling against

8. _____ locution   a roundabout way of speaking

9. _____ plus   an amount over or above what is needed

10. _____ ject   throw or cast forward

11. _____ abortion   in favour of abortion

12. _____ standard   below standard

13. _____ operative occurring after a surgical operation

14. _____ feit   an excessive amount; overindulgence

15. _____ ition   passage from one position, state, stage, or subject to another

Check your answers with those in the Answer section at the end of the book.

ADDITIONAL IMPORTANT PREFIXES

Prefix	Meaning	Origin	Example Word
in-		(Latin)	*in*considerate—*not* considerate
im-*		(Latin)	*im*mature—*not* mature
il-*	not or never	(Latin)	*il*legal—*not* legal
ir-*		(Latin)	*ir*religious—*not* religious
un-	not, the opposite of	(Old English)	*un*accustomed—*not* accustomed
multi-	many, much	(Latin)	*multi*coloured—having *many* colours
micro-	small	(Greek)	*micro*film—a photograph on film of pages of books, newspapers, or records that can be preserved in a very *small* space
re-	again or back	(Latin)	*re*ject—throw *back*
			*re*juvenate—make young *again*
mis-	wrong	(Old English)	*mis*deal—deal *incorrectly*
con-		(Latin)	*con*centric—having the *same* centre
com-**	together with,	(Latin)	*com*bine—join *together*
col-**	jointly	(Latin)	*col*laborate—work *together*
cor-**		(Latin)	*cor*relate—be *jointly* related
pseudo-	false, pretended	(Greek)	*pseudo*-scientific—*falsely* presented as scientific
retro-	backward, back to	(Latin)	*retro*active—applying *back to* a previous time

* Use each of these negative prefixes in the following manner: *il*—before l; *im*—before b, m, p; and *ir*—before r. (These are all variations of the prefix *in*.)

** Use *col*—before l; *com*—before b, m, p; and *cor*—before r. (These are all variations of the prefix *con*.)

● EXERCISE 1.3

By referring to the list just given, add the appropriate prefix to create the word that suits the given definition.

1. _____ national   dealing with or concerning many nations

2. _____ nym   a fictitious or false name used by an author to conceal his or her identity

3. _____ spect   a looking back to; thinking about the past

4. _____ conceive   have the wrong idea about

5. _____ usual   not usual

6. _____ defatigable   never getting tired; tireless

7. _____ meter   an instrument for measuring very small distances, angles, objects, etc.

8. _____ relevant   not related to the subject; off topic

9. _____ cur   agree in opinion; work together

10. _____ silient   springing back; returning to the original form or position after being bent

11. _____ intellectual   giving the appearance of intelligence

12. _____ cosm   the world in miniature

13. _____ construe   get the wrong meaning

14. _____ iterate   say again

15. _____ talented   having many skills

Check your answers with those in the Answer section at the end of the book.

● EXERCISE 1.4—REVIEW

By relying only on your knowledge of prefixes or by reference to the various lists previously given, choose the appropriate meaning for each of the following words.

1. *sub*liminal
   a) an ointment used for superficial burns
   b) a happy state
   c) below the conscious state

2. *inter*im
   a) a storm without hail
   b) a time between
   c) a shout of warning to those ahead

3. *post*prandial
   a) an instrument for telling the time by the position of the sun
   b) after dinner
   c) a person or vehicle that carries mail

4. qua*d*raphonic
 a) reproduction of sound over four separate transmission channels
 b) not genuine or real
 c) an attractive subject in a photograph

5. *uni*lingual
 a) remaining in a place
 b) joining together
 c) having knowledge of only one language

6. *mis*nomer
 a) an error in naming
 b) a proper title of an important person
 c) a group of musical notes in the lower clef

7. *im*pervious
 a) kingly or regal
 b) not able to be influenced or affected
 c) rational and informed

8. co*ll*usion
 a) anything thin and slight such as a spider's web
 b) a conspiracy; an acting together for some wrong purpose
 c) a glue-like liquid that dries very rapidly and leaves a tough, waterproof, transparent film

9. *un*daunted
 a) frightened
 b) small and active
 c) not afraid; not discouraged

10. *micro*fiche
 a) an instrument that measures distance
 b) a very small flat sheet of film that contains a very tiny copy of printed or other graphic matter
 c) a special cooker for seafood

11. *bi*cuspid
 a) a tooth having two points
 b) past or gone by
 c) guardianship or care

12. *cent*enarian
 a) a mythical creature having the head, trunk, and arms of a human and the body and legs of a horse
 b) a person who has reached the age of one hundred
 c) a member of a business and professional club

13. *contra*vene
 a) an artery in the leg
 b) a minor offence
 c) do or act against

14. *retro*gress
 a) forward action
 b) go backward into a worse condition
 c) a meeting for Members of Parliament

15. *inane*
   a) not sensible
   b) with consideration
   c) like a child

Check your answers with those in the Answer section at the end of the book.

II. ROOT WORDS

A root—the basic component of a word (in Latin, Greek, or English)—is situated at the beginning, middle, or end of a word depending on the prefixes or suffixes required to express the meaning of the word.

● EXERCISE 1.5

The following is a list of common roots with their meanings and origins. A sentence follows each of the sample roots to illustrate its meaning. Read each one carefully, then think of two other words containing the same root meaning and write them in the spaces provided.

1. *lingua*—tongue; language (Latin)
   He was completely *bilingual*; he could speak English and French fluently.

   Two other words containing the same root meaning are
   a) _trilingual_ ✓   b) _tetralingual_

2. *cap, capit*—head (Latin)
   Because of his ability to lead and inspire others, Eric was chosen to be the *captain* of the team.

   Two other words containing the same root meaning are
   a) _capital_ ✓   b) _caption_ ✓

3. *pos, pon*—put or place (Latin)
   To *compose* an essay, you must collect the facts and put them together in a logical and effective fashion.

   Two other words containing the same root meaning are
   a) _possibility_   b) _upon_

4. *duce, duct*—lead (Latin)
   After overeating during the holidays, many people go on diets to *reduce*.

   Two other words containing the same root meaning are
   a) _deduce_ ✓   b) _ductile_

5. *spec, spect, spic*—see or look (Latin)
   The *spectators* watched the game.

   Two other words containing the same root meaning are
   a) _special_   b) _suspect_

6. *aud, audit*—hear or listen (Latin)
Because she was just *auditing* the course, she only had to listen; she didn't have to write the exams.

Two other words containing the same root meaning are

a) audition ✓   b) audio

7. *tract*—pull or draw (Latin)
The *tractor* pulled the hay wagon.

Two other words containing the same root meaning are

a) subtract ✓   b) abstract ✓

8. *cred*—believe (Latin)
That was an *incredible* story; I didn't believe a word of it.

Two other words containing the same root meaning are

a) credibility ✓   b) credit ✓

9. *rupt*—break (Latin)
He was rushed to the hospital with a *ruptured* appendix.

Two other words containing the same root meaning are

a) bankruptcy ✓   b) corrupt ✓

10. *ject*—throw or hurl (Latin)
The noisy patrons were *ejected* from the lounge when they refused to leave of their own accord.

Two other words containing the same root meaning are

a) subject ✓   b) interject ✓

11. *dict*—say or speak (Latin)
I will *dictate* the spelling words to the class.

Two other words containing the same root meaning are

a) dictionary ✓   b) dictator

12. *ped, pod*—foot (Latin)
At concerts, a conductor stands on a *podium* so that all members of the orchestra can easily see and follow his directions.

Two other words containing the same root meaning are

a) tripod ✓   b) pedestrian ✓

13. *scribe, script*—write or writings (Latin)
In the morning edition of the paper, the news reporter *described* the horror and tragedy of the fires in California.

Two other words containing the same root meaning are

a) subscribe   b) subscription ✓

14. *derm*—skin (Greek)
I went to see a *dermatologist* about my skin problems.

Two other words containing the same root meaning are

a) dermabrasion   b) subdermal

15. *port*—carry, bring (Latin)
We purchased a small *portable* television set so that we could watch TV in any room in the house.

Two other words containing the same root meaning are
a) _transport_ ✓   b) _reporter_ ✓

16. *phobia*—hatred or fear of (Greek)
Because I suffer from *claustrophobia,* I feel nervous whenever I step into an elevator. I am terrified that I will be trapped in that small enclosed space.

Two other words containing the same root meaning are
a) _Arachnophobia_ ✓   b) _controphobia_

17. *pathy, pathos*—feeling (Greek)
I have a great deal of *empathy* for students in English because I remember struggling to understand the relevance of all the facts my English teachers tried to teach me.

Two other words containing the same root meaning are
a) _sympathy_ ✓   b) _telepathy_ ✓

18. *vent, vene*—come (Latin)
At a *convention,* people with the same affiliations come together to share experiences and learn about their general area of interest.

Two other words containing the same root meaning are
a) _adventure_ ✓   b) _ventricle_

19. *loqua, loqui, locu*—talk (Latin)
Loquacious people love to talk.

Two other words containing the same root meaning are
a) _colloquial_ ✓   b) _locution_

20. *thesis, theses*—a placing (Latin/Greek)
Parentheses are special marks placed around a group of words that the writer would like to add to a statement.

Two other words containing the same root meaning are
a) _antithesis_ ✓   b) _thesis_ ✓

Check your answers with those in the Answer section at the end of the book.

● EXERCISE 1.6

By using your knowledge of root words and prefixes or by referring to the previous lists, write the meanings of the following words.

1. retract _to pull or draw back_ ✓

2. unilingual _one language_ ✓

3. centipede _one hundred feet legs_

4. retrospect _to see or look back_ ✓

5. incredible <u>*hot believable* ✓</u>
6. antithesis <u>*opposite placing contrasting idea*</u>
7. intervene <u>*to come between* ✓</u>
8. circumlocution <u>*around talk around about way of talking*</u>
9. antipathy <u>*opposed feeling* ✓</u>
10. interrupt <u>*to come and break between* ✓</u>

Check your answers with those in the Answer section at the end of the book.

III. SUFFIXES

A suffix is one or more letters attached to the end of a word that change its meaning or function. Your knowledge of these common suffixes (of Latin, Greek, or English origin) will help you to define and use words more accurately.

EASILY DEFINED SUFFIXES

Suffix	Meaning	Example Word
-ful	full of	beauti*ful*—*full* of beauty
-less	without or less	penni*less*—*without* a penny
-ous	abounding in, plenty of	spaci*ous*—*plenty of* space
-hood	state or condition	liveli*hood*—*condition* of living
-al	relating to	person*al*—*relating to* a person
-ward	in the direction of	home*ward*—*in the direction of* home
-er } -or }	the person who	farm*er*—*the person who* farms inspect*or*—*the person who* inspects
-ee	the person to whom	employ*ee*—*the person to whom* employment is given
-ible } -able }	able to	aud*ible*—*able to* be heard believ*able*—*able* to be believed

● EXERCISE 1.7

Look at the suffixes of the word choices given below, and choose the appropriate word for each space in the following sentences.

employee
employer

1. The _____ hired the _____ to begin work on Monday.

spacial
spacious

2. My _____ sense is not great, but even I could tell that the apartment was _____ enough for the two of us.

merciless
merciful
mercy

3. The victim cried for _____ but the assailant was _____ and refused to be _____ in his treatment.

fear
fearful
fearless

4. The courageous soldier was _____ in the face of grave danger and showed no visible signs of _____ even though all others in the company were very _____ and shook and trembled as the enemy approached.

educational
educable

5. People are most _____ when they are young. This is the time when most learning takes place. Therefore, to develop the mind and make full use of your potential, you should stay in school and take advantage of every _____ opportunity.

Check your answers with those in the Answer section at the end of the book.

THE DEFINITIONS OF MORE DIFFICULT SUFFIXES

Suffix	Meaning	Example Word
-ist	a person who	special*ist*—*a person who* specializes
-ish	inclined to be	fool*ish*—*inclined to be* a fool
-ise -ize	make or act	advert*ise*—*make* known or public / dramat*ize*—*act* as one in a drama or play
-ism	a practice or doctrine	critic*ism*—the *practice* of criticizing
-itis	an inflammation of	appendic*itis*—*an inflammation of* the appendix
-ive	likely to	imitat*ive*—*likely to* imitate
-ology	study of	bi*ology*—*study of* living organisms
-let	little or small	book*let*—*small* book
-cide	killer/killing of	insecti*cide*—*killing of* insects

● EXERCISE 1.8

Add the appropriate suffix to each of the following root words.

1. geno _____   systematic measures for the extermination of a national, cultural, religious, or racial group
2. pamph _____   a small book
3. radi _____   the study of radioactive waves or X-rays
4. dermat _____   inflammation of the skin
5. pass _____   likely to submit without resistance
6. gar _____   inclined to be showy or gaudy
7. horticultur _____   one skilled in growing flowers, fruits, vegetables, etc.

8. hypnot _____ the practice or theory of artificially inducing a sleep-like state
9. vapour _____ make or change into vapour
10. real _____ one who views things as they are
11. pessim _____ one who tends to see only the gloomy side of life
12. soci _____ the study of the origin, development, organization, and functioning of human society
13. minim _____ make smaller; reduce to the smallest possible amount or degree
14. styl _____ inclined to conform to the present styles, especially in dress
15. act _____ likely to act or to be in motion
16. rivu _____ a small stream
17. tonsil _____ inflammation of the tonsils
18. sui _____ the act of deliberately killing oneself
19. optim _____ the doctrine or practice of looking at the best side of life
20. verbal _____ make or put into words

Check your answers with those in the Answer section at the end of the book.

THE NEXT STEP

If you feel confident about this section, proceed to the pretest for "Context Clues."

PRETEST: CONTEXT CLUES

Read each of the following and circle the correct meaning of the word suggested by the sentence clues. This exercise tests your ability to interpret the meanings of words by the way they are used in a sentence or paragraph.

1. Good is the *antithesis* of evil.

antithesis means
a) highest degree
b) equal
c) opposite
d) lowest form

2. The mayor's *innocuous* remarks could not possibly have hurt anyone's feelings.

innocuous means
a) sarcastic
b) angry
c) harmless
d) long-winded

3. The dilapidated old railway station marred the *aesthetics* of the scenic park area.

aesthetics means
a) ugliness
b) beauty
c) transportation
d) layout

4. After she had won a million dollars, she developed a very *opulent* lifestyle; as a matter of fact, from that point on, she insisted on having only the best.

opulent means
a) rich
b) poor
c) precise
d) careless

5. Many impersonators and cartoonists gain popularity by exaggerating the *idiosyncrasies* of politicians.

idiosyncrasy means
a) perfect manners
b) specific habits
c) acts of imitation
d) moments of brilliance

6. The speaker was so *verbose* that, after fifteen minutes, the audience became restless.

verbose means
a) funny
b) true
c) honest
d) wordy

7. I am more of a loner than my *gregarious* sister; I prefer the company of a good book whereas she loves to be with other people.

gregarious means
a) nice
b) sociable
c) miserable
d) unfriendly

8. Mr. Morris was so concerned about his students that, to many of them, he became a *surrogate* father.

surrogate means
a) surprise
b) called by name
c) substitute
d) mean

9. Because Bill did not make enough money to cover his expenses, he took a second part-time job to *augment* his income.

augment means
a) increase
b) check
c) reduce
d) spend

10. The children were so *mesmerized* by the storyteller that they couldn't keep their eyes away from her.

mesmerized means
a) recognized
b) unhappy about
c) spellbound
d) disappointed

Check your answers with those in the Answer section at the end of the book.

If you had eight or more answers correct, write the Unit One Post-Test. If you had fewer than eight answers correct, complete the lesson that begins on the following page.

CONTEXT CLUES

Words are very rarely used in isolation. Except for one-word commands, such as "come" or "go," words are generally used with several others to convey a message. If you can learn to define a word by using the ideas expressed in all the other words surrounding it—which we refer to as context clues—then you will have developed a very useful vocabulary skill. For example, there are clue words or ideas in the following sentence that should indicate the meaning of the word *vitriolic*.

> She was so angry and bitter about having to work the late shift that even her responses to simple questions were *vitriolic*.

Given the clue words *angry and bitter*, which describe the person's mood, you can assume that vitriolic has somewhat the same meaning; therefore, if you guessed that vitriolic means bitter, angry, sharp, sarcastic, or any other caustic quality, you would be correct.

Learning to guess the meanings of words both by their construction and by the way they are used in a sentence or paragraph is an excellent vocabulary skill that not only will help you to define words, but will also give you a better overall understanding of what you have read. These skills, however, must be learned and practised so that you can easily adapt them to your natural reading habits.

There are several context-clue methods that will help you unlock the meaning of words.

I. WORDS OF EXPLANATION

These clue words are often introduced by phrases such as *in other words*, *that is*, *or*, and *that is to say*. For example, look for clue words that will unlock the meaning of the word *procrastinate*.

> People should not procrastinate about doing routine duties; *that is*, they should never put off until tomorrow what they can possibly do today.

The clue words *that is* are followed by an explanation of what the word *procrastinate* means.

NOTE: The clue word *or* can be used in two ways:
1) to indicate a choice

> Willie *or* Andy will represent us. (one or the other)

2) to explain the meaning of the preceding word. Usually commas are placed around the explanation.

> Colloquial, *or* informal, expressions should not be used in formal reports.
> (Here, the word *colloquial* is explained as meaning *informal*.)

II. SENTENCE ACTION

Often, the action in a sentence describes the situation—which, in turn, gives the reader a reasonable understanding of an unknown word. For example, look at the action in the following sentence to see if you can determine the meaning of the word *allay*.

> To *allay* her fear of darkness, the child slept with her night light on.

The description of the child's action should indicate to the reader that *allay* must mean *relieve* or *lessen*.

● EXERCISE 1.9

By using the two context-clue methods, write the meaning of each of the italicized words in the following sentences.

1. Children are often *pugnacious,* or quarrelsome, just to gain attention.

   pugnacious means _____

2. The slick car vendor *inveigled* the foolish young man into buying an expensive sports car rather than an affordable used one.

   inveigled means _____

3. At one time or another, we all encounter our *nemesis* in life; that is, we are punished, in some way, for our wrongdoings.

   nemesis means _____

4. His movements were so *lethargic* it took him forever to finish the job.

   lethargic means _____

5. Chemical dependency has been recognized as a *pernicious* disease. Did you know that this illness can cause great harm or even death if the afflicted person does not seek help or treatment?

   pernicious means _____

6. After playing five sets of tennis, she was totally *enervated;* she didn't have one ounce of energy left!

   enervated means _____

7. Everyone laughs at Rona's *facetious* remarks; her quick wit is a refreshing change from serious conversations.

   facetious means _____

8. In days of old, people wore *amulets* to ward off evil spirits.

   amulet means _____

9. Making a good speech involves the skill of *kinesics;* communicating with appropriate and effective gestures and facial expressions greatly enhances what one has to say.

   kinesics means _____

10. Because of her seemingly natural business *acumen,* or keen insight in business ventures, Lisa's suggestions and advice were always well respected by her colleagues.

   acumen means _____

Check your answers with those in the Answer section at the end of the book.

III. CIRCUMSTANCES

Look at the circumstances described in the sentence or group of sentences in which the word appears. If you can assess and analyze the whole situation, this general information may help you to get the gist of the word. For example, look at the whole situation presented in the following group of sentences to see if you can determine the meaning of the word *juxtaposition*.

> To solve any kind of problem, arrange all possible solutions in *juxtaposition*. Then try to visualize the result of each of the various combinations. After carefully analyzing all reasonable conclusions, you should be able to solve the problem by selecting the choice that seems to be the most effective.

Examining the total concept of this paragraph, you should note that many solutions have to be considered (and probably compared) if you are to arrive at the best solution; therefore, juxtaposition must mean *placed close together or side by side (as done for comparison or contrast)*.

IV. SIMILARITIES AND DIFFERENCES

Many times, the writer will tell you what the unknown word does *not* mean; or he or she will state exactly what the word does mean. For example, the following sentence describes the opposite meaning of the word *commodious*.

> The bedrooms of our summer cottage are certainly not *commodious*. They are so small that there is barely room for a bed and a dresser.

From the clues in the sentence, the reader knows that commodious means the opposite of small and crowded; therefore, the word must mean *spacious and roomy*.

● EXERCISE 1.10

By using these last two context-clue methods, write the meaning of each of the italicized words in the following sentences.

1. *Apocalyptic* environmentalists present a bleak view of the future of the planet if we do not change our wasteful habits.

   apocalyptic means __end of the world prophesying events of great significance__

2. Parents usually do not appreciate the *cacophonous* sounds of heavy metal music. The volume, the harshness, and the unmelodious tones all grate on their nerves.

   cacophonous means __harsh sound__ ✓

3. No one could possibly describe Mary as *ingenuous*. Not only is she suspicious of other people's actions but often she herself is dishonest.

   ingenuous means __naive__ ✓

4. Teenagers have *insatiable* appetites. They are constantly looking for something to eat!

   insatiable means __can't be satisfied__ ✓

5. Her *indolence* was the main reason she failed. She was always late to class, had a million excuses for not doing her homework, and did not put any effort into her program.

   indolence means __laziness__ ✓

6. Staying up all night and cramming for that exam proved to be a *nugatory* exercise; when I sat down at the exam and read the questions, my mind went blank!

   nugatory means __futile__ ✓

7. Most people enjoy tuning in to a radio station that presents an *eclectic* music selection. Programs that include everything from classical to modern jazz, blues, and even country and western give their audiences the opportunity to learn and experience something from every phase of the music world.

   eclectic means ___*a variety made up of a selection from various sources*___

8. Naturally, Ted became more *amenable* to the idea of being transferred to another city when the company offered him a promotion.

   amenable means ___*responsive* ✓___

9. The new computer system's two file servers will be *in tandem*; therefore, if one is down, the other will take over and the only disruption will be a slightly reduced operating speed.

   in tandem means ___*working together one following the other*___

10. *Plagiarism* is similar to stealing. If students copy other people's work without giving proper credit to the original source, and submit this written work as their own, they are committing a crime. In a college or university setting, this crime is punishable by a failing grade, or, in some cases, expulsion.

    plagiarism means ___*copying others work and handing it as theirs* ✓___

Check your answers with those in the Answer section at the end of the book.

● EXERCISE 1.11—REVIEW

Write the meaning of each italicized word by using the four context-clue methods presented in this lesson; namely,

- look for words of explanation.
- look at the action in the sentence(s).
- look at the circumstances that involve the unknown word.
- look for clues of similarities or differences.

1. The two older men were both so *garrulous* that no one else had an opportunity to say a word!

   garrulous means _____

2. *Egotism,* or self-centredness, is often the cause of many misunderstandings or quarrels.

   egotism means _____

3. The good news was *disseminated* quickly. In a matter of minutes, people all over the world knew that the hostages had, at last, been freed.

   disseminate means _____

4. His *affable* nature made him a friend to all.

   affable means _____

5. I hate *strident* sounds, such as chalk or fingernails screeching on a blackboard.

   strident means _____

6. We do not have a *nepotism* clause in our hiring policy. As long as the prospective employee has the proper job qualifications, anyone—including relatives—can work here.

   nepotism means _____

7. *Pedantic* people really annoy me. Their constant need to impress you with their knowledge is both tiring and boring.

   pedantic means _____

8. Some people have a difficult time making up their minds. They *vacillate* for hours or even days before finally making a decision.

   vacillate means _____

9. NATO and UNICEF are *acronyms* that are so commonly used that many of us have forgotten what words these letters originally represented.

   acronym means _____

10. The chairperson reminded the members of the committee to restrict their discussion to issues that were *germane* to the problem. Too many unrelated ideas were being introduced.

    germane means _____

11. The lecturer was anything but *succinct* in her discussion; she talked for what seemed like hours about the same issue.

    succinct means _____

12. Documented facts are an *integral* part of any report. Without well-supported proof for what you are proposing, your whole report will be considered worthless by any professional person.

    integral means _____

13. Communication problems often arise when words are not correctly arranged within a sentence. Good writers observe the rules of *syntax* to ensure that their messages will be clearly understood.

    syntax means _____

14. Expressing the same idea more than once is *redundant*.

    redundant means _____

15. It is easy to listen in class if the professor is confident about the subject matter, has a good speaking voice, and does not *deviate* from the main topic.

    deviate means _____

Check your answers with those in the Answer section at the end of the book.

V. COMBINING WORD CONSTRUCTION AND CONTEXT CLUES

Often, a written passage will contain more than one word whose exact meaning you do not understand; however, by using both word construction and the context as clues, you may still be able to interpret the paragraph.

● EXERCISE 1.12

By using clues about both word construction and context, write the meaning of each italicized word in the following passages. Do not concentrate on the word alone; see it in relation to the paragraph.

City-lovers are often *mesmerized* by the never-ending changes of the "*streetscape*" of the city. People can walk down the same street a hundred times and be fascinated by things that they had not taken the time to be aware of before. *Gargoyles,* ugly statues believed to ward off evil spirits, are often part of an historic building; and even though these are *grotesque* in appearance, they add to the character and beauty of the street scene. Various architectural designs, colours of buildings, signs in windows, and menus on display at the front of a restaurant, all contribute to the *kaleidoscope* of the city scene that never fails to enchant those who are ready to appreciate their *diverse,* but *unique,* surroundings. Although years go by and changes do take place, the city holds a fascination that never *palls;* there will always be people interested in what is going on around them.[1]

1. *mesmerized* means ___fascinated ✓___
2. *streetscape* means ___the look of the street___
3. *gargoyle* means ___ugly statues ✓___
4. *grotesque* means ___ugly ✓___
5. *kaleidoscope* means ___various designs in different colours continuous change of patterns and colours___
6. *diverse* means ___a variety ✓___
7. *unique* means ___one of a kind ✓___
8. *palls* means ___never end becomes tiresome___

Many new young executives are *cognizant* of the risks they are taking in beginning a new business venture. None of them are satisfied with *mediocrity* as they realize that only a *herculean* effort in their first years will help them achieve a *lucrative* business; that is, one that will provide reasonable profits for them to get established. These *entrepreneurs* are willing to work long, hard hours to create their own commercial *enterprise* and eventually reap the *monetary,* or financial, rewards that accompany success.

9. *cognizant* means ___consciously aware ✓___
10. *mediocrity* means ___just okay average ability___
11. *herculean* means ___very strong ✓___
12. *lucrative* means ___profitable ✓___
13. *entrepreneur* means ___a motivated self-employed individual I can't fit it in___
14. *enterprise* means ___a business an important undertaking___
15. *monetary* means ___financial ✓___

Check your answers with those in the Answer section at the end of the book.

In your own reading, if no clues are given about difficult words and your understanding of a passage is hampered, circle the word, consult your dictionary or the glossary at the end of your text, and write the meaning of the word in the top or bottom margin for future reference.

● EXERCISE 1.13

For each unknown word, there are four clues (a, b, c, d) to help you guess its meaning. How many of the clues do you need to guess the word that is being described?

1. a) If you have forgotten to include a message in a letter, you might add this at the end.

    b) It is usually represented by only two letters.

    c) This word literally means *to write after*.

    d) Sometimes advertisers use this to draw the reader's attention to special features of their product.

    The word is ___P.S.   postscript___.

2. a) This is the name given to a meeting of many people with similar interests and expertise about a subject.

    b) At these get-togethers, people participate in various activities such as listening to notable speakers, having workshops, networking with others in their fields, etc.

    c) By this exchange of information, participants hope to gain more skill in their field.

    d) These meetings are usually held over three days or more in a central location to attract as many members as possible.

    The word is ___convention___.

3. a) This is the act of sending something to another person or place.

    b) This word is also commonly used when one sends messages electronically such as by fax.

    c) It is also the name given to the main part of the gear system in a motor vehicle.

    d) In a motor vehicle, this can be automatic or manual but the more common form nowadays is automatic.

    The word is ___transmission___.

4. a) This word can be used to identify people who set up their stalls on the streets and sell their products.

    b) In olden times, these people would call out their products as they walked down the streets.

    c) Today, these might be young people who ride up and down the streets on a special tricycle with a refrigerator box selling ice cream.

    d) This word is also used to describe people who sell illegal drugs.

    The word is ___dealers   peddlers___.

5. a) This is a word to describe people who are able to get along well with others in a group.

    b) These people are usually very friendly and cheerful.

    c) They are good listeners as well as interesting conversationalists.

d) Others are generally comfortable being with these people because they are easy to talk to and fun to be with.

The word is *Sociable*   .

Check your answers with those in the Answer section at the end of the book.

 **COLLABORATIVE EXERCISE 1.14**

Form teams of three members each. Pairs of teams work together: Team A and Team B. Each team should decide on ten words that could be explained by the combined construction of two or more elements: namely, prefixes, roots, suffixes, as well as context clues. Each of these words is recorded on a separate piece of paper and put in a box or envelope for the opposite team members.

Team A begins by trying to identify a word; Team B observes, times, listens for any infractions of the rules, and keeps score for Team A (ten points for each correct response). The time limit for each team is six minutes, with a maximum time limit of two minutes per team member. Gestures may be used with the clues. As soon as one member guesses three words correctly or reaches the maximum two-minute time allotment, the next member of the same team quickly takes over.

The game proceeds as follows (Exercise 1.13 can be used as a model):

a) The first member of Team A chooses a word from Team B's box and tries to explain the meaning of the word to another member of Team A (only one) without using any part of the word. Context clues, gestures, and the meanings of the various parts are the only kinds of clues that can be used. Although only four clues per word were used in the model exercise, the player can use as many clues as necessary.

b) Using any part of the word disqualifies the word.

c) The second Team A member then follows the same procedure with the third Team A member.

d) The third Team A member then takes over and follows the same procedure with the first Team A member until all words have been identified or the total time limit is reached.

Team B then follows the same procedure using the words composed by Team A.

THE NEXT STEP

If you feel confident about this section, write the Unit One Post-Test at the end of this unit.

FREEWRITING

This assignment is separate and can be done before or after the Post-Test for this unit.

GETTING TO KNOW YOURSELF AS A WRITER

One activity that students commonly dislike is writing. They don't know what to write about, where to start, or how to express themselves. Freewriting is a good activity for both personal and academic reasons; for example, you can use this form of writing

- to unlock your mind and get you started in the writing process
- to generate ideas about a particular topic
- to speculate about observations, data, and other information
- to respond to information you read, hear, or see—e.g., books, media, speakers, films
- to summarize lessons or lectures
- to let off steam when you are frustrated

Once you identify your purpose, begin to write anything that comes to mind, including any random thoughts or frustrations. Do not worry about errors in spelling, grammar, punctuation, organization of ideas, or paragraphing. As this is a preliminary step in the writing process, you can leave these types of technicalities to future formal writing activities. Therefore, keep your hands on the keyboard, or your pen or pencil on the paper, and write your thoughts as quickly as you can for ten or fifteen minutes without stopping.

Use the suggestions listed below as a guide. You can add any relevant information you like:

1. Introduce yourself and tell where you are from, as well as any interesting or special facts about yourself or your family.

2. Tell about your past education experience and about your activities, achievements, clubs, etc., during your last school experience. You might also discuss your favourite subject and teacher.

3. Explain why you chose this education facility to further your education. What are your plans for the time you are here? What are your future plans?

Do not worry if you do not have time to complete this activity. Just write as much as you can in the given time.

The purpose of this first freewriting activity is to give you practice in producing as much writing on a topic as you can in a limited time period. If your instructor does not ask to see these pieces of writing, complete them independently. Keep them in one place so you can use them for future recommended grammar and composition exercises. The best way to improve your writing ability is to write, write, write!

POST-TEST FOR UNIT ONE

If you feel confident about the skills presented in this unit, complete the Post-Test that follows; however, **do not attempt this test if you have not completed the required work.**

Once you have completed the whole test, check your answers with those suggested at the end of this unit. A marking scheme has been provided to give you a realistic idea of your ability in this area. Your goal should be 80 percent or better with no more than one error in any section.

I. Using just your knowledge of prefixes, select the correct meaning for each word in the following questions, and record your answers in the spaces provided.

1. *microcosm* means
   a) a critical evaluation or analysis
   b) a small world
   c) a contrary purpose
   d) a large wagon with a canvas cover

2. *trimester* means
   a) a third part of a school year
   b) every two months
   c) incorrect instructions
   d) an athletic contest comprising five different track and field events

3. *interstice* means
   a) a periodic payment, usually a fixed moderate amount of money
   b) a structure forming the foundation of a building
   c) a small or narrow space between things or parts; chink
   d) the outer boundary

4. *antipodal* means
   a) something required beforehand
   b) on the opposite side of the earth
   c) taking an affirmative stand
   d) after childbirth

5. *confabulate* means
   a) talk together informally and intimately; chat
   b) tell through legends
   c) disclose or reveal
   d) charge over the basic rate

6. *pseudonym* means
   a) sacred song
   b) partly suede
   c) false name
   d) argument against

II. Using the clue words listed in each question, determine the meaning of the root word.

1. decapitate, per capita, caption
   The root *cap* or *capit* means
   a) feeling
   b) place
   c) head
   d) foot

2. spectacles, spectator, inspect
   The root *spec* or *spect* means
   a) lead
   b) carry ✓
   c) believe
   (d) see

3. intervene, convention, circumvent
   The root *vene* means
   a) break
   (b) come ✓
   c) lead
   d) fear

4. loquacious, eloquent, soliloquy
   The root *loqua* or *loqui* means
   a) feeling
   (b) speak ✓
   c) place
   d) language

5. aqueduct, introduce, produce
   The root *duct* or *duce* means
   a) water
   (b) lead ✓
   c) make
   d) break

6. disrupt, interrupt, rupture
   The root *rupt* means
   a) talk
   (b) break ✓
   c) fear
   d) pull or draw

Deduct one mark for each error in Sections I and II.

TOTAL MARKS FOR SECTIONS I and II _____ 10 _____ /12

III. By using your knowledge of root words and prefixes, write the meanings of the following words.
   1. monophobia _One fear_ fear of being alone
   2. postscript _Write after_ ✓
   3. contravene _to act against_ ✓
   4. prediction _guess before hand_ ✓
   5. inaudible _Cant hear_ ✓
   6. circumvent _to spread around_ ✓

Deduct two marks for each error in Section III.

TOTAL MARKS FOR SECTION III _____ 10 _____ /12

IV. From the list below, add the appropriate suffix to match the definition of the word. Clues that illustrate the meaning of the suffix are italicized.

-ful	-ly	-er	-ible	-ist	-ism	-ive	-let
-less	-hood	-ee	-able	-ish	-itis	-ology	-cide

1. termin <u>ology</u> ✓   the *study of* terms
2. fool <u>ish</u> ✓   *inclined* to be a fool
3. ring <u>let</u> ✓   a *small* curl
4. special <u>ist</u> ✓   *one who* devotes time to one area of study or business
5. merci <u>less</u> ✓   *without* mercy
6. employ <u>ee</u> ✓   the *person to whom* employment is given

Deduct one mark for each error in Section IV.

TOTAL MARKS FOR SECTION IV _____ 6 /6

V. Use context clues to determine the meaning of the following italicized words. Record your answers in the spaces provided.

1. The hostess gave a last-minute, *cursory* glance around the room before she greeted her guests at the door.

   cursory means __quick__ ✓

2. Poor sports are known for their *acrimonious* behaviour after a game. Their bad manners and bitterness are usually clear to anyone who pays attention to them.

   acrimonious means __bad sharp or bitter in temper, language, or manner__

3. The *periphery* of a rectangle is called the perimeter.

   periphery means __sides outside boundary__

4. Smoking is not a *salutary* act. Many serious illnesses have been attributed to this habit.

   salutary means __healthy__ ✓

5. Hospitals offer many *ancillary* services, such as physiotherapy, ambulance service, specialty treatment centres, research areas, and outpatient clinics, all of which are closely related to in-hospital services, but independently operated.

   ancillary means __secondary assisting__

Deduct two marks for each error in Section V.

TOTAL MARKS FOR SECTION V _____ 4 /10

VI. By using any or all of the vocabulary skills you have learned in this unit, write the meanings of *any five* of the italicized words in the following paragraph.

For years, many people were satisfied to be weekend sports *spectators;* but through advertising and medical advice, they are becoming more *cognizant* of the importance of fitness in their daily lives. The *fallacy* that running and jogging are dangerous to people's well-being is now being *refuted.* In fact, documented medical reports indicate that a person who regularly participates in some type of athletic activity feels better and is increasing his or her chances for a longer and more *salubrious* life. Therefore, people, particularly those who suffer from *hypochondria,* should join a health club and get active! They will discover that their imagined illnesses or feelings of *lethargy* will gradually disappear. With this renewed level of fitness and focus, they can also *recapture* the *zest* and energy they enjoyed in their earlier years. A different attitude and better health mean they will have a greater chance of living a longer, more satisfying life.

1. *spectator* means ~~consciously aware~~
2. *cognizant* means _consciously aware_ ✓
3. *fallacy* means _false belief_ ✓
4. *refuted* means _taking back_ ✓
5. *salubrious* means _____
6. *hypochondria* means _____
7. *lethargy* means _tiredness_ ✓
8. *recapture* means _to get again_ ✓
9. *zest* means _____

Deduct two marks for each error in Section VI.

40

TOTAL MARKS FOR SECTION VI _____ 10 _____ /10

Answers are on the following pages.

ANSWERS FOR UNIT ONE POST-TEST

I. 1. (b) *microcosm* means a small world

2. (a) *trimester* means a third part of a school year

3. (c) *interstice* means a small or narrow space between things or parts; chink

4. (b) *antipodal* means on the opposite side of the earth

5. (a) *confabulate* means talk together informally and intimately; chat

6. (c) *pseudonym* means false name

II. 1. (c) decapitate, per capita, caption
The root *cap* or *capit* means head

2. (d) spectacles, spectator, inspect
The root *spec* or *spect* means see

3. (b) intervene, convention, circumvent
The root *vene* means come

4. (b) loquacious, eloquent, soliloquy
The root *loqua* or *loqui* means speak

5. (b) aqueduct, introduce, produce
The root *duct* or *duce* means lead

6. (b) disrupt, interrupt, rupture
        The root *rupt* means break

III. 1. monophobia fear of being alone
   2. postscript (message) written after
   3. contravene come against; oppose
   4. prediction prophecy; telling or saying something before it happens
   5. inaudible not able to be heard
   6. circumvent come or go around; avoid or get the better of

IV. 1. termino*logy* the *study of* terms
   2. fool*ish* *inclined* to be a fool
   3. ring*let* a *small* curl
   4. special*ist* *one who* devotes time to one area of study or business
   5. merci*less* *without* mercy
   6. employ*ee* the *person to whom* employment is given

V. 1. *cursory* means hasty; superficial
   2. *acrimonious* means sharp or bitter in temper, language, or manner
   3. *periphery* means outside boundary
   4. *salutary* means good for the health; healthy
   5. *ancillary* means assisting; auxiliary

VI. 1. *spectator* means one who sees or watches
   2. *cognizant* means aware
   3. *fallacy* means a false idea; mistaken belief
   4. *refuted* means called back; proved to be false or incorrect
   5. *salubrious* means healthful
   6. *hypochondria* means an abnormal condition characterized by a depressed emotional state or imagined ill health
   7. *lethargy* means overpowering tiredness or drowsiness; inactivity caused by loss of interest or concern
   8. *recapture* means have again; bring back; gain or get again
   9. *zest* means enjoyment; satisfaction; sense of well-being

READING FOR COMPREHENSION

OVERVIEW

In order to understand a piece of writing fully, you must be able to recognize the writer's plan of attack. The writer obviously has some strong viewpoints or important information to convey, and had to consider and organize his or her thoughts in order to transmit this message effectively. When reading, you should be able to interpret the message just as the writer intended you to. Of course, skilled writers (and most textbook writers would be classified as such!) are able to write in a way that enables a reader to reach an understanding without too much effort; but a skillful reader is also necessary to complete the communication circuit—one who can discern the writer's exact meaning or interpretation. The skills presented in this section should help you to become a more interpretive reader. Learning to recognize main ideas and to interpret the writer's pattern of development will improve your comprehension and retention skills.

In addition, Unit Two contains the second in the series of freewriting exercises, designed to give you practice in transferring your thoughts into written words. Learning to express your opinions and feelings effectively is the focus of these activities.

LEARNING OBJECTIVES FOR UNIT TWO

Upon completion of this unit, you should be able to:

1. Identify the topic in a given paragraph.

2. Identify the main idea
   a) as the first sentence
   b) in mid-paragraph
   c) at the end of a paragraph
   d) as an implied, rather than stated, expression

3. Distinguish among the three basic patterns of paragraph development, namely, those developed by
   a) one or more examples or reasons
   b) steps in a sequence
   c) point of comparison or contrast

4. Predict and interpret an author's organization by using any or all of the following:
   a) clue words given in the main idea
   b) transition words used within the paragraph
   c) clue words or phrases used within the paragraph

5. Using an outline format, write organized notes from an article by identifying the main ideas as well as the major and minor points.

6. Using a given newspaper article, identify the main message.

Check Internet resources for additional news articles that will help you with reading, outlining, and collaborative exercises (see pages 469–70).

PRETEST: MAIN IDEAS

Each of the following ten paragraphs on motivation is followed by four statements, one of which expresses the main idea of the paragraph. Read each paragraph carefully and completely; then circle the letter that correctly identifies the main-idea statement (the author's main point). This exercise tests your ability to recognize the stated or implied main idea of a paragraph.

Mysteries of Motivation[1]

1. The top management of any organization must make a sincere effort in meeting "creature comforts," providing security, and offering incentives for good performance. However, the more important elements of motivation must be dealt with on a personal level between a superior and his or her subordinates. This day-to-day contact of genuine interest and concern between the two divisions is necessary to foster good rapport.

   a) The top management of any organization must make a sincere effort towards making their employees happy.
   b) Management should offer incentives for their employees' good performance.
   c) Motivation must be dealt with on a personal level between a superior and his or her subordinates.
   d) Day-to-day contact is important.

2. Some managers and supervisors will draw the line at this point, protesting that they have more practical and pressing matters to worry about than "wet nursing" their employees. But the fact is that they cannot escape the influence of motivation, or of its opposite, demotivation. The motivation of each individual in a work team is what goes to make up its morale—and bad morale can spell grief to the leader of any team.

   a) Some managers and supervisors have more practical and pressing matters to worry about than "wet nursing" their employees.
   b) Managers and supervisors say they must draw the line at some point.
   c) Demotivation is bad for morale.
   d) The motivation of each individual in a work team is what goes to make up its morale.

3. The results of surveys of workers' attitudes in recent years underline the importance of motivation at the ground level. They show that present-day employees place a strong emphasis on challenge, opportunity, and recognition of performance. In addition, these workers appear to be more willing than their counterparts of a generation ago to quit a job that does not offer these things. An old-line manager or supervisor might write them off as spoiled brats or prima donnas. But by failing to take account of their personal priorities, he or she could very well have to live with the consequences of a high turnover, which include having to function on a more or less permanent basis with a half-trained staff.

   a) The results of surveys of workers' attitudes in recent years underline the importance of motivation at the ground level.
   b) Workers today appear to be more than willing to quit a job.
   c) Managers have to live with the consequences of a high turnover, which include having to function with a half-trained staff.
   d) Supervisors should write off unhappy employees as spoiled brats or prima donnas.

4. On the other hand, bosses who make a serious effort to understand their subordinates become better motivated themselves because they come closer to fulfilling their own ego and self-expression needs in the process. Motivation must, in fact, work two ways because superiors must be open to their subordinates' influence if they expect the subordinates to be open to theirs. The cross-motivation that comes from healthy superior-subordinate relationships gives rise to an ideal working climate not only for the people directly concerned but for the organization as a whole.

   a) Bosses who make a serious effort to understand their subordinates become better motivated themselves.
   b) Superiors must be open to their subordinates' influence.
   c) Cross-motivation that comes from healthy superior-subordinate relationships gives rise to an ideal working climate.
   d) Superiors should come closer to fulfilling their own ego and self-expression needs.

5. In other words, cross-motivation keeps everybody happy. And when we get right down to the core of the matter, that is what motivation is all about. The philosopher William James identified its nucleus long before the term ever entered the vocabulary. He wrote that if we were ever questioned about identifying life's chief concern, our common answer would be happiness. He concluded that how to gain, how to keep, and how to recover happiness is in fact the secret motive of all we do—and all we are willing to endure.

   a) How to gain, how to keep, and how to recover happiness is the secret motive of all we do.
   b) The result of cross-motivation is that it keeps everybody happy.
   c) William James identified motivation's nucleus long before the term ever entered our vocabulary.
   d) If we were ever questioned about what our chief concern was, most of us would identify it as happiness.

6. If a person's work adds to his or her happiness, then the job in itself becomes the ultimate motivator. But for this to be so, the work must be valued and recognized as such. For the manager or supervisor, this implies a continuing effort to accentuate the importance of what the subordinate is doing in the overall context of the organization. It is noteworthy in this regard that the most fiendish punishments the military mind can devise entail having a prisoner do something entirely useless, like scrubbing a cell floor with a toothbrush or painting a pile of rocks.

   a) Some military people have fiendish minds.
   b) The worst thing about being in the military is that you might have to scrub floors with a toothbrush or paint a pile of rocks.
   c) Managers must accentuate the importance of what the subordinate is doing.
   d) If a person's work adds to his or her happiness, then the job becomes the motivator.

7. However, motivation is a matter of human understanding—of the superior understanding the subordinate. If and when that state is achieved, it becomes a process of encouraging people to go as far as possible towards meeting their aspirations—in plainer language, their hopes and dreams. This requires giving them an opportunity to show what they can do. Their efforts must then be recognized and rewarded to the extent that this is possible within the system. They must be made to feel wanted within that system. This is done by making them aware of how their efforts contribute to the whole.

   a) Motivation is a matter of human understanding.
   b) If and when the state of human understanding is achieved, it becomes a process of encouraging people to go as far as possible towards meeting their aspirations—their hopes and dreams.
   c) Employees' efforts should be recognized and rewarded.
   d) Employees should be made aware of how their efforts contribute to the whole organization.

8. It comes down to treating people with respect for their individuality and consideration for their feelings. It means caring about others—about their personal well-being. It means giving them a chance to show what they can do even if that is sometimes inconvenient. It means encouraging and helping them to meet their full potential in their careers.

   a) Motivation means caring about others.
   b) Motivation means encouraging and helping others to meet their full potential in their careers.
   c) Motivation has many meanings.
   d) Motivation means treating people with respect for their individuality.

9. When you think about it, motivation is not much different from friendship. A friend attempts to understand you and to help you as far as possible to achieve your aims. A friend is concerned about your happiness and tries within the limits of his or her ability to make you happy. A friend is someone who supports you and knows that he or she can count on your support in return.

   a) Motivation and friendship are similar.
   b) A friend is someone who supports you and knows that he or she can count on your support.
   c) Friendship is extremely important.
   d) Both a supervisor and a friend will attempt to understand you and help you achieve your aims.

10. Above all, a friend is someone who will go out of his or her way to do things for you. The motive for this is nothing more than the knowledge that you would do the same for him or her. And so it is with mutual motivation in the plant, office, or school. The bosses who are most concerned about their subordinates get the most out of them in the form of high-quality work.

   a) Mutual motivation produces the highest-quality work.
   b) A friend is someone who will go out of his or her way to do things for you.
   c) Bosses should be concerned about their subordinates.
   d) There are many similar motives for friendship and motivation.

Check your answers with those in the Answer section at the end of the book.

If you had eight or more answers correct, proceed to the Pretest for "Organizational Patterns in Reading." If you had fewer than eight answers correct, complete the lessons on the following pages.

MAIN IDEAS

When writers write, they do so to convey a message. There is some special fact or story or viewpoint that they want to send to someone else. Since they usually have one purpose and one message, your duty as a reader is to interpret that message; and, of course, it would be wonderful if it were the same one that the writer had intended you to receive. However, this very simple method of communication becomes very complex when either the writer does not convey the message clearly or the reader does not interpret it correctly. This unit, on comprehension skills, is intended to give you a better understanding of how to decode messages.

For the most part, what we read is contained in books, magazines, newspapers, etc.; therefore, we can assume that the writer has good communication skills and has learned to communicate ideas in a clear and meaningful fashion. However, different readers do not always get the same meaning from a written passage—and some readers do not get any meaning at all from what they read!

To begin with, you must realize that every paragraph, article, chapter, or book has one central theme—some concept that the author is giving to the reader. That concept may be a simple one or it may be very complex. Your responsibility as a reader is to receive and understand the idea or ideas that the writer is sending. If you can quickly determine this main idea as you are reading, then all the details will quite naturally fall into place, and your interpretation and understanding will be exact.

Use the following formula to locate the writer's most important idea in a paragraph.

1. First, identify the topic by asking, "Whom or what is the paragraph about?" **Limit yourself to one or two words.**

2. Second, determine the main idea by asking, "What fact or point of view is the writer presenting about the topic?" **Express this idea in a complete sentence.** In order to see all other details in relation to the main idea, this statement must be written as a complete thought. (Thoughts that pass through our heads are transmitted in sentences; none of us can think in "bits and pieces" and make any sense!)

3. Finally, look at the remaining sentences in the paragraph to see if they prove or elaborate this main idea. Writers very rarely make unqualified statements and usually support their ideas with proof, examples, or a story that verifies their point of view.

I. RECOGNIZING MAIN IDEAS IN PARAGRAPHS

Although main ideas can be located in different places in different paragraphs, you can easily locate the most important theme by using the formula given above: identify the topic and then consider what the writer is saying about that topic. The main idea will be the controlling statement, or all-encompassing idea, of the paragraph or article. All other given facts will support or relate to this statement. Read the following examples and look at the graphic explanation of the various paragraph patterns.

A. The Main Idea Could Be the First Statement

Main-idea sentence ———————————→ **In planning a report, one must give serious thought to the needs and temperament of the person for whom it is being prepared.** Some people want all details carefully and completely explained. Others, however, prefer concise, well-documented deductions. On the other hand, many employers demand tables and graphs that clearly and succinctly present all information at a glance. And there are still those who would "run a mile" from any vestige of statistical data.[2]

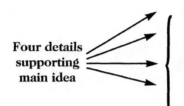

Four details
supporting
main idea

1. The topic is *planning a report.*

2. The main-idea statement that controls all other sentences in the paragraph is:

   In planning a report, one must give serious thought to the needs and temperament of the person for whom it is being prepared. (This is the main idea.)

3. Each of the four remaining sentences provides the evidence/proof/support for the main idea by giving examples of what various types of people might like in a report.

B. The Main Idea Could Be in the Middle of the Paragraph

The writer might wish to introduce only the topic in the initial sentence. This topic could be presented as either a statement or a question.

NOTE: If a question is near the beginning of the paragraph (either the first, second, or third sentence), then the main idea will be the answer to that question, regardless of its position in the paragraph.

   In the following example, the first sentence is a topic sentence. (Only the topic is mentioned; the writer expresses no opinion or overall idea.) A question is next, and then comes the main idea (which, you will note, is the answer to the question). This pattern may also be reversed; that is, the question may be first, followed by a topic sentence and then the main idea.

Topic sentence ———————————→ The term "critic" seems to have such a negative connotation that most people do not associate this term with anyone but professionals who are trained

Question ———————————→ to judge. But who are the real critics of the world?

Main-idea sentence ———————————→ **Although none of us may readily admit this fact, the truth is we are all critics.** The person who dislikes a particular product or the way others bring up their children is a critic. The individual who reprimands another for some aspect of business or who tunes out one radio station for another is also a critic. These people are discriminating according to their personal preferences and individual standards.[3]

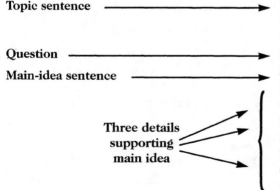

Three details
supporting
main idea

1. The topic is *critics*.

2. The main idea that controls the other sentences in the paragraph is:

   Although none of us may readily admit this fact, the truth is we are all critics.
   or
   The truth is we are all critics. (This is the main idea.)

   The first sentence is a topic sentence in which the writer mentions only the subject matter, not a point of view. The second sentence is a question; the main idea, you can see, is the answer to that question. In this case, the main-idea sentence follows the question but this need not be the pattern.

3. Each of the three remaining sentences provides evidence, proof, or support for the main idea by giving examples of actions that make us all critics.

C. The Main Idea Could Be the Last Sentence in the Paragraph

In these cases, the writer first provides positive or negative facts that lead to his or her general conclusion or main idea.

Topic sentence

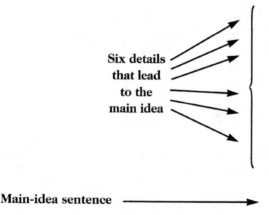

Six details that lead to the main idea

Society could not exist without criticism. Surprisingly enough, discontentment is often the first sign of progress for a person, a business, or even a nation. Finding fault is not always negative. Identifying weaknesses in a system, wanting changes, or recommending different methods for accomplishing goals is often an initial step towards improvement. A person who is unhappy with his or her situation will look for ways to change. Businesses often get new ideas by listening to their customers' complaints, and most governments operate according to the wishes of the people. If the people are displeased, those in power are wise to listen to their **Main-idea sentence** ⟶ electorate. **Therefore, criticism of the constructive sort, accompanied by positive suggestions, is known to accelerate advancement in every facet of society.**[4]

1. The topic is *criticism*.

2. The main idea that controls the other sentences in the paragraph is:

   Criticism of the constructive sort, accompanied by positive suggestions, is known to accelerate advancement. (This is the main idea.)

   The first sentence is a topic sentence. It states the topic but does not express the writer's viewpoint. The other sentences provide the evidence that leads to the main idea. A hint here is the word *therefore*. It announces that this sentence contains the conclusion and the main point.

3. Each of the six preceding sentences provides evidence, proof, or support by giving reasons why and examples of how criticism can bring about positive changes.

● EXERCISE 2.1

Determine the main idea in each of the following paragraphs by reading each one completely and then applying the formula discussed above.

1. Perhaps the highest use of books is not as sources of information but as friends. Besides being great teachers, books can also be great comforters. They not only expand one's understanding of the world and its varied inhabitants but also provide an escape from disturbing or unalterable situations. To be lost for a little while in another time or place with this "consoling friend" is a great healer for all kinds of woes. Books are well known for keeping one company for five minutes in a bus depot or occupying one's whole day; in fact, many exciting tales can keep one awake for an entire night! Developing a close association with literary works is being a promoter of thought as well as having the means to seek refuge from almost all miseries of life.[5]

   a) What is the topic? (Try to limit yourself to one or two words.) *books as friends*

   b) What is the author saying about this topic? *Books can be great comforters and can provide an escape from disturbing situations.* ✓
   (This is the main idea.)

2. The majority of Canadians continue to enjoy the fruits of American culture without feeling any less Canadian for it. They will laugh at comic strips, snicker at soap operas, chew gum, and eat turkey and pumpkin pie at Thanksgiving—a feast which we celebrate in October instead of November in a typical variation on an American theme. They will use American slang and terminology, and read the books on the *New York Times* bestseller list.[6]

   a) What is the topic? (Try to limit yourself to one or two words.) *Canadians* ✓

   b) What is the author saying about this topic? *Canadians enjoy American culture with out feeling less Canadian for it.* ✓
   (This is the main idea.)

3. How do most of us make decisions? Sometimes we may arrive at a conclusion by using rational thinking. We make observations, weigh the alternatives, and then choose what we consider to be the best choice for that situation. Other times, however, we make decisions without any conscious thinking act at all, as we so often do about the minor things in life. Our wardrobe selection, our meal menus, or our plans for entertainment usually are considerations that do not require a great deal of thought; they are routine decisions that we automatically make. No matter how conscientious we may try to be, we all use these two basic decision-making techniques.[7]

   a) What is the topic? (Try to limit yourself to one or two words.) *decisions* ✓

   b) What is the author saying about this topic? *No matter how conscientious we are, we all use these two basic decision-making techniques.* ✓
   (This is the main idea.)

4. What age does one have to be before being considered an adult? Actually, being "grown up" does not depend only on one's chronological age but also on one's emotional maturity. There are many people who are adults intellectually and physically but are children emotionally. They are the ones who throw temper tantrums when they don't get their own way or who resort to violence or swearing when something breaks down. On the other hand, there are many children

who are mature beyond their years. Their quiet acceptance of things they cannot change and their ability to cope in difficult situations make them more grown up than some adults.[8]

a) What is the topic? (Try to limit yourself to one or two words.) *adults being grown up*

b) What is the author saying about this topic? *Being "grown up" doesn't just depend on chronological age but on emotional maturity as well*

(This is the main idea.)

5. There is no greater test for a young person today than that of choosing a career. This task is one of life's most important challenges. Preparing for tomorrow and recognizing which path is the best one to follow is not easy for most. The brightness of one's future is dependent upon making the right career choice and taking advantage of opportunities when they arise.[9]

a) What is the topic? (Try to limit yourself to one or two words.) *Career*

b) What is the author saying about this topic? *Choosing a career is one of life's most important challenges for young people*

(This is the main idea.)

6. A person's emotional maturity determines his or her ability to work effectively with other people. There is no credit due to you for being old in years; that is something that just happens. But to be mature in thinking is a credit to you because you have worked towards it and developed it. Maturity is a state of mind, not a date on a calendar.[10]

a) What is the topic? (Try to limit yourself to one or two words.) *Maturity*

b) What is the author saying about this topic? *Maturity is a state of mind, not a date on a calendar*

(This is the main idea.)

7. People take many complex things for granted. They no longer marvel over automobiles or airplanes. Reaching a destination in a matter of minutes or hours is an expected deduction. Radio, television, telephone, or computers provide communication and entertainment on demand. These things seem so very simple and accepted because someone, ages ago or half a century ago, was ingenious enough to invent them.[11]

a) What is the topic? (Try to limit yourself to one or two words.) *taking complex things for granted*

b) What is the author saying about this topic? *People take many complex things for granted.*

(This is the main idea.)

8. The record of things to be recalled is contained in books, in the minds of parents, in universities and colleges, and in business files. What are books but the thoughts of people of their time put down in type? What has a university or college to proffer except what it has absorbed of the past, to be communicated to every new generation with interpretation and adaptation? What has any mother to pass on to her children except the accumulated

wisdom of mothers of the past and lessons of her own experience? What is the purpose of all our office work from the clay tablets of Babylon to the high speed printout of today's electronic machines except to provide the history of transactions?[12]

a) What is the topic? (Try to limit yourself to one or two words.) *transactions* ✗
   record of thing to be recalled

b) What is the author saying about this topic? *The purpose the written word* ✗
   is to provide a history of transactions
   (This is the main idea.)

9. The monogram *CSA* might be found on anything from a mobile home to an electric toothbrush. Wherever it is, it means that the product has measured up to the standards that have taken experts an average of six months to formulate and write. Every CSA-approved product has been subject to rigorous testing. The association's laboratories put them through such paces as crashing a steel ball on the centre of a bathtub to check for cracking, and twisting an electrical cord up to 10 000 times.[13]

a) What is the topic? (Try to limit yourself to one or two words.) *CSA* ✓

b) What is the author saying about this topic? *Every CSA-approved product* ✓
   has been subject to rigorous testing
   (This is the main idea.)

10. Who among us doesn't dream of being successful? This common goal, however, can have many different meanings. For some, success is measured in dollars; while for others, it is measured by the number of friends they have. Real success, however, is a matter of attaining a lifestyle in which one is comfortable with oneself. If, for example, a wealthy man lives his life hating the world and everyone in it, including himself, can he be looked upon as successful? The same is true for a poor man who always appears happy and has countless friends. Is he not more successful than the wealthy man? The poor man is comfortable with himself and has accepted his lifestyle; therefore, he can be credited with leading a very successful life. Although success is everyone's goal, there are many different viewpoints about how one achieves this desired state.

a) What is the topic? (Try to limit yourself to one or two words.) *Success* ✓

b) What is the author saying about this topic? *Real success is a matter of* ✓
   attaining a lifestyle in which one is comfortable with oneself
   (This is the main idea.)

Check your answers with those in the Answer section at the end of the book.

II. Implied Main Ideas

Main ideas are not always stated in exact words or in one particular position in a paragraph. Many times, the main idea is not stated at all, but is strongly suggested or implied from all the information given in the paragraph. If you apply the formula you used in the previous exercise, you should readily determine the main point that the writer is making. Look at the following example.

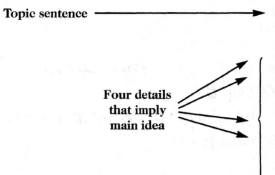

Topic sentence —————————→ Manners are nothing more than modes of behaviour which may have little or nothing to do with kindness or civility. Historians tell us that in the Europe of the Middle Ages, the prevailing manners were simple and sincere. In the fourteenth century, however, their role began to change as the merchant classes sought to better their social standing by duplicating the style of the aristocracy. The aristocracy closed ranks by making its manners more esoteric. Thus snobbery—both in the sense of social climbing and in the sense of looking down one's nose at others—came into being.[14]

Four details that imply main idea

1. The topic is *manners*.

2. The main idea is implied by the given facts.

    Manners have developed throughout the ages because of people's need to continue to distinguish the various classes. (This is the main idea. Your wording may be different but the suggestion of development is the important idea to convey.)

    The first sentence is a topic sentence. It states the topic but does not express the writer's viewpoint. The other sentences provide the evidence that leads to the main idea. A hint here is the chronological listing of the series of events.

3. Each of the four sentences traces the history of manners, the topic, and provides evidence/proof/support for the main idea.

● EXERCISE 2.2

Determine the main idea implied by each of the following paragraphs by reading each one completely and then applying the formula.

1. In the early part of this century, marriage between young people was an arrangement made between the parents—or even nations—to join two people for reasons other than love. As time progressed, it did become more acceptable for young people to choose their own lifetime partners. The young man, however, had to declare his honourable intentions to his lady's parents before he was allowed to court her. Then, of course, it became more fashionable for young people to meet and date before they made the "big decision." Until the 1960s though, a young man still continued to treat his "date" with more formal respect: he always saw her to and from her front door, bought her gifts of candy or flowers, and showed her every courtesy. With today's young people, formal courtesies—including dating—seem to have disappeared; and their marriage, if there is one, has become a legal agreement in which both parties indicate "their rights"—and, in some cases, state renewable dates for a renegotiated contract!

    a) What is the topic? (Try to limit yourself to one or two words.)

    _____

    b) What is the author saying about this topic?

    _____

    (This is the main idea.)

2. Every person is guilty, to some degree, of being a junk collector. In fact, the act of cleaning or moving often uncovers some archaic articles that, although they have lost their usefulness, are repacked just in case they are needed again at some future time. However, this instinctive

habit is also shared by animals and birds. Pack rats and magpies are notorious for stashing away every object that strikes their fancy. Even chimpanzees and whisky-jacks share the habit of assembling junk.[15]

a) What is the topic? (Try to limit yourself to one or two words.)

_____

b) What is the author saying about this topic?

_____

(This is the main idea.)

3. A person who gathers genuine friends has a collection that is unique and priceless. For in this, as in all other forms of collecting, a couple of basic rules must apply to make it worthwhile. First, never collect just for show, but for intrinsic value. And second, never collect to impress others or to meet their standards. Collect according to your own standards to satisfy you.[16]

a) What is the topic? (Try to limit yourself to one or two words.)

_____

b) What is the author saying about this topic?

_____

(This is the main idea.)

4. In the mid-1960s a wave of disquiet swept through the middle classes of North America and Western Europe. Something was happening among the young people of the day which the elders could not quite understand. Parents and grandparents had, after all, worked long and hard to build a society in which their offspring would want for very little materially. They had secured for the next generation a degree of political and economic freedom never known in the world before. And yet there were clear signs that a considerable and influential segment of the younger population was turning its back on the fruits of their parents' labour. Bewildered and a little hurt, the adults asked why.[17]

a) What is the topic? (Try to limit yourself to one or two words.)

_____

b) What is the author saying about this topic?

_____

(This is the main idea.)

5. One feature of the military is pride in appearance. The "spit and polish" of a perfectly groomed young recruit on parade is a feature that most ordinary citizens would find onerous to endure themselves. It is an interesting fact that when people lose their pride, their appearance is usually the next thing to go. A film director who wants the audience to identify a character as having "gone to seed" not only would dress him or her shabbily and untidily but would also make sure that he or she was rather dirty as well.

a) What is the topic? (Try to limit yourself to one or two words.)

_____

b) What is the author saying about this topic?

_____

(This is the main idea.)

Check your answers with those in the Answer section at the end of the book.

● EXERCISE 2.3—REVIEW

In some of the following paragraphs, the main idea is stated at the beginning, in the middle, or at the end of the selection. In other paragraphs, the main idea is implied rather than expressed in words. Underline the expressed main ideas and write any implied main ideas in the margin.

The Practical Writer[18]

1. Some writers deliberately muddy the meaning of their words, if indeed they meant anything to begin with. When most people write, however, it is to get a message across. This is especially so in business and institutions, where written words carry much of the load of communication. The written traffic of any well-ordered organization is thick and varied— letters, memos, reports, policy statements, manuals, sales literature, and what-have-you. The purpose of it all is to use words in a way that serves the organization's aim.

2. Unfortunately, written communications often fail to accomplish this purpose. Some organizational writing gives rise to confusion, inefficiency, and ill-will. This is almost always because the intended message did not get through to the receiving end. Why? The main reason is usually that the message was inadequately prepared.

3. An irresistible comparison arises between writing and another craft which most people have to practise sometimes, namely cooking. In both fields there is a wide range of competence, from the great chefs and authors to the occasional practitioners who must do the job whether they like it or not. In both, care in preparation is of the essence. Shakespeare wrote that it is an ill cook who does not lick her fingers; it is an ill writer who does not work at it hard enough to be reasonably satisfied with the results.

4. In the working world, bad writing is not only bad manners; it is bad business. The victim of an incomprehensible letter will at best be annoyed and at worst decide that people who can't say what they mean aren't worth doing business with. Write a sloppy letter, and it might rebound on you when the recipient calls for clarification. Where one carefully worded letter would have sufficed, you might have to write two or more.

5. Muddled messages can cause havoc within an organization. Instructions that are misunderstood can set people off in the wrong direction or put them to work in vain. Written policies that are open to misinterpretation can throw sand in the gears of an entire operation. Ill-considered language in communications with or between employees can torpedo morale.

[margin note: bad writing can cost you]

Mysteries of Motivation[19]

6. To motivate people, the dictionaries tell us, is to cause them to act in a certain way. This is done by furnishing them with a motive to do your bidding. By the strictest definition, the most elementary form of motivation would be if a hold-up man were to stick a pistol in your face and growl: "Your money or your life." He instantly arouses a motive in you for doing what he wants you to—the motive of staying alive.

7. In the lexicon of management science, the system of reward and punishment is known as the "carrot and stick" approach, the carrot being dangled in front of a donkey's nose and the stick applied smartly to his hindquarters. In this fashion he is alternately enticed and impelled towards his master's goal. Whether the donkey ever gets to eat the carrot in this analogy is not made clear in management literature. We can be sure, however, that he gets to feel the stick.

[handwritten margin note: management makes use of the reward and punishment system known as the "carrot and stick" to entice and impelle the worker towards his master's goal]

8. The modern worker is clearly motivated by much more than the carrot of pay and advancement and the stick of discipline and insecurity, although it would be foolish to underestimate the continuing effectiveness of these devices. Money might not be everything—otherwise movie stars would be the happiest people on earth—but there is no evidence that the mass of humanity has ceased to have a strong desire for the comfort and possessions that money will buy. The "stick," at the very least, is what makes us get up in the morning and go to work even when we don't feel like it. It is part of normal human nature to stay clear of trouble and to want the assurance of a steady, well-paid job.

Check your answers with those in the Answer section at the end of the book.

THE NEXT STEP

If you feel confident about this section, proceed to the Pretest for "Organizational Patterns in Reading."

PRETEST: ORGANIZATIONAL PATTERNS IN READING

I. Each of the following main-idea sentences suggests how the paragraph will be developed. Read each sentence and circle the letter identifying the most appropriate type of development. This exercise tests your ability to recognize a writer's method of paragraph development from among the following styles: one or more examples or reasons, sequence of steps or events, and points of comparison or contrast.

1. The life history of the butterfly presents some remarkable changes in this insect.

   Developed by a) example or reason
                 b) sequence
                 c) comparison or contrast

2. Swimming in a pool is quite different from swimming in a lake.

   Developed by a) example or reason
              b) sequence
              c) comparison or contrast

3. Morale, which is one of the most important elements in the working force, can be fostered in many ways.[20]

   Developed by a) example or reason
              b) sequence
              c) comparison or contrast

4. Happiness is what one believes it to be.

   Developed by a) example or reason
              b) sequence
              c) comparison or contrast

5. When you think about it, motivation is not much different from friendship.[21]

   Developed by a) example or reason
              b) sequence
              c) comparison or contrast

6. Manners are simply modes of behaviour that have developed throughout the centuries.[22]

   Developed by a) example or reason
              b) sequence
              c) comparison or contrast

II. Read the following paragraphs and identify each one's pattern of development.

The Search for Happiness[23]

1. Opinions differ from age to age as to what happiness is. Popular "how to" books of the 18th century were chiefly concerned with the subject of how to die a good death. People of the 19th century were most interested in reading books that told them how to make a good living. Most of the books in the 20th century are devoted to telling us how to live happily.

   The above paragraph was developed by
   a) example or reason
   b) sequence
   c) comparison or contrast

2. Many people—perhaps the majority of people—would say that the greatest happiness that they could achieve would be the freedom and ability to do what they want to do. It is difficult, however, to be sure just what one wants today, let alone next year or twenty years from now. Human beings are changeable. What may seem supremely good today may be completely out of date within a few months.

   The above paragraph was developed by
   a) example or reason
   b) sequence
   c) comparison or contrast

3. Happiness arises largely from the mental qualities of contentment, confidence, serenity, and active good will. It includes the pain of losing as well as the pleasure of finding. It thrives best in a crowded life. The men and women who are recorded in history and biography as most happy were people with always somewhat more to do than they could possibly do. Every waking hour of their lives was occupied with ambitious projects, literature, love, politics, science, friendship, commerce, professions, trades, their religious faith, and a thousand other matters. The secret of happiness may be found by making each of these interests count to its utmost as part of the fabric of life.

    The above paragraph was developed by
    a) example or reason
    b) sequence
    c) comparison or contrast

4. Seeking happiness, however, requires a plan. We need to know the sort of happiness we want, what the ingredients are, what are our strongest wants, and what we have to start with. Then we should train ourselves to keep the program simple and free from complications. We must learn to control our egos after being praised and to bounce back quickly from disappointment, to seize and create opportunities to put our special abilities to work, to seek excellence in everything we do, and to remain modest. Finally, we must continually review and periodically revise our goals. Happiness is right there for us, if we cultivate it.

    The above paragraph was developed by
    a) example or reason
    b) sequence
    c) comparison or contrast

Check your answers with those in the Answer section at the end of the book.

If you had eight or more answers correct, proceed to the Pretest for "Outlining." If you had fewer than eight answers correct, complete the lessons on the following pages.

ORGANIZATIONAL PATTERNS IN READING

Once you have determined the author's main viewpoint in a reading selection, the next important step for you to take is to see just how the main points have been supported. If you can anticipate, for example, that the author plans to give reasons to support the theory, then you would be able to concentrate on seeking these out as you read. Therefore, you would automatically create a "purpose" to your reading; as a result, not only would your concentration improve but so would your interpretive skills.

Most of the time, writers place their main-idea statement at or near the beginning of each paragraph. This statement, or the statements that follow, often provide clues about how the paragraph is being developed. Basically, the writer will develop the major details of a paragraph in one of three commonly used patterns:

1. One or more examples or reasons that illustrate the point
2. Sequence of steps or events that give logical development of the topic
3. Points of comparison or contrast that illustrate similarities to, or differences from, another familiar topic

I. PARAGRAPHS DEVELOPED BY ONE OR MORE EXAMPLES OR REASONS

Using this first method, the writer may give more information about a point or relate an incident that verifies or supports the main idea. The following paragraphs illustrate this pattern.

The main idea is developed by the use of one illustration to support or give further explanation.

Straight thinking is based upon knowledge. How can a man think if he doesn't know? Dr. W.E. McNeill told the Autumn Convention at Queen's University how *Charles Darwin* gathered biological facts for twenty years without seeing any binding relationship. Then, according to Dr. McNeill, while Darwin was walking through an English country lane, the idea of

> evolution came to him suddenly. That's what **thinking is—the flashing emergence of an idea after the facts have been mulled over for a long time.**[24]

In this paragraph, the writer could have developed the main-idea sentence by providing several examples of, or reasons for, the statement; however, only one story is cited, which very capably illustrates the point.

Read the following paragraph to see how the writer has used additional information to explain the main point.

The main idea is developed by an explanation of intuition and examples of intuitive types of people.	People who have intuition have a very rare gift. **Individuals who can effortlessly and accurately anticipate outcomes or truths without having total knowledge of all the facts are extremely valuable to their professions.** *In science*, these intuitive researchers are the ones who discover cures for illnesses or uncover secrets of the world because their minds can see beyond their research. *In business*, these insightful managers are said to have "horse sense" because they instinctively know the needs of their clients or markets and can react positively to them before their competitors can. It is not surprising that intuition plays an important part in the lives of many successful people.[25]

In a paragraph developed by more than one example or reason, plural words such as *many, several, numerous*, etc., are often used in the main-idea statement. Read the following statements, which give clue words about the paragraph's development.

> People today realize the *many* advantages of keeping physically fit.

The writer will probably go on to tell you what some of these advantages are.

> *Some* very interesting facts about the case were revealed during the trial.

The clue words "some very interesting facts" imply that the writer will give examples of these facts.

> Unfortunately, we encountered a *few* problems during our trip.

It is obvious that the writer will elaborate on these problems.

> During the year, *many* important measures were taken to ensure that the company's procedures were up to date.

The writer will now explain what those measures were.

Clue words that suggest that the writer is presenting examples or reasons can also appear in the paragraph itself, as illustrated in the following example:

The main idea is developed by four examples of what people might want in a report.	In planning a report, one should give serious thought to the needs and temperament of the person for whom it is being prepared. *Some people* want all details carefully and completely explained. *Others*, however, prefer concise well-documented deductions. *On the other hand, many employers* expect to see tables and graphs that clearly and succinctly present all the information at a glance. *And still, there are those* who would "run a mile" from any report that contained a vestige of statistical data.[26]

Although the main-idea sentence does not really give clues to tell the reader that specific examples will follow, the words that introduce each example of what people might want in a report (some ... others ...) identify the pattern of development.

II. PARAGRAPHS DEVELOPED BY SEQUENCE

In a paragraph developed by examples, the writer can present data in any order without substantially changing the meaning or effectiveness of the message. However, to explain a process, give instructions, or relate a story or event, he or she must use a *particular order* to relay the message to the reader without adding confusion.

Read the following statements and notice the italicized clue words, which should alert you to a specific sequence that will be developed.

> Finally, the story about what really had happened *began* to unfold.

If the writer indicates that "a story" is going to be told, naturally he or she will start at the beginning and relate it step by step.

> According to psychologists, children must pass through natural *stages* in their emotional *development* if they are to be emotionally stable adults.

There are two clue words here that should alert the reader that a specific order of events will follow: *stages* and *development*. The writer most likely will start with a description or identification of the first stage and follow each one until completion.

> To obtain our passports as quickly as possible, we were advised to *follow* this *procedure*.

Obviously, the writer must explain in logical sequence what the procedure is.

> *Changing a tire* is an easy task *if you know how*.

Although a direct clue word has not been given, the writer has hinted that he or she is going to explain how to change a tire.

> *During this last decade*, there have been *a series* of changes in secondary school curricula.

The writer will now probably present information, in chronological order, about the specific type of changes that were made and will begin with the first major change of the decade.

Other clue words that can appear in the paragraph and alert you to the major steps in a sequence are numerical words (first ... second ... etc.) or order words (next ... then ... finally ...) or any combination of both. Historical development is easy to follow because the dates and facts presented give you clues about the paragraph's development, as illustrated in the example that follows:

Although the main idea in this paragraph is unstated, the first sentence introduces the initial change and the dates clearly outline the sequence of events in the gradual development and acceptance of our present metric system. (The latter, by the way, would be the main idea!)

To overcome the confusion of measurement, Revolutionary France proclaimed the metre and kilogram as the sole standard measures for all purposes *in the late 1700s*. They were multiplied and subdivided in units of 10, with decimal points replacing the awkward fractions employed for conversion in the English scheme. Although a simultaneous attempt to impose a 10-hour day and a standard 30-day month failed, the simplicity and adaptability of the metric system gradually won recognition the world over. *In 1875, the Treaty of the Metre* was signed, setting up the International Bureau of Weights and Measures at Sèvres, near Paris. Then new standards for the kilogram and the metre were made. One of these—a platinum-iridium cylinder kept at Sèvres—is still the world standard for the kilogram. The old metal standard for the metre has since been superseded by physics. A metre is now officially "1650763.73 wave lengths of the orange-red line of krypton 86." *In 1893*, the United States scrapped its metal standards for the pound and the yard and redefined them in terms of the international kilogram and metre. *In 1951*, Canada did likewise. Since then, our official pounds and yards have been defined as ultra-precise fractions of the kilogram and metre. Pounds and yards ceased to exist as standards entirely when the British government followed suit *in 1959*. To get in step in matters of trade and technology with virtually all the rest of the world, Great Britain, Canada, and the United States *in recent years* have all decided to adopt the improved metric system known as "SI," for Système Internationale d'unités.[27]

III. Paragraphs Developed by Comparison or Contrast

It is sometimes easier for a writer to put a main point across by comparing or contrasting it to something more familiar to the reader or to some facts already established. If you can quickly recognize this pattern of development, then you can look for ways in which the persons or objects are similar or different.

The following statements give italicized clue words that should indicate that the pattern of development is either comparison or contrast.

It was amazing to see how *similar* the two girls really were.

The writer would now present ways in which the girls were alike (comparison pattern).

Women are now seeking *equality* in status with men.

If people or objects are said to be equal or striving for equality, then the writer will present facts that show how they are the same (comparison pattern).

The moth and the butterfly have *similar* stages of development.

The writer will probably now present information that indicates what the similar stages are.

Points of contrast are illustrated by either negative words or clue words italicized in the following statements. Contrast conveys the ways that people, objects, or ideas differ.

The gears in recent models of ten-speed bicycles *do not operate in the same way* as they did in earlier models.

By telling you that the gears "do *not* operate in the same way," the writer indicates that he or she will now present ways in which they are different (contrast pattern).

Parents' and teenagers' viewpoints about present-day issues often *differ*.

The writer will, most likely, describe some present-day issues and indicate ways in which opinions are dissimilar (contrast pattern).

There are many words and phrases which should clearly alert the reader to the comparison or contrast patterns of paragraphs. The following paragraph illustrates an effective use of the comparison pattern.

The main-idea statement illustrates the comparison pattern. Three major points of similarity follow.

An irresistible comparison arises between writing and another craft which most people have to practise sometimes, namely cooking. In both fields there is a *wide range of competence*, from the great chefs and authors to the occasional practitioners who must do the job whether they like it or not. In both, *care in preparation* is of the essence. Shakespeare wrote that it is an ill cook who does not lick her own fingers; it is an ill writer who does not *work at it hard enough to be reasonably satisfied with the results.*[28]

By using comparison, the writer has capably pointed out facts about the writing process that the reader will easily remember because the points have been compared to a craft that everyone has had some experience with: cooking.

In many paragraphs, you might have to look just beyond the main idea to see the author's method of development. But training yourself to recognize these major points and to be aware of how the writer is supporting a viewpoint will not only help you to interpret the meaning but should also help you to recall the essence of the writer's message.

Before you begin the exercise that follows, review the facts and clues about the three basic paragraph designs:

1. **Example or Reason.** The main-idea statement may discuss just one issue; in fact, the sentence could contain the word "one." Following the statement will be a further explanation or definition of *what* the writer means, or there could be a short illustration or story that verifies the main point.

   The main-idea statement could also contain *plural terms*, which would suggest that more than one example or reason will be presented. Clue words in the paragraph, such as *some ... other*, *first ... and*, *one ... another*, will identify the major details.

2. **Sequence of Steps or Events.** The main-idea statement will indicate a process or indicate a time period which suggests that *a particular order of facts or events* will follow. Other clue words might be *story, history, stages, development, steps, process,* and *procedure*—all of which indicate a specific order.

3. **Points of Comparison or Contrast.** This type of main-idea statement usually discusses *how* two people or items are *similar or dissimilar*. The clue words to look for that show comparison are *similar, alike, the same,* and *equal*. Clue words that indicate points of contrast are *dissimilar, unlike, not the same, opposite,* and *different from*.

After this unit, specific identification of paragraph development will not be emphasized; but your understanding and recalling ability will depend on how quickly and effectively you can recognize the writer's main idea and interpret major points of development.

● EXERCISE 2.4

By using the clue words presented in this section, anticipate the method of paragraph development that you would expect to follow these main-idea statements, and underline the clue words. If necessary, refer to the examples previously presented to help you become more familiar with the characteristics of the three basic designs.

1. As children <u>grow</u> from infants to adolescents, their attitudes towards their parents <u>change</u>.
   Developed by _Sequence_ ✓

2. There are usually <u>many</u> different motives for reading.
   Developed by _Example or Reason_ ✓

3. A crowd is a temporary grouping of people in physical proximity.
   Developed by _Example or Reason_ ✓

4. <u>From</u> the earliest times to the present, humanity has believed in a form of higher power.
   Developed by _Sequence_ ✗ _Example_

5. Children are too often handy targets for adult frustrations.
   Developed by _Example or Reason_ ✓

6. Books are good for us.
   Developed by _Example or Reason_ ✓

7. Two books I have recently read, *Gone with the Wind* and *Ashes in the Wind*, are incredibly <u>alike</u>.
   Developed by _Comparison_ ✓

8. Jealousy is an emotional response that fosters aggression.
   Developed by _Example or Reason_ ✓

9. The function of one's eye is <u>similar</u> to the function of a camera.
   Developed by _Comparison_ ✓

10. Effective speech-making means avoiding vague and clumsy words that often cause misinterpretation.
    Developed by _Example or Reason_ ✓

Check your answers with those in the Answer section at the end of the book.

● EXERCISE 2.5

In each of the following paragraphs, underline the main idea or write it in the margin, and indicate the paragraph's pattern of development.

1. The average reader can read an average book at the rate of 300 words a minute. That means 4500 words in a quarter of an hour, or 1 642 500 words in a year. <u>If you spend just fifteen minutes a day, you can read twenty average-length books between January 1 and December 31.</u>[20]   ✓
   Developed by _Example_

2. There is a difference between politeness and courtesy. According to Dr. Samuel Johnson, politeness is fictitious benevolence. Courtesy, on the other hand, has benevolence built in. One cannot be genuinely courteous without having a genuine regard for the feelings and general welfare of one's fellows. Politeness is a quality of the head; courtesy, of the heart.[30]

   Developed by _____Contrast ✓_____

3. A minority of the killers and mutilators of the road go beyond carelessness to wanton recklessness. Some—not all of them young—get a thrill out of willfully breaking traffic laws. Some bully their fellow road users by racing down pedestrians, forcing their way into traffic flows, and cutting perilously close in front of other vehicles when passing. Some lose their tempers and employ their vehicles as weapons to threaten the objects of their anger. Terrifyingly enough, some persist in driving while under the influence of alcohol or drugs. Drivers like these are public menaces, and they should be publicly condemned as such.[31]

   Developed by _____example ✓_____

4. Trans Canada Airlines went to work in the 1930s to establish a route across the country. It added larger Lockheed 14s and, on April 1, 1939, inaugurated a transcontinental passenger service between Montreal and Vancouver. The flying time of the first east-west flight was 16 hours, 5 minutes, with five intermediate stops. As early as 1943, TCA spread its wings over the Atlantic, operating the Canadian Government Trans-Atlantic Air Service, which carried priority passengers and mail in Lancaster bombers to and from Britain. This war effort paved the way for routine postwar transatlantic crossings by North Stars, then Super Constellations, then DC-8s, and the present giant Boeing 747s and Lockheed L-1011s. In the meantime, TCA, renamed Air Canada, has grown into one of the ten largest airlines in the world.[32]

   Developed by _____example sequence_____

5. Some people treat danger with greater equanimity than others. For instance, it comes naturally to a man born into a warrior class in an Eastern country to fear being branded a coward more than the prospect of sudden death. Similarly, a person with a genuine faith that he or she will enter into a happier state through dying is apt to be less afraid of mortal peril than one who thinks of death as the ultimate extinction. Some societies place a relatively low premium on human life so that they pay less attention than others to physical risks.[33]

   Developed by _____example ✓_____

Check your answers with those in the Answer section at the end of the book.

THE NEXT STEP

If you feel confident about this section, proceed to the Pretest for "Outlining" on the following page.

◆ PRETEST: OUTLINING

This exercise tests your ability to sense organization in detailed paragraphs or to use outlining as a note-taking technique.

1. Read the article that follows.

2. Record the most important information in outline format according to the following specifications:
    a) use Roman numerals (I, II, III, etc.) to indicate complete main-idea statements.
    b) use capital letters to identify major details (use words or word phrases if possible).
    c) use Arabic numbers (1, 2, 3, etc.) to indicate minor details (again, use words or word phrases if possible).

3. Record your answers on a separate sheet of paper.

The Urge to Collect[34]

Although people have habits of collecting things, this matter of instinct is not exclusive to human beings. Pack rats and magpies are notorious for stashing away every object that strikes their fancy. Chimpanzees and whisky-jacks share a habit of assembling jumbles of trash.

Psychologists have attributed people's urge to collect to many innate desires. Sigmund Freud, that monumental spoilsport, put down the urge to collect as a sublimation of sexual desire. This hardly seems to accord with the ways of pack rats and the rest, unless these creatures are more complicated than we think. Other psychologists have tied collecting to an unsatisfied lust for power. This would explain why some of the most powerful people in history have been among history's greatest collectors as well.

It is sufficient to say, therefore, that a great many different people collect a great many different things for a great many different reasons. It might even be said that we are all collectors whether we know it or not. For who among us does not collect something, be it rubber bands, paper bags, derelict wallets or handbags, desiccated ball-point pens, single cuff links, or earrings? What spouse does not notice a tendency in his or her partner to collect certain foodstuffs, such as various cheeses or teas, or current "specials" at the food market? How many are also reluctant to part with broken fishing tackle, odds and ends of material, or obsolete neckties or jewellery? What is a home without keys for which there are no locks, unstrung tennis rackets and unsmoked pipes, sweaters that will never be worn again, and musical instruments that will never again be played?

It takes a superhuman effort of will to throw out everything in a household that should be thrown out, and most of us prove to be only too human when the moment of decision arrives. Sophisticated collectors would dismiss this as mere "accumulation," as opposed to the active practice of collecting, which entails buying, selling, trading, labelling, cataloguing, and maintaining contact with fellow enthusiasts. Still, it takes no special powers of analysis to see that our reluctance to part with useless items goes beyond the delusion that they "might come in handy someday." They may be rubbish, but it is our own rubbish—part of our uniqueness as human beings.

Check your answers with those in the Answer section at the end of the book.

If you had errors of any kind, complete the lesson that begins on the following page. If you successfully completed this Pretest, write the Unit Two Post-Test.

OUTLINING

An outline is a visual written record of an author's skeleton of ideas. If you can learn to see this framework within a written work, you will be better able to interpret the ideas the author is attempting to convey. Comprehension can only improve with your ability to see the organization of another's work.

In the previous sections of this unit, you have learned to recognize main ideas and anticipate methods of development. In this section, you will learn to put both of those skills together to see the author's "total picture."

Outlining is not only an excellent skill to use in note-taking from textbooks and lectures, but it is also a skill you will use as a basis for all of your written compositions, essays, and reports. You will find that your effectiveness and success in future reading and writing assignments in all classes will depend on your ability to organize—both as you read and as you write!

I. OUTLINE FORMAT

Outlines should be clearly and neatly written so that your interpretation is recorded correctly. There should be no doubt about the importance and relevance of any point. Note that

- the Roman numeral identifying the main idea is placed at the left-hand margin.
- capital letters, which indicate the major points of development, are indented five spaces. Each of these points should contain similar word patterns; for example, if one major point begins with an action word, all other major points should begin with action words. If one begins with a noun, all other major points should begin with nouns.
- minor details that support the major points of development are identified by Arabic numbers and indented ten spaces from the left margin. They, too, are written in concise phrases.
- if a second line is required to provide complete information for any point, it should begin under the first word of the previous line—not in the left-hand margin.

Read the following paragraph and study the outline format that follows.

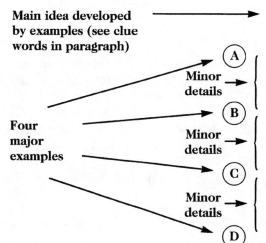

Main idea developed by examples (see clue words in paragraph)

Minor details

Four major examples

Minor details

Minor details

In planning a report, one should give serious thought to the needs and temperament of the person for whom it is being prepared. Some people want all details carefully and completely explained. They need to study every phase of the research to determine the worth of the report. If a great deal of money or work is to be invested, the reader wants the reassurance that all questions have been answered. Others, however, prefer concise, well-documented deductions. They are interested in the results and recommendations and will ask for any other data if they feel it is necessary. These readers have faith in the integrity of the researchers. Many employers expect to see tables and graphs that clearly and succinctly present all the information at a glance. To them, "a picture is worth a thousand words"; from this type of report, they can assimilate more information in a shorter period of time. And, still, there are those who would "run a mile" from any report that contained a vestige of statistical data.[35]

Outline Format

Main idea expressed as a complete sentence.

Four major details give examples of the kinds of reports different employers want.

Each minor point tells more about the preceding major detail.

I. In planning a report, one should give serious thought to the needs and temperament of the person for whom it is being prepared.

A. Some want all details explained
   1. need to study every phase of the report
   2. want reassurance if money or work is to be invested

B. Others prefer concise deductions only
   1. only interested in results and recommendations
   2. have faith in researchers

C. Employers expect tables and graphs
   1. "picture is worth a thousand words"
   2. can assimilate more information faster

D. Some dislike statistics

● EXERCISE 2.6

Outline the following paragraphs in the given formats. The main idea must be written as a complete sentence; the details should be clear, but brief.

1. Money represents different things to different people. For the poor, it means survival and the fulfilment of the basic needs of life, such as food and shelter. Middle-class citizens, who usually can save enough money from their pay cheques to enjoy some of the luxuries of life, see money as a security symbol. However, to the wealthy, who usually do not want for any materialistic items, money is a power symbol that allows them to do or gain whatever they desire.

I.   (Main idea developed by _____)

   A.

   B.

C.

2. The chief function of a family meeting is for members to discuss matters of common interest and to agree on what is to be done. Although every member of a family has rights, responsibilities, and privileges, there are times when the group must act as a unit. To do this effectively, all members should have input about any serious issue or problem facing the family rather than leaving the decision-making to one or two people. This practice teaches members to respect each other's rights and opinions. Despite any differences, the individuals also learn to negotiate what is best for all to live in harmony as a group. If every family encouraged this method of communication, more people would feel the security that this unit is supposed to provide.[36]

I.   (Main idea developed by _____)

    A.

    B.

    C.

    D.

    E.

● EXERCISE 2.7

Outline the following paragraphs in the spaces provided. For each paragraph, identify the main idea and write it as a complete sentence; then locate and record the major and minor details. The format for the first two paragraphs is given. Please note that minor details may follow only *some* of the major points, not necessarily all of them.

1. Communication is a process of transmitting a message from the sender to the receiver. First, the message is mentally considered by the sender and put into oral or written words. Then the message is conveyed to the receiver by any one of several means. One of the most common methods of relaying information is by telephone. Another means of communicating is by a written letter, memo, or telegram. And the third effective means of conveying a message is by personal contact. Once the message is given, it is up to the recipient to decode and interpret what has been sent.

I.   (Main idea developed by _____)

    A.

    B.

      1.

      2.

      3.

   C.

2. Although this method appears to be a simple process, communicating effectively seems to be a major problem in today's society. Many times, the sender does not clearly and completely prepare the message before he or she puts it into words. Information might be missing or incomplete. Also, if a letter or memo is poorly written, contains ambiguous statements, or has a multitude of mechanical errors, the true meaning will be clouded. In addition, the manner in which a message is presented could negatively affect the true intent of the sender. The tone of one's voice, the sloppiness of a written document, or the inappropriate dress or manners of the sender will change the original intent and content of the communiqué. As well as all of these possible errors, it should also be noted that the recipient must be capable of reading and correctly interpreting what he or she receives. This seemingly basic procedure, therefore, requires skillful messengers and recipients to make a successful communication circuit.[37]

I.   (Main idea developed by _____)

   A.

      1.

      2.

   B.

      1.

      2.

      3.

   C.

   D.

3. In the early 1800s, phrenology, a medical theory that bumps and depressions on people's skulls indicated their ability and personality traits, was a popularly used practice. At that time, it was believed that the brain was shaped according to its used or unused parts. For example, if a person used one particular area, that portion of the brain would grow from the exercise and create a bump. Any part of the brain that wasn't used would form an indentation. Using this theory, physicians studied people in jails and insane asylums to determine if the behaviour patterns these prisoners had displayed correlated with the shapes of their heads. The doctors discovered that many thieves had bumps above their ears. A great number of destructive people, those who gained pleasure from others' pain, seemed to have bumps behind their ears. Also, these researchers found that several inmates who were classified as "sex deviates" had large bumps at the back of their heads. Although this theory was short-lived, there may be a carry-over from it in our language today. Carefully consider what someone is implying if he or she says that you have "rocks in your head"!

4. It takes a superhuman effort to throw out everything in a household that should be thrown out, and most people prove to be only too human when the moment of decision arrives. Almost all homemakers have a collection of supermarket bags, old magazines, last year's telephone directory, or boxes of outdated clothes and footwear that just might be useful some day in the distant future. Children are often reluctant to part with favourite, old, ragged toys that are no longer a part of their everyday lives. How could they part with these priceless treasures that hold such memories of the past and are an important part of every child's security? Other members of the family insist on keeping sports equipment, even when these articles are just collecting dust in the basement. One never knows when skiing will once again be the sport of the year, and those old skis will be there, waiting for the owner to strap them on again. Regardless of how organized and tidy one is, everyone will likely have a horde of personal treasures that just might come in handy some day.[38]

Check your answers with those in the Answer section at the end of the book.

II. ORGANIZATION OF MORE THAN ONE PARAGRAPH

Even if articles consist of many paragraphs, each paragraph will have its own organization and importance to the total picture. To outline more than one paragraph, simply identify the main idea of each paragraph by successive Roman numerals. Each paragraph, then, will contain its own organization. Study the following example and accompanying outline for the first three paragraphs; then continue to complete the outline by following the same procedure.

The Practical Writer[39]

From time to time, most educated people are called upon to act as writers. Although they may not think of themselves as professional writers when they dash off a personal note or a memo, this is exactly what they are! They are practising a difficult and demanding craft and are expected to live up to its challenge. Their purpose must be the same as any author's. They must find the right words and put them in the right order so that the thoughts that are represented can be understood.

I. From time to time, most educated people are called upon to act as writers.
   A. are "professional writers"
   B. are practising the craft and must live up to its challenge
   C. have same purpose as any author
      1. find and use words in an understandable way

Although some writers deliberately muddy the meaning of their words, most people write to get a message across. Businesses depend on written words to carry the load of their communications. Letters, memos, reports, sales literature, and manuals are all part of an organization's structure. Every facet of a business depends on using words in a way that serves the goals of that organization.

II. Although some writers deliberately muddy the meaning of their words, most people write to get a message across.
   A. businesses dependent on written words
      1. letters, memos, etc., part of structure
   B. every facet of business relies on words that serve the goals of the organization

Unfortunately, written communications often fail to accomplish this purpose. Some organizational writing gives rise to confusion, inefficiency, and ill-will. Somehow, the intended message did not get through to the receiving end. In most cases, the reason was a simple one—the message was inadequately prepared!

III. Unfortunately, written communications often fail to accomplish this purpose.
   A. confusion, inefficiency, ill-will created
   B. intended message not received
      1. inadequately prepared message

● EXERCISE 2.8

Continue by completing outlines for the last four paragraphs.

An irresistible comparison arises between writing and another craft which most people have to practise sometimes, namely cooking. In both fields there is a wide range of competence, from the great chefs and authors to the occasional practitioners who must do the job whether they like it or not. In both, care in preparation is of the essence. Shakespeare wrote that it is an ill cook who does not lick her own fingers; it is an ill writer who does not work at it hard enough to be reasonably satisfied with the results.

Unlike bachelor cooks, however, casual writers are rarely the sole consumers of their own offerings. Reclusive philosophers and schoolgirls keeping diaries are about the only writers whose work is not intended for other eyes. If a piece of writing turns out to be an indigestible half-baked mess, those on the receiving end are usually the ones to suffer. The reader of a bad book can always toss it aside, but in organizations, where written communications command attention, it is up to the recipient of a sloppy writing job to figure out what it means.

The reader is thus put in the position of doing the thinking the writer failed to do. To make others do your work for you is, of course, an uncivil act. In a recent magazine advertisement on the printed word, one of a commendable series published by the International Paper Company, novelist Kurt Vonnegut touched on the social aspect of writing: "Why should you examine your writing style with the idea of improving it? Do so as a mark of respect for your readers. If you scribble your thoughts any which way, your readers will surely feel that you care nothing for them."

In the working world, bad writing is not only bad manners, it is bad business. The victim of an incomprehensible letter will at best be annoyed and at worst decide that people who can't say what they mean aren't worth doing business with. Write a sloppy letter, and it might rebound on you when the recipient calls for clarification. Where one carefully worded letter would have sufficed, you might have to write two or more.

Muddled messages can cause havoc within an organization. Instructions that are misunderstood can set people off in the wrong directions or put them to work in vain. Written policies that are open to misinterpretation can throw sand in the gears of an entire operation. Ill-considered language in communications with employees can torpedo morale.

Check your answers with those in the Answer section at the end of the book.

III. READING THE NEWSPAPER FOR COMPREHENSION

In the previous exercises, you learned about various reading techniques and developed many skills to help you improve your reading comprehension. Now, you should apply those skills to your everyday reading materials—for example, the newspaper. In addition to a daily information source, newspapers are an excellent resource for research materials for essays or reports; therefore, it is important that you understand how this information is organized and presented.

Paragraphs in a newspaper must be short. Most times they are one, two, or three sentences long—seldom longer. Why? First of all, because of the limited space, paragraphs cannot contain well-developed ideas or always begin with a main-idea sentence. A reporter writes a straight news story in an inverted triangle style with the most important news given first. Thus, the reader will get the essentials of the story at the beginning; and the editor, if he or she lacks space, will be able to cut off the last few paragraphs without affecting the sense of the story. Secondly, short paragraphs present a good visual picture for the readers. People are more inclined to read short bits of information than solid blocks of writing. Since there is a lot of news to read in the newspaper, the readers want to scan the articles and read bits and pieces of all that interests them. If information was presented as solid blocks of writing, most of the news would probably be unread.

Now, look at the various kinds of information that are in the newspaper.

TYPES OF NEWSPAPER ARTICLES

A newspaper is made up of several types of information:

1. News stories about international, national, and local events.

2. News about sports, business, science, education, and lifestyles; human interest stories; feature stories; and other special interest stories.

3. Editorials—the editor's opinions on a current news event.

4. Columns—daily or weekly stories written by one particular journalist under his or her special headline.

   a) Some columns comment on and explain the news or politics—internationally, nationally, provincially, and/or municipally.

   b) Other columns are written about special interests such as hobbies, manners, cooking, gardening, business, pets, health, personal problems, general maintenance, etc.

5. Reviews of plays, books, movies, music, travel destinations, television programs, etc.

6. Special features such as letters to the editor, cartoons, comics, puzzles, etc.

7. Advertisements—both general advertisements integrated throughout the paper and those specifically located in the classified ads sections. Some are written in the same style as a newspaper story but the "article" will be identified at the very top as "Advertisement."

The first two types of stories are based on facts; editorials and columns are based on personal opinions from reported facts.

Factual Stories

No personal feelings or biases are supposed to enter into a straight newspaper story. The journalist's job is to report the current events and stories factually, accurately, and impartially. In most reporting, the news writer summarizes the main facts in the first paragraph and adds details in the following paragraphs. Many news stories are accompanied by one or more pictures that attract the reader's attention and also illustrate the news item.

Editorials

One of the ways we gain more depth into the news of the day is to read the opinions of knowledgeable commentators. Editorial writers review what is happening or has happened and provide the readers with comparative information; background data; and others' viewpoints based on facts, experience, research, biases, etc. The purpose of editorials is to encourage readers to think beyond the facts and react to the issues by either agreeing or disagreeing with the original issue or with the critic.

THE STRUCTURE OF NEWS STORIES

All news stories consist of three parts:

1. **The Headline.** This is an eye-catching summary, usually printed in large, heavy type at the head of the story. It gives a quick idea of the content of the story. Many times there will be a subheading underneath the headline that highlights a detail of the story.

2. **The Lead.** The first paragraph or the first two paragraphs are called "the lead." In this initial part of the article, the writer usually summarizes the content and identifies the source of the information (that is, indicates the person who released or provided this data). In the lead, the journalist also answers the questions *where, when, who, what,* and *why.* **The lead is the main idea. The details that support this main idea will be contained in the paragraphs that follow.**

3. **The Body.** The body of the article follows the lead paragraph or paragraphs. In this section, the writer elaborates on the information given in the lead and provides the supporting facts for the story. The paragraphs are organized so that the most important details are given first and the least important ones last.

It is the reader's task to comprehend what the writer has said.

Look at the example on the following page. Notice how the first two paragraphs answer the five main questions. The rest of the article fills in the details.

E-MAIL NOT REPLACING LETTERS YET

ASSOCIATED PRESS

MINNEAPOLIS, Minn. — Sure, e-mail is making inroads, but don't count out the old-fashioned letter, envelope and stamp mail just yet.

Thomas Leavey, director general of the International Bureau of the Universal Postal Union, said postal services represent 27 percent of the world's communications market, compared with e-mail's 4 percent.

Phones and faxes carry more than either form, but about half the world's population still lacks phone access, said Leavey, a former assistant U.S. postmaster general. He spoke in Minneapolis last week as part of an International Telecommunication Union conference.

That's why postal service, though erratic in some countries, remains "a trusted third party" in communications, he said. Postal volume is expected to continue growing about 2.5 percent per year until 2005.

Whatever e-mail's advantages, "snail mail" still has a place, he said.

"There still is a warm feeling you get about mail, just as about the newspaper on your doorstep," he said.

But in some countries, the old and the new are converging.

In Ghana, post offices are offering e-mail addresses and computer terminals for customers to exchange electronic messages, he said. In Brazil, postal kiosks are offering electronic ways to order merchandise from catalogs.[40]

MAIN IDEA

Source: Thomas Leavey, who is the director general of the International Bureau of the Universal Postal Union and former assistant U.S. postmaster general

Where: at the International Telecommunication Union conference in Minneapolis

When: last week (check dateline)

What: Although e-mail is increasing in popularity, the old-fashioned way of sending letters via the postal service is still the more popular method.

Why: Postal services represent 27 percent of the world's communications market compared with e-mail's 4 percent.

SUPPORTING DETAILS
(Note that the story can be cut at any point after the lead.)

— phones and faxes are more common than either form but about half the world's population still lacks phone access

— even though it's sometimes erratic in some countries, it is still a trusted form of communication

— people like the warm feeling associated with having something delivered to their homes

— in some countries, such as Ghana and Brazil, the post offices are offering computer-access services.

● EXERCISE 2.9

Read the following articles and find the essential information.

1. Read the title and the lead paragraph(s); then quickly identify the source and the answers to the questions *where, when, who, what,* and *why.*

2. Briefly record the supporting details.

ANNE FRANK HIDING PLACE RESTORED FOR DOCUMENTARY

TORONTO STAR

AMSTERDAM, Netherlands—The secret annex where Anne Frank and her family hid from the Nazis during World War II has been restored for a documentary film on the teenage diarist's life.

It is the first time the four-room annex has been refurbished to appear as it did during the two years recorded in Anne's famous diary, K.P.D. Broekhuizen, the deputy director of the Anne Frank Foundation, said yesterday.

The small wing at the rear of a brick house has been maintained as a museum by the foundation and attracts hundreds of thousands of visitors each year.

Filming is scheduled to begin next week on the $136 000 documentary, which will be marketed internationally next year, Broekhuizen said.

The film portrays a modern-day boy reading Anne's diary while visiting the annex where she, her parents, her sister and four other Jews hid, Broekhuizen said.

It will include superimposed images of the Frank family from photos and "as little play acting as possible," said Broekhuizen.

To restore the annex, researchers used descriptions from the diary as well as records kept by Anne's father, Otto, and the recollections of Miep Gies, a non-Jewish friend who smuggled food to the family.

Anne's two years in hiding began on a rainy day in July 1942, when her parents told her they would go into hiding in the building on the Prinsengracht where Otto ran his pectin trading company.

That day, Anne wrote of the hidden annex, describing its layout, furnishings and even the 150 cans of vegetables cached to sustain them.

The Franks were betrayed in the fall of 1944 and deported to Nazi extermination camps.

Anne and her sister, Margot, are believed to have died in late February or early March 1945 in Bergen-Belsen, weeks before it was liberated by the Allies. Her father was the only survivor.[41]

MAIN IDEA

Source:

Where:

When:

Who:

What:

Why:

SUPPORTING DETAILS

—

—

—

—

—

—

—

—

—

COKE SET TO TAP INTO BOTTLED WATER

THE GUARDIAN

WASHINGTON — Coca-Cola is about to take the plunge into the fast-growing bottled water business by selling its own brand of purified waster from the tap or wells, with some added minerals.

The world's biggest soft drinks company is expected to start selling water throughout the United States in May. The company even has a brand name in the works — Dasani.

Coke has hesitated to diversify into the water business because the secret of its success is simplicity — it sells concentrate to bottlers. Other companies then add water and carbonation and distribute the resulting drinks, and water sales could undercut its profits from soft drinks.

But bottled water has become too big a market for Coke to ignore, and its executives believe that if people want to drink water, it might as well be purified tap water from Coca-Cola.

Its archrival, PepsiCo., has entered the market with its Aquafina brand, now the top-selling water brand at corner shops and gas stations.

Bottled water is a $4 billion a year business, up from $2.65 million in 1990, says Beverage Marketing Corp., a New York consultancy. Sales of plastic bottles of water have been the largest, rising 25 percent over the past two years.

The largest player is Perrier, with the Poland Spring and Arrowhead brands. This week, Danone, the French owner of Evian and Dannon, agreed to buy AquaPenn Spring Water, the 10th largest firm in the United States, for $110 million.[42]

MAIN IDEA

Source:

Where:

When:

Who:

What:

Why:

SUPPORTING DETAILS

—

—

—

—

—

—

—

—

—

—

3. Use the same procedure on three to five current newspaper articles.

Check your answers with those in the Answer section at the end of the book.

COLLABORATIVE EXERCISE 2.10

Step 1: With two or more group members, choose a current news story that is of interest to all members of the group. Each member should have a copy of the article. You can choose the article from your local newspaper or from a news source on the Internet.

Step 2: Then, individually, read and identify the essential information as you have done in the previous exercises by recording the answers to the five questions.

Step 3: Once you clearly understand the message, write down what you consider to be the major point(s), issue(s), or conclusion(s) of the news story.

Step 4: Next, all members should come together to discuss the facts and issues as each one has recorded them. Have all identified the same content as being essential? Have all identified the same issues or conclusions of the news story? If you missed any details, add them to your notes.

Step 5: What is your opinion about these issues? Do you agree or disagree? Why? Think of good reasons or examples to support your opinion. Discuss your opinion with those members who have a similar view.

Step 6: Then debate, for no longer than fifteen minutes, with those who have the opposite point of view. Each side should take turns presenting a strong reason or example for their viewpoint. Now, with information from both sides, reconsider your point of view. Do you still have the same viewpoint or have you changed your mind with the information presented by the other team?

Step 7: With a show of hands, decide which is the dominant opinion.

THE NEXT STEP

If you feel confident about this section, write the Unit Two Post-Test at the end of this unit.

 # FREEWRITING

This assignment is separate and can be done before or after the Post-Test for this unit.

GETTING TO KNOW YOURSELF AS A WRITER

To prepare yourself for future writing assignments, continue to do the freewriting activities. You will use these exercises for future grammar and composition exercises. Even if your instructor does not request these pieces of writing, complete these activities and keep them in one place for future reference. Learning to improve your writing skills is much more valuable and meaningful if you can apply specific skills to your own work.

Write for ten to fifteen minutes, without stopping, on one of the choices given below or on ones assigned by your instructor. Try to express your feelings as you would if you were talking to a close friend.

NOTE: Do not worry if you do not have time to finish this activity. It is more important to write as much as you can in the given time.

1. Describe one of the following. Your first sentence should identify what you are about to describe.
   a) The significant events that happened on the first day of a new job
   b) The method you use to study for a test in a particular subject (e.g., math, physics, economics, history, English)
   c) How to repair a specific object or item

2. Select a current newspaper article. Identify the main message and then write a letter to the editor in response. State whether you agree or disagree with the writer and give reasons for your opinions.

POST-TEST FOR UNIT TWO

If you feel confident about the skills presented in this unit, complete the following Post-Test. **Do not attempt this test if you have not completed the required work.**

Once you have completed the whole test, check your answers with the suggested ones at the end of this unit. A marking scheme has been provided to give you a realistic idea of your ability in this area. Your goal should be to achieve 80 percent or more.

1. Read the following articles.

2. In the spaces provided, write the main-idea statement from each paragraph and indicate which of the methods of paragraph development discussed in this unit has been used. (One paragraph has an implied main idea.)

   (Deduct two marks for each main-idea or paragraph-development error.)

   TOTAL MARKS FOR IDENTIFYING MAIN IDEAS _____/10

   TOTAL MARKS FOR IDENTIFYING PARAGRAPH DEVELOPMENT _____/10

3. In the spaces provided, outline any three paragraphs from the articles that follow.

   (Deduct two marks for each error in outline format or content.)

   TOTAL MARKS FOR OUTLINING _____/30

Depression in College Students[43]

Why are college students, a more competent and advantaged group than the general population, such easy prey to depression? There are many possible reasons. Many students are living away from home for the first time. They must cope with situations that require new kinds of adaptive behaviours. In addition, because colleges bring together the most talented and achieving students from many high schools, staying at the top is much harder, and competition is fierce. Many students who have always been near the top of their classes can't face the prospect of a less outstanding position. Often students aren't sure what career they want to follow. They may spend time feeling guilty about the money their parents are spending on their education and feel an obligation to be successful even when they have no clear idea of what to do with their lives. At first, they may have few people to whom they can turn for comfort or reassurance. Their old friends are back home, and the effort required to make new friends may cause some anxiety. Severe loneliness and feelings of isolation result.

I. _____
_____
_____
_____
_____
(Developed by _____
_____)

Self-destruction is also a serious problem among college students. The suicide rate for the college population is 50 percent higher than for the general population. Each year 100 000 North American college students threaten suicide and some 1000 actually kill themselves. During a nine-year period, 23 students enrolled at the University of California at Berkeley committed suicide (Seiden, 1966). Compared to their non-suicidal classmates, these students appeared to be moody, drove themselves harder, and were depressed frequently. Their

II. _____
_____
_____
_____
_____
(Developed by _____
_____)

depression often took the form of extreme agitation. Most of them gave recurrent warnings of their suicidal intent. The major precipitating factors seemed to be worry about schoolwork, concerns about health, and difficulties in their relationships with others.

Although most students who feel depressed do not seek professional help either within the college or from outside sources, perhaps the one effective way to reduce this problem is to make them aware, as soon as possible, that what they are experiencing is not unique. The majority of students have the same discomforts. This might help them decide more intelligently how to deal with depression and where to seek help. Rather than attributing academic difficulties to intellectual deficiencies, the student might be made aware that emotional stress and depression may cause sadness and less motivated behaviour, which also might interfere with academic performance.

III. _____
_____
_____
_____
_____
(Developed by _____
_____)

Child Labour[44]

During the nineteenth century, many young children were put to work in factories and were denied the opportunity to attend school. The majority of these youngsters faced life as unskilled labourers; however, gradual improvements changed this unfair practice. The founding conference of the Canadian Labour Union in 1873 supported a resolution to prohibit the employment of children under ten in manufacturing establishments where machinery was used. In the late 1800s, various provincial factory acts were passed. These prohibited the employment of boys under twelve and girls under fourteen. Also, a limit of sixty hours of work per week for women and children was established. During the twentieth century, major advances were made. At present, the federal government and all provinces have passed child labour laws. The Canadian Labour Code allows the employment of individuals under the age of seventeen only if they are not required, under provincial law, to be in attendance at school and if the work is unlikely to endanger their health or safety. In addition, no one under seventeen is permitted to work during the hours from 11 p.m. to 6 a.m.

I. _____
_____
_____
_____
_____
(Developed by _____
_____)

Japanese and Canadian Management Styles[45]

Japanese managers are more likely than Canadian managers to practise participative management; that is, to manage by consensus. Performance in Japanese firms tends to be evaluated more on group, or team, accomplishments. In this Eastern country, subordinates are encouraged to participate in the decision making that will affect them in order to get their commitment to the decision. In Canadian firms, however, performance tends to be evaluated more on the individual's accomplishments. Although it ordinarily takes Japanese

I. _____
_____
_____
_____
_____
(Developed by _____
_____)

managers longer than Canadian managers to make decisions, the Japanese can usually implement their decisions more quickly because most of the opposition to a decision will have been eliminated before it is made. On the other hand, Canadian managers make decisions more quickly but typically spend more time implementing them. It is likely that Japanese and Canadian styles of management will become more alike as firms in these two nations compete more aggressively for sales in the global business environment.

SUGGESTED ANSWERS FOR UNIT TWO POST-TEST

Depression in College Students

I. There are many possible reasons for the competent and advantaged group of college students to suffer from depression. (An implied main idea developed by examples)

    A. living away from home for the first time
        1. must cope and adapt to new situations

    B. more competition and more students in class
        1. can't face prospect of less outstanding position

    C. not sure of their career choice
        1. guilty feelings about cost of their education
        2. feel obligated to parents

    D. no one to turn to for comfort or reassurance
        1. miss friends from home
        2. difficulty forming new friendships
        3. feelings of loneliness and isolation

II. Self-destruction is also a serious problem among college students. (Developed by *examples*)

    A. suicide rate 50 percent higher than general population
        1. 100 000 threaten suicide and 1000 actually kill themselves

    B. in a nine-year period, twenty-three suicide victims from University of California
        1. were moody, drove themselves harder, and were depressed frequently
        2. were often extremely agitated
        3. gave recurring warnings of their intentions

    C. worry about schoolwork, concerns about health, and difficulties in relationships major factors

III. Perhaps one effective way to reduce this problem is to make students aware that what they are experiencing is not unique. (Developed by *details* of an explanation)

    A. help them make intelligent decisions about how to get help

    B. make them aware of effects of emotional stress

Child Labour

I. Gradual improvements changed the child labour practices of the nineteenth century. (Developed by *sequence* of events. The second sentence of the paragraph, with a few necessary added details for clarity, is the main-idea sentence.)

   A. in 1873, children under ten prohibited in manufacturing firms

   B. in 1800s, various provincial factory acts passed
      1. prohibited employment for boys under twelve and girls under fourteen
      2. limit of sixty hours per week for women and children

   C. in twentieth century, major advances
      1. federal and provincial governments passed child labour laws
      2. those under seventeen can work if not required by province to be in school and if work is not dangerous to health or safety
      3. no one under seventeen can work from 11 p.m. to 6 a.m.

Japanese and Canadian Management Styles

I. Japanese managers are more likely than Canadian managers to practise participative management. (Developed by *contrasting details* of how these two countries differ in management styles)

   A. Japanese performance evaluation based on team effort
      1. subordinates participate in decision making and thus are committed to it

   B. Canadian performance evaluation based on individual effort

   C. Japanese take longer to make decisions but implement them more quickly

   D. Canadian managers make decisions more quickly but take more time implementing them

   E. competition will force both to become more similar in style

DEVELOPING GOOD STUDY SKILLS

 ## OVERVIEW

Learning to recognize the main idea, anticipating the author's pattern of development, and seeing the "skeleton" of major and minor supporting points will improve your comprehension skills. If you continue to use what you have just learned, your retention of the ideas in a chapter or passage will also improve, as you will be training your brain to read for ideas and not for the words that are expressed on paper. In other words, you will have developed a system for finding out what is important.

In addition to using these skills for comprehension and note-taking in research projects, you can also use these same techniques to take notes in lectures. Most speakers have a specific message to give their audience; if you become skilled at recognizing the key portions of the lecture (that "skeleton of ideas") and can record them in a meaningful outline format, then you not only will gain a better understanding of the lecture but will also have excellent notes for study purposes.

LEARNING OBJECTIVES FOR UNIT THREE

Upon completion of this unit, you should be able to:

1. Apply preview techniques to textbook and research reading.

2. Use comprehension skills from Unit Two by highlighting or underlining the key words in the main ideas and major supporting details.

3. Write brief and concise marginal notes to enhance highlighted or underlined portions of an excerpt. These notes will serve one or all of the following purposes:
   a) defining difficult vocabulary words that have been circled in the text
   b) identifying paragraph content by using a descriptive title
   c) summarizing a complex portion of the text with a clear, concise statement
   d) writing a brief, inferred main idea beside the related paragraph (underlining may be required to make the message complete)

4. By highlighting the key words in the main message and using marginal notes, create a readable and complete synopsis of an article.

5. Identify the main message in a given newspaper article and write a letter to the editor in response.

6. Use comprehension skills to improve listening ability in lectures.

7. Write meaningful notes at lectures using suggested techniques and knowledge of comprehension skills.

 Check Internet resources for additional news articles for reading, underlining, note-taking, and collaborative exercises (see pages 469–70).

STUDYING WRITTEN MATERIALS

There is **no** Pretest for this section. Instead, you should work through each and every exercise and evaluate your skills as you progress. If you encounter difficulties, see your instructor for assistance.

The comprehension skills you have learned so far can also be transferred to your textbooks to help you to identify the theme of the chapter or article for your future reference. Underlining or highlighting and making marginal notes as you read makes the content "come alive"! You already have the necessary skills to accomplish this task.

I. IDENTIFYING THE MAIN MESSAGE BY UNDERLINING

Read the following paragraph and note that the underlined portions identify the main idea and the necessary supporting points.

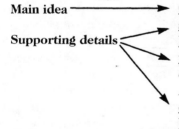

Main idea

Supporting details

Communication is a process of <u>transmitting a message from the sender to the receiver.</u> First, the <u>message</u> is mentally <u>considered by</u> the <u>sender and put into words.</u> <u>Then</u> the message is <u>conveyed to</u> the <u>receiver</u> by any one of several means. One of the most common methods of relaying information is <u>by telephone.</u> Another means of communicating is <u>by written letter, memo, or e-mail.</u> And the third effective means of conveying a message is <u>by personal contact.</u> <u>Once</u> the message is <u>given,</u> it is <u>up to</u> the <u>recipient to decode</u> and <u>interpret what has been sent.</u>

In applying this technique, your objective should be to mark *just the key words* in the main idea and supporting details. What you hope to produce is a readable and meaningful message of underlined parts of the text. Therefore, eliminate any unnecessary wording. It is important to include the following:

1. the topic

2. the action or viewpoint expressed

3. the circumstances or results

Try to underline or highlight only meaningful phrases of two or more words and avoid marking complete lines or paragraph blocks. This latter practice creates more problems than it solves; since all the words leap out at you, their importance and relevance remain a mystery, and you are faced with two tasks: trying to find the skeleton of ideas and trying to read "between the lines" marked in the text!

To find out if you have the correct message, read only what you have underlined. For example, read the underlined portions of the following paragraph and note how the main message has been identified. What you underline should provide you with a readable and meaningful synopsis of the passage.

Key words in
main idea

Key words in
supporting details

Other necessary
words included
to make message
flow

Although this method appears to be a simple process, communicating effectively seems to be a major problem in today's society. Many times, the sender does not clearly and completely prepare the message before he or she puts it into words. Information might be missing or incomplete. Also, if a letter or memo is poorly written, contains ambiguous statements, or has a multitude of mechanical errors, the true meaning will be clouded. In addition, the manner in which a message is presented could negatively affect the true intent of the sender. The tone of one's voice, the sloppiness of a written document, or the inappropriate dress or manners of the sender will change the original intent and content of the communiqué. As well as all of these possible errors, you should note that the recipient must be capable of interpreting what he or she receives. This seemingly basic procedure, therefore, requires skillful messengers and recipients to make a successful communication circuit.

● EXERCISE 3.1

In the following paragraph, underline or highlight the key words in the main idea and necessary supporting points.

It takes a superhuman effort to throw out everything in a household that should be thrown out, and most people prove to be only too human when the moment of decision arrives. Almost all homemakers have a collection of supermarket bags, old magazines, last year's telephone directory, or boxes of outdated clothes and footwear that just might be useful some day in the distant future. Children are often reluctant to part with favourite, old, ragged toys that are no longer a part of their everyday lives. How could they part with these priceless treasures that hold such memories of the past and are an important part of every child's security? Other members of the family insist on keeping sports equipment, even when these articles are just collecting dust in the basement. One never knows when skiing will once again be the sport of the year, and those old skis will be there, waiting for the owner to strap them on again. Regardless of how organized and tidy one is, everyone will likely have a horde of personal treasures that just might come in handy some day.[1]

Check your answers with those in the Answer section at the end of the book.

Note that words such as *however, but, unfortunately, as a result, consequently, similarly,* etc., are necessary for the meaning of the paragraph. These words indicate a change of thought, a result, or a condition—all of which are necessary to create the flow of the message.

II. USING PREVIEW TECHNIQUES

To gain thorough comprehension of a long factual article or a chapter of a textbook, first preview the selection:

1. Read the title and the author's name or source of information.

2. Read the lead paragraph(s), if there is one.

3. To create a purpose for your reading, read subtitles as they occur and change them into questions.

4. Read the first sentence of each paragraph.

5. As you scan this material, circle any unknown words that you happen to see.

6. Look at any pictures, charts, graphs, or diagrams as you meet them and read their captions.

7. Read the final paragraph, summary, or list of questions that concludes the writing selection. (Chapters often end with summaries or questions.)

By following this technique and by making it a natural procedure, you will understand and remember content better than you ever have before. By forming questions of subtitles, you will be giving a purpose to your reading task; and by reading just the first sentence of each paragraph, you will be skimming most of the author's main ideas. Therefore, you will have a general idea of the scope and limits of the author's message and will be ready to accept and interpret the supporting details when you read completely through the selection.

● EXERCISE 3.2

1. Preview the following excerpt from the article "What Use Is Education?" Sample vocabulary words have been circled, although some of these words may not necessarily be unknown to you. If there are other words whose meanings you do not recognize, please circle those as well.

2. Before you begin to underline, define the circled words in either the top or the bottom margin. You could use the word skills presented in Unit One or you could consult your dictionary.

3. Now, read the first part of the article. As you read, underline or highlight the most important words from the main idea and important details. As you read through the article, you may find that there are complete paragraphs that do not require underlining. This information is necessary for you to understand the author's ideas and viewpoints but may not be essential for your recall ability.

4. Use the following questions to help you identify the main message.

   a) What is the article about?
   b) What is the author saying about this topic?
   c) Who is involved?
   d) When does this occur?
   e) Where does it take place?
   f) Why is this important?
   g) What conditions are present?
   h) What results will take, or have taken, place?

All of these questions may not always be appropriate, some may need to be repeated, and they need not be asked in this specific order. Try to follow the flow of the article with your choice of questions. Remember, your underlined or highlighted portions should create a meaningful and complete message.

Source of information]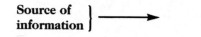

The Royal Bank of Canada
Monthly Letter

Title ———————————————————▶   **What Use Is Education?[2]**

[*A student wrote to the editor of the* Monthly Letter, *Royal Bank of Canada, and questioned <u>why young people should</u> continue in school and <u>get an education. The following letter was the response.</u>*]

The commonplace thing to do would be to enlarge upon the material aspects of a good education, and to tell you that the principal benefit is in helping you to get a good job, etc. We are sure you already know about that. A young <u>person who does not make the best of all the <u>learning opportunities of school</u> years will be at a disadvantage in competition</u> with others in later life.

We are not going to suggest to you that you should fill yourself chock-full of information, for the <u>real benefit of your education</u> will be <u>knowledge and understanding</u> and not a long list of memorized facts. The <u>main purpose of education</u>, as we see it, <u>is</u> to <u>teach one to think,</u>

Subtitle ———————————▶   **Learning to Think**

It is only by learning how to think, and by <u>learning how to sift out things worth thinking about,</u> that you can <u>put yourself in the best position for enjoying a happy life.</u> This is a very important reason for wishing to continue at school and get an education. <u>Education,</u> when of the right sort, <u>helps you</u> to see things <u>clearly, to distinguish between the essential and the (trivial,)</u> and to <u>give you</u> a frame of mind and system of <u>thought and judgement that will fit</u> you into your place <u>in life.</u>

of little significance or value

<u>Without education</u> (1) you could <u>never hope to really understand</u> the world or its people or <u>what goes on in it</u>; (2) you <u>could not handle yourself graciously</u> and with ease in an environment that is not always so well disposed towards you as your home and your school; (3) you <u>could never relate</u> yourself properly <u>to the problems of others</u> or achieve <u>the peace of mind and understanding</u> which one must have <u>to support one through the crises</u> that come to try all of us.

We believe it is very much worthwhile for you to study and we hope that you will pursue your education so successfully that you will have a very happy life. You will realize, we are sure, that <u>everyone faces problems</u> and difficulties at <u>some time or other</u> and everyone suffers distress and sorrow. These seem to be inescapable. But the <u>educated person</u> is in a much <u>better position to cope</u> with these things, <u>to solve</u> these problems, and <u>to master</u> some of the <u>difficulties,</u> and <u>thus</u> in the end to be less <u>disturbed and grieved</u> by it all. An educated individual is, we think, <u>entitled</u> to count upon life holding out prospects <u>of achievement and security</u>—not the kind of security that is dependent upon one's ideals, capability and understanding.

What we are trying to say is that <u>education is absolutely essential</u> but we are not referring to a mass of what, in an old-fashioned way, we called "book learning" and nothing else. What we are after is the education that will teach you to think and

A manner of personal conduct behaviour

reason, which will improve your material prospects, which will add to your poise and (deportment,) which will develop your judgement and which, all in all, will round you out for a fully successful and happy life. That is the kind of life we wish for you.

Subtitle ⟶ **A Sense of Values**

One of the most frightening things in our world is ignorance; not merely lack of knowledge, but more than anything else the ignorance that consists in not knowing that there are better things, better ways of doing things, and a social responsibility to try to see and do these better things.

Education will help you to think clearly and reach good judgements about the relative importance of the various kinds of activity that make up human life. What are these activities? There are some that minister directly to self-preservation, like obtaining food and keeping healthy; others are concerned with the raising of offspring; some have to do with social and political relations; and there are activities associated with the leisure part of life. All of these (clamour) for attention, effort and time. The value of any of them exists for you in relation to the values you give the others.

a loud out cry

An ancient Greek philosopher said the purpose of education is to persuade you to like what you ought to like, and to dislike what you ought to dislike. Education will open up to you the opportunity to follow the true, the beautiful and the good, to avoid vulgarity and false sentiments by providing you with standards by which to judge values. It will enable you to decide what will contribute toward your happiness in life. Without education, how can you (discern) what is good for you? what is right or wrong? what is true or false? what is lovely or ugly?

to recognize

Check your answers with those in the Answer section at the end of the book.

If you have a tendency to underline too much or too little, be aware that what you have underlined should be meaningful to you as you read—these portions should represent a "skeleton" of the author's ideas.

● EXERCISE 3.3

Now continue the process for the second section and try to correct any problems you have encountered.

1. Preview.
2. Define unknown words.
3. Read thoroughly and underline or highlight.

This Changing World

We in Canada are very conscious of our natural resources, because our economy is founded on them—our forests and our farmlands, our minerals and our waterpower, our fisheries and our wildlife. But all these resources are useless without two others: the intelligence and the initiative of our people.

And where do we get these personal qualities? From the accumulated intellectual talent of our people given to us through the discipline of education.

We need knowledge and enterprise more than people ever before needed them, because we are living in a period of the most profound social and cultural transition. Young people of today do not realize it, for this is the only sort of world they know, but during the past sixty years our world has become increasingly strange and frightening.

Less than two generations ago, the life of ordinary people was fairly routine. Crisis was something that came only once in ten years, like an earthquake or a political joust about tariffs or a spot of sabre-rattling—and these were handled with dexterity and aplomb by experts.

Today, we live with crises at home and abroad, and not only the catastrophe-relief people, the politicians and the military are involved: we are all in it. That is why we need education, to gain knowledge and attain wisdom.

We cannot estimate with any certainty what changes may be brought about in the lifetime of you who are now young: changes due to medical science, interplanetary communication, atomic energy, increasing population, exhaustion of certain natural resources, conquest of the polar and tropical regions, aggression by despotic powers. You cannot face these prospective changes with intelligence or serenity if you have only the education that was adequate a half century ago.

Young people have more and more to learn as our culture grows more complex. Education gives us the tools with which to deal with material forces that were once our enemies, and turn them into slaves to do our bidding, but education must go on to teach us how to live and behave in this new society.

Scientific technology has broken up the placid life familiar to our grandparents. It has converted the person of general competence into a specialist.

Our ancestors had to be content so long as they were just one potato row ahead of starvation; tomorrow, science will have moved forward another step, machines will run machines, labour will be upgraded in terms of skill, and there will then be no appeal from the judgement that will be pronounced on the uneducated person.

What Is Education?

Education should be useful. We don't mean useful in the sense of making us adept in manipulating gadgets. Every young person reading this letter wants something better than that. You wish to be fit to perform justly, skilfully, magnanimously and with personal satisfaction, all the offices of life.

Learning sheer fact is not all of education. The three R's do not constitute education, any more than a knife, fork and spoon constitute a dinner. Some of the greatest bores are people who have memorized a great deal of information and love to talk about it.

The aim of an educational institution is to give students a living fund of knowledge from which they may generate ideas. When you can bring relevant background to bear on a problem, assemble pertinent data, grasp relationships, appraise the values involved, and make a judgement: when you can do that you are an educated person.

Then you need not fear becoming bewildered by change or thrown into a panic by misfortune, because you will be able to determine three vital things: where you are, where you are headed, and what you had better do under these circumstances.

In seeking that education, be imaginative. The first ten or twelve years of your life were its romantic stage. When you looked through a telescope to study the stars you saw not lumps of matter floating in space but the glory of the sky. In secondary school you pass through the age of precision. You must learn things correctly, exactly and completely, because these things form the bank account on which you will be drawing all through your life. After secondary school you enter the period of generalization. You will begin to apply what you have learned, transferring particularities of knowledge to the problems of general living. As one peak is climbed, farther ranges will appear upon the horizon, beckoning to you. You cannot climb them until you reach them, but there they are, eternally luring you.

But, you may say, "so-and-so made good in life without having had an extensive formal education." Quite true. Many men and women did not have the opportunity that is open to every young person in Canada today. They left school and went to work before completing high school; some did not go any further than public school. But they continued to learn while they worked.

They succeeded in spite of handicaps and not because of them. They had a daemon in them that prodded, and a vital energy that strengthened them to attain education by home study, or in evening classes, or in other ways. Sir Winston Churchill, who contributed so greatly to the world in war and in peace, once told an audience in Boston: "I have no technical and no university education, and have just had to pick up a few things as I went along."

Young people in Canada today need not endure hardship and suffer delay. So far as is in their power and so far as their knowledge carries them, people of the older generation have made it possible for young people to become educated to the utmost extent of their capability and their desire.

Don't expect—and don't desire—that education shall be poured into you. You will see more interesting and useful things when you look for them yourself. You can't profit by accepting facts without questioning, by accepting words instead of trying to understand ideas. You need to explore the many sides there may be to a question.

If you walk all around the opinion of a famous [person], question it, and then embrace it, the opinion is no longer his [or hers] but yours. When you learn how a danger occurs, you may take steps to avoid it; if you want to <u>escape being fooled</u>, <u>find out how the fooling is done</u>; go behind the puppet show to see with what skill the little figures are manipulated.

Check your answers with those in the Answer section at the end of the book.

III. ADDING MARGINAL NOTES

Most times, your underlined portions of a selection will be sufficient for you to gain a good comprehension of the article; however, there will be times when these underlined portions become clearer and more effective with an added marginal note. Marginal notes should be concise, clearly written groups of words that serve one of the following purposes:

1. defining meanings of unknown words (use the top or bottom margin for definitions)

2. identifying content by giving it a title

3. summarizing a complicated section (concise wording is essential)

4. expressing an implied main idea

The following examples demonstrate each of these four points in turn.

A. Define Unknown Words in the Top or Bottom Margin

You have already been doing this as part of your previewing techniques. Scan the three paragraphs that follow and circle any unknown words. These should be written in the top or bottom margin of the page. Do not place them in side margins as they will become confused with notes you need to include as you read.

B. Add a Title to Help Identify Content

In the following paragraph, the underlined portions identify specifics, while the marginal note indicates the general topic.

Results of poor communications

<u>Muddled messages</u> can <u>cause havoc within an organization.</u> <u>Instructions</u> that are <u>misunderstood</u> can <u>set people off in</u> the <u>wrong direction</u> or put them to work in vain. Written policies that are open to <u>misinterpretation can throw</u> sand in the gears of an <u>entire operation. Ill-considered language</u> in communications with employees <u>can torpedo morale.</u>

C. Use a Marginal Note to Summarize a Complex Portion of Text

Minimal or no underlining of the text is necessary, since the marginal note performs the same function, but with greater concision.

Therefore, think before you begin to write.

<u>The intellectual discipline required to make thoughts come through intelligibly on paper pays off in clarifying your thoughts in general.</u> When you start writing about a subject, you will often find that your knowledge of it and your thinking about it leave something to be desired. The question that should be foremost in the writer's mind, "What am I really trying to say?", will raise the related questions, "What do I really know about this? What do I really think about it?" A careful writer has to be a careful

thinker—and in the long run careful thinking saves time and trouble for the writer, the reader, and everybody else concerned.

D.   Use the Margin to Identify an Implied Main Idea

The underlined portions of the text will provide the needed details.

Avoid using vague or ambiguous terms.

The problem is that <u>many people believe</u> that <u>they have thought out ideas and expressed them competently</u> on paper <u>when they</u> actually <u>haven't.</u> This is <u>because they use</u> nebulous <u>multi-purpose words that</u> may <u>mean one thing to them and something</u> quite <u>different to someone else.</u> An example of this type of multi-purpose word is the verb "involve," which is used variously to mean "entail," "include," "contain," "imply," "implicate," "influence," etc. "It" has developed a vagueness that makes it the delight of those who dislike the effort of searching for the right word. Consequently, "it" is much used, generally where some more specific word would be better and sometimes where it is merely superfluous.[3]

Be direct to make your message clear.

Reread the notes and underlined portions of each of the above paragraphs to see the effectiveness of this study skill. Remember, though, that marginal notes should be limited to be effective. Do not write as much in the margin as the author has presented in the text. Also, do not mimic the words of the text. If the author has said it best, underline it! If you can say it better or more concisely, write it! Every single paragraph does not require your comments.

● EXERCISE 3.4

Write a marginal note for each of the following paragraphs. Try to use each of the following types:

- a title to classify the underlined portions

- a summary of a complex paragraph

- an implied main idea to identify the central theme

Evolution of marriage over time methods of courtship and marriage have changed

1.   In the ear<u>ly part of this century, marriage </u>between young people <u>was an arrangement m</u>ade between parents—or even nations—to <u>join two people for reasons other than love.</u> As <u>time progressed,</u> it did become <u>more acceptable fo</u>r young people <u>to choose their own</u> lifetime <u>partners.</u> The <u>young man</u>, however, <u>had to declare his honourable intentions to</u> his la<u>dy's parents b</u>efore <u>he </u>was allowed to <u>court her.</u> <u>Then,</u> of course, <u>it became more fashionable for</u> young people <u>to meet and date before</u> they made the <u>"big decision."</u> <u>Up until the 1960s</u>, though, a <u>young man still continued to show formal respect for his da</u>te and always saw her to and from her front door, bought her gifts of candy or flowers, and showed her every courtesy. With <u>today's young people,</u> <u>formal courtesies</u>—including dating—seem to <u>have disappeared</u>; and <u>marriage,</u> if there <u>is </u>one, has become <u>a legal agreement</u> in which both parties indicate their rights—and, in some cases, state <u>renewable dates for a renegotiated contract!</u>

writing / cooking
writing un cooking are
similar

2. An irresistible comparison arises <u>between writing and</u> another craft which most people have to practise sometimes, namely <u>cooking</u>. In both fields there is a <u>wide range of competence</u>, from the great chefs and authors to the occasional practitioners who must do the job whether they like it or not. In both, <u>care in preparation is of the essence</u>. Shakespeare wrote that it is an ill cook who does not lick her fingers; it is an ill writer who does not <u>work at it hard enough to be reasonably satisfied with the results.</u>[4]

bad writing
bad writing is bad
business

3. <u>In the working world, bad writing is not only bad manners</u>; it is <u>bad business</u>. The victim of an incomprehensible letter will at best be annoyed and at worst decide that <u>people who can't say what they mean aren't worth doing business</u> with. Write a sloppy letter, and it might rebound on you when the recipient calls for clarification. Where one carefully worded letter would have sufficed, you might have to write two or more.[5]

bad writing
bad writing can effect
moral

4. Muddled messages can cause havoc within an organization. <u>Instructions that are misunderstood</u> can set <u>people</u> off in the wrong direction or put them <u>to work in vain</u>. <u>Written policies that are open to misinterpretation</u> can throw sand in the gears of an entire operation. <u>Ill-considered language in communications with or between employees can</u> torpedo morale.[6]

motivation
motivate people to do
your bidding

✗5. To <u>motivate people</u>, the dictionaries tell us, is to <u>cause them to act in a certain way</u>. This is done by furnishing them with a <u>motive to do your bidding</u>. By the strictest definition, the most elementary form of motivation would be if a hold-up man were to stick a pistol in your face and growl: "Your money or your life." He instantly arouses a motive in you for doing what he wants you to—the motive of staying alive.[7]

carrotandstick
~~reward~~
~~punish~~
entice workers towards
goal with a reward

✗6. In the lexicon of management science, the <u>system of reward and punishment</u> is known as the "carrot and stick" approach, the carrot being dangled in front of a donkey's nose and the stick applied smartly to his hindquarters. In this fashion he is alternately <u>enticed and impelled towards his master's goal</u>. Whether the donkey ever gets to eat the carrot in this analogy is not made clear in management literature. We can be sure, however, that he gets to feel the stick.[8]

Check your answers with those in the Answer section at the end of the book.

● EXERCISE 3.5

Continue with the last section of the article "What Use Is Education?" This time, remember to

1. preview,
2. define words (top or bottom margin),

3. read completely and underline or highlight, and

4. use marginal notes where you feel they would be effective.

Special Training[9]

Choosing a career today is not the docile following in your parents' footsteps that was common a half century ago. There are attractive professions and businesses and crafts that were not heard of, some not even imagined, when today's university graduates were born.

It is not desirable that you should pursue technical education to the exclusion of general or cultural education. Supervisors will tell you that workers who have had practice in learning at school usually turn out to be better at learning in a factory. They catch on more quickly, not only to the "how" of the job but to the "why" of it. They have a quicker and surer grasp of problems. They are more likely to think up time- and labour-saving ideas. They have the broad outlook and the capacity for straight thinking that are essential to promotion and advancement.

The earthworm has not only digging skill but a sense of the principles involved in digging a good hole at the proper depth and in the right direction. We, on the higher stratum of the animal kingdom, need no less. It is principles, and not mere data, we need if we are to find our way through the mazes of tomorrow.

If you are going in for commerce, do not imagine for a moment that all you need is training in reading, writing and arithmetic. Even the addition of bookkeeping, shorthand and typing is not enough. You need an intelligent knowledge of the realities of modern economic life.

People in business believe that more attention should be given in schools and colleges to the art of communicating ideas. There is not much prospect for advancement in commercial firms unless you can express your thoughts competently. You cannot buy or sell, give instructions to subordinates, make a report, win friends or influence people, unless you can say clearly and appealingly what it is in your mind to say.

If you are going to learn a trade, don't be satisfied to become a specialist in "know-how" rather than in knowledge. The sort of person you are to be is more important in the long run than the sort of skills you acquire.

Really useful training in a trade will provide you with some general principles and a thorough grounding in their application to certain concrete details. It will give you a base on which you may build a bigger and better job. It will habituate you to use all your brain instead of just the fragment that directs your fingers.

Should you be going on to university, you need to know that the function of higher education is twofold: to disseminate knowledge already stored up, and to spur you to acquire new knowledge. What training there is in a university is directed toward conditioning the mind to think; to pushing back the barriers of the past and extending the boundaries of what is known; to discovering problems to be solved.

Compare your answers with those suggested in the Answer section at the end of the book.

IV. USING UNDERLINING TECHNIQUES FOR NEWSPAPERS

If you are using the newspaper as a research source, then highlighting an article effectively will be an invaluable research skill for essays and reports. Use the same approach and skills you have practised in this unit.

What is the essence of what the writer has said? Identify the main message.

1. Read the title and the lead paragraphs. Quickly identify the source of information and the answers to where, when, who, what, and why questions.

2. Highlight the main message by identifying the overall theme and the supporting information.

3. Look at the major issues identified and the supporting evidence or prospective solutions.

● EXERCISE 3.6

Read the following newspaper articles and highlight the main ideas and supporting details. Use marginal notes if necessary. Make sure your highlighted portions and marginal notes provide a readable summary.

1.

'GREEN' HOUSE WILL POWER ITSELF AND RECYCLE WASTE

TORONTO (CP)—A Toronto architect is building a self-sufficient house that will generate its own electricity, compost its sewage, store rainwater for drinking and recycle dirty water.

The house, designed by Martin Liefhebber Architect Inc., will operate completely independent of basic public utilities or city services.

"This is the house of tomorrow," said Chris Ives, an engineer in the research division of the Canada Mortgage and Housing Corp.

The design was one of two winners of CMHC's healthy housing design competition last year. It was among the leading housing technology on display earlier this week as part of the Canadian Home Builders' Association's annual conference in Toronto.

"It may sound space-age and implausible to some," Ives said. "But all of the technology used in Martin (Liefhebber's) design is already available on the market."

The features of the house will include:

—Twelve roof-top solar panels that turn the heat of the sun into electrical currents to be stored in large batteries in the basement. A device called an inverter transforms the energy into 110 volts of power.

—A composting tank in the basement that processes sewage and will provide one cubic foot of fertilizer for the garden about every four years.

—A second tank in the basement that filters waste water from the kitchen sink and shower. The water will then be pumped up to a roof-top greenhouse where plants indigenous to swamps will play the final role in cleansing it for re-use.

—Drinking water will be supplied by rain and snow caught by an external tank and stored in a larger one in the basement with a capacity of 20 000 litres. The storage tank will contain lime to neutralize the acid caused by air pollution. "Drinking rainwater is a lot healthier than the stuff that comes out of Lake Ontario," Liefhebber said.

—A masonry stove made from soapstone will provide additional heating for the house, for cooking, and will only require about $175 worth of wood for the winter season.

A first-floor solarium filled with plants will help clean the air, and thick walls and large windows facing south will help to retain heat. A solar-powered pump will provide cooling in the summer.

"A design like this won't work if a family continues to use lots and lots of water and lots and lots of electricity," Ives said.

A family would have to be willing to give up their clothes dryer and blow dryer. But they can keep the microwave, television and VCR.

The house will be equipped with an energy efficient refrigerator, which uses about one-fifth as much power, Liefhebber said.

The two-storey, 900-square-foot [83.6 square metres] house will cost about $100 000 to build, he said. CMHC estimates it would likely sell for a market price of about $160 000.

Construction is set to begin in May, but Liefhebber still has to complete a few stages of the municipal approval process.

The prototype is being built for an individual who owns a piece of unserviced land in Riverdale, an east end district of Toronto.

The lot has garages on either side and it would cost about $150 000 to establish connections to sewage and other city services, Liefhebber said.

It costs about $10 000 on average to hook up a new house to water, sewage, drainage and hydro if the necessary infrastructure is already in place, he said.[10]

2.

PEPSI TURNING BLUE TO LURE MARKETS

LONDON (Reuter) —Escalating its battle against soft drinks giant Coca-Cola Co. and others for a stake in emerging markets, PepsiCo Tuesday unveiled "Project Blue," with a new blue can and advertising campaign in 24 countries outside the United States.

Running a far second behind giant Coca-Cola in the world market, Pepsi has lacked a unified image, critics say. For example, in Germany, a can of Pepsi looks one way, and in Latin America, another. Some of Pepsi's billboards are more than 20 years old and, critics say, the soft drink tastes different wherever you are.

But PepsiCo said those days are over.

Launched in Britain, "Project Blue" is a $500 million project to claw back market share from arch-rival Coke, senior executives said.

In a razzmatazz media launch here, Pepsi introduced a new electric blue can, scrapping the old red, white and blue. It also flew in supermodels Claudia Schiffer and Cindy Crawford and tennis star Andre Agassi to publicize a series of television commercials they were hired to make.

In addition, Pepsi unveiled a $190 000 marketing exercise—a Concorde supersonic airliner painted in Pepsi's new colours.

But it was unclear how Pepsi intended to use the blue Concorde because aviation experts said the plane could fly at supersonic speeds only if painted pure white due to the heat generated at high speed.

"We have to be big in the new emerging markets, that's where the real battle is being fought," said John Swanhaus, senior vice president, international sales and marketing.

Swanhaus said that sales growth in emerging sectors was in excess of 20 percent a year compared with only 4 percent or 5 percent in the maturer drinks markets.

Pepsi has moved into Asia, Eastern Europe and the Middle East in recent years, where growth in sales of soft drinks has spiked higher from a very low base, he said.

Swanhaus, speaking at London Gatwick Airport where Pepsi unveiled its new blue cola can, said Pepsi was actually outselling Coca-Cola in China where it has already invested over $500 million.

But it's still an uphill struggle. Outside the United States, Coke outsells Pepsi about three to one.

Coke is the U.S. market leader, with about 43 percent to Pepsi's 31 percent, according to Beverage Marketing, a trade publication.

However, Swanhaus said, Pepsi has been gaining share internationally.

While Swanhaus said the United States and Canada were expected to follow suit and change their brand designs shortly, a spokesperson for Pepsi International said this was news to him.

Keith Hughes, a spokesperson for Pepsi International, based in Purchase, N.Y., said from London "that's not the way I would see it. We're very excited about it but I don't think there are any specific plans at this point" to change the Pepsi cans in the United States and Canada.

Pepsi worked with San Francisco-based corporate image consultants Landor Associates, basing the new can on the success of Pepsi Max, a popular diet drink sold overseas in a blue can.

In British markets, Swanhaus said Pepsi had been squeezed not only by Coca-Cola, but also by supermarkets' own brands of colas and Richard Branson's Virgin Cola.

"To compete in the own-brand markets you have to be price-competitive, innovative and imaginative. We're trying to be more relevant to the teen market, which is not an easy segment to get through to," he said.

As part of Pepsi's big marketing push, it is rolling out a series of five new TV commercials in Europe—TV takes the largest share of Pepsi's advertising budget—and will increase its use of neon billboards in central London's Piccadilly Circus district.[11]

3.   Repeat the process for a current newspaper article.

Compare your answers to questions 1 and 2 with those suggested in the Answer section at the end of the book.

THE NEXT STEP

If you feel confident about this section, proceed to "Listening and Note-Taking."

LISTENING AND NOTE-TAKING

The communication circuit includes four distinct, but related, skills. Writing and speaking are activities that transmit messages, as writers and speakers impart information, wisdom, knowledge, experience, theory, instructions, etc., to others. The other two communication skills, reading and listening, involve receiving information, as readers and listeners are the recipients of all that writers and speakers impart. To be a good communicator, you must learn to use all of these skills effectively.

Of all the communication skills, people spend the most time listening; however, many do not consider listening to be a skill. In this section, we will focus on listening skills and relate them to the reading skills you have already reviewed.

I. COMPARING READING SKILLS WITH LISTENING SKILLS

Reading and listening skills have many similarities. Both include the skills of recognizing and comprehending that "skeleton of ideas" set out by writers and speakers. Therefore, the reading skills you have recently learned and applied—namely, locating the main idea and/or theme, identifying patterns of development, distinguishing between major and minor points, recognizing the conclusion, and comprehending the total message—are all equally important skills to apply in the listening process.

On the other hand, when you read, you usually have the opportunity to reread, study, and reconsider the content with no time restrictions. However, when you listen to a speaker, you require increased decoding skills. Listening means more than just hearing or paying attention. Active listening involves a high degree of thinking, as you must simultaneously hear and decode the speaker's message. At the same time, listeners must also be alert to predicting outcomes and understanding inferences. You do not usually get the chance to hear the lecturer again. Therefore, it is extremely important to be well versed in the skills of recognizing and comprehending main ideas, patterns of development, supporting ideas, and conclusions as well as in the ability to envision the total message just as the speaker intended.

And so, listening is not merely an activity that can be assumed but a skill that requires learning and practice. By mastering the reading skills in this chapter, you are also setting the foundation for improving your listening skills.

II. Assessing Your Listening Skills

Many common problems interfere with effective listening habits. Assess your listening skills with the following checklist. Then identify and begin remedying any factors that are negatively affecting your listening capabilities.

☐ Do you have good intentions to listen but, at some point in the lecture, find that your mind has wandered to thoughts, plans, or ideas that are not related to the speaker's topic?

☐ Are you an on-and-off listener? Is your mind sometimes focused on the speaker and sometimes wandering?

☐ Are you easily distracted by noise or movement?

☐ Are you sometimes tired, disinterested, or bored in a listening situation?

☐ At times, does a speaker's accent, appearance, or mannerisms capture your attention or "turn you off"?

☐ If the speaker's message seems disorganized or difficult to understand, do you often just stop listening?

☐ While listening, do you have difficulty determining what is relevant and what is not?

☐ Do you try to grasp or write down everything that the speaker says?

☐ Do you enjoy listening to a speaker whose views you totally agree with?

☐ Do you often get angry or annoyed with a speaker whose views you totally disagree with?

☐ Do you sometimes let your emotions have control over you while you are listening?

☐ After a lecture, are you often vague about what the speaker's main message was?

If you compared the skill of listening with the skill of flying an aircraft, how secure would you feel flying with a pilot having any one of these common problems of attentiveness? The more points you have identified in this checklist, the more you need to learn and practise listening skills.

III. Improving Your Listening Skills

There are many different types of lecturers: some who are very organized; some who are extremely disorganized; some who will often stray off the topic; some who speak with interesting voices; some who speak with monotone voices; some who speak loudly with conviction; others who are difficult to understand; some whose view you will strongly agree or disagree with; some whose mannerisms will be distracting. Regardless of the type of lecturer you encounter, the ultimate responsibility for knowing the content is yours. Therefore, make a sincere effort to eliminate any negative listening practices and receive the maximum benefits from every lecturer's experience, wisdom, knowledge, theories, and instruction.

Be Prepared Mentally and Physically

Reading chapters in advance of the lecture will enhance your overall comprehension of the subject matter.

Choose a seat close to the front of the lecture theatre or classroom and sit within the "V" audience range of the speaker's position at the front of the room and within his or her focus of attention. (The speaker would be positioned at the point of the V and you should be somewhere between the extensions.)

Be a little early and make sure that you have the needed materials for the lecture: several pencils or pens, sufficient lined paper, course materials, etc.

Ideally you should be well rested and mentally focused for the lecture. You cannot be attentive if you are sleepy or disinterested in the topic.

LEARN TO AVOID DISTRACTIONS

Some listeners have such poor listening skills that any noise or movement immediately captures their attention and their listening skills are forgotten. Often people must either study or work in a busy environment, so make a sincere effort to eliminate this bad habit.

If you are within the speaker's focus of attention and are mentally prepared for the presentation, you have already taken important steps in reducing distractions. Practise ignoring others' actions or noise. If people around you are disruptive, either request their cooperation or move to another seat, whichever is less distracting to your focus. Also, some listeners focus on the speaker's appearance, mannerisms, or accent instead of on the content of the presentation. Avoiding any type of distraction requires both effort and practice. Make up your mind to focus on receiving the content of the lecture.

LEARN TO KEEP AN OPEN MIND

Don't jump to conclusions or form strong opinions while you are listening. If you are in total agreement with someone's viewpoint, you may have the tendency to stop listening critically and miss many of the points the speaker is expressing; or you may assume facts that were not mentioned in the presentation. Therefore, if the speaker's views are similar to your own, maintain your listening skills, listen for specific points and supporting evidence for his or her theories, and/or consider the questions that would challenge what he or she is saying. Are there any points the speaker did not include?

On the other hand, if you are in total disagreement with someone's viewpoint, you may be so busy being frustrated, mentally arguing, or feeling angry that you stop listening. Remember: you are not required to accept this person's point of view as yours; but you are required to know the exact content and supporting evidence that this speaker is conveying. In this situation, remain calm; try to bury any emotions; and listen for the specific points and supporting evidence for the theories. Also, consider the questions that would challenge what he or she is saying. Are there any points the speaker did not include?

LEARN TO CONCENTRATE

Focus on receiving the content of the lecture. Be alert to "signal words" that will give you clues about the pattern of development. If the lecturer stresses or repeats information, mark it as important in your notes.

Since a person's mind can hear and accept information faster than a speaker can talk, use your extra thinking time wisely. Either review to see how the content is developing, anticipate the next points, identify important factors, copy information from any visuals used, or write questions or comments about what has been said. All your thinking processes should be related to the content.

One good method for improving listening skills is to develop good note-taking techniques. Taking effective notes forces you to be an active listener. Most lectures contain the following components:

1. An introduction to capture your attention and stimulate your interest

2. A thesis statement and focus for the specific topic

3. The development of each part or stage of the thesis. The speaker may begin with any one of the patterns of development to support the information or theory of the lecture. To keep your attention and/or to provide a more relaxed atmosphere, he or she may also include personal experiences, irrelevant comments, or jokes; these are fun to listen to but recognize that it is not necessary to remember these "extras." Most speakers will reconfirm important information by repetition, restatements, and illustrations at strategic places in the lecture.

4. A conclusion that will give the results, make predictions, give advice, and/or summarize the main points. These points are vital for you to record and remember; therefore, keep attentive until the lecturer completes his or her whole message. Do not stop listening!

IV. Developing Effective Note-Taking Skills

In addition to improving your comprehension, using good note-taking skills is a time saver as well. Well-written, well-spaced, clearly written notes make studying easier. Having meaningful notes to review will give you a sense of confidence at exam time.

Preparatory Steps

1. Have sufficient paper and plan to write on only one side of each page. Number your pages as you take notes. Use lined notebook paper; do not use scrap paper or the backs of handouts.

2. Leave spaces between items in your lecture notes.

3. Write down the essential information: the topic (as specifically as you can), the date, and the lecturer's name.

4. Identify and write down your purpose in listening to this lecture. The grade you want in this subject is a good reminder of your purpose if you cannot identify a specific one.

5. Throughout your note-taking, write legibly; do not scribble or doodle on your pages.

6. Leave a good bottom margin on each page so that you can add any missed information or write your own comments at a later time.

Specific Method for Taking Notes during a Lecture

Take notes in a format that makes it easy for you to comprehend and learn the material. Although these notes may be written in your own style, that style should be a good basis for your examination study notes and questions.

1. Use titles and subtitles whenever appropriate.

2. Write the thesis statement, main ideas, and emphasized points in complete sentences.

3. Use an outline format with good indentations that will clearly identify main ideas, major details, and minor points. Specific numbering and lettering is not essential at this point but clear indentations are extremely important.

4. Record major and minor details using meaningful words or phrases. Include verbs in these phrases whenever possible. Try to use parallel structure in recording your points and make sure that the topic or subject of your developing points is clearly identified.

5. It is important to include clear transitional, directional, or signal words that indicate how

facts are related. In following this practice, you will see the speaker's pattern of development and will be better able to anticipate and understand other facts in the presentation.

6. Use numbers, abbreviations, formulas, diagrams, pictographs, pictures, maps, drawings, arrows, your own comments (enclose the latter in brackets or mark them in a special way), etc. For example, look at the following symbols, abbreviations, and shortened words:

Examples of Common Symbols and Abbreviations

&	and	=	equal
e.g.	example	∵	but
w/	with	∴	therefore
w/o	without	i.e.	that is
vs	opposed or against	c/o	in care of
#	number	%	percent
<	less than, reduced	%age	percentage
>	greater than, increased	etc.	and so on
@	each/for each/at	//	parallel
+	plus or in addition	–	minus

Examples of Shortened Words

Some students find that, in context, many words are still understandable without some letters, especially vowels or endings. Can you recognize the following shortened words?

pkg	package	smpl	sample
cont	continue	bkgrd	background
imp	important	govt	government
info	information	abbrev	abbreviation
acct	account	exam	examination
shrt trm	short term	fwd	forward
intro	introduce/introduction	attn	attention
dept	department	subj	subject
org	organization	chpts	chapters
concl	conclude/conclusion	cap	capital
assoc	association	wtg	writing
ques	question	pt	point

A caution: use shortened writing sparingly until you can easily recognize the meanings of your own shortened versions of words. With practice, your shortened forms will become an automatic and understandable method for recording lecture notes more quickly and accurately.

7. If you miss something important the speaker has said, leave an extra space in your notes; relax and pick up what he or she is currently saying. If the point was important, you can be sure that he or she will repeat it. If that doesn't happen, you can get that information from another student or from the lecturer after the lecture. Don't lose any more information by trying to find out that one point.

8. If you recognize the speaker's organization and plan, you will more easily tell the difference between what is important and what is not so important. Personal experiences and stories usually demonstrate a specific point. Focus on noting what that point is. Also listen for opinion words such as *seems*, *in my opinion*, *appears*, etc. If the opinion being expressed is relevant, use these same words to record it. This will help you differentiate between facts and opinions later on.

9. As you listen, use the extra space beside your notes or at the bottom margin for any questions or comments about the lecture.

10. During your free thinking time, copy notes from overhead transparencies, black boards, flip charts, etc., and write them at the appropriate place in your notes; or if you are not sure how to incorporate them into your notes, write them on the back of the page opposite to the related notes.

11. After the lecture and before you leave the lecture hall, fill in any missing information and put your notes in good order.

12. As soon as possible (preferably later that day), review your notes for the whole lecture. Do you understand the content? If so, try to envision the whole message, summarize the main points, and write any possible text questions that could help you recall the specific content. If you do not understand the lecture, discuss the content with someone from the class who does; then fill in the missing content in your notes, try to envision the whole message, summarize the main points, and write any possible text questions that will help you recall specific content and give you a solid basis for the next lecture.

EXAMPLE OF EFFECTIVE NOTE-TAKING

Sept. 23   Lecture by J. Baker

Skills of Listening & Taking Notes in Lectures

My purposes: 1) need to understand & remember content
                 of lectures better
              2) want an A grade this year!

Good communicators are skillful in all 4 comm. skills.

givers { writers → exper., info → readers } receivers
of info { speakers → theories, etc. → listeners } of info
         info should be same at each
              end of the circuit

Although most time is spent listening, listening often
    not thought of as skill! ..... not taught.
∴ relate reading skills to listening skills

Reading & Listening have many similarities
    — must recognize same "skeleton of ideas"
         e.g. —main idea
              —pattern of dev.
              —major & min. pts
              —conclu.
    — must understand overall message

<u>However</u>, listening requires more than above pts.

  – must have higher degree of thinking

     – hear + decode @ same time

     – be alert to outcomes

     – understand inferences

  – cannot hear lecture a 2nd time

∴ m<u>ust</u> practise this skill.

Assess listening skills (see p. ___ quest) + improve

* Regardless of type of lecturer, we are
resp. for knowing content of lecture!

∴ a) Be prepared mentally + physically

    – read chpts. before lect.

    – choose seat at front

      – in "V" aud. range

    – be early for class

    – have nec. supplies

    – be rested

    – be focused

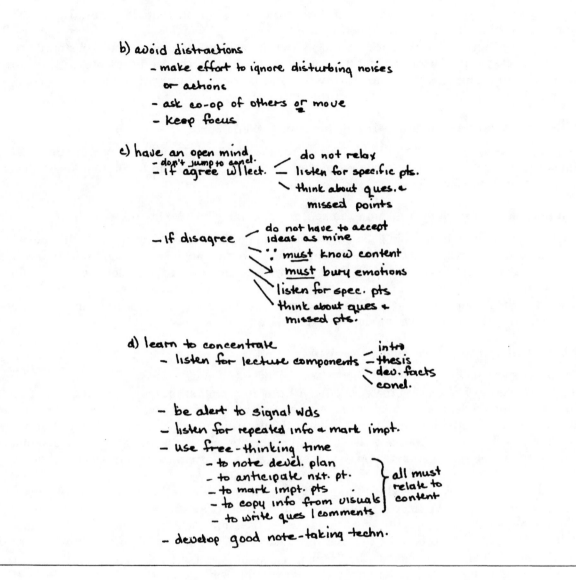

OTHER CONSIDERATIONS ABOUT NOTE-TAKING

Is spelling important?

Spelling is not important when you are taking notes unless the misspelling causes you to misunderstand the content. You should take time to correct any spelling errors in your after-lecture review, as misspellings on examinations do matter!

What about any questions you have about the lecture?

If the questions are about the facts of the lecture itself, talk to other students to clarify or add any information you do not understand or you have missed. If, however, there is something that requires more clarification, make an appointment to talk to the professor as soon as possible.

What about using tape recorders during a presentation?

Some students make a practice of using tape recorders for all their lectures. Taping lectures means that you will not feel the need to use and develop your listening and note-taking skills. This activity increases your work load significantly, as you are committed to listening to each lecture at least twice. Also, you will not get the full benefit of the lecturer's message, as you will miss the body language clues included with what he or she has said. If the lecturer has used visuals of any type, you will not connect these with the sequence of the verbal content.

Are copies of past examinations from your course available?

Before your course begins, it would be a good idea to obtain copies of past examinations. You will have a good idea of what is expected of you during the course and will also learn about the lecturer's style and focus.

Is it necessary to write up your notes in sentence/paragraph style?

If you have taken your notes in good outline fashion and have used sentences for the thesis, main ideas, and important sentences, as well as having used meaningful words and phrases with good transitional words, then there is no need to rewrite your notes in complete sentences. In fact, your outline information will give you instant recall, as you can see the total picture by quickly reviewing the "skeleton of ideas." Reading paragraphs takes much more time, and this is not an easy way for you to recall the importance and relevance of the facts.

What about copying notes from a classmate?

Use other students' notes sparingly. If you are absent or if you have missed a few facts, it is good to copy information from a classmate, but record this information in your own note-taking style, if possible. If the student is an excellent note-taker, you may gain some valuable points about how to take notes effectively. However, do not rely on this student for all your notes; try to improve your own style. If the student does not take notes in a manner that is easy for you to understand, have someone read the information to you so you can take the information in your own style.

Therefore, the keys to good listening and note-taking skills are learning to establish your and the speaker's purpose; to improve your focus on the speaker's content; and through your practice at recognizing the components of most lectures, to comprehend the speaker's total message. Remember that it is important to listen for ideas rather than focus on every word and fact. Skilled note-takers can envision the "skeleton" of the speaker's message, identify patterns of development, and gain good comprehension of the subject matter.

 ## COLLABORATIVE EXERCISE 3.7

1. One class member acts as a lecturer and reads aloud any one of the paragraphs in Units Two or Three. If possible, the speaker should use a microphone to ensure that everyone can hear; and he or she should speak clearly and use the appropriate intonation, as most lecturers would. Others listen and take notes. Using the Answer section at the back of this text as a guide, each person can then compare their note-taking skills with the information and levels of relevance suggested in the answers. Try this same exercise with two other readers.

2. Once the members of the group feel they have mastered note-taking skills for these short passages, they should use the same procedure with any of the longer passages in Units Two or Three.

Remember: The most important factor in these exercises is for you to *hear* and *recognize* the theme, pattern of development, and key words and phrases. Then, you must practise *recording* these in a meaningful fashion.

THE NEXT STEP

If you feel confident about the skills presented in this unit, write the Unit Three Post-Test on the following page.

 # FREEWRITING

This assignment is separate and can be done before or after the Post-Test for this unit.

Write for ten to fifteen minutes, without stopping, on the topics given below or on ones assigned by your instructor. Try to express your feelings as you would if you were talking to a close friend.

NOTE: Do not worry if you do not have time to finish this activity. It is more important to write as much as you can in the given time.

Respond to one of the following:

1. What person from the past would you most like to meet? Give at least three reasons for your choice.

2. What is your favourite holiday? Describe three or more customs, events, or activities that make this a special occasion.

3. Respond to one of the articles you highlighted in this unit. Write to the editor or to an interested party and give your opinion(s) about the "green" house. Support your opinion(s) with at least three examples, facts, or reasons.

POST-TEST FOR UNIT THREE

If you feel confident about the skills presented in this unit, complete the Post-Test that follows; however, **do not attempt this test if you have not completed the required work.**

Once you have completed the test, check your answers with the suggested ones at the end of this unit. A marking scheme has been provided to give you a realistic idea of your ability in this area. Your goal should be to achieve 80 percent or more.

1. Preview the article.
   a) Read the title and source of information.
   b) Skim the article by reading the first sentence of each paragraph and the last paragraph.
   c) As you skim, glance over the material and circle any unfamiliar words not already identified.

2. Write the definition of each circled word in the top or bottom margins. Make sure the synonyms you have chosen are suitable replacements for the circled words.

3. As you read the article thoroughly, highlight or underline the key phrases in the main ideas and supporting details to provide a readable and comprehensive summary of the selection.

4. Use at least four marginal notes. Remember that both your underlining and your marginal notes should provide you with a readable summary of the article.

The Royal Bank of Canada
Monthly Letter

Section 1

On Reading Profitably[12]

Our printing presses are devouring a great tonnage of paper, and authors are covering it with words telling all that has ever been thought, felt, seen, experienced, discovered and imagined. Never before has so much information, guidance and entertainment been so readily available to everyone. Our problem is to make the best use individually of what is printed.

There are many different motives for reading. We may seek knowledge, relaxation, comfort, background, inspiration, or something that will enable us to compose all these into a way of life. In earlier days [humanity] flourished with merely barbaric flashes of thought, but in this period of civilization we need a coordinating philosophy built upon and making use of all the experiences of the past.

The accumulated factual knowledge of the past few hundred generations of human beings is too great to be acquired through experience in a lifetime. We must take it (vicariously) from books. Books push out the boundaries of our ignorance, factually into the past and speculatively into the future.

Consider this: we have only three ways of evaluating human existence: the study of self, which is the most dangerous and most difficult method, though often the most fruitful; the observation of our fellow persons who may hide their most revealing secrets from us; and books, which, with all their errors of perspective and judgment, are constant, detailed and always at our beck and call.

It is interesting and useful to read how crises similar to our own in form, though perhaps not in magnitude, were handled by our predecessors. Books unroll the great scroll of history so that things that are remote in time and place help us to judge things that are near at hand today.

Section 2

Books Are Friends

Perhaps the highest use of books is not as sources of information about nations, people or foreign lands, but as friends. Reading is one of the most effective means of getting away from disturbing and unalterable circumstances. Intimate association with noble works—literary, philosophic and artistic—is a promoter of thought, a refuge from almost all the miseries of life.

Books are good for us because they tend to shake us up. Our environment is confusing. It is made up of a tangle of complicated notions, in the midst of which individuals are inclined to sit apathetically. Greek philosophy, we recall, leaped to heights unreached again, while Greek science limped behind. Our danger is precisely the opposite: scientific data fall upon us every day until we suffocate with uncoordinated facts; our minds are overwhelmed with discoveries which we do not understand and therefore fear.

What we find in books can make us look again at things we have taken for granted, and question them; it can arouse us to appreciate once more the ideas and ideals that are being stifled under the flow of technical marvels. If a book moves us to thought, even to angry thought, the chances are that it is doing us a good turn.

Section 3

Lastly, in this brief tabulation of the value of reading, consider the benefit good reading is to the person who seeks ability in self-expression. The person who wishes to excel in conversation and another who must make letters and orders clear: both need to read wisely.

From whence come the quotations we run across continually in conversation, correspondence, public addresses and articles? All branches of the English-speaking world would include these six sources in any list: the Bible, the plays of Shakespeare, *Aesop's Fables, Alice in Wonderland*, the classic myths, the Gilbert and Sullivan operettas. The French-speaking world turns similarly to the Bible but otherwise is more likely, of course, to use expressions from the fables of La Fontaine and the great works of Racine, Corneille and Molière.

We are not interested in reading as critics, but as human beings in search of some human values. If a book gives you the feeling that you are being inspired, informed, helped, or entertained, never mind what anybody else says about it, it is good.

Literary theorists are often mistaken. Shakespeare's plays attracted enormous and enthusiastic audiences, so it seemed clear to the theorists of the period that there must be something wrong with them. Said William Hazlitt, the essayist: "If we wish to know the force of human genius we would read Shakespeare. If we wish to see the insignificance of human learning we may study his commentators."

Section 4

Reading for the Business Person

The person in business who never, in spite of good resolutions, gets around to reading books that are not directly associated with a particular trade, is being deprived of the habits, the skills, the understanding, and the increased freedom of thought which a well-balanced pattern of reading would provide.

Reading in technical books, learned journals and trade magazines may be necessary, depending on one's way of making a living, but this reading should not be the end. A person who has to fit life into a groove during every working day may become a unique individual in reading. He or she may have a dual life: as a business person among scholars and a scholar among business people.

A skilled artisan, extremely wise in matters of a particular art, is cheating himself of the greatness in life that might be his if he reads nothing else but technical books and light magazines and newspapers.

Reading furnishes the tools and material to take us out of blind-alley conversation. But it goes further. It advances our prospect of getting out of the routine of our profession, business or art.

Section 5

Search for Knowledge

The person who reads wisely and widely often finds that he or she has the enormous advantage of knowing more about a subject than others do. Knowledge builds self-confidence and self-reliance.

Some people profess to despise knowledge based upon books, but one must suspect that they are envious. There is no surer sign of intellectual ill-breeding, says Sir Arthur Quiller-Couch in *On the Art of Writing*, than to speak, even to feel, slightingly of any knowledge one does not happen to possess oneself.

It is true that knowledge is not necessarily a good in itself; it needs to be assimilated by the intellect and the imagination before it becomes positively valuable. We are wise to soak ourselves in as many facts and ideas as we can, so that our minds have material with which to work.

Books will provide us with the material information we can use to answer vital questions. When we are puzzled as to why human beings behave as they do we cannot find the answer in our surroundings but in the long perspective of history.

A person reading well-selected books becomes a denizen of all nations, a contemporary of all ages. In books one meets all kinds of people, the wisest, the wittiest and the tenderest.

Whether you read Jane Austen, dealing with her little community of country gentlefolk, clergymen and middle-class persons, or James Michener, ranging over the world and an infinity of characters, you are adding to your own experience that of others. You tend to become many-sided and to take large views. You expand your range of pleasures; your taste grows supple and flexible.

Section 6

You may be so fortunate as to find in books not only the record of things as the author saw them, but shadows of things to come. If non-Germans had taken the trouble to read *Mein Kampf* when it was written in 1924 they would have found Hitler's entire program spelled out in all its shocking detail; it was half a century after Thoreau's death before his doctrine of civil disobedience was applied by Mahatma Gandhi in India.

Fires stirred by the writings of Malthus, Adam Smith and Tom Paine have never died down. Controversies continue to rage. Some two-thirds of the world's rapidly increasing population suffer from malnutrition. This makes the issues raised by Malthus in 1798 as vital today as they were then. When Paine wrote in 1775 that oft-quoted line: "These are the times that try men's souls," he wrote for our time also. It was seventy years ago that Einstein published his article on the use of atomic energy, giving the world the most celebrated equation in history: $E = mc^2$. Where the atomic age, then born, will lead [humanity], no one knows.

It is because we are called upon to apply intelligent thought to these and other problems that it is necessary for us to read with industry and discernment.

SUGGESTED ANSWERS FOR UNIT THREE POST-TEST

Although your answers may not be identical to those suggested, assess your work as objectively as possible using the following guide. On the charts provided, circle your score for each section.

Give yourself one mark for each correct definition that is properly placed in the top or bottom margin.

TOTAL MARKS FOR VOCABULARY _____ /6

Assess your use of underlining in each of the six marked sections on a scale of 1 to 5 by comparing your answer to the one suggested in the answer section.

	Poor	Weak	Average	Good	Excellent
Section 1	1	2	3	4	5
Section 2	1	2	3	4	5
Section 3	1	2	3	4	5
Section 4	1	2	3	4	5
Section 5	1	2	3	4	5
Section 6	1	2	3	4	5

TOTAL MARKS FOR UNDERLINING _____ /30

Your marginal notes may not be similar to the ones identified in the answer section; however, assess each of your four notes on a scale of 1 to 3, taking the following factors into consideration:

- conciseness of note
- appropriateness to content
- originality of wording
- correct placement in margin

	Poor	Needs improvement	Okay	Excellent
Note 1	0	1	2	3
Note 2	0	1	2	3
Note 3	0	1	2	3
Note 4	0	1	2	3

TOTAL MARKS FOR MARGINAL NOTES _____ /12

Assess the overall effectiveness of your work using the following scale:

needs improvement = 0   average = 1   good = 2

OVERALL EFFECTIVENESS _____ /2

Section 1

What does "reading profitably" mean?

On Reading Profitably

Our printing presses are devouring a great tonnage of paper, and authors are covering it with words telling all that has ever been thought, felt, seen, experienced, discovered and imagined. <u>Never before has so much information, guidance and entertainment been so readily available to everyone.</u> <u>Our problem is to make the best use</u> individually <u>of what is printed.</u>

There <u>are many different motives for reading.</u> We may <u>seek knowledge, relaxation, comfort, background, inspiration,</u> or something that will enable us to compose all these into a way of life. In earlier days [humanity] flourished with merely barbaric flashes of thought, but <u>in this period of civilization</u> we <u>need a co-ordinating philosophy</u> built upon and <u>making use of all the experiences of the past.</u>

<u>The accumulated factual knowledge</u> of the past few hundred <u>generations</u> of human beings <u>is too great</u> to be acquired through experience in a lifetime. <u>We must take it</u> (vicariously) <u>from books.</u> Books push out the boundaries of our ignorance, factually into the past and speculatively into the future.

Consider this: <u>we have</u> only <u>three ways of evaluating human existence:</u> the <u>study of self</u>, which is the most dangerous and most difficult method, though often the most fruitful; the <u>observation of our fellow persons</u>, who may hide their most revealing secrets from us; <u>and books</u>, which, with all their errors of perspective and judgment, are constant, detailed and always at our beck and call.

<u>It is interesting and useful to read how crises</u> similar to our own in form, though perhaps not in magnitude, <u>were handled by our predecessors.</u> <u>Books</u> unroll the great scroll of history so that things that are remote in time and place <u>help us to judge things that are near at hand today.</u>

vicariously—second-hand

Section 2

In what ways are books friends?

Books Are Friends

Perhaps the highest use of books is not as sources of information about nations, people or foreign lands, but as friends. Reading is one of the most effective means of getting away from disturbing and unalterable circumstances. Intimate association with noble works—literary, philosophic, artistic—is a promoter of thought, a refuge from almost all the miseries of life.

Books are good for us because they tend to shake us up. Our environment is confusing. It is made up of a tangle of complicated notions, in the midst of which individuals are inclined to sit apathetically. Greek philosophy, we recall, leaped to heights unreached again, while Greek science limped behind. Our danger is precisely the opposite: scientific data fall upon us every day until we suffocate with uncoordinated facts; our minds are overwhelmed with discoveries which we do not understand and therefore fear.

What we find in books can make us look again at things we have taken for granted, and question them; it can arouse us to appreciate once more the ideas and ideals that are being stifled under the flow of technical marvels. If a book moves us to thought, even to angry thought, the chances are that it is doing us a good turn.

Section 3

Ways that good reading habits help people

Sources of quotations we use or hear

Lastly, in this brief tabulation of the value of reading, consider the benefit good reading is to the person who seeks ability in self-expression. The person who wishes to excel in conversation and another who must make letters and orders clear: both need to read wisely.

From whence come the quotations we run across continually in conversation, correspondence, public addresses and articles? All branches of the English-speaking world would include these six sources in any list: the Bible, the plays of Shakespeare, *Aesop's Fables*, *Alice in Wonderland*, the classic myths, the Gilbert and Sullivan operettas. The French-speaking world turns similarly to the Bible but otherwise is more likely, of course, to use expressions from the fables of La Fontaine and the great works of Racine, Corneille and Molière.

We are not interested in reading as critics, but as human beings in search of some human values. If a book gives you the feeling that you are being inspired, informed, helped, or entertained, never mind what anybody else says about it, it is good.

Critics often look for faults in well-liked literary works.

Literary theorists are often mistaken. Shakespeare's plays attracted enormous and enthusiastic audiences, so it seemed clear to the theorists of the period that there must be something wrong with them. Said William Hazlitt, the essayist: "If we wish to know the force of human genius we would read Shakespeare. If we wish to see the insignificance of human learning we may study his commentators."

apathetically—indifferently; unemotionally

Section 4

Why is reading important to the business person?

Reading for the Business Person

The <u>person in business who never</u>, in spite of good resolutions, gets around to <u>reading</u> books that are <u>not</u> directly <u>associated with a particular trade</u>, is <u>being deprived of</u> the habits, the skills, the understanding, and the increased freedom of thought which a <u>well-balanced pattern of reading</u> would provide.

<u>Reading in technical books</u>, <u>learned journals</u> and <u>trade magazines</u> is <u>necessary</u> according to one's way of making a living, but this reading <u>should not be the end</u>. A person who has to fit life into a groove during every working day may become a unique individual in reading. He or she may have a dual life: as a business person among scholars and a scholar among business people.

A <u>skilled</u> artisan, extremely wise in matters of a particular art, is <u>cheating himself</u> of the greatness in life that might be his <u>if he reads nothing</u> else <u>but technical books</u> and <u>light magazines and newspapers</u>.

<u>Reading</u> furnishes the tools and material to take us out of blind-alley conversation. But it goes further. It <u>advances our prospect of getting out of the routine of our profession, business or art</u>.

Section 5

How do you increase knowledge?

Those who discount the value of book learning are really envious that they do not have this knowledge.

Search for Knowledge

The <u>person who reads wisely</u> <u>and widely</u> often finds that he or she <u>has the</u> enormous <u>advantage of</u> knowing more about a subject than others do. Knowledge builds <u>self-confidence and self-reliance</u>.

Some people profess to despise knowledge based upon books, *but* one must suspect that they are envious. There is no surer sign of intellectual ill-breeding, says Sir Arthur Quiller-Couch in *On the Art of Writing*, than to speak, even to feel, slightingly of any knowledge one does not happen to possess.

It is true that <u>knowledge</u> is <u>not necessarily a good in itself</u>; it <u>needs to be assimilated</u> <u>by the intellect and the imagination before it becomes positively valuable</u>. We are wise to soak ourselves in as many facts and ideas as we can, so that our minds have material with which to work.

<u>Books</u> will <u>provide us with</u> the <u>material information</u> we can use <u>to answer vital questions</u>. When we are puzzled as to why human beings behave as they do we cannot find the answer in our surroundings but in the long perspective of history.

A person reading well-selected books becomes a denizen of all nations, a contemporary of all ages. <u>In books one meets all kinds of people</u>, the wisest, the wittiest and the tenderest.

No matter what authors' books you read, you broaden your outlook and expand your reading tastes.

Whether you read Jane Austen, dealing with her little community of country gentlefolk, clergymen and middle-class persons, or James Michener, ranging over the world and an infinity of characters, you are adding to your own experience that of others. You tend to become many-sided and to take large views. You expand your range of pleasures; your taste grows supple and flexible

artisan—craftsperson
denizen—inhabitant; resident

Section 6

Political theorists often wrote of their beliefs ... which later became facts of life.

Throughout the centuries, situations do not really change.

You may be so fortunate as to find in <u>books not only</u> the <u>record</u> of <u>things as the author saw them,</u> <u>but</u> shadows of <u>things to come</u>. If non-Germans had taken the trouble to read <u>*Mein Kampf*</u> when it was written in 1924 they would have found <u>Hitler's entire program</u> spelled out in all its shocking detail; it was half a century after <u>Thoreau's</u> death before his <u>doctrine of civil disobedience</u> was <u>applied by Mahatma Gandhi in India</u>.

Fires stirred by the writings of Malthus, Adam Smith and Tom Paine have never died down. Controversies continue to rage. <u>Some two-thirds of the world's</u> <u>rapidly increasing population suffer</u> <u>from malnutrition</u>. This makes the <u>issues raised</u> by Malthus <u>in 1798 as vital today as they were then</u>. When Paine wrote in 1775 that <u>oft-quoted line</u>: "<u>These are the times that try men's souls,</u>" he wrote for our time also. It was <u>seventy years ago</u> that <u>Einstein published</u> his article on the <u>use of atomic energy</u>, giving the world the most celebrated equation in history: $E = mc^2$. <u>Where the atomic age</u>, then born, <u>will lead</u> [humanity], <u>no one knows</u>.

It is <u>because we are called upon</u> to <u>apply intelligent thought to these and other problems that it is necessary for us to read with</u> industry and discernment.

industry—diligence; perseverance
discernment—good judgment; comprehension

MAKING THE CONNECTION

 OVERVIEW

This unit, which focuses on the use of words as well as sentence structure, encourages you to apply skills learned in previous units. Both the dictionary and thesaurus are introduced as basic reference texts and their use is encouraged for all your future written assignments.

Because sentences are the fundamental method of expressing thoughts and ideas, it is necessary for students to learn to build and shape written sentences with deliberate structure and careful word selection. In this unit, you will learn the importance of presenting ideas simply and clearly in complete sentences and of trying to convey your messages as dynamically in writing as you would in person. Sentence combining is also a feature of this unit.

In addition, the importance of and the relation between reading and writing skills are emphasized in the section on précis writing. You will be required to use reading skills to identify the main message of a selection and writing skills to summarize this message effectively and correctly in your own words.

The series of freewriting activities continues. With each effort, you should find that words are beginning to flow more easily from your head to your paper. In this exercise, you will combine reading skills with your writing ability.

LEARNING OBJECTIVES FOR UNIT FOUR

Upon completion of this unit, you should be able to:

1. Use both the dictionary and the thesaurus for proofreading skills and word selection; specifically,
    a) proofread and correct commonly misspelled words with the aid of a dictionary
    b) find synonyms and antonyms in a thesaurus to replace ineffective or repetitious expressions
    c) locate words in a thesaurus to express a general or vague idea in specific terms
    d) practise an "economy of words" and eliminate redundant expressions

2. Identify the three requirements of basic sentence structure; namely,
    a) identify the subject, the predicate, and the combination of the two that creates a complete thought
    b) distinguish and correct various types of sentence fragments
    c) distinguish and correct run-on sentences

3. Refine sentence structure to improve style and tone; specifically,
    a) use coordinating and subordinating conjunctions to improve basic sentence structure
    b) distinguish the changes in emphasis or meaning caused by variations in sentence patterns
    c) use semicolons with transitional phrasing to connect two related thoughts
    d) critique short, choppy sentence structures and combine the given ideas by using underlining skills and other refining techniques to produce better-quality sentences

4. Use a combination of reading, underlining, and sentence-refining techniques to appraise and condense a given passage to a half or a third of its original length, without changing the author's original intent.

5. Identify the main message of a given newspaper article and prepare a commentary letter to your classmates or an organization.

6. Using the summarizing skills presented in this unit, write an abstract of an article.

 Check Internet resources for grammar and summary writing exercises, as well as for additional news articles for summarizing, evaluating, and collaborative exercises (see pages 469–70).

SPELLING AND VOCABULARY

There is **no** Pretest for this section. You will learn how to use a dictionary and thesaurus as reference books for proofreading and composition skills.

Throughout this text, you will need to perfect your skills in spelling, grammar, and punctuation. Spelling should be the easiest to master; however, your proofreading habits and ability to recognize correct spellings will determine your success in this area.

I. USING A SPELL-CHECKER

A spell-checker is a wonderful software addition to a word processing program, as it will identify misspelled words as you type your paragraphs, essays, or letters. However, this software feature should not replace the need for you to proofread your work. Although the following exaggerated paragraph is perfect according to a spell-checker, it contains many errors that can be picked up only by careful proofreading.

> I no that this paragraph is perfect bee cause I used my spell checker, witch, buy the weigh, automatically corrected all my miss steaks as I rote. Four me, righting is sew much easier now that I can depend on this soft wear two point out awl my airs as I rite. It has all ready saved me lodes of thyme as now their is no knead for me to revue and proof reed this a sign meant as care full lea as I wood have had too be for I had this wonderful spell checker!

Remember that while spell-checkers are good to use, they will check only the spelling of words; they do not check the meanings of words or whether the words suit the context of your message.

II. USING THE DICTIONARY

Whether you consider yourself to be a good or a poor speller, please adhere to the following suggestions:

1. Be critical of what you have written.

2. If you tend to make careless mistakes, read your written work aloud.

3. Underline words that you suspect could be errors.

4. Double-check the spelling of these words in a good dictionary. If two spellings are given, the preferred spelling is listed first.

5. Use the guide words at the top of each dictionary page to help you locate information quickly.

6. Be aware of the different kinds of information available in the dictionary: namely,
    a) spelling (preferred spellings are listed first)
    b) syllabication

   c) pronunciation (the pronunciation key is located on the cover page)

   d) part of speech (i) all verb forms (e.g., *bring, brought*)

               (ii) plural forms (e.g., *crisis—crises*)

               (iii) degrees of adjectives or adverbs (e.g., *slow, slower, slowest*)

               (iv) grammar usage (e.g., use of prepositions such as *in* or *into*)

   e) derivations

   f) meanings (words are often illustrated in sentences)

   g) synonyms and antonyms

No matter how good or poor a speller you are, there will always be words that cause you difficulty. If you can recognize these troublesome words and take the time and effort to criticize your written work, your spelling problems should be minimal. After you have looked up a word four or five times, you probably will be able to recognize and write that word in its correct form.

● EXERCISE 4.1

Often people make spelling errors because they mispronounce words and write them according to the way they say them. The following words, taken from students' work, represent just some of the most commonly misspelled words. Find out which words are your "spelling demons."

Circle the correctly spelled word in each pair. If you are uncertain of any spellings, look up the word in your dictionary. Also, check your pronunciation of any word that you discover you consistently misspell.

1. accidently   accidentally

2. acquire   aquire

3. accommodate   accomodate

4. across   accross

5. adjurn   adjourn

6. alchol   alcohol

7. alright   all right

8. alot   a lot (the synonym "many" is the preferred word choice)

9. analysized   analyzed

10. apparant   apparent

11. arguing   argruing

12. asending   ascending

13. association   assosciation

14. atomsphere   atmosphere

15. athletics   atheletics

16. attitute   attitude

17. audiance   audience

18. basicly   basically

19. bilingal   bilingual

20. boundary   boundry

21. bussiness   business

22. canidate   candidate

23. caos   chaos

24. children   childern

25. choosen   chosen

26. college   collage (post-secondary institution)

27. congratulations   congradulations

28. consensus — (concensus) ✗
29. consistant — (consistent) ✓
30. (cruel) — crule ✓
31. decidions — (decisions) ✓
32. developement — (development) ✓
33. differant — (different) ✓
34. (disasterous) — disastrous ✗
35. (discus) — discuss (talk) ✗
36. drasticly — (drastically) ✓
37. embarrassing — (embarasing) ✗
38. emotionally — (emotionly) ✗
39. (esential) — essential ✗
40. exaggerate — (exagerate) ✗
41. expecially — (especially) ✓
42. excercise — (exercise) ✓
43. existence — (existance) ✗
44. (familiar) — familar ✓
45. February — (Febuary) ✗
46. (friends) — freinds (close associates) ✓
47. finial — (final) ✓
48. (fourty) — forty ✗
49. goverment — (government) ✓
50. (gradual) — gradule ✓
51. grammer — (grammar) ✓
52. (grievous) — grievious ✓
53. (guarantee) — garantee ✓
54. heighth — (height) ✓
55. hinderance — hindrance ✗
56. hunerd — (hundred) ✓
57. humors — (humorous) (funny) ✓
58. ilegal — (illegal) ✓
59. incidentally — (incidently) ✗
60. inisiate — (initiate) ✓
61. interduce — (introduce) ✓
62. (interest) — intrest ✓
63. knowlege — (knowledge) ✓
64. (liason) — liaison ✗
65. lisence — (licence) ✓
66. maintenance — (maintainance) ✗
67. (marijuana) — marjana ✓
68. mediocer — (mediocre) ✓
69. mischievious — (mischievous) ✓
70. misspell — (mispell) ✗
71. modren — (modern) ✓
72. neccessary — (necessary) ✓
73. (officially) — officialy ✓
74. opinon — (opinion) ✓

75. pachients   (patients) ✓
76. payed   (paid) (received or spent money) ✓
77. (preperation)   preparation ✗
78. prespiration   (perspiration) ✓
79. possitive   (positive) ✓
80. posess   (possess) ✓
81. pratice   (practice) ✓
82. (prescribe)   perscribe ✓
83. priviledge   (privilege) ✓
84. (professional)   proffessional ✓
85. pernounce   (pronounce) ✓
86. (psychology)   phsycology ✓
87. quantity   (quanity) ✗
88. (questionaire)   questionnaire ✗
89. realisticly   (realistically) ✓
90. reconize   (recognize) ✓
91. refrences   (references) ✓
92. registrar   (registrer) (the person who admits students to a ✗
                       post-secondary school)

93. relevant   (relevent) ✗
94. (rememberance)   remembrance ✗
95. sarcasticly   (sarcastically) ✓
96. secratery   (secretary) ✓
97. sence   (sense) ✓
98. (separate)   seperate ✓
99. skiing   (sking) ✗
100. (speach)   speech ✗
101. (strict)   strick (rigid or severe) ✓
102. submite   (submit) ✓
103. substancial   (substantial) ✓
104. sucess   (success) ✓
105. tangant   (tangent) ✓
106. their   (thier) ✗
107. tommorrow   (tomorrow) ✓
108. tragedy   (tradgedy) ✗
109. (until)   untill ✓
110. (writing)   writting ✓

Check your answers with those in the Answer section at the end of the book.

Make a list of the words that you misspell and try to conquer these "spelling demons." Aim for perfection in this area because incorrect spelling is considered unprofessional in any career. Recognizing and correcting these kinds of errors in your work will always be an asset in your chosen field. You might find it helpful to use a pocket telephone book as your own personal speller. Use the letter tabs to list alphabetically the correct spelling of your most common errors.

● **EXERCISE 4.2**

Correct all spelling errors in the following paragraphs. Use a dictionary if you have doubts about the spelling of any words.

1. What does it take today to be a success? Some people believe that if they graduate from collage or university they will be garanteed a well-paying job in the proffession of thier chosing. Even though a good education is neccessary, it is not the only factor. Posessing a possitive attitute, demonstrating a willingness to learn, and expecially having pachients to implement the knowlege they sence they have accquired are all esential elements in getting ahead. And so, if "opportunity knocks" but doesn't promise all that young people hoped it would, they should reconize that some of the simple tasks can be the first step in their career developement. No one knows the meaning that today's actions will have on tommorrow. Being sucessful means making the best of present situations, being intrested in the job (even if it is very boring), and being ready and watchful for new doors to open.

2. Childern are well known for their crulety to one another. Last Febuary, one of the contenders in the speach contest continually mispernounced the words "relevant" and "atomsphere." Apparantly, everytime she made these disasterous mistakes, young schoolmates in the front row began to create a little bit of caos with their whispering and giggling. Knowing their reactions must be directed at her, the poor canidate became embarased and forgot her lines. Even with prompting, she could not recover her composure. Finially, she left the stage in tears. All her pratice and preperation were runed because she had payed attention to her mischievious freinds instead of concentrating on getting her information accross to the audiance. There were no congradulations; instead, her potential moment of glory had turned into an unforgetable tradgedy!

Check your answers with those in the Answer section at the end of the book.

III. USING A THESAURUS

The thesaurus is a handy book that contains synonyms and antonyms for most English words or expressions. You can probably recall wasting precious time trying to think of the right word or expression to use in your essays. Perhaps you find that you often repeat words simply because you cannot think of others to use. If so, then you should be using a thesaurus.

There are two types to choose from: one arranged in categories of synonyms; and the other arranged in a dictionary format. Both reference texts have their advantages and disadvantages. It is important that you choose the one that will best suit your needs.

The original thesaurus is the reference version, arranged in categories of synonyms. The main advantage of this format is that you are given a wide range of synonyms, antonyms, and idioms to peruse to find just the right term to fit your purpose. Words are arranged by degrees within categories; therefore, writers can easily find specific words to replace common, vague, or overused words; and precise or more formal expressions to replace casual expressions or slang. However, some word choices may not be as up to date as in a dictionary-format thesaurus. Also, those who are not familiar with this format will have to take a little time to learn how to use the text.

The easier to use of the two types of thesaurus is arranged in dictionary format; no special instructions are necessary for you to use this reference text. Most often, this format contains more up-to-date word selections; but word replacement choices are very specific, and related antonyms and idioms are not easy to locate. The one exception, however, is *The Random House Thesaurus*. In this book, each meaning is introduced by one or more example sentences or phrases that illustrate the meaning for the list of synonyms that follow. Also, related antonyms are included at the end of each entry.

Excerpts from both types of thesaurus are illustrated in this section. Decide which is better suited to your needs; then take time to read the front section of your chosen text to learn about its specific features and instructions for use.

THE ORIGINAL VERSION: A TREASURY OF SYNONYMS AND ANTONYMS

A. Use the Synopsis of Categories to Locate General Expressions

Use this portion of the thesaurus on those occasions when you are groping for that missing piece to the puzzle; you have the ideas that you want to express but you cannot find the words to say precisely what you mean.

For example, you may want to express the fact that you are giving information. Although the word *give* has many connotations, none express your exact feelings. Look in the synopsis of categories under either "Formation of Ideas" or "Communication of Ideas" (see, for example, *Roget's Thesaurus*). There you will find a wide range of vocabulary words that will help express your exact feelings. It may be the verb form of "Prediction" (511) or "Teaching" (537) that will give you the missing piece to your puzzle. These categories, as well as the many words listed in close proximity, should provide you with a wide selection of terms from which to choose the right expression.

B. Use the Index to Find Synonyms and Antonyms

1. The alphabetically arranged index at the back of the thesaurus is useful when you want to locate a specific word.

2. If, for example, you find that you have overused the word *strange*, or that this word is too basic for your essay, you could look up the following information in the index:

   strange—   unrelated 10
               exceptional 83
               ridiculous 853
               wonderful 870
               —bedfellows 713
               —to say 870

   NOTE: A dash (—) before these words indicates that the listed word would be used at the beginning of a phrase (e.g., *strange* bedfellows, *strange* to say).[1]

3. Select the appropriate interpretation (say, *exceptional*); turn to the numbered item in the book (Section 83) and choose the preferred synonym listed under the term *Adj.* (short for *adjective*, meaning descriptive).

4. The antonym (the opposite meaning) will be listed under *Adj.* in the section immediately before or after Section 83. In this case, the antonym for *exceptional* would be listed in Section 82 or 84.

Knowing the location of antonyms is particularly helpful if you wish to avoid using the negative term *not*; for example, suggested word replacements for *not exceptional* are *conventional*, *ordinary*, *customary*, etc. Any of the latter words would usually be better to use than the term *not exceptional*.

5. If a suitable synonym or antonym is not listed in Section 83, then peruse all sections before and after the section, as other degrees of the word will be listed in this general category.

6. Note the meanings of the following symbols:

n.—noun   adj.—adjective (descriptive of nouns)
v.—verb adv.—adverb (descriptive of actions)

Pay particular attention to the kind of synonym you wish to replace. For example, if you wish to find a synonym for the word *speak* in the following sentence, you would turn to Section 582 and locate the synonyms listed under *v.* (verb).

The astronaut received several invitations to *talk to* various groups about his experiences in space.

Look at the listing of synonyms given in *Roget's Thesaurus,* Harper Paperback Edition (HarperCollins Publishers, 1946; reprinted 1991).

165   COMMUNICATION OF IDEAS   581–584
V. **silence,** muzzle, muffle, suppress, smother, gag, strike dumb, dumfound.

Adj. **dumb,** mute, mum; tongue-tied; voiceless, speechless, wordless; silent, etc. *(taciturn),* 585; inarticulate.

582. SPEECH.—*N.* **speech,** locution, talk, parlance, word of mouth, prattle.

oration, recitation, delivery, speech, address, discourse, lecture, harangue, sermon, tirade, soliloquy, etc., 589; conversation, etc., 588; salutatory; valedictory.

oratory, elocution, eloquence, rhetoric, declamation; grandiloquence.

speaker, spokesman, mouthpiece, orator, rhetorician, lecturer, preacher, elocutionist, reciter, reader; spellbinder.

V. **speak,** talk, say, utter, pronounce, deliver, breathe, let fall, rap out, blurt out.

soliloquize, etc., 589; tell, etc. *(inform),* 527; address, etc., 586; converse, etc., 588.

declaim, hold forth, harangue, stump [*colloq.*], spout, rant; recite, lecture, sermonize, discourse, expatiate.

Adj. **oral,** lingual, phonetic, unwritten, spoken.

eloquent, oratorical, rhetorical, elocutionary, declamatory, grandiloquent.

583. [Imperfect Speech] STAMMERING.—*N.* **inarticulate**[2]

Locate a suitable synonym under the term *V* (verb). The most suitable word would probably be "address." However, other synonyms could be located in Section 586 on page 166.

585–590   INTELLECT   166
585. TACITURNITY.—*N.* **taciturnity,** silence, muteness, curtness; reserve, reticence.

man of few words; Spartan.

V. **be silent,** keep silence; hold one's tongue, say nothing; render mute.

Adj. **silent,** mute, mum, still, dumb.

taciturn, laconic, concise, sententious, close, close-mouthed, curt; reserved; reticent.

586. ADDRESS.—*N.* **address,** allocution; speech, etc., 582; appeal, invocation, salutation, salutatory.

Note the words listed in Section 586 under the term *V* (verb). Only choose words that you know will suit the sentence. If you have any doubts, refer to the dictionary or choose another word.

→ *V.* **address,** speak to, accost, apostrophize, appeal to, invoke; hail, salute; call to, halloo.

lecture, preach, harangue, spellbind.

587. RESPONSE, etc., *see* **Answer** 462.

588. CONVERSATION.—*N.* **conversation,** colloquy, converse, interlocution, talk, discourse, dialogue, duologue.

chat, tattle, gossip, tittle-tattle; babble.

conference, parley, interview, audience, reception; congress, etc. *(council)*, 696; powwow.[3]

C. Use the Index to Locate General Information on a Topic

If you require information on a general subject or any portion of it, refer to the index. For example, "Music" is listed under Section 415. Here you will find references to specific terms, kinds of music, musicians, musical instruments, etc.

THE DICTIONARY FORMAT

The astronaut received several invitations to talk to various groups about his experiences in space.

Now look at the listing of synonyms given in *The Random House Thesaurus,* First Balantine Books Edition (Random House Inc., 1984; reprinted 1993).

talent

yarn. **2** *Don't tell tales out of school:* fib, lie, falsehood, untruth, fabrication, falsification; piece of gossip, scandal, rumor.

talent *n. You have a talent for drawing:* special ability, gift, facility, genius, aptitude, knack, bent, flair.

talented *adj. a talented musician:* gifted, accomplished; proficient, competent, capable.

talk *v.* **1** *Can the baby talk yet? We talked for hours:* utter words, speak; converse, bandy words, discuss, chat, chatter, gab, gossip, prattle, babble, rap, jaw. **2** *You'd better talk with a lawyer:* confer, consult, speak; negotiate, parley. **3** *He's talking nonsense!:* utter, speak, say, express; intone, enunciate; state, proclaim, pronounce, declare; preach, pontificate. —*n.* **4** *Let's have a little talk:* conference, consultation, powwow.

This example is similar to the meaning of the sentence, but you must change some words to the verb form.

→ **5** *The speaker gave a short, humorous talk:* address, lecture, speech, oration, sermon. **6** *There's been some talk about closing the office:* gossip, rumor, hearsay; report, word. **7** *The kids' hip talk is sometimes hard for adults to follow:* idiom, language, lingo, slang, cant, jargon, argot. *Ant.* **1** be silent, be mute; listen.

talkative *adj. The talkative man monopolized the conversation:* loquacious, voluble, effusive, garrulous, talky, gabby, prolix, long-winded, windy, wordy, verbose.

tally

Ant. reticent, taciturn, uncommunicative, close-mouthed, tight-lipped.

talker *n.* **1** *The senator is a marvelous talker:* conversationalist; speaker, lecturer, orator, speechmaker. **2** *She's quite a talker—I couldn't get in a word!:* loquacious person, voluble person, garrulous person, chatterbox, windbag, gabber; gossip, rumormonger, scandalmonger.

tall *adj.* **1** *The boy is four feet tall:* high, in height. **2** *Basketball players are tall. a tall mountain:* of more than average height, long-limbed; high, lofty, towering, soaring, elevated. **3** *a tall tale:* hard to believe, implausible, preposterous, exaggerated, embellished, false. *Ant.* **1** wide, broad; long, deep. **2** short, low. **3** believable, credible, plausible, reasonable.

tally *n.* **1** *The final tally was 200 votes for and 150 against:* count, reckoning, mark, score; total, sum. —*v.* **2** *The judges tallied the scores:* record, mark down, register, list; count, add, sum up, total, reckon. **3** *The checkbook stubs don't tally with my bank statement:* match, jibe, square, correspond, agree, accord, concur, harmonize.

tame *adj.* **1** *a tame monkey. Greg is too tame to stand up for his rights:* domesticated, domestic; docile, gen-[4]

● EXERCISE 4.3

1. Use the thesaurus to replace very basic words in your written work. Replace the italicized words with more suitable expressions from the thesaurus.

   a) How much money did she plan to *put into* mutual funds? ~deposit~ ~invest~

   b) You cannot *make* me do anything I don't *want* to do. ~compel~ ~desire~

   c) That was a *good* meal! ~excellent~

   d) Lisa felt that she *got* a better understanding of herself from her psychology classes. ~received~

   e) The victim *told* in detail all the events that happened the night of the crime. ~expressed~ ~related~

2. Use the thesaurus to avoid negative terms. Replace the negative expressions italicized in the following sentences.

   a) Her reasoning is definitely *not right*, as she jumps to conclusions without having all the facts. ~incorrect~

   b) Some people are *not sensitive* to the needs of others. ~insensitive~

   c) I am *not going to continue* my subscription to that magazine. ~cease~

   d) Her comments were *not related* to the topic being discussed. ~unrelated~

   e) There was *no agreement* among the school board members on the choice of the new administrator. ~disagreement~

3. Use the thesaurus to replace slang or casual word usage. Replace the italicized words with more suitable expressions given in the thesaurus.

   a) Because the owners were renovating their business, customers were asked to *put up with* a few inconveniences. ~endure~

   b) It was Evan's job to *weed out* the problems in the project. ~remove~

   c) Good employees *stick to* established company policies. ~follow~ ~abide~

   d) It is difficult at times to *make out* another person's handwriting. ~comprehend~ ~decipher~

   e) Did you *find out* how much you will have to pay for car insurance? ~ascertain~

Check your answers with those in the Answer section at the end of the book.

IV. WORDINESS

Some students tend to use many words to explain themselves when really one word or phrase would be more effective. Examine the following wordy expressions and note the suggested correction for each.

1. in the year 1996	in 1996	
2. the exact same	the same	
3. basic fundamental	basic *or* fundamental	(not both)
4. in my opinion, I think	in my opinion *or* I think	(not both)
5. in my opinion, I believe	in my opinion *or* I believe	(not both)

6.	the course program	course *or* (not both) program
7.	at this point in time	now *or* today *or* presently
8.	at that point in time	then
9.	a whole lot *or* a lot	many *or* several
10.	final outcome	outcome
11.	end result or end product	result *or* product
12.	in the event that ...	if ...
13.	with reference to ...	concerning ... *or* about ...
14.	necessary requirements	requirements *or* necessary supplies/qualifications
15.	people who live in Canada	Canadians
16.	people who live in the city	city dwellers
17.	students who go to high school/college/university	high school students/college students/university students
18.	He seems to be happy.	He seems happy.
19.	She appeared to be angry.	She appeared angry.
20.	Is it true that people today seem to be reading less?	Do people today read less?

● EXERCISE 4.4

Improve the quality of the following sentences by eliminating wordy expressions. Some redundancies are mentioned in the preceding list; others should be obvious if you proofread critically.

1. ~~In my opinion,~~ I believe that high schools should place more emphasis on the ~~basic~~ fundamentals of English and mathematics.

2. Although it is true that students who go to high school have a much better general education, at this point in time, their basic ~~fundamental~~ skills seem to be weak.

   High school students have a much better general education, but their basic skills seem to be weak.

3. In the ~~years of the~~ 1990s, a ~~whole lot of~~ *Many* changes were made in the education system to improve the ~~course~~ programs in communication and math skills.

4. Although everyone ~~who is a~~ student cannot be at the ~~exact~~ same level in these basic skills, ~~in my opinion~~ I believe that when these changes have been in effect for a few more years, students will demonstrate ~~a whole lot of~~ improvements in their everyday work.

Many

5. ~~At that point in time, it may be true that~~ Then More students may ~~wish and~~ desire to remain in school and be better prepared for the work force.

6. My teacher who teaches English at the college has agreed to supply my prospective employer with the ~~necessary~~ required report with reference to my excellent written communication skills.

My English teacher at the college agreed to supply my prospective employer with the required report about my excellent written communication skills

7. In the event that students who are potential graduates from college or university can demonstrate the necessary job skills required for work during their field placements, both the employers and the students will benefit positively from the end results of an effective educational and learning experience.

If potential graduates can demonstrate job skills required for work during their field placement both employers and students benefit from an effective educational learning experience

8. At this point in time, new employees who have just begun their jobs at banks seem to have a lot of opportunities for advancement and upward mobility within this structure of the corporations.

New bank employees have a lot of opportunities for advancement within ~~this structure~~ the corporation.

Check your answers with those in the Answer section at the end of the book.

THE NEXT STEP

If you feel confident about this section, proceed to "Sentence Structure."

SENTENCE STRUCTURE

There is **no** Pretest for this section. Please work through each phase of "Sentence Structure."

A sentence is a group of words expressing a complete thought. It is completely independent; it can stand alone. Each complete thought begins with a capital letter and ends with proper punctuation. However, even adding a capital letter and end punctuation to a group of words does not necessarily mean that you have created a sentence; the word group must also give a clear message!

I. BASIC SENTENCE STRUCTURE

A sentence requires three components to make it correct and complete.

1. It must have a *subject* that identifies who or what is being discussed.

2. It must have a *predicate* that contains the action and/or gives information about the subject.

3. The combination of a subject and predicate must also express a complete thought or give a clear message to the reader.

Examine the following sentences and note these three components.

Subject (*who or what is being discussed*)   +   *Predicate*   =   *Complete thought*

Many trees were blown down during the storm.

Subject (*who or what is being discussed*)   +   *Predicate*   =   *Complete thought*

Traffic along the expressway moved slowly because of the foggy conditions.

Sentences that command give that effect by omitting the subject "you"; however, this term is still understood.

Predicate   +   Subject (*who or what is being discussed*)   =   *Complete thought*

Finish your dinner.   (**you** is understood)

● EXERCISE 4.5

Underline the subject (‿‿‿‿‿) and the predicate (_____) in each of the following sentences and indicate if the word group is a complete thought (C). Note the examples:

The noise in the hallways is often distracting   = C

Shut the door. (you is understood)   = C

1. Full-time jobs are becoming more and more difficult to find.
2. Members of the ski team are planning to compete in the college races.
3. The new residence is heated by solar energy.
4. Take out the garbage.
5. Everyone was looking forward to the holidays.
6. That report was due last Friday.
7. Go directly to the office after the meeting.
8. A list of the prize winners was posted on the bulletin board.
9. You should have a study plan for all courses.
10. You need good communication skills in every kind of career today.

Check your answers with those in the Answer section at the end of the book.

II. BASIC SENTENCE PATTERNS

All sentences in the preceding exercise are arranged in natural order; that is, all sentences begin with the complete subject which is followed by the complete predicate. If you are composing any message, however, you need to add variety to this one pattern to make your message more interesting to the reader. Examine the following sentence patterns:

Natural Order

Subject   +   *Predicate*   =   *Complete thought*

The five airplanes flew silently above the clouds.

Reversed Order

Predicate   +   *Subject*

Silently above the clouds flew the five airplanes.

Mixed Order

Predicate is divided

Subject

Silently above the clouds the five airplanes flew.

Questions are often formed by changing the sentence pattern. Note the following examples:

Subject + *Predicate*

You did answer those questions. (a statement)

Predicate is divided

Subject

Did you answer those questions? (a question)

Where are you going?

When did she leave?

● EXERCISE 4.6

Identify the subject (⌣⌣⌣⌣⌣⌣) and predicate (_____) as illustrated in the above examples. Indicate the sentence pattern: natural order, reversed order, mixed order.

1. The old man walked slowly down the street. _____

2. On the exam were several difficult questions. _____

3. What have you done with my report? _____

4. In the autumn all the leaves fall off the trees. _____

5. On the first page was a list of the candidates' names and addresses. _____

6. I was very tired by the end of the day. _____

Check your answers with those in the Answer section at the end of the book.

● EXERCISE 4.7

Follow each direction for changing the sentence patterns of sentences in Exercise 4.6. Rewrite the sentences in the spaces provided.

1. Write sentence #1 in reversed order.

   _____

2. Write sentence #1 in mixed order.

   _____

3. Write sentence #2 in natural order.

   _____

4. Write sentence #4 in natural order.

   _____

5. Write sentence #6 in mixed order.

   _____

Note that the sentence order cannot be changed for Sentence #3 without creating an awkward sound. Consider the various methods but choose the best one to relay your message.

Check your answers with those in the Answer section at the end of the book.

III. SENTENCE FRAGMENTS

Students often mistakenly punctuate partial word groups as complete sentences. This error is one of the most common in all written work. Fragments are created if one of the three requirements for sentence structure is omitted; that is, if the subject or predicate is missing or if the thought is incomplete.

MISSING SUBJECTS

A sentence fragment is created when the writer neglects to include the subject of the sentence in his or her message.

Fragment	Suggested Correction
	add a subject
Met the new neighbour.	We met the new neighbour.
Hope to see you soon.	I hope to see you soon.
Talk to you tomorrow.	Pat will talk to you tomorrow.

MISSING PREDICATES OR PORTIONS OF MISSING PREDICATES

Another kind of sentence fragment is created when the writer neglects to include a complete verb (the action word or helper word).

Fragment	Suggested Correction
	add a predicate
The man in the grey suit.	The man in the grey suit is my boss.
	add a subject and a predicate
	or I know the man in the grey suit.
	change form of action word
	Marcus picked up his books.
	add a helper to make the action complete
Marcus picking up his books.	or Marcus is picking up his books.
	treat this as descriptive, add a predicate
	or Marcus, picking up his books, left the room.
	add a predicate
The one who arrives first.	The one who arrives first wins the race.

● EXERCISE 4.8

In the space provided, correct the following fragments by adding any necessary words.

1. The colour of the water.
   ✓ *The colour of the water was blue.*

2. The workers who built the bridge.
   The workers who built the bridge did a good job.

3. Plan to leave at three o'clock.
   I plan to leave a 3 o'clock.

4. Suyin finding an error in her work.
   Suyin found an error in her work.

5. Was reading the sports section of the newspaper.
   I was reading the sports section of the newspaper.

6. Happy the storm was over.
   I'm happy the storm is over.

7. Sorry Fritz had to miss the party.
   I'm sorry Fritz had to miss the party.

8. All cars that don't pass a safety check.
   All cars that don't pass a safety check are unsafe.

Check your answers with those suggested in the Answer section at the end of the book.

MISSING SUBJECTS AND PREDICATES

This kind of fragment will usually be next to a complete sentence. To correct this error, attach the word group to the sentence it describes.

Fragment	Suggested Correction
	attach to sentence
In the middle of the night. The telephone rang.	In the middle of the night the telephone rang.
	attach to sentence
We walked. Across the street.	We walked across the street.
With renewed willpower and determination to lose some weight. I went on a diet.	With renewed willpower and determination to lose some weight, I went on a diet.
	attach to sentence

INCOMPLETE THOUGHT

This kind of fragment contains a subject and a predicate but does not convey a complete message. There are two ways to correct this error.

1. Delete the initial word. The meaning of the expression will be slightly changed, but the group of words will be a complete sentence.

2. Attach the incomplete descriptive fragment to a sentence. The whole word group will now be complete.

Fragment	Suggested Correction
	omit "Although"
Although I had studied.	I had studied.
	attach to a subject and a predicate
	or Although I had studied, <u>I didn't pass the test.</u>
	omit "Ever since"
Ever since I have started a regular exercise program and watch what I eat.	I have started a regular exercise program and watch what I eat.
	or Ever since I have started a regular exercise program and watch what I eat, <u>I feel and look so much better.</u>

add a subject and a predicate

● EXERCISE 4.9

Correct sentence fragment errors in the following exercise by adding or deleting words or by attaching the fragment to an existing sentence and correcting the punctuation.

1. During the spring and summer seasons. We often go for long drives in the country.
   ✓ *During the spring and summer seasons, we often go for long drives in the country.*

2. Because it rained.
   ✓ *It rained.*

3. Although I had been there before.
   ✓ *I had been there before.*

4. If you plan to leave as soon as this class is over.
   ✗ *If you plan to leave as soon as this class is over, I'll see you later.*

5. If you need some help. Please telephone me at home or at work.
   ✓ *Please telephone me at home or at work, if you need some help.*

6. Although I have had a driver's licence for six years and I have never had a speeding ticket.
   Although I have had a driver's licence for six years and I have never had a speeding ticket.

7. I enjoy playing all sports. Because they are a lot of fun.

✓ I enjoy playing all sports, because they are a lot of fun.

8. Ali promised to meet us at the bus station. Which is near the new post office building.

✓ Ali promised to meet us at the bus station, which is near the new post office building

Check your answers with those suggested in the Answer section at the end of the book.

● EXERCISE 4.10—REVIEW

Correct sentence fragment errors in the following paragraph.

After studying house designs and decorating techniques for two years, Sara decided to take a business management course. She felt this extra training would give her the skills she would need, To open her own company. In the beginning *she* had to work long hours, Doing the ordering, the accounts, deliveries, as well as decorating customers' homes. Because she couldn't afford to hire anyone to help her. Her work was excellent. Because she made sure that her customers were always satisfied. As more people learned about her talents, Her company expanded, *and she* Hired some assistants. Today, Sara being one of the city's most successful businesswomen.

Check your answers with those suggested in the Answer section at the end of the book.

IV. CORRECTING RUN-ON SENTENCES

Run-on sentences, a very common error in English, are two or more sentences punctuated as one. Occasionally, students will use just a comma between two complete thoughts; however, this punctuation mark is not sufficient and may confuse the reader. As you will learn in later units, the comma has very specific functions and cannot be used alone as an "end-of-sentence" punctuation mark.

To avoid this kind of sentence structure error, proofread your work aloud. Your voice will naturally pause at the end of each complete thought. Reread portions of any suspected run-on sentences to make sure that each group of words makes sense by itself.

Use appropriate end punctuation—period (.), question mark (?), or exclamation mark (!)—as well as a capital letter between the two sentences.

Error:	The highway was crowded with traffic, it took me two hours to get home.
	or
	The highway was crowded with traffic it took me two hours to get home.
Correction:	The highway was crowded with traffic. It took me two hours to get home.
Error:	What have you done about your tuition fees they were due last Thursday.
Correction:	What have you done about your tuition fees? They were due last Thursday.
Error:	I'm late I know I have missed the bus now, how am I going to get to my interview for nine o'clock.
Correction:	I'm late! I know I have missed the bus. Now, how am I going to get to my interview for nine o'clock?

● EXERCISE 4.11

In the spaces provided, correct these run-on errors by separating the sentences and adding the appropriate punctuation.

1. Will you leave the light on I might be late.

Will you leave the light on? I might be late

2. Planning a trip is very easy paying for it is the difficult part.

Planning a trip is very easy. Paying for it is the difficult part.

3. Plastic materials cause pollution they do not decompose as other waste products do.

Plastic materials cause pollution. They don't decompose as other waste products do.

4. When you answer the phone don't use a different tone of voice, Try to speak naturally and just be yourself.

5. First you should consider all the benefits of travelling then you should decide if it is really worth the expense.

6. Olena was the one who did all the work. Why should others receive the credit for her efforts.?

7. I have one serious fault. I am always late!

8. I have tried various solutions to solve this character defect. So far none of them have worked.

9. Psychologists say that it is not really difficult for people to overcome bad habits. All they require is the right attitude and the determination to change.

10. What have you done about your problems? If you haven't yet acknowledged their existence, how can you expect to change?

Check your answers with those in the Answer section at the end of the book.

● EXERCISE 4.12—REVIEW

Correct sentence fragments and run-on sentences in the following exercise. You may need to correct the punctuation, add any necessary words, or delete unnecessary words to make the statements clear and complete.

1. Maria had made a record number of real estate sales last month. She was given a promotion. Which she really deserved.

2. If you finish your assignment by eleven, You should plan to meet me for lunch. Perhaps we could eat at the new restaurant downtown. I understand they have an excellent salad bar.

3. No matter what you decide to do, You should discuss your decision with a counsellor. Why don't you listen to his or her ideas. Before you actually make your plans? then you can consider all the options available to you.

4. After all the work I put into writing that essay, *I got an A!*

5. Shut all the windows before you leave. It might rain while we are away.

6. Skiing is a great way to meet people. If you excel at this sport you can join a racing team, *and* Compete at all levels and travel to other ski areas.

7. Hutoshi finally finished her project. Which had been very difficult and had taken up all of her free time. She now intended to celebrate.

8. Whenever we sit down to dinner, *the dog begs for food.*

9. To begin a research paper, first jot down your purpose in one statement. Next write a few questions that you feel need to be asked. then go to the library or other resource centres for the answers. Finally sort your information to see what other data should be investigated. These are just the beginning steps of preparing a research project.

10. To my amazement, for each ticket I had purchased for the lottery, I won either a free ticket or two dollars. Hoping to be the big winner now that I had five free tickets and ten extra dollars in my pocket.

Check your answers with those suggested in the Answer section at the end of the book.

V. REFINING SENTENCES

Now that you know how to correct sentences by making them conform to the basic subject-followed-by-predicate structure, you are ready to start refining your writing.

One difficulty with constantly repeating the basic sentence pattern is that, while your sentences may be grammatically correct, they may become very repetitive. If you have a tendency to write a series of short, choppy sentences, the quality of what you have written will be reduced.

The style and the quality of your writing can be greatly improved by avoiding the use of vague terms such as *it* or *this*, by varying your wording using a dictionary or a thesaurus, and by using a variety of sentence patterns to create rhythm and tone. Following are several ways to add interest to your basic sentences.

COORDINATING CONJUNCTIONS

Use coordinating conjunctions to join two or more similar words, actions, word groups, or sentences. The most commonly used coordinating conjunctions are

and   or   but

AND indicates that factors are similar in some way or expresses a continuing idea.

Example 1:

> Pina completed the math question quickly. She completed it accurately.

In these sentences two similar words (quickly, accurately) describe the same situation. To avoid being repetitious, write the part that is common to both sentences and then use a coordinating conjunction to join the similar portions.

> Pina completed the math question quickly **and** accurately.

Example 2:

> Pina completed the math questions quickly. She then left the room.

There are two actions that apply to Pina in these sentences. Therefore, write the part that is common to both sentences (Pina) and use a coordinating conjunction to join the continuing action.

> Pina completed the math questions quickly **and** then left the room.

Example 3:

> Simone put on her favourite record. She sat in a comfortable chair. She relaxed. She let the worries of the day fade away.

In this instance, there are several continuing actions that Simone performed. Write the common part of the sentences (Simone). Use commas to separate each of the actions and a coordinating conjunction to join the last one.

> Simone put on her favourite record, sat in a comfortable chair, relaxed, **and** let the worries of the day fade away.

However, unrelated ideas cannot be joined.

> **Error:**   Thank you for considering my application and I am looking forward to hearing from you in the near future.

Because there is no continuous action in this pair of statements, they cannot be joined by a conjunction. Use a period between these two separate thoughts or rewrite the message using one of the other refining techniques discussed in this chapter.

> **Correction:**   Thank you for considering my application. I am looking forward to hearing from you in the near future.

OR indicates that factors are similar in some ways but indicates or offers a choice.

Example 4:

> Natasha will go. Boris will go.

If only one is to perform the action, use *or* to indicate the choice.

> Natasha **or** Boris will go.

Example 5:

> Clean up your room. Suffer the consequences.

The conjunction *or* joins the two actions and offers a choice.

> Clean up your room **or** suffer the consequences.

BUT indicates either two contrasting descriptions or a change of idea.

Example 6:

> The researcher conducted a hasty study of the case. She was also thorough.

In this example, there is one idea with two contrasting descriptions. Because this contrast seems to be an addition to the main idea, use commas to indicate the change.

> The researcher conducted a hasty, **but** thorough, study of the case.

Example 7:

> We planned to arrive on time. We were delayed by the heavy flow of traffic.

These sentences describe a change in a situation. Use *but* to express the change.

> We planned to arrive on time **but** were delayed by the heavy flow of traffic.

Example 8:

> Mr. Kovac arrived at the office early this morning. He was late for our meeting at nine o'clock.

These sentences represent two contrasting ideas. Use *but* to express the contrast.

> Mr. Kovac arrived at the office early this morning **but** he was late for our nine o'clock meeting.

AND, OR, BUT—a combination of these can be used to keep the sentence flowing.

Example 9:

> Slang expressions should not be used in business. They should not be used in writing.
> They are acceptable jargon in everyday speech. They should be kept there!

Here we have two negative ideas combined with a change of thought and added to a continuing idea.

> Slang expressions should not be used in business or writing, **but** they are acceptable jargon
> in everyday speech **and** should be kept there!

● EXERCISE 4.13

In the following groups of sentences, identify the ideas as continuing, contrasting, or offering a choice. Then combine the sentences using the most appropriate coordinating conjunction to convey the correct message.

1. Be sure to take your key.
   Be sure to lock the door behind you.

   _____

2. The speaker looked confident.
   He was really nervous.

   _____

3. Catrin had carefully cut all the savings coupons out of the newspaper.
   She forgot them at home.

   _____

4. Next year I may apply for the accounting program.
   I may apply for the business administration course.

   _____

5. Mario is planning to leave as soon as this class is over.
   He is going to type up his late assignment.
   He is going to submit it before five o'clock.

   _____

   _____

6. Dana stayed up all night studying for her midterm test.
   The next day she was too drowsy to think clearly.

   _____

7. You should not dwell on your past mistakes.
   You should not concentrate on problems that might occur in the future.
   You should only pay attention to what you can do about today.

   _____

   _____

8. We were sure the boy had committed the crime.
   We were sure that the boy was lying about his whereabouts.
   We had no evidence to support our theory.

   _____

   _____

9. I tried to sleep.
   The thought of tomorrow's exam kept me awake.

   _____

10. Allan repaired his watchband with a paper clip.
The clip snapped.
The watch slipped off his wrist.

_____

_____

Check your answers with those suggested in the Answer section at the end of the book.

SUBORDINATING CONJUNCTIONS

Use subordinating conjunctions to relate two sentences that do not have equal status. One will express a dominant theme; the other will relate the circumstances or time elements that are also involved. For example:

> We were late.
> We missed the train.

It seems that "missing the train" is the more important fact; therefore, this is the dominant theme. Join the sentences as follows:

Because we were late, <u>we missed the train.</u>

subordinate idea   *dominant theme*

or <u>We missed the train</u> because we were late.

dominant theme   *subordinate idea*

Subordinating conjunctions help to relate the conditions or circumstances of a fact of lesser importance to the more dominant theme.

Following is a list of the most commonly used subordinating conjunctions.

A. To Indicate a Time Relationship

after	before	since	until
when	while	as (two simultaneous occurrences)	

B. To Indicate a Conditional Relationship

even though	because	since	though	if
as though	as if	so that	unless	although

dominant theme   *subordinate idea*

I like a cold drink { before / after / while / when } I eat supper.

The subordinating conjunction here shows the time relationship.

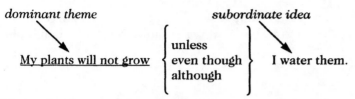

NOTE: A subordinate clause that begins a sentence is followed by a comma.

> Before I eat supper, I like a cold drink.

> Even though I water my plants, they will not grow.

● EXERCISE 4.14

Use subordinating conjunctions to relate the ideas in the following sentences. Identify the dominant theme and try to use a different subordinating conjunction for each of the ten sentences.

1. You haven't enough money for coffee. You will have to drink water.

   _____

2. I studied hard enough for the exam. I still didn't pass.

   _____

3. She stared at me. She didn't know me.

   _____

4. We went for coffee. The concert was over.

   _____

5. The recipe was a failure. I followed the directions carefully.

   _____

6. I like to have a glass of wine. I eat a gourmet dinner.

   _____

7. I was exhausted after a hard day at work. I could not sleep.

   _____

8. We had raced to the airport. We discovered that the plane would be late.

   _____

9. I had tickets for the concert. I could not go. I was sick.

   _____

10. I have known you for a while. I would like you to meet my family.

    _____

Check your answers with those suggested in the Answer section at the end of the book.

CREATING THE RIGHT EMPHASIS

Some sentences change meaning when one idea is emphasized and the other is subordinated. For example, compare the messages that are created by combining the same ideas in two different ways.

> Rob has a college diploma.

> He has no related job experience.

Version 1:

> Although Rob has a college diploma, he has no related job experience.

This message suggests that Rob would not be a good employment risk. If you change the dominant theme, however, you also change the meaning. Note the emphasis in the following:

Version 2:

> Although he has no related job experience, Rob has a college diploma.

In this version, it seems that Rob's college diploma is the more important job factor and the fact that he has no related job experience is not detrimental to his candidacy for employment. Therefore, if you want to emphasize a particular message, make sure that you place that main thought in the dominant theme and the lesser idea in a subordinate clause.

● EXERCISE 4.15

In the following sentences, use an appropriate subordinating conjunction to convey the message as instructed.

1. The accident victim has fully recovered. His head injury had been very serious. *(Emphasize the seriousness of the head injury.)*

2. Syed had a speech impediment. He was a popular dinner speaker. *(De-emphasize Syed's speech impediment.)*

3. The money was turned over to the authorities. The boys had been tempted to keep it. *(Emphasize the fact that the boys had wanted to keep the money.)*

4. Chanda never missed an episode of her favourite soap opera. She had a very busy work schedule. *(De-emphasize Chanda's busy work schedule.)*

5. I get nervous. I drink coffee. *(Emphasize your nervousness.)*

Check your answers with those suggested in the Answer section at the end of the book.

TRANSITIONAL WORDS

Use a semicolon (;) and, if appropriate, a transitional word or group of words to connect two related and complete thoughts. Transition means *to carry over*. The following transitional words or groups of words can help to relate two sentences in a more meaningful way; however, the statement following the transitional word group is the accented one.

HOWEVER **NEVERTHELESS** }	indicate that a change follows.
CONSEQUENTLY **THEREFORE** **AS A RESULT** }	indicate that a result (either positive or negative) follows.

The highway was congested with traffic; **consequently**, it took me two hours to get home.

or

The highway was congested with traffic; **as a result**, it took me two hours to get home.

● EXERCISE 4.16

In the spaces provided, join the two sentences by using a semicolon (;) and a transitional word or group of words to relate the two thoughts.

1. Al was at a party last night; *consequently,* He had difficulty concentrating on his work in the morning.

2. I really enjoy the sunny, warm, tropical weather, *however,* I don't enjoy the reptiles that also like that climate!

3. I set the clock fifteen minutes ahead of time; *As a result,* I am never late for any appointments.

4. It had been ten years since Anu had attended any school; *However,* Her writing skills were excellent.

5. The lighting is poor in the bedroom; *Therefore,* I cannot study there.

6. To me, the doctor's handwriting seemed almost illegible; *Nevertheless,* The pharmacist had no problem deciphering the prescription.

7. Mahdi never did any homework in math; *As a result,* He failed the course.

8. Repairs were being made to the highway; *Therefore,* Traffic had to be rerouted.

9. The sun shone brightly; It was extremely cold.

   However,

10. The students encountered many problems learning the new computer program; After many frustrating hours, the majority finally mastered the technique. *However,*

Check your answers with those suggested in the Answer section at the end of the book.

UNDERLINING

To identify the key parts of a sentence and combine them into one effective statement, you may find it helpful to use your underlining skills. To further improve your sentences, limit the number of times you use the words *it* and *this*; instead, omit these terms or replace them with the name of the action or expression.

Example 1:

It is important to <u>keep</u> yourself <u>physically fit.</u> It is <u>good for your mind and</u> it is good for <u>your body</u>.

Suggested Correction:

Keeping physically fit is good for your mind and your body.

Example 2:

You should <u>proofread your work</u> and <u>plan your writing assignments.</u> <u>This course will help</u> <u>you</u> do that.

Suggested Correction:

This course will help you to proofread your work and plan your writing assignments.

Example 3:

<u>Anita has a bird.</u> The bird's name is <u>Pretty Boy.</u> He <u>likes to sit on her chrome microwave.</u> He <u>admires himself.</u>

Suggested Correction:

Anita has a bird named Pretty Boy who likes to sit on her chrome microwave and admire himself.

● EXERCISE 4.17

Underline the key parts of the following sentences and combine those ideas into one effective sentence.

1. It is good to take <u>Vitamin C every day</u>. It will <u>prevent colds</u>. Many people believe that.

   Taking Vitamin C everyday will prevent colds.

2. Today more <u>women</u> are participating in <u>weight-training programs</u>. It helps them to <u>keep</u> their body muscles toned. It helps them stay in <u>good physical condition</u>.

   Weight-training programs keep the body in good physical condition, by keeping the muscles toned.

3. <u>James Clavell</u> is a very successful <u>writer</u>. He has written many interesting <u>novels</u>. These novels are about the history of Japan.

✓ *James Clavell writes novels about the history of Japan*

4. Our friends have a new burglar <u>alarm</u>. This alarm is <u>very sensitive</u>. A leaf falling off a plant will set it off.

Our friends New buglar alarm is very sensitive.

5. It is a good idea to <u>preview</u> your <u>exams before</u> you <u>write</u> them. This might <u>help</u> you to <u>plan</u> your time wisely. This might <u>result in</u> your achieving a better grade.

✓ *Previewing your exam before you write it helps plan your time & get a better grade.*

Check your answers with those suggested in the Answer section at the end of the book.

Sometimes, making structural changes can alter the emphasis, or main idea, of a passage. You should be aware of this and choose the version that best expresses what you want to say. For example, there are two ways of correcting the following badly written passage:

> My favourite season is winter. The snow is great for sports. Skiing, snowmobiling, and skating are my favourite sports.

Suggested Corrections:

> My favourite season is winter. At this time of year, the snow is great for skiing, snowmobiling, and skating.
>
> *or*
>
> Winter, my favourite time of year, is a great time for skiing, snowmobiling, and skating.

The main topic in the first suggested correction is "my favourite season," and the sentence that follows presents one reason for saying so; other reasons could follow. However, in the second corrected version, the theme of the passage is "winter is a great time for skiing, snowmobiling, and skating." What follows should be a discussion of each of these three points. Notice that both versions contain the same information; it is the style in which the information is presented that makes the difference in emphasis.

● EXERCISE 4.18

Combine the following sentences by using the techniques discussed in this unit. Your objective should be to produce a clearly focused passage.

1. The weather at this time of year gives me a cozy feeling. I like to curl up in front of the fireplace on a cold winter day. I like to read a good book. This helps me forget the freezing world outside.

✓ *The weather at this time of year gives me a cozy feeling. To help forget the freezing world outside I like to curl up in front of the fire place and read a good book.*

2. His marks have been steadily improving since last September. I think he's going to pass his year. That will be a surprise to everyone!

✓ *Since last September his marks have been steadily improving. I think he's going to surprise everyone and pass his year.*

3. I was biking to the park. My jeans got caught in my bicycle chain. I fell and badly scraped my arm.

While I was biking to the park my jeans got caught in the chain. As a result I fell and scraped my arm.

4. There are many advantages to having a hobby. It teaches you to relax. You have something to do with your leisure hours. It always gives you a sense of satisfaction to see a project completed or to collect another unique item.

   ✓ *Having a hobby teaches you to relax and you always have something to do with your leisure time. You will always get a sense of satisfaction when you see a project completed*

5. Some drivers like to compete on the highway. They use stoplights for racing signals. They break speed limits. They swerve in front of other drivers. They are public menaces. They are often the cause of many accidents. They should receive stiff penalties for these kinds of infractions.

   ✓ *Some drivers like to compete on the highway. For example they use stoplights for racing signal break speed limits and swerve in front of other drivers. These public menaces cause many accidents and should receive stiff penalties for their infractions.*

Check your answers with those suggested in the Answer section at the end of the book.

● EXERCISE 4.19—REVIEW

Each of the following paragraphs contains sentence structure errors discussed in this unit. Revise and rewrite the paragraph. Eliminate any short, choppy, repetitive sentence pattern. Add good transitional words and sentence variety that will help to improve the quality of the message. Eliminate any wordy expressions.

1. Combine the following article into five or six sentences. Use underlining techniques to identify the most important factors.

   At this point in time, people who live in Canada seem to be unhappy. They are unhappy about the high cost of living. They are unhappy with wage restraints. The situation is grim according to many people. But shopping plazas are crowded. Lots of people are buying luxury items. Microwave ovens, video games, and video players are expensive. People should stop complaining. They should learn to live within their means. They should learn that true happiness stems from who you are, not from what you have.

2. Combine the following article into six or seven sentences. Use underlining techniques to identify the most important factors.

In my opinion I think that health insurance rates should be increased for people who indulge in self-destructive habits. People who drink alcohol excessively develop many serious health problems. It has been proven that most accidents are caused by drinking drivers. Smoking is another self-destructive habit. Excessive smoking also causes illnesses. Lung cancer and emphysema are two serious health problems caused by smoking. People with these habits require extra medical care. One solution is that they should be the ones who pay higher insurance rates. They might even realize the dangers. They might quit their destructive habits. This solution might solve our present hospital bed shortage. It might also help more people live longer and healthier lives.

3. a) With a coloured pen or pencil, proofread three of your freewriting exercises and identify errors in spelling and sentence structure.

   b) Choose one of these three freewriting exercises to edit. Using sentence combining and refining techniques, rewrite and produce an improved version of your original.

Check your answers to questions 1 and 2 with those suggested in the Answer section at the end of the book.

THE NEXT STEP

If you feel confident about this section, proceed to "Summary and Précis Writing" on the following page.

Summary and Précis Writing

There is **no** Pretest for this section. In the following lessons, you will learn how to summarize the main points of a written passage. To do this task effectively, you must use all the skills previously explained in this unit.

On many occasions your main task for essays or reports will be to collect data on a particular topic. One of the skills you will need for this type of assignment is the ability to summarize, or précis, a long informative article without losing the author's original intent, content, or tone. A summary is a condensed version of an excerpt; it is always written in your own words (paraphrased) and is approximately one-half to two-thirds the length of the original script. A précis is a very condensed summary of a published work that is approximately one-third the length of the original article. Both involve a combination of the reading skills we have already discussed and the sentence-combining skills you have just completed. Therefore, for this exercise, use underlining and marginal notes to help you recognize and understand the author's main points; then, clearly and effectively, write this message in your own words using the guidelines that follow. Please note that all passages cannot be reduced as drastically or as rigidly as the ones presented in this section; knowledge gained from previous units should help you determine the relevant ideas in any written passage.

Remember, too, that any condensed or quoted article from a published source must be credited to the original author. Footnotes, endnotes, or in-text citations must identify your source of information. Check the correct procedure for references with either your dictionary (check the information in the back) or an English handbook.

I. The ABC's of Summary and Précis Writing

A. Use Your Reading Skills

1. Preview the article.

2. Define any unknown words (top or bottom margin).

3. Read thoroughly and underline the most important words in the author's main ideas and supporting major details.

4. Make any necessary marginal notes that identify content or summarize or explain an implied idea.

B. WRITE YOUR SUMMARY

From your underlining and marginal notes, identify the topic and then write a main-idea sentence that expresses the all-encompassing idea of the passage. You may find this same idea at both the beginning and end of the passage; however, try to use your own wording to capture the theme. Link together the supporting ideas and try to simplify difficult or wordy portions. Double space your rough draft so that you can easily make any necessary revisions on this same copy. With minor revisions and polishing, this step could be considered a summary. Your goal is to create a paraphrased version that is approximately one-half to two-thirds the length of the original without changing the tone or the intent of the author.

Follow the DO's and DON'T's listed below.

DO ...

1. follow the same paragraphing as the original unless the condensed version is very brief.

2. try to link ideas together so that your written passage is a smooth version of the original.

3. use effective transitional expressions, such as *however, therefore, as a result, according to,* etc., that help to relate ideas. Also, use techniques discussed in sentence-combining skills.

4. make sure you retain the same tone and emphasis as the author.

5. proofread your summary or précis. Check to see that the message will be just as clear to a reader, who has not seen the original, as it is to you. Check for errors in spelling and sentence structure.

6. count the number of words in your first draft.
   a) All words should be included—even small ones such as *a, an, the, in, to,* etc.
   b) Contractions count as two words, e.g., *won't, I'll, isn't,* etc.
   c) Hyphenated terms—*air-conditioned, well-travelled,* etc.—count as two words.
   d) Numbers or abbreviated terms are counted for each number or letter, e.g., 29 would count as two words.

7. revise your summary until you are satisfied that your own version has captured the author's ideas without plagiarism.

DON'T ...

1. write one-sentence paragraphs. Attach the single sentence to a related paragraph.

2. include your own opinions.

3. take direct quotations from the article. Present the details of the information in your own words. Using more than three consecutive words from the source without the use of quotation marks is plagiarism.

4. omit relevant details.

5. write in short, choppy sentences or use unnecessary words. Be alert to sentence fragments or run-on sentence errors. Use your thesaurus and dictionary to ensure effective and correct word usage.

C. Condense Your Summary

To produce a précis, revise your summary to approximately one-third the length of the original. A précis consists of the central theme and a very condensed version of the supporting facts.

1. Combine sentences where and when possible.
2. Eliminate unnecessary details.
3. Try to eliminate wordy expressions.
4. Use your thesaurus to replace words or word groups more effectively.
5. Revise until your final copy meets the required length of one-third of the original.

The following example demonstrates how to apply the ABC's of précis writing. Study the method and suggested answers given for each step. Although counting words at the end of the first stage is optional, it does provide a guide to the length of your final revision.

A. Use Your Reading Skills

1. Define unknown words.

2. Underline the main message.

   Subordinate—place in lower rank
   Wholesome and constructive thinking in the family will penetrate all society. The person who learns within the family to accommodate others, to subordinate, when necessary, personal interest to the interest of the group, and to tolerate in others fads and habits he would condemn in himself: that person has learned many of the lessons necessary to becoming a good worker, a good leader and a good citizen.[5]

   (67 words)

B. Write Your Summary

1. Identify the topic.

2. Use your own words to write a main-idea statement that expresses the central theme of the passage. Remember you may find this idea expressed at either the beginning or end of the passage; in some cases, it will be in both places.

3. Identify and link together the details that support this theme.

4. Simplify difficult or wordy passages. Use your thesaurus.

5. Combine sentences by using the refining techniques presented in the grammar section.

   Developing good thinking skills *taught* within the family unit can positively affect all facets of society. Family members who *learn to* practise being considerate, *cooperate* cooperative, selfless, and tolerant of others' *cope with* different man- nerisms or customs *are* have learned *well-prepared* the essentials of what it takes *to accept* to be a responsible member of the *roles in life* workforce and of society as a whole.

   (This is a summary of the paragraph.)   (54 words)

C. Condense Your Summary (23 to 28 words)

1. Keep or condense your main-idea statement.

2. Use sentence-combining skills.

3. Eliminate unnecessary details or combine and condense related ones.

4. If necessary, use your thesaurus for more explicit expressions.

5. Follow the do's and don't's listed earlier.

> Good thinking skills taught within a family can affect all society. Members who learn to cooperate and cope with others are well-prepared to accept responsible roles in life.

(29 words)

● EXERCISE 4.20

Read and underline the important details in each of the following paragraphs. Write first drafts and polish them to form summaries; then condense each version to approximately one-third the original.

1. **A. Use your reading skills.**
   - Define unknown words.
   - Underline the main message.

> If the family were to be swept away, the world would become a place of regimentation, chaos and desolation. Why? Because the family fulfils at least three vital functions: it provides sustenance and trains its members in the art of surviving; it provides the earliest group association, teaching the art of social living; and it is the primary place where the values and knowledge of culture are passed from generation to generation.[6]

(72 words)

B. Write your summary.
   - Identify the topic.
   - Use your own words to write a main-idea statement that expresses the central theme of the passage.
   - Identify and link together the details that support this theme.
   - Simplify difficult or wordy passages. Use your thesaurus.
   - Combine sentences by using the refining techniques presented in the grammar section.

C. Condense your summary (24 to 28 words). Because this version is approximately one-third the original, it is a précis.
   - Keep or condense your main-idea statement.
   - Use sentence-combining skills.
   - Eliminate unnecessary details or combine and condense related ones.
   - If necessary, use your thesaurus for more explicit expressions.
   - Follow the do's and don't's of summarizing listed earlier.

2. A. **Use your reading skills.**
    - Define unknown words.
    - Underline the main message.

In a democratic egalitarian society, dignity attaches itself not so much to social status as to conduct. Given the basic knowledge of manners taught in most homes and schools, a person may become as much of a gentleman or lady as he or she chooses to be. It is simple in theory but difficult in practice, because being a real gentleman or lady means running a continuous check on one's words and actions to ensure that they do not needlessly offend or disconcert anyone.[7]

(84 words)

B. **Write your summary.**
    - Identify the topic.
    - Use your own words to write a main-idea statement that expresses the central theme of the passage.
    - Identify and link together the details that support this theme.
    - Simplify difficult or wordy passages. Use your thesaurus.
    - Combine sentences by using the refining techniques presented in the grammar section.

C. **Condense your summary.** (28 to 32 words)
    - Keep or condense your main-idea statement.
    - Use sentence-combining skills.
    - Eliminate unnecessary details or combine and condense related ones.
    - If necessary, use your thesaurus for more explicit expressions.
    - Follow the do's and don't's listed earlier.

3. A. **Use your reading skills.**
   - Define unknown words.
   - Underline the main message.

Bosses who make a serious effort to understand their subordinates become better motivated themselves, because they come closer to fulfilling their own ego and self-expression needs in the process. Motivation must, in fact, work two ways, because superiors must be open to their subordinates' influence if they expect the subordinates to be open to theirs. The cross-motivation that comes from healthy superior-subordinate relationships gives rise to an ideal working climate, not only for the people directly concerned, but for the organization as a whole.[8]

(87 words)

   B. **Write your summary.**
   - Identify the topic.
   - If possible, use your own words to write a main-idea statement that expresses the central theme of the passage. Remember you may find this idea expressed at either the beginning or end of the passage; in some cases, it will be in both places.
   - Identify and link together the details that support this theme.
   - Simplify difficult or wordy passages. Use your thesaurus.
   - Combine sentences by using the refining techniques presented in the grammar section.

   C. **Revise and write the final copy.** (30 to 35 words)
   - Keep or condense your main-idea statement.
   - Use sentence-combining skills.
   - Eliminate unnecessary details or combine and condense related ones.
   - If necessary, use your thesaurus for more explicit expressions.
   - Follow the do's and don't's listed earlier.

4. A. **Use your reading skills.**
   - Define unknown words.
   - Underline the main message.

"I don't give a damn about what other people think of me," a well-known rock star was recently quoted as saying. She might as well have said that she doesn't give a damn about other people, period; it amounts to the same thing. A certain degree of submersion of one's own will in deference to others is implicit in any effort to be kind and civil. If you insist on doing just what you want, you are liable to trespass on other people's sensibilities, if not their rights.[9]

(91 words)

B. **Write your summary.**
   - Identify the topic.
   - Use your own words to write a main-idea statement that expresses the central theme of the passage.
   - Do not use direct quotations. Present the information (if it is relevant) in your own words.
   - Identify and link together the details that support this theme.
   - Simplify difficult or wordy passages. Use your thesaurus.
   - Combine sentences by using the refining techniques presented in the grammar section.

C. **Condense your summary.** (30 to 35 words)
   - Keep or condense your main-idea statement.
   - Use sentence-combining skills.
   - Eliminate unnecessary details or combine and condense related ones.
   - If necessary, use your thesaurus for more explicit expressions.
   - Follow the do's and don't's listed earlier.

5. A. **Use your reading skills.**
   - Define unknown words.
   - Underline the main message.

The intellectual discipline required to make thoughts come through intelligibly on paper pays off in clarifying your thoughts in general. When you start writing about a subject, you will often find that your knowledge of it and your thinking about it leave something to be desired. The question that should be foremost in the writer's mind, "What am I really trying to say?" will raise the related questions, "What do I really know about this? What do I really think about it?" A careful writer has to be a careful thinker—and in the long run careful thinking saves time and trouble for the writer, the reader, and everybody else concerned.[10]

(111 words)

B. **Write your summary.**
   - Identify the topic.
   - Use your own words to write a main-idea statement that expresses the central theme of the passage.
   - Do not use direct quotations. Present the information (if it is relevant) in your own words.
   - Identify and link together the details that support this theme.
   - Simplify difficult or wordy passages. Use your thesaurus.
   - Combine sentences by using the refining techniques presented in the grammar section.

C. **Condense your summary.** (36 to 41 words)
   - Keep or condense your main-idea statement.
   - Use sentence-combining skills.
   - Eliminate unnecessary details or combine and condense related ones.
   - If necessary, use your thesaurus for more explicit expressions.
   - Follow the do's and don't's listed earlier.

II. SUMMARY AND PRÉCIS OF A LONGER WORK

Some students are overwhelmed when faced with the task of reducing a lengthy passage. The solution is to summarize each paragraph individually. In some ways, writing a précis of a longer work is easier, as some paragraphs can be summarized to a greater degree than others without altering the meaning. Therefore, reduce each section and then revise overall until you have the desired length. Study the following example.

A. Use your reading skills.

- Preview.
- Define unknown words.
- Highlight or underline.
- Make necessary marginal notes.

B. Write your summary.

- Write the main idea and supporting details.
- Simplify wordy or difficult passages (with your thesaurus).
- Combine sentences.

For all their vulnerability, Canadians still tend to view the possibility of disaster with benign fatalism. While warning that disaster can strike anywhere and anytime, EPC officials note that few Canadian families have even taken the elementary precaution of preparing a portable survival pack containing clothing, blankets, first-aid supplies, and food and water for seven to 14 days. Most have never given a thought to seeing that there are live batteries for their radios, over which information and instructions in case of a mass emergency would be broadcast. Not many have ever heard of the vital rule of always keeping the tanks of their cars half-full in case they are called upon to evacuate.

(119 words)

Canadians still do not treat the possibility of disaster seriously. Although there have been warnings that disasters can occur anywhere and anytime, few Canadians have bothered to prepare a basic 14-day survival kit that would include the necessities of food, clothing, water, and first-aid materials. Most have not considered having extra batteries for portable radios so they could receive information and instructions, nor have they practised always keeping a half tank of gas in their cars in case of an emergency evacuation.

(84 words)

Canadians have a sanguine tendency to leave emergency action to the public authorities. A report of a crippling week-long blizzard in the Niagara region in 1977 underscores the folly of this approach. Essential equipment proved to be less reliable than expected. The telephone system was swamped, one snow plough got lost in a white-out, and another got so badly stuck that it could not be dug out for six days. The police radio system was useless, not because the radio did not work, but because the patrol cars could not move.

(93 words)

Canadians tend to rely on public authorities for an emergency plan in any type of disaster. However, total reliance on others is not wise. In 1977, during a week-long blizzard in Eastern Ontario, essential snow removal equipment, as well as telephone and police services, could not function effectively because of heavy snow and white-out conditions.

(58 words)

benign—kindly, favourable
sanguine—cheerful and hopeful

In other words, people in that particular emergency were left very much to their own devices. Despite the best efforts of EPC and provincial and municipal agencies, the same could happen to anyone in any emergency that might occur. It is only prudent to plan to fend for yourself in any accident or disaster. From the most minor mishap to the most devastating disaster, coping with danger is up to you.[11]

(73 words)

Therefore, people in that emergency were left to solve their own problems. Because major or minor types of disasters can happen any time, it is wise for all to have an emergency plan of action. No matter what type of catastrophe, people are responsible for their own safety and well-being.

(51 words)

Total: 192 words

C. **Condense your summary.**

- Use sentence-combining skills.

- Eliminate unnecessary details.

- Use your thesaurus for explicit expressions.

- Follow the do's and don't's listed earlier.

First Draft (Recopied): A Summary

likelihood   *predicted*
Canadians still do not view the possibility of disaster seriously. Although there have been warnings
catastrophes
that disasters can occur anywhere and anytime, few Canadians have bothered to prepare a basic
fourteen (one word not two)
14-day survival kit that would include the necessities of food, clothing, water, and first-aid materi-
or
als. Most have not considered having extra batteries for portable radios so they could receive infor-

mation and instructions; nor have they practised always keeping a half tank of gas in their cars in

case of an emergency evacuation.

(84 words)

experts
Canadians tend to rely on public authorities for an emergency plan in any type of disaster.
unwise
However, total reliance on others is not wise. In 1977, during a week-long blizzard in Eastern
maintenance   *crippled*
Ontario, essential snow removal equipment, as well as telephone and police services, could not

function effectively because of heavy snow and white-out conditions.

(58 words)

fend for themselves   *various*
Therefore, people in that emergency were left to solve their own problems. Because major or minor

types of disasters can happen any time, it is wise for all to have an emergency plan of action. No
should take responsibility
matter what the catastrophe, people are responsible for their own safety and well-being.

(50 words)

Total: 191 words

Now compare the original version with the précis that follows.

Original (285 words)

For all their vulnerability, Canadians still tend to view the possibility of disaster with benign fatalism. While warning that disaster can strike anywhere and anytime, EPC officials note that few Canadian families have even taken the elementary precaution of preparing a portable survival pack containing clothing, blankets, first-aid supplies, and food and water for seven to 14 days. Most have never given a thought to seeing that there are live batteries for their radios, over which information and instructions in case of a mass emergency would be broadcast. Not many have ever heard of the vital rule of always keeping the tanks of their cars half-full in case they are called upon to evacuate.

Canadians have a sanguine tendency to leave emergency action to the public authorities. A report on a crippling week-long blizzard in the Niagara region in 1977 underscores the folly of this approach. Essential equipment proved to be less reliable than expected. The telephone system was swamped, one snow plough got lost in a white-out, and another got so badly stuck that it could not be dug out for six days. The police radio system was useless, not because the radio did not work, but because the patrol cars could not move.

In other words, people in that particular emergency were left very much to their own devices. Despite the best efforts of EPC and provincial and municipal agencies, the same could happen to anyone in any emergency that might occur. It is only prudent to plan to fend for yourself in any accident or disaster. From the most minor mishap to the most devastating disaster, coping with danger is up to you.

Précis (90 words)

Canadians do not treat the likelihood of disaster seriously. Although catastrophes have long been predicted, few have prepared the basic fourteen-day survival kit or practised the elementary precautions of having an extra supply of radio batteries and gas for emergency evacuations.

(43 words)

Canadians' total reliance on experts for emergency planning is unwise. In 1977, a week-long blizzard in Ontario crippled essential maintenance, telephone, and police services.

(25 words)

Therefore, those people had to fend for themselves. Because disasters can happen any time, people should take responsibility and have emergency plans.

(22 words)

● EXERCISE 4.21

Write a précis of each of the following articles.

A. Use reading skills—underlining and marginal notes—to identify the main message.

B. Write your summary (double spaced); follow the do's and don't's suggested earlier.

C. Condense your summary; use sentence-combining skills and your thesaurus.

1. A. Read and underline.

In some cities the world is quite literally represented. Canadians are particularly favoured in this respect. Thanks to immigration and the Canadian tradition of encouraging ethnic diversity, few cities in the world are as cosmopolitan as our three largest ones. Smaller places such as Winnipeg and Hamilton are not far behind.

(51 words)

Within three blocks of a single street in Montreal, for instance, you will find Russian, Creole, Japanese, Spanish, Italian, Chinese, French, Arab, and West Indian restaurants, plus American-style bars and a British-style pub or two. Nor is this street unique for its variety in the cosmopolitan heart of Montreal. Whole districts of our cities have assumed the character of the country of origin of most of their residents. Hence there are parts of Toronto where you would swear you were in Lisbon or Athens, and streets in Vancouver that might be in Hong Kong.

(96 words)

B. Write your summary.

Ethnic diversity is only one of the reasons why Canadians should explore their own cities before looking farther afield. If there is variety within Canadian cities, there is also great variety among them. A person from, say, Calgary will find a world of difference from what he or she is used to at home in the salty old seaport and garrison atmosphere of Halifax. And vice versa: for someone from Halifax to visit Calgary is to sample an entirely unfamiliar air of cowboys and Indians, oil and cattle—the air of both the old and the new West.[12]

(97 words)

Total: 244 words

C. **Condense your summary.** (81 to 88 words)

2. A. Read and underline.

B. Write your summary.

Since most us live in crowds, we are faced with the problem of having to establish our distinctive identities within an existing social framework. People who insist on doing precisely what they want with no self-discipline and no regard to the impact of their actions on those around them are likely to end up in jail, where individualism is not encouraged at all. In his immortal work, *On Liberty*, John Stuart Mill struck the balance between the individual and society quite neatly. "The liberty of the individual must be thus far limited; that he must not make a nuisance of himself to other people," he wrote.

(108 words)

Individualism, then, is not anti-social; rather the opposite. A person's identity is not his or hers alone; it is only complete when it is rounded out by loved ones and friends. Individualism is strength, so a true individualist is strong enough to tolerate the habits and opinions of people who differ from him or her. A true individualist respects the individuality of everyone else.

(65 words)

"This is my way; what is your way? The way doesn't exist," wrote the philosopher Friedrich Nietzsche. In this perplexing world, finding one's own way and then sticking to it is something that comes naturally only to a lucky few. Most of us lose our way from time to time, straying down the wrong streets and going up blind alleys. It is all very exhausting. It would be much less trouble to take directions from those who assure us they know the way. But wait! "Most of the greatest evils that man has inflicted upon man have come through people feeling quite certain about something which, in fact, was false," Bertrand Russell tells us. Quite certainly, what he says is true.[13]

(122 words)

Total: 295 words

C. **Condense your summary.** (97 to 106 words)

Check your answers with those suggested in the Answer section at the end of the book.

III. SUMMARIZING AND RESPONDING TO A NEWSPAPER ARTICLE

Not every newspaper presents all the news factually. Sometimes the writers and editors will try to influence readers' opinions by "slanting" a news story. When you read a newspaper, you must determine if a news story has been reported accurately with data and opinions based on verifiable facts or whether the information has been slanted by facts and opinions based on prejudices.

Newspapers sometimes use headlines to mould readers' opinions. Be alert for "slanting" words in headlines and in the story itself. Do descriptions present the writer's bias (for example, watch for terms like *hard-working team, the exciting production, another attempt/failure/success, dynamic speech*, etc.)? These simple examples illustrate how easy it is to persuade readers to believe preconceived opinions about a subject. Judge headlines as critically as you judge news stories. Avoid reading only the headlines in glancing through the paper; read every lead as well. Remember that, because a headline is only a title, it must express ideas simply and briefly.

To be an intelligent reader of the newspaper, you need to grasp the overall information given in a story and evaluate its accuracy. If you can assess what was actually said by knowing the difference between facts and the writer's opinions, then you can arrive at your own conclusions about the article and form your own sound opinions.

Use the following method to read and assess newspaper articles:

1. First, identify the essence of what the writer has said.

   a) Read the title and the lead paragraph; quickly identify the source, and look for answers to where, when, who, what, and why questions.

   b) Highlight the main message by identifying the overall theme and the supporting information.

   c) Look at the major issues identified and the supporting evidence or prospective solutions.

   When you record the information, do so accurately. Do not change the tone or theme of the writer and make sure that you attribute the information to the writer.

2. Once you clearly understand the main message, consider the following questions:

   a) What are the issues and conclusions?

   b) What reasons has the writer given?

   c) Has the writer tried to influence your thinking by using emotional language or opinions?

   d) What evidence has the writer provided?

      i) Is it complete and/or based on fact?

      ii) If statistics are provided, are they accurate and complete?

      iii) Are there any flaws or errors in the information?

      iv) Did the writer refer to testimonies from others? From whom? Do you consider the source or sources reliable? Why or why not?

      v) Are there any factors that the writer omitted? Are all sides of the controversy/issue given or is this story one-sided? It is just as important to consider what the writer did *not* say.

3. Now, consider if you agree or disagree. If you are presenting your own viewpoint as well as a summary, put your comments in a separate paragraph after the summary. Make sure you identify the source of information for the summary. Clearly specify that your comments are your own opinions and provide evidence for your feelings.

● EXERCISE 4.22

For each of the following articles, write an editorial or a letter to the editor. To do this, first write a summary of the article. Remember to credit the source of information and state where and, if possible, when the article was published.

Using the questions given in the method for reading and assessing newspapers (number 2, page 159), assess each article's content. Do you agree or disagree with the story? Why? Write your own opinions in a second paragraph.

To indicate your opinion, use such words as *seem, might, could, possibly, believe, claim, think, feel, according to, in _____'s opinion*, etc. Provide facts to support your point of view.

By the paragraphing and wording of your editorial or letter, make sure the reader will clearly understand the difference between the summarized facts of the news story as it was reported and your opinions about the topic.

1.

SMART CARDS A TOUGH SELL IN U.S., PROPONENTS CONCEDE

By Patricia Lamiell

ASSOCIATED PRESS

New York — As they eulogized an electronic-cash card trial, bankers and technology experts were asking fundamental questions: Why have the little cards embedded with silicon chips—known as smart cards—not taken off in the United States, and how can they be made more attractive?

The trial's sponsors, Citibank, Chase Manhattan Corp., Visa USA and MasterCard USA, were not calling the enterprise a complete failure. It produced "a lot of good learning," Michael Tempora, vice president for U.S. chip-card products at MasterCard, said last week

The main goal of the pilot was to create a reader that could accept different types of cards, one from Citibank that used Visa technology, and another from Chase that used technology from MasterCard and its smart-card partner, Mondex. On that admittedly modest goal, the sponsors succeeded.

But the card readers broke frequently. And merchants weren't happy about allocat-ing precious counter space to yet another device, even if it was free. So merchants dropped out of the program. Of the 600 merchants who accepted the machines a year ago, fewer than 400 remained at the end of last month. And that number had dwindled to close to 200 by the time the pilot was shut down last week, Citibank spokesman Mark Rodgers said.

That was an easy decision for merchants to make, because smart cards weren't catching on with their customers, either. About $1 million worth of business was transacted with the cards over a year's time, a fractional percentage of the total commerce for the stores in the 36-block test area.

"People have plenty of payment choices today in the United States," said David Weisman, a technology analyst with Forrester Research Inc. in Cambridge, Mass. "We have a very good telecommunications structure that allows for credit and debit cards to work in most situations. There are a lot of things that are going to keep smart cards from catching hold here."

Bankers and smart-card experts said several things need to fall into place before smart cards take off here, as they have in Europe and parts of Asia and Latin America.

Consumers need a financial incentive to use them, such as those provided by loyalty or rewards programs, or even discounts. "Compensation is essential," said Jerome Svigals, an electronic banking consultant in Redwood City, Calif.

The cards have to do more than just serve as an electronic purse. The few successful trials in the United States have been in controlled settings like college and corporate campuses and military bases, where people have to use them not only to pay for things but to gain access to buildings and computer files, get food at the cafeteria, or check books out of the library, the experts said.

"You have to have a critical mass of people, a well-defined set of applications, and a much more controllable environment" than was available in the Manhattan trial, said Paul Beverley, vice president of marketing for smart cards at Schlumberger USA which made about 35 percent of the cards that were used in that trial.

The growth of electronic commerce should provide a big boost to smart cards, analysts said. "Smart cards are terrific enablers for secure transactions over the Internet," said Ronald Braco, senior vice president at Chase.[14]

Source: **Who:**

Where: **What:**

When: **Why:**

SUPPORTING DETAILS

SUMMARY

YOUR OPINIONS

2.

DEVELOPING NATIONS HOSTILE TO GREENHOUSE GAS PROPOSAL

BUENOS AIRES (AP) — A U.S. backed proposal for the developing world to assert a bigger role in combating global warming has won a cool reception at the U.N. climate summit.

Developing nations led by China blocked efforts Monday to add discussion of voluntary quotas for poorer nations to the agenda of the conference, the biggest gathering since a landmark global warming treaty in Kyoto, Japan.

The issue of poorer nation participation in arresting global warming is one of the touchiest under the 1997 treaty.

Spurred on by China and other foes of voluntary commitments, the 163 summit nations decided by consensus Monday to block the issue from even reaching the agenda as they kicked off their two-week conference.

"To say the least, we are disappointed that it appears that countries will not have an opportunity to explore this matter in any detail," U.S. negotiator Melinda Kimble told delegates.

But she later told a news conference she was heartened when Argentina sought to advance the issue at all.

"What we are beginning to see, with the issue of developing nations, is a debate on the next steps," said Kimble, a U.S. acting assistant secretary of state. "This is very much a step forward."

Before their work concludes Nov. 13, the 163 assembled nations are to debate several contentious issues meant to put Kyoto's words into deeds.

History was made last December in Kyoto, when governments set 2012 as the deadline for cutting back on greenhouse gases in the United States, Japan, the 15-nation European Union and 21 other industrial nations.

Although the cuts currently apply only to those 38 nations, greenhouse emissions in India and China are expected by 2015 to exceed those of the biggest polluter, the United States.

Many scientists believe the Earth is gradually warming because of five gases, chiefly carbon dioxide from power plant and automobile consumption. Critics say dire warming scenarios remain unproven and do not warrant potentially costly shifts away from fossil fuels.

After industrial nations agreed in Kyoto to slash greenhouse gas emissions, U.S. officials arrived here with hopes the conference would produce further agreements on implementation that would make the pact easier to sell to a critical U.S. Congress.

The United States is not among the 38 signatories of the accord so far, and a Republican-led U.S. Senate remains skeptical, absent greater efforts by the developing world. Yet, many developing countries argue their economies cannot assume costly greenhouse gas reductions that quotas would require. They point out industrialized nations in the North loaded the atmosphere with carbon dioxide to begin with.[15]

Source: Who:

Where: What:

When: Why:

SUPPORTING DETAILS

SUMMARY

YOUR OPINIONS

3. Repeat the process with current newspaper articles.

Check your answers for the summary portions of questions 1 and 2 with those in the Answer section at the end of the book. Opinions, of course, will vary.

COLLABORATIVE EXERCISE 4.23

In groups of six to eight, choose a story that is of interest to the group. Choose one from your local newspaper, the Internet, or the one that is given below. Write individual summaries of the major points of the story. Remember to credit the source of information and state where and when the article was published.

1. A. Using the questions given in the method for reading and assessing newspapers (number 2, page 159), assess the article's content. Do you agree or disagree with the actions or viewpoints taken in the story? Work with two or more group members with similar opinions or divide your group and take opposing views.

   B. Now gather as many reasons as you can to support your opinions. (You can use other sources, as well, if you require more information.)

   C. Next, listen to and debate with the group members with opposite opinions. Make notes of their points of view. Can you convince others to change their minds with your points or are you convinced by them to change your position?

GROUP RE-CREATES ATOMIC BOMB HORROR OF HIROSHIMA

Yomiuri Shimbum

The first full panoramic picture of Hiroshima after the nuclear bomb was dropped on the city during World War II can now be viewed on the Internet.

Members of a civic group, Heiwa Hakubutsukan o Tsukuru Kai (preparatory committee for establishing a peace museum), led by Director Susumu Hani, created the image by using a computer to edit photographs of Hiroshima that were taken about two months after the atomic bomb devastated the city.

Hiroshima Peace Memorial Museum officials were pleased with the effects of the picture, saying it offers a previously unseen view of the city after the attack.

The original photographs were taken in October 1945 by Shigeo Hayashi of Tokyo, who is now 80 years old and a member of the group. He took the photographs while serving on a team researching the damage caused by the atomic bombs in Hiroshima and Nagasaki.

He took 12 photographs from the roof of the Hiroshima Chamber of Commerce and Industry building about 320 meters north of the center of the blast, and 22 from the Chugoku Shimbum building about 900 meters east of it.

Last July, the group drew up plans to create a panoramic image that would convey the full horror of the atomic bombing, and the task was completed in September.

By scrolling through the group's Web site on the Internet, it is possible to see images of the Atomic Bomb dome, primary school buildings, and a collapsed bridge. Close-up shots are also posted.

"It's an epoch-making creation because it allows viewers to see what the city was like from the viewpoint of the photographer," said Tsutomu Iwakura, executive director of the group. "We would like to appeal to as many people as possible to realize the importance of peace."

To access pictures and more information about this story on the following Web site:[16]

Go to → hhtp://yahoo.com/
then type in → Hiroshima Peace Museum

D. Put this information in writing. In the first paragraph, write a summary of the facts as they were presented in the news article. In the second paragraph, begin with the words, "Some people believe ..." and present some of the stronger opposition points to your group's opinion. In the third paragraph, begin with the words, "However, more convincing evidence indicates ..." and present the viewpoints of your group.

E. Now, read your editorials aloud to hear how news can be slanted according to opinions.

SUMMARY

OPPOSING OPINIONS

YOUR OPINIONS AND YOUR GROUP'S OPINIONS

2. Repeat the process with current newspaper articles. **Check your answers for the summary portions of questions 1 and 2 with those in the Answer section at the end of the book. Opinions will vary.**

IV. WRITING AN ABSTRACT

An abstract is a very concise summary of a report or research paper. Even if the paper is very long, the abstract is usually one paragraph in length and contains approximately 75 to 100 words for a study paper or review. (It may be slightly longer for a thoroughly researched study.) The purpose of an abstract is to encourage others to read or listen to your findings. Research papers in journals usually begin with an abstract. Conference brochures commonly contain a form of abstract from each of the presenters so that conference members can choose the presentations they are most interested in. Often an instructor will ask students to write an abstract of given information to determine how well they understand the content.

An abstract should contain the following information:

1. The purpose of the report, research, or study paper
2. A thesis or hypothesis statement
3. A brief explanation of the methods used to gather information (if primary research was involved, such as surveys, experiments, observations, etc.)
4. The highlights of the major findings
5. The results or conclusions of the study

Your abstract should follow the same order of information as the study paper. To write an abstract, write brief answers to the following questions:

1. What is the paper about?

2. What main question or problem does the paper focus on?

3. If primary research was used, how would you describe the test groups or methods employed?

4. What are the main themes from each section?

5. What was the result or what did you conclude from the study or information?

Now, in a single paragraph, write your answers to these questions. Follow the rules for writing and revising a summary or précis given earlier until you have met the length requirement.

● EXERCISE 4.24

Write an abstract for the article entitled "On Reading Profitably" contained in the Post-Test for Unit Three. Since this is your first attempt at writing an abstract, you may wish to follow the underlined version of the article in the answer key.

Compare your abstract with the one suggested in the Answer section at the end of the book.

THE NEXT STEP

If you feel confident about this unit, write the Unit Four Post-Test.

▶ POST-TEST FOR UNIT FOUR

If you feel confident about the skills presented in this unit, complete the Post-Test that follows. **Do not attempt this test if you have not completed the required work.**

Once you have completed the whole test, check your answers with the suggested ones at the end of this unit. A marking scheme has been provided to give you a realistic idea of your ability in this area. Your goal should be to have no more than two minor errors in the spelling and thesaurus categories and no more than two major errors in sentence structure and composition skills.

I. Circle the spelling errors in the following lists and write your corrections beside the misspelled word. Refer to your dictionary if you are in doubt about any spelling.

separate	tragedy	success
secratary	questionnaire	references
misspell	opinon	realistically
liaison	introduce	existence
exercise	familiar	candidate
association	aquire	accomodate
adjourn	analyzed	accidentally
development	congradulations	bussiness
differant	grammer	Febuary
knowledge	fourty	relevant

(Deduct one mark for each error.)

TOTAL MARKS FOR SPELLING _____ /5

II. Use a thesaurus to replace the italicized words in each of the following sentences. (Include section numbers if you are using the original version of the thesaurus.)

1. Please *glance at* this report by Friday and send your written opinions about the proposal to Ms. Chung.

A suitable replacement for *glance at* is _____

(found in section _____)

2. What have you *seen* from all of the examples that have been presented?

A suitable replacement for *seen* is _____

(found in section _____)

3. During this past year, there were *no disagreements* among the council members.

A suitable replacement for *no disagreements* is _____

(found in section _____)

4. The members of the group were asked to *come together* in the lecture theatre at eight o'clock for a short meeting.

A suitable replacement for *come together* is _____

(found in section _____)

5. Gossip magazines are popular because they *let out* such interesting information about famous people.

A suitable replacement for *let out* is _____

(found in section _____)

(Deduct one mark for each error.)

TOTAL MARKS FOR USING A THESAURUS _____ /5

III. Proofread and correct any errors in sentence structure. Add or delete words to eliminate sentence fragments; correct faulty or missing punctuation in run-on sentences. Use the spaces provided to rewrite any sentence that needs reworking.

1. Good jobs are very difficult to find these days. Part of the reason being so many candidates with the same qualifications.

2. Going for Sunday walks in the fields with the sound of the wind rustling through the trees. Hearing the birds singing their songs. Feeling the peacefulness of living in the country. But most of all, feeling free of all the hustle and bustle of the city.

3. Most of us, at one time or another, allow our childhood feelings to resurface when we do, we tend to be as spontaneous, open, and happy as we probably were as children.

4. Listening is a difficult business research indicates that most people speak approximately 125 words per minute they are capable of listening at a rate of 600 words a minute what they do with their "spare time" determines how well they comprehend an oral message.

5. Reading facts about stars and space. Fascinated by the information and what I can see through my telescope.

(Deduct two marks for each incorrect answer. Because there can be more than one correct answer for any of these questions, ask your instructor to check your work.)

TOTAL MARKS FOR SENTENCE STRUCTURE _____ /10

IV. By using one or a combination of the refining techniques discussed in this unit, join each of the following groups of sentences.

1. Many summer vacationers leave the business of the city to seek the peace and tranquility of nature. The campgrounds are often more crowded than their own neighbourhoods.

2. The library was closed. I couldn't get the research material I needed. My project was not completed by the due date.

3. Eva's apartment is always neat and clean. The interior of her car is littered with empty packages and food cartons. I prefer to take the bus home from work.

4. That family had faced a long period of adversity. They maintained an optimistic outlook and tried to make the best of each crisis.

5. Some students must pay all their own educational expenses. They are willing to make many sacrifices to get an education. They attend classes all day and they work long hours at part-time jobs. Then they have to study in any free time they have.

(Deduct two marks for each error.)

TOTAL MARKS FOR REFINING SENTENCES _____ /10

V. Improve the quality of the following paragraph by underlining key parts and combining them into four or five effective sentences. Your purpose should be to eliminate short, choppy sentence structure and, by using sentence variety and good transition words where appropriate, to create an interesting and informative paragraph. Avoid the use of the vague terms *it* and *this*.

Leukemia is a cancer. It affects the blood-forming organs of the body. It can affect people of different ethnic groups and people of all ages. There is no cure for this disease. Treatments prolong life expectancy. There are many drugs and doses to treat leukemia. Persons are usually hospitalized for initial assessment and treatment. Once remission is achieved, they can usually live comfortably at home. They should be careful to avoid persons who may transmit infections. Infections are the prime cause of death in leukemia victims.

(Deduct one mark for each sentence or composition error.)

TOTAL MARKS FOR SENTENCE COMBINING _____ /5

VI. Write a précis of the following article by using the steps suggested in Unit Four.

    A. Use your reading skills—underline and make marginal notes to identify your main message.

    B. Write your first draft.

    C. Revise your rough copy; use sentence-combining skills and your thesaurus.

    If possible, have your instructor check your condensed version.

(Deduct up to five marks for incomplete or overdone underlining and marginal note-taking. Deduct up to ten marks for composition errors, i.e., repetitious sentence structure, using the terms *it* or *this*, repetitious word usage, short simple sentences, sentence fragments, spelling errors, and exceeding the recommended number of words for the final copy.)

TOTAL MARKS FOR PRÉCIS WRITING _____ /15

A. Read and underline.

B. Write your summary.

Language can assist people in identifying social background within a particular culture. Most Canadians are able to identify dialects and accents of their own language. For example, many people recognize a distinctive style of speaking that is common among Newfoundlanders, and Newfoundlanders can recognize various mainland accents. Such recognizability is by no means peculiar to the English language; the same holds for French, German, or any other language that is spoken where cultural diversity exists.[17]

(75 words)

C. Condense your summary. (35 to 45 words)

Answers are on the following pages.

ANSWERS TO UNIT FOUR POST-TEST

I. separate   tragedy   success

(secretary)   questionnaire   references

misspell   (opinion)   realistically

liaison   introduce   existence

exercise   familiar   candidate

association   (acquire)   (accommodate)

adjourn   analyzed   accidentally

development   (congratulations)   (business)

(different)   (grammar)   (February)

knowledge   (forty)   relevant

II.
1. Suitable replacements for *glance at* are *examine* or *review* (other words do not suit the context), found in section 457.

2. Suitable replacements for *seen* are *comprehended, understood, perceived, learned,* or *discovered,* found in section 490.

3. Suitable replacements for *no disagreements* are *agreement, unanimity,* or *harmony,* found in sections 23/488/714.

4. Suitable replacements for *come together* are *assemble, meet, congregate,* or *convene,* found in section 72.

5. Suitable replacements for *let out* are *disclose, uncover, divulge, reveal,* or *publish,* found in section 529.

III. Answers other than the ones suggested below may be correct. Ask your instructor to check your work.

1. a) Because so many candidates have the same qualifications, good jobs are difficult to find these days.

   b) Good jobs are difficult to find these days; this situation is, in part, caused by the increasing number of candidates with the same qualifications.

2. a) I enjoy going for Sunday walks in the fields with the sound of the wind rustling through the trees. Hearing the birds singing their songs and feeling the peacefulness that country living provides is truly refreshing. But, most of all, I appreciate the freedom from all the hustle and bustle of the city.

   b) Going for Sunday walks in the fields with the sound of the wind rustling through the trees, hearing the birds singing their songs, and feeling the peacefulness of the country are all the wonderful moments I treasure. But, most of all, I love the feeling of freedom from the hustle and bustle of the city.

3. a) Most of us, at one time or another, allow our childhood feelings to resurface; and when we do, we tend to be as spontaneous, open, and happy as we probably were as children.

   b) Most of us, at one time or another, allow our childhood feelings to resurface. When we do, we tend to be as spontaneous, open, and happy as we probably were as children.

4. a) Listening is a difficult business. Research indicates that most people speak at approximately 125 words per minute; however, they are capable of listening at a rate

of 600 words a minute. What they do with their "spare time" determines how well they comprehend an oral message.

b) Listening is a difficult business. Although research indicates that most people speak at approximately 125 words per minute, they are capable of listening at a rate of 600 words a minute. Therefore, what they do with their "spare time" determines how well they comprehend an oral message.

5. a) I enjoy reading facts about stars and space; this information, as well as the astonishing sights I can see through my telescope, absolutely fascinates me.

   b) I am fascinated by what I read about stars and space and by what I can see through my telescope.

IV. Answers other than the ones suggested below may be correct. Ask your instructor to check your work.

1. a) <u>Although</u> many summer vacationers leave the business of the city to seek the peace and tranquility of nature, *the campgrounds are often more crowded than their own neighbourhoods.*

   b) Many summer vacationers leave the business of the city to seek the peace and tranquility of nature, <u>but</u> *the campgrounds are often more crowded than their own neighbourhoods.*

   c) Many summer vacationers leave the business of the city to seek the peace and tranquility of nature; <u>however,</u> *the campgrounds are often more crowded than their own neighbourhoods.*

2. a) <u>Because</u> the library was closed, *I couldn't get the research material I needed;* <u>as a result,</u> *my project was not completed by the due date.*

3. a) <u>Although</u> Eva's apartment is always neat and clean, *the interior of her car is littered with empty packages and food cartons;* <u>consequently,</u> *I prefer to take the bus home from work.*

4. a) <u>Even though</u> that family had faced a long period of adversity, *they maintained an optimistic outlook and tried to make the best of each crisis.*

   b) That family had faced a long period of adversity; <u>nevertheless,</u> *they maintained an optimistic outlook and tried to make the best of each crisis.*

   c) That family had faced a long period of adversity, <u>but</u> *they maintained an optimistic outlook and tried to make the best of each crisis.*

5. a) <u>Because</u> some students must pay all their own educational expenses and are willing to make many sacrifices to get an education, *they attend classes all day, work long hours at part-time jobs, and then study in any free time they have.*

   b) <u>Because</u> some students must pay all their own education expenses, *they are willing to make many sacrifices to get an education;* <u>therefore,</u> *they attend classes all day, work long hours at part-time jobs, and then study in any free time they have.*

V. Your answer will probably differ in some ways from the suggested one below. To be sure you have combined sentences effectively, have your instructor check your answer.

Leukemia, a cancer which affects the blood-forming organs of the body, can affect people of different ages and ethnic groups. Even though there is no cure for this dreaded disease, the life expectancy of diagnosed victims can be prolonged by medication. Those afflicted are usually hospitalized for initial assessment and treatments; however, once remission occurs, they can usually live comfortably at home. Because infections are the prime cause of death in leukemia victims, they should be careful to avoid persons who may transmit any viruses.

VI. Your answers will probably differ in some ways from the suggested ones below. To be sure you have completed this exercise effectively, have your instructor check your answers.

A. Read and underline.

<u>Language</u> can <u>assist people in identifying social background</u> <u>within a particular culture</u>. <u>Most Canadians</u> are <u>able to identify dialects and accents</u> of their <u>own language</u>. For example, <u>many</u> people <u>recognize</u> a distinctive style of speaking that is common among <u>Newfoundlanders, and Newfoundlanders</u> can <u>recognize</u> various <u>mainland accents</u>. Such recognizability is by no means peculiar to the English language; the <u>same</u> holds <u>for</u> French, German, or <u>any other language</u> that is spoken <u>where cultural diversity exists</u>.

(75 words)

B. Write your summary.

Language often reveals one's social background within a culture. By listening to someone speak, most Canadians can determine where the person is from. For example, most recognize the distinctive accent of Newfoundlanders and similarly, the Islanders recognize various mainland dialects. Such linguistic differences exist in any country where diverse cultures coexist.

(51 words)

C. Condense your summary.

Language often reveals one's social and cultural background. Canadians, for example, recognize the distinctive Newfoundland accent and Islanders recognize mainland dialects. Such linguistic differences exist in any country with diverse cultures.

(31 words)

PUTTING THE BASICS TOGETHER

OVERVIEW

Unit Five deals with the integration of spelling, grammar, punctuation, and composition. Once again, both the dictionary and the thesaurus are recommended as main reference books for all writing tasks. In this section, you will also use the dictionary to find irregular plurals of nouns and you will apply this knowledge to grammatical sentence structures as you learn or review how to ensure correct subject-verb agreement in sentences.

The use of the comma is extremely important to someone else's correct interpretation of your work; however, many people tend to punctuate sentences by guess rather than by knowledge. This section introduces three basic uses of the comma and provides simplified information about its correct use.

In Units Two, Three, and Four, you learned how to comprehend a written passage by following the writer's plan. In this unit, you will develop that same kind of plan for your own compositions. Since this format is the basis for all reports and essays, using this skill will help you to improve the quality of your writing. You can use the freewriting exercises from the first three units as preliminary brainstorming activities to help you get started with the planning stage of the writing process.

LEARNING OBJECTIVES FOR UNIT FIVE

Upon completion of this unit, you should be able to:

1. Apply the basic rules for pluralizing nouns.

2. Use the dictionary to determine the number of a word or to find the correct spelling of the plural form.

3. Identify the subject of a sentence and make the verb agree in number.

4. Apply the following three basic rules for using the comma:
   a) before a conjunction in a compound sentence
   b) after each item in a series
   c) after an introductory word or group of words

5. Limit and focus the topic for a one-paragraph writing plan.

6. Use brainstorming techniques in the preliminary writing process.

7. Write effective main-idea and concluding sentences for a one-paragraph writing plan.

8. Identify and use a specific pattern of organization to develop a topic.

9. Use the standard outline format with the following details:
   a) the main idea written as a complete sentence
   b) major and minor points

10. Write concluding sentences that summarize, give advice, make a prediction, or give the result of the paragraph discussion.

 Check Internet resources for grammar and composition exercises (see pages 469–70).

PRETEST: SPELLING—PLURAL FORMS

Correct any spelling errors in the following sentences. Pay particular attention to words that are plural. Use the dictionary to find plural forms of words.

1. The owners of that complex are my two brother-in-laws.

2. The Cortez are our next-door neighbours.

3. Two attornies were hired by the defendants because they wanted their cases tried separately.

4. Mosquitos are the worst summer pests.

5. It seems to me that all the Harries in this city answered our advertisement for an ambitious young salesperson.

6. We ordered several cargoes of tomatos during the summer season.

7. We now have five secretarys in our main office.

8. John likes four teaspoonsful of sugar in his coffee.

9. You should enclose any words of explanation in parenthisises.

10. Omar arranged the cans neatly on the shelfs.

Check your answers with those in the Answer section at the end of the book.

If you had eight or more sentences correct, go on to the Pretest for "Subject-Verb Agreement." If you had fewer than eight sentences correct, complete the lessons on the following pages.

SPELLING–PLURAL FORMS

A noun is a word that names a person, place, or thing. Nouns can be either singular or plural. Plural nouns refer to more than one person, place, or thing. An example of each is given below.

Persons:	the eight Andersons
Places:	several restaurants
Ideas or objects:	different philosophies

Dictionaries indicate the correct plural form for any irregular noun. For example,

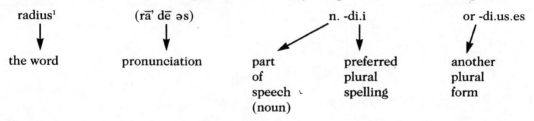

radius[1]	(rā' dē əs)		n. -di.i	or -di.us.es
↓	↓		↓	↓
the word	pronunciation	part of speech (noun)	preferred plural spelling	another plural form

Therefore, the preferred plural spelling of radius is *radii*. Another acceptable form would be *radiuses*; however, when two spellings are given, use the preferred form, which is usually listed first.

Read the following lesson on plurals; then complete the exercise that follows.

I. SIMPLE PLURALS

Most words in English form their plurals by adding *s* to their singular forms.

Singular	Plural
program	programs
textbook	textbooks
Mr. Brown	the Browns (family)

● EXERCISE 5.1   ⑩

Write the plural form of each of the following nouns.

1. accident ___accidents___ ✓
2. instrument ___instruments___ ✓
3. neighbour ___neighbours___ ✓
4. resident ___residents___ ✓
5. Mr. Smith ___the Mr. Smiths___ (family)
6. mechanism ___mechanisms___ ✓

II. WORDS ENDING WITH A HISSING SOUND

When, however, the singular form of a word ends with a "hissing" sound (such as church, tax, glass, topaz, brush), add *es* to form the plural.

Singular	Plural
mass	masses
brush	brushes
bench	benches
tax	taxes
Mr. Jones	the Joneses (family)

● EXERCISE 5.2

Write the plural form of each of the following nouns.

1. address*es*
2. boss *es*
3. Mrs. Blatz*es* (family)
4. box*es*
5. lunch*es*
6. dish *es*

III. WORDS ENDING WITH Y

There are three rules for making plurals of nouns ending with *y*.

Rule 1: If *y* is preceded by a vowel (a, e, i, o, u), just add *s*.

Singular	Plural
valley	valleys
key	keys
play	plays

Rule 2: If *y* is preceded by a consonant, change the *y* to *i* and add *es*.

B, C, D, F, G, H, J, K, L, M, N, P, Q, R, S, T, V, W, X, Z

Singular	Plural
lady	ladies
salary	salaries
library	libraries

Rule 3: To pluralize any proper noun ending with *y*, just add *s*.

Singular	Plural
Mary	Marys
Mr. Kenney	the Kenneys (family)

● EXERCISE 5.3

Write the plural form of each of the following nouns.

1. attorney*s*
2. secretary *secretaries*
3. inventory *inventories*
4. Sally*s*
5. turkey*s*
6. Mr. Murphy *the Murphys* (family)

IV. WORDS ENDING WITH *O*

There are two rules for making plurals of nouns ending with *o*:

Rule 1: When o is preceded by a vowel (a, e, i, o, u) simply add *s*.

Singular	Plural
radio	radios
portfolio	portfolios

Rule 2: When o is preceded by a consonant, add *es*.

Singular	Plural
tomato	tomatoes
cargo	cargoes

Exceptions: 1. All musical terms, words of foreign origin, and abbreviated words ending with *o* add an *s* in their plural forms.

Singular	Plural	
piano	pianos	
solo	solos	} musical terms
soprano	sopranos	
bistro	bistros	
kimono	kimonos	} words of foreign origin
kilo	kilos	
photo	photos	
disco	discos	} abbreviated words
memo	memos	

2. For some words, both plural forms are acceptable. Check your dictionary and use whichever form is listed first (this is the preferred form).

Singular	Plural
zero	zeros or zeroes
motto	mottos or mottoes
memento	mementos or mementoes

● EXERCISE 5.4

Write the plural form of each of the following nouns. Check your dictionary if you have any doubts.

1. hero~~es~~ _____
2. ditto~~es~~ dittos _____
3. banjo ~~es~~ banjos _____
4. auto s _____
5. zero s/es _____
6. innuendo s/es _____

V. WORDS ENDING WITH *F* OR *FE*

There are two ways of forming the plurals of words that end with *f* or *fe*. In some cases, simply add *s*; in others, change the *f/fe* to *v* and add *es* to form the plural. Because there is no hard and fast rule, always refer to a dictionary for clarification.

These words just add *s*:

Singular	Plural
chief	chiefs
belief	beliefs
gulf	gulfs
sheriff	sheriffs
proof	proofs

These words change the *f/fe* ending to *v* and add *es*:

Singular	Plural
self	selves
life	lives
thief	thieves
calf	calves
wolf	wolves

● EXERCISE 5.5

Write the plural form of each of the following nouns. Check your dictionary if you have any doubts.

1. loaf _loaves_ ✓
2. wife _wives_ ✓
3. handkerchiefs ✓

4. waif _waifs_ ✓
5. half _halves_ ✓
6. leaf _leaves_ ✓

VI. COMPOUND WORDS

To form the plural of a compound word, add *s* to the more important word.

Singular	Plural
mother-in-law	mothers-in-law
editor-in-chief	editors-in-chief
lieutenant-governor	lieutenant-governors

Words ending in *-ful* form their plurals by adding *s* at the end of the word.

Singular	Plural
spoonful	spoonfuls
armful	armfuls

● EXERCISE 5.6

Write the plural form of each of the following nouns.

1. father-in-law _fathers-in-law_ ✓
2. mouthfuls ✓
3. library technicians ✓

4. general managers ✓
5. tablespoonfuls ✓
6. cupfuls ✓

Check your answers with those in the Answer section at the end of the book.

VII. IRREGULAR PLURALS

Note the entries and preferred plural spellings of the following irregular plural forms, taken from the *Random House Dictionary,* First Ballantine Books Edition, 1980.

> child n., pl. *children*
>
> man n., pl. *men*
>
> crisis n., pl. -*ses* (the plural form is *crises*)
>
> datum n., pl. *data*
>
> mathematics n., no plural form (mathematics is singular)
>
> measles n., no plural form (measles is singular)
>
> radius n., pl. -*dii*, -*diuses* (two plural forms are acceptable: *radii*—preferred plural; *radiuses*—acceptable plural)[1]

● EXERCISE 5.7

Write the plural forms of each of the following nouns. Check your dictionary if you have any doubts.

1. phenomenon s ✓
2. analysis analyses ✓
3. alumnuses alumni
4. mouse mice ✓
5. news news ✓
6. criterion criteria ✓

VIII. CONFUSING HOMONYMS (WORDS THAT SOUND THE SAME)

Avoid confusing a word with its homonyms. Recognize the different meanings for each of the following.

residents: (plural form) people who live in a place
residence: a home

presents: (plural form) gifts
presence: attendance

adolescents: (plural form) young people
adolescence: the teen years

attendants: (plural form) people who assist or accompany
attendance: presence at a function

patients: (plural form) people receiving medical treatment
patience: the ability to tolerate

correspondents: (plural form) people who communicate by letter, or journalists
correspondence: written communication

● EXERCISE 5.8

Underline the correct form of the homonym in each of the following sentences.

1. Your (presents, <u>presence</u>) is required at the meeting, as we must have a quorum in (attendants, <u>attendance</u>) to vote on the issue.

2. Because she had been up all night, she didn't have much (patients, <u>patience</u>) with anyone.

3. Most people have encountered all kinds of traumatic problems during their (adolescents, <u>adolescence</u>).

4. Ella is living in (residents, <u>residence</u>) while she is at college.

5. We expected to receive some (correspondents, <u>correspondence</u>) from them while they were away.

6. Because of the nearness of the forest fire, most of the (residence, <u>residents</u>) of Fort Hope had to be evacuated.

7. During the summer the police arrested several (adolescence, <u>adolescents</u>) for acts of vandalism.

8. Several St. John Ambulance (attendance, <u>attendants</u>) were required at the rock concert to care for the usual casualties.

9. Teenagers often try the (patients, <u>patience</u>) of their parents.

10. Katerina received so many (presence, <u>presents</u>) for her seventh birthday that she didn't know which one to play with first.

Check your answers with those in the Answer section at the end of the book.

● EXERCISE 5.9—REVIEW

Write the plural of each of the following nouns. Consult your dictionary, if necessary.

1. country _countries_
2. business _businesses_
3. index _indexes_
4. sister-in-law _sisters-in-law_
5. roof _roofs_
6. Ms. Maki _the Makis_ (family)
7. datum _data_
8. woman _women_
9. handful _handfuls_
10. mumps _____

11. mosquito _mosquitoes_
12. secretary _secretaries_
13. parenthesis _parentheses_
14. priority _priorities_
15. soprano _sopranos_
16. athletics _____
17. resident _residents_
18. jury _juries_
19. Mr. Curtis _the Curtises_ X (family)
20. derby _derbies_

Check your answers with those in the Answer section at the end of the book.

THE NEXT STEP

If you feel confident about this section, proceed to the grammar Pretest on the following page.

PRETEST: SUBJECT-VERB AGREEMENT

Underline or circle the correct form of the verb to make it agree with its subject.

1. Neither of your answers (is, <u>are</u>) correct. X

2. A stack of dirty dishes (was, <u>were</u>) left in the sink. X

3. Either the vegetables or the meat (has, <u>have</u>) an odd smell. X

4. One of those boys (has, <u>have</u>) to be guilty. X

5. Professor Goodwin and her husband (is, <u>are</u>) leaving today for Ireland. ✓

6. Spaghetti and meatballs (is, <u>are</u>) a good Italian meal. X

7. Mr. Singh's new Honda (<u>doesn't</u>, don't) use very much gasoline. ✓

8. Physics, as well as mathematics, (requires, <u>require</u>) skill in logic. X

9. There (don't, <u>doesn't</u>) seem to be a solution to that problem. ✓

10. (Is, <u>Are</u>) parentheses required around that information? ✓

Check your answers with those in the Answer section at the end of the book.

If you had eight or more sentences correct, go on to the Pretest for "Basic Uses of the Comma." If you had fewer than eight correct, complete the lessons on the following pages.

SUBJECT-VERB AGREEMENT

I. SENTENCES IN NATURAL ORDER

In order to understand the principles governing subject-verb agreement, you must first be able to recognize the two main parts of a sentence—namely, the **subject** and the **predicate**, which were introduced in Unit Four. Remember that

1. the subject is who or what is being discussed; and
2. the predicate, which contains the "action" of the sentence, gives information about the subject or tells what action the subject is performing.

● EXERCISE 5.10

Draw a vertical line to separate the subject from the predicate, as illustrated in the following example.

The directors of the division/met to discuss the new programs.

complete subject
(who or what is being discussed)

complete predicate
(what the subject is doing)

1. The coffee in the cafeteria is reasonably priced.
2. The applicants for the job were asked to fill out a special form.
3. Most first-year students at post-secondary institutions are required to take an English course.
4. Many new and exciting programs are being planned for the future.
5. People who live in glass houses shouldn't throw stones.

Check your answers with those in the Answer section at the end of the book.

FINDING THE SIMPLE SUBJECT

To find the simple subject, which must agree with the verb, cross out any descriptive groups of words. In studying the following examples, you should note that the simple subject comes first in most sentences.

The woman ~~in the flowered dress~~/is André's sister.

The people ~~who lived in that city~~/were upset about the excessive air pollution.

Students ~~who wrote that test~~/were finished classes for the day.

The man ~~lying on the beach~~/was getting a terrific tan.

184

● EXERCISE 5.11

Draw a vertical line to separate the complete subject from the predicate; then find the simple subject by crossing out any descriptive word groups.

1. Solar-heated houses, which are still in the experimental stage, are ideally suited to sunny northwestern Ontario.

2. The problems that she encountered were impossible to solve.

3. Mentally handicapped children in our present society appear to have a better chance to live more rewarding and independent lives.

4. The person responsible for that action was justifiably punished.

5. The boy running up the stairs was the thief.

6. All the students in the pie-eating contest were asked to wear aprons.

7. Textbooks are getting more and more expensive every year.

8. The water level in the lake is high this year.

9. Some grocery stores stay open all night for the convenience of shift workers.

10. Sandi was thrilled to receive a special invitation to the gala event of the year.

Check your answers with those in the Answer section at the end of the book.

II. SENTENCES IN INVERTED ORDER

Up to this point, all the examples and exercises presented to you have illustrated sentences in their natural order—that is, ones in which the subject is first and the predicate is second. However, many sentences are written in reversed or mixed order; that is, the subject is either at the end or in the middle of the sentence.

When are **you** leaving?	(Whom or what are you discussing?) The subject is "you."
In the doorway stood **two strangers**.	(Whom or what are you discussing?) The subject is "two strangers."
Is **Javed or Kim** planning to attend the workshop?	(Whom or what are you discussing?) The subject is "Javed or Kim."
Here comes **your dog**.	(Whom or what are you discussing?) The subject is "your dog."
There were **many people** waiting to see the parade.	(Whom or what are you discussing?) The subject is "many people."

● EXERCISE 5.12

Use a wavy line (‿‿‿‿‿‿) to identify the simple subject in each of the following sentences.

1. How well does he understand the French language?

2. What is Oksana planning to do after class?

3. Does Pascal or Rod know about your plans?

4. Into the room stomped the angry instructor.

5. During the night the thieves burglarized the house.

6. There could be more than one answer to that question.

7. Down the long aisle walked the bride with her father.

8. Where are you going for your vacation?

9. For some people, learning seems to be an easy task.

10. Across the lake sped the motor boat with a water-skier in tow.

11. After two days of rain usually comes a Monday.

12. Amongst the pile of debris, she found a valuable antique tray.

Check your answers with those in the Answer section at the end of the book.

Now that you have a better understanding of subjects and predicates you can proceed to learn about subject-verb agreement.

III. SUBJECT-VERB AGREEMENT

Most people can easily recognize the singular and plural forms of nouns and pronouns; but what they do not realize is that verbs also have singular and plural forms. Examine the verb forms in the following sentences.

singular subject   *singular verb*

He <u>walks</u> to work every day.

plural subject   *plural verb*

They <u>walk</u> to work every day.

Notice that the singular verb in the present tense ends with s—the plural verb does not contain s.

NOTE: An easy way to remember this grammatical rule is to identify the subject as singular ⓢ or plural ⓟ. If the identified subject is ⓢ, add an s to the verb. If the subject is ⓟ, make sure the verb does not contain s.

ⓢ   *singular subject = s on verb*

Everyone is here.

ⓟ   *not singular = no s on verb*

All are here.

(s)   *singular subject = s on verb*

The **style** has changed.

(p)   *not singular = no s on verb*

The **styles** have changed.

These examples are very straightforward and most students would naturally use the correct verb agreement; however, many times errors are made if the sentence pattern varies or if an interrupting group of words separates the subject from the verb. Note the subject and correct verb agreement in the following examples. (Remember: To find the subject, ask "whom or what is being discussed?")

1. Varied sentence patterns

(p)

Have the **styles** changed?

(s)

Here is your **assignment**

(s)

Where was **he** going?

2. Interrupting groups of words

(p)

Styles around the world have changed.

(s)

Each of the students has a copy.

Notice that the first word or words in the complete subject are usually considered to be the simple subject.

● **EXERCISE 5.13**

Underline and identify the simple subject as (s) (singular) or (p) (plural); then draw an arrow to the verb and make it agree in number with the subject.

1. One of the chairs were broken.

2. Too many cooks spoils the soup.
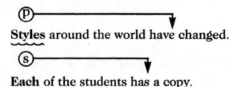

3. What were Pavel doing with your books?

4. Every one of the members were informed of that meeting.

5. When do Mico start his new job?

6. The people who live at the end of our block has invited us to their neighbourhood party. *have*

7. There are no time for such trivial details.

8. The one sport that I really enjoy playing are tennis. *is*

9. At the top of our list of necessary household expenditures were my request for a new car. *has*

10. How much does three cans of pop cost? *do*

11. Last year there was no houses in that area. *were*

12. What is the main objectives of the proposal? *are*

13. Unless there is very bad weather conditions, the buses usually are on time. *are*

14. The recent discovery of holes in the ozone layer have many people worried about the future of earth. *has*

15. Recently there has been many changes in the tax laws. *have*

Check your answers with those in the Answer section at the end of the book.

IV. RECOGNIZING SINGULAR SUBJECTS

The following words are always considered singular and require a singular verb to agree.

either/neither
everyone/someone/anyone
everybody/somebody/anybody
each/one
nobody/nothing

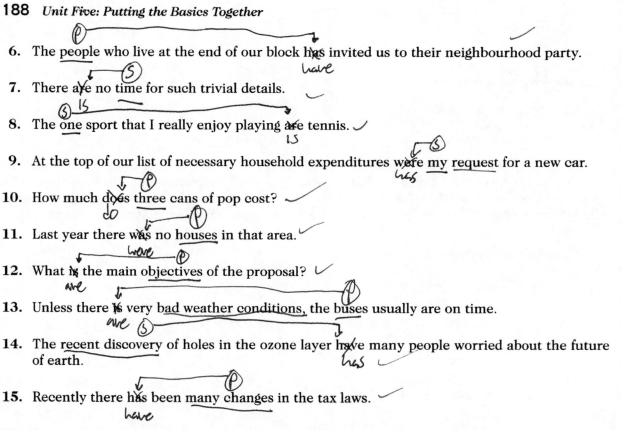

Either is a good choice.

Everyone has problems.

When word groups interrupt, the verb must still agree with the simple subject.

Either of those books is a good choice.

Everyone ~~in the world~~ has problems.

● EXERCISE 5.14

Identify the simple subject as ⓢ (singular) or ⓟ (plural) and make the verb agree in number. If a sentence is correct, mark it "Correct."

1. Every one of the new students in residence receive an invitation to the first-year dance. /
   receives

2. Each person in the room have time to fill out the questionnaire.
   has

3. One of my books are missing. ✓
   is

4. Do anyone know where Dieter lives? ✓
   Does

5. Either steak look good to me. ✗
   looks

6. Somebody at the back of the bus were singing. ✓
   was

7. One of the children was ill. *correct* ✓

8. Neither boy claim to be the culprit. ✓
   claims

9. Nobody in our group was responsible for the accident. *Correct* ✓

10. Nothing have ever been solved by anger. ✓
    has

Check your answers with those in the Answer section at the end of the book.

V. COMPOUND SUBJECTS USING *EITHER/OR*, *NEITHER/NOR*, *AND*

The only words that can affect the number of the simple subject are the words *or, nor,* and *and.* Joining words, such as *or, either ... or ..., neither ... nor ...,* suggest a choice. These words may join two or more singular words, plural words, or a mixture of both.

1. **Always make the verb agree in number with the word that follows *or* or *nor*.**

   Julian or **Hans** was responsible for delivering the package to you.

   Hamburgers or **hotdogs** were what the children wanted.

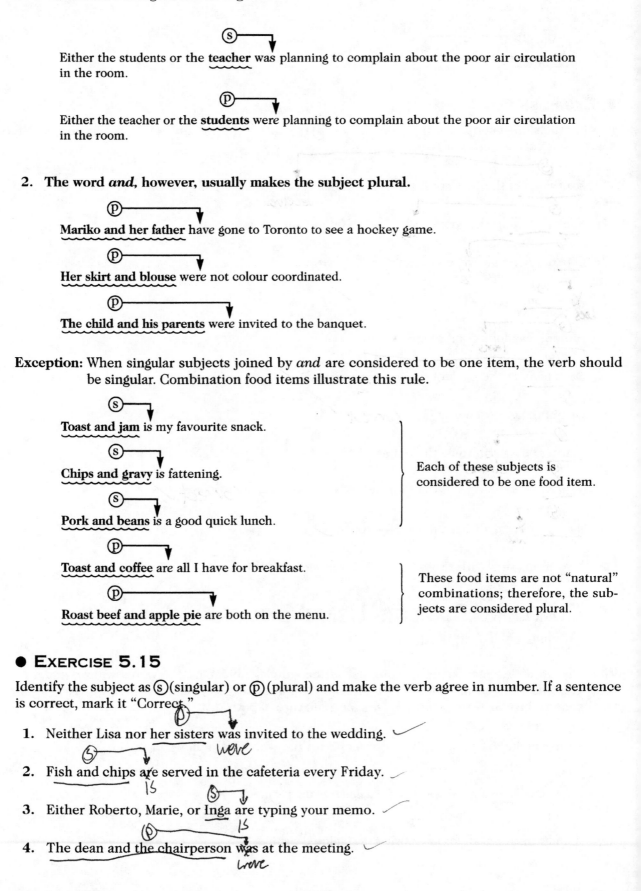

Either the students or the **teacher** was planning to complain about the poor air circulation in the room.

Either the teacher or the **students** were planning to complain about the poor air circulation in the room.

2. **The word *and*, however, usually makes the subject plural.**

Mariko and her father have gone to Toronto to see a hockey game.

Her skirt and blouse were not colour coordinated.

The child and his parents were invited to the banquet.

Exception: When singular subjects joined by *and* are considered to be one item, the verb should be singular. Combination food items illustrate this rule.

Toast and jam is my favourite snack.

Chips and gravy is fattening.

Pork and beans is a good quick lunch.

Each of these subjects is considered to be one food item.

Toast and coffee are all I have for breakfast.

Roast beef and apple pie are both on the menu.

These food items are not "natural" combinations; therefore, the subjects are considered plural.

● EXERCISE 5.15

Identify the subject as ⑤(singular) or ℗ (plural) and make the verb agree in number. If a sentence is correct, mark it "Correct."

1. Neither Lisa nor her sisters was invited to the wedding. *were*

2. Fish and chips are served in the cafeteria every Friday. *is*

3. Either Roberto, Marie, or Inga are typing your memo. *is*

4. The dean and the chairperson was at the meeting. *were*

5. Hot dogs and ice cream was what she served for dinner. ✓ *were*

6. Don't Antonio or Carlos ever get tired of watching soccer games on television? ✓ *Doesn't*

7. Both Markus and Stefan intend to apply for that job. *Correct* ✓

8. Neither my memo nor my letters have been typed yet. *Correct* ✓

9. Bruno, Sacha, and Rohan is your new instructors. ✓ *are*

10. Roast turkey with all the trimmings and hot apple pie is what I ordered for dinner. *are*

11. Neither Ivana nor her friends was willing to help with the clean-up after the party. ✓ *were*

12. Either the switches or the power are off because not one of the appliances are working. ✓ *is*

13. Both Edna and Michelle in our class sings off key. ✓ *sing*

14. At the end of the sales season, only a black Mercedes and a red Corvette was left in the showroom. ✓ *were*

15. Neither the blinding snowstorm nor the freezing cold keep the mail carriers from delivering the mail. ✓ *keeps*

Check your answers with those in the Answer section at the end of the book.

VI. TRICKY SUBJECT-VERB AGREEMENT

Some words that are plural in form are really singular in meaning. Subjects such as *mathematics*, *civics*, *economics*, and *physics*; diseases such as *measles* and *mumps*; and terms such as *news*, *mechanics*, and *athletics* are singular in meaning and require singular verbs.

No news is good news.

Mumps is a communicable disease.

Words that indicate a singular unit of time, weight, money, or distance also require a singular verb.

Ten dollars was an outrageous price to pay for that meal.

Fifteen minutes is an eternity if you are waiting for someone.

Did you know that **three kilometres** is almost two miles?

Many foreign words are included in our everyday vocabulary. If you do not recognize their plural forms, you should consult your dictionary to ensure that you are using the correct form of the word and the correct verb to agree. Some of these more commonly used words require careful checking to make sure that the subject and verb agree. For example,

criterion—criteria

What criteria were used to screen the applicants?

datum—data

The **data** on the recent fires have been sent to the provincial authorities.

crisis—crises

For police officers, crises are daily occurrences.

● EXERCISE 5.16

Identify the subject as ⓢ (singular) or ⓟ (plural) and make the verb agree in number. If a sentence is correct, mark it "Correct."

1. Parentheses is needed around incidental information.

2. Physics, chemistry, and mathematics was part of the prerequisites for that program.

3. Fifty cents are not much to pay for a cup of coffee.

4. What were the basis for her argument?

5. The mechanics of using a computer effectively are difficult for me to understand and remember.

6. Measles seem to be more infectious during the school year.

7. Ten minutes were all she needed to solve that mathematical problem.

8. Where is the data you collected?

9. News of the catastrophes were flashed around the world in minutes.

10. Two litres of milk are in that container on the kitchen table.

11. Do you think $500 are too much rent to pay for this apartment?

12. The phenomena of space is being observed by hundreds of scientists.

13. Mathematics are not easy if you do not have a head for numbers.

14. After my holiday spending spree, there are only $25 remaining in my bank account.

15. The criteria for the entrance exams for that university was very complex. Applicants had to score high both in the interview and on each test in order to be accepted.

Check your answers with those in the Answer section at the end of the book.

● EXERCISE 5.17—REVIEW

Identify subjects as ⓢ (singular) or ⓟ (plural) and make the verb agree in number. If a sentence is correct, mark it *"Correct."*

1. Neither of these problems are difficult.

2. There don't seem to be a logical answer to that question.

3. The people who live in Hamilton is sometimes upset about the pollution levels.

4. Many new and exciting programs are being planned for the future.

5. Do Anja or Martina know your exciting news?

6. Fifteen dollars are an excellent price for that chair.

7. Either the chesterfield or the chairs has to be moved.

8. Both the icy road conditions and poor visibility was cited as the cause of the accident.

9. Either the neighbours or Mrs. Wong plan to circulate the petition.

10. How much do one of those apples cost?

11. Where is my keys?

12. Often, there are just too many things to do in a day!

13. Mathematics are my favourite subject.

14. Stefan and Marta was married in July of this year.

Unit Five: Putting the Basics Together

15. Someone at the game were blowing a bugle to encourage the home team on to victory. [was]

16. Hamburgers and hot dogs is most commonly served at barbecues. [are]

17. Hours flies by like minutes when I am working at the computer. [fly]

18. Neither Willy nor Larry were able to be master of ceremonies at the reception. *correct* [was]

19. Is the answers to these questions in the back of the book? [are]

20. Spaghetti and meatballs are one of our favourite family meals. [is]

21. In essays, parentheses is needed around any added information; however, these marks should be used sparingly. [are]

22. Strawberries and cream were the only dessert choice.

23. Two metres of material are not enough for me to make that dress. [was] [is]

24. The doctor said that the cause of my sinus problems are dust and pollen. [is]

25. Bacon and eggs are always a popular item on the breakfast menu. [is]

26. For business-minded people, there is many ways to make money. [are]

27. Both the conductor and his assistant was from Germany. [were]

28. Either of these protein foods are a good substitute for meat. [is]

29. The errors in his essays was the reason for his poor mark. [were]

30. The media was invited to a special press conference called by the president of the major corporation. [were]

31. Either Kim or Jon are welcome to represent the staff at the meeting, but not both of them.

32. The consultant's analyses of the various problems in the organization was very helpful to the administration. [were]

33. Neither of the descriptions about tonight's movies sound very interesting. [sounds]

34. A list of honour students are posted in the main hall for everyone to see.

35. Everybody in the room were celebrating the team's victory. [was]

36. Either of these topics are a good choice for your essay. [is]

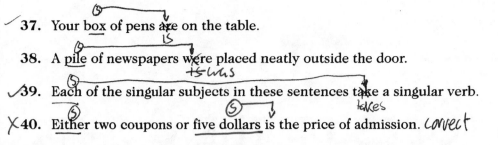

37. Your box of pens are on the table.

38. A pile of newspapers were placed neatly outside the door.

39. Each of the singular subjects in these sentences take a singular verb.

40. Either two coupons or five dollars is the price of admission. *correct*

Check your answers with those in the Answer section at the end of the book.

THE NEXT STEP

If you understand the principles of subject-verb agreement, proceed to the Pretest for "Basic Uses of the Comma."

PRETEST: BASIC USES OF THE COMMA

Insert commas, where necessary, in the following sentences. Some sentences may not require any commas. This exercise tests comma use in compound sentences, in a series, and after introductory words.

1. Do you plan to spend your vacation travelling, camping, or staying at home?

2. When you encounter problems, it is best to seek the advice of a professional counsellor or clergy.

3. The person of my dreams must have intelligence, a sense of humour, and the ability to listen.

4. Using the stairs in an office or apartment building would be an excellent way for workers to stay in shape, but not many people use this easy form of exercise in their daily lives because using the elevator is faster and more convenient for them during their busy schedules.

5. To win at any game of cards, you must practise and be able to remember each card that has been played.

6. What we hope for, and what we get are usually two different things.

7. He had difficulty deciding if he should save his winnings or invest them or buy the car he had always wanted.

8. In some small cities, you can drive to a nearby lake or quiet park area in just a few minutes and spend a relaxing afternoon or evening away from the hustle and bustle of daily life.

9. Papers, books, magazines, etc. were scattered around the room.

10. Acting on the advice of Mr. Tanaka, I decided to invest in some stock.

Check your answers with those in the Answer section at the end of the book.

If you had eight or more sentences correct, go on to "Outlining." If you had fewer than eight sentences correct, complete the lessons on the following pages.

BASIC USES OF THE COMMA

Using commas effectively is really not difficult. This lesson outlines three basic uses.

I. USE A COMMA BEFORE THE CONJUNCTION IN A COMPOUND SENTENCE

1. If a conjunction (*and, but, or*) joins two complete thoughts, a comma is usually placed before the conjunction. Note this use of the comma in the following examples.

   During the telethon the telephones rang incessantly, *and* we did our best to answer all calls calmly.

   We had planned a fishing trip to Whitefish Bay, *but* the sudden downpour of rain quickly made us change our minds.

2. However, if the compound sentences are very brief, no comma is required.

   She knocked at the door *but* no one answered.

   I did well on that test *but* I had studied for it.

   I laughed *and* she cried.

3. In the following sentences, the conjunctions do not join two complete thoughts; therefore, no commas are required.

   She didn't know if she should laugh *or* cry.

   I turned off my alarm *and* went back to sleep.

   My brother *and* I have similar hairstyles.

● EXERCISE 5.18

Add any necessary commas.

1. I sent in my application as soon as I heard of the vacancy, but I have not yet received a reply.

2. She quickly ate her breakfast and rushed off to work.

3. "Hotdogging" is an exciting new sport for skiers, but a person must have a great deal of courage to attempt some of those stunts.

4. Today was nice, but tomorrow is supposed to be nicer.

5. You should send in your confirmation fee as soon as possible, or you will lose your opportunity for admission to that program.

6. The phone rang and two of us raced to answer it. ✓

7. You can take the supplies we have in stock, or wait for the new shipment to arrive. ✗

8. Have you completed packing for your trip to Europe, or are you waiting until the day before ✓ you leave?

9. What she says and what she actually does are two different things. ✓

10. The heavy waves tossed the small craft around in the water like a toy, but the skilled crew ✓ finally managed to guide their boat into a protective bay along the coast.

Check your answers with those in the Answer section at the end of the book.

II. USE A COMMA TO SEPARATE ITEMS IN A SERIES

1. Commas are placed after each item in a series. Include a comma before the conjunctions *and, but, or*.

   His diet lunch consisted of a boiled egg, one piece of Melba Toast, and a cup of black coffee.

   Spring means raking leaves, planting gardens, and taking off storm windows.

2. If a series of descriptive words is used in front of a noun, place a comma after each word in the series that can be attached by the word *and*.

   The tired, old, homeless man fell asleep on the park bench.
   (The tired *and* old *and* homeless man—you would not use *and* after homeless)

   The poor, old, tired, weather-beaten, and homeless man fell asleep on the park bench.
   (If *and* is placed at the end of the series before the noun, use a comma before the conjunction.)

3. If a series is used at the beginning or in the middle of a sentence, do not separate the final item in the series from the rest of the sentence.

   She searched through desks, boxes, and files to find the missing documents.

4. Put a comma after the term *etc.* when it ends a series in mid-sentence.

   We were pleased to learn that the hotel would look after room arrangements, decorations, food, beverages, etc., for our planned party.

5. Occasionally, a writer will intentionally use a conjunction between every item in a series. This use of the conjunction creates a special effect. Commas are not required.

   He didn't know if he should phone or write or visit her in the hospital.
   (Continual use of *or* indicates indecisiveness.)

   He had to mow and rake and water the lawn before he could go out to play.
   (Continual use of *and* indicates tediousness.)

● EXERCISE 5.19

Add any necessary commas. If a sentence is correctly punctuated, mark it *"Correct."*

1. The little mouse ran down the stairs, around the table, and under the sofa. ✓

✗ 2. The child didn't know if she should buy pop, or gum, or candy with her quarter.

3. Tying strings around fingers, writing messages on mirrors, and leaving notes on doors are ✓ some of the ways people try to remember things.

X **4.** Newspapers, books, toys, etc.,littered the living room. C

X **5.** He rushed home,changed his clothes,and left for the airport. C

✓**6.** What you do,where you go, and how you spend your money is your own business.

7. The proper placement of periods, commas,and semicolons is necessary for the reader to interpret the message correctly.

✓**8.** Students can achieve good marks if they have a consistent study program,devote more time to troublesome subjects,and develop good self-discipline.

X **9.** Chico claimed that the alarm ringing in the morning,the clatter of dishes in the kitchen,the blare of the radio,etc., were the reasons for her cranky behaviour.

✓**10.** More wind and rain and cloud cover were predicted for the next five days. C

Check your answers with those in the Answer section at the end of the book.

III. USE A COMMA AFTER AN INTRODUCTORY WORD OR GROUP OF WORDS

Often, you will use a group of words as an introduction to a main thought. If you use an introduction, you must place a comma after it. In effect, this signals the reader that the main idea is yet to come. Now, reread this paragraph and see how many examples you can find that deal with commas placed after an introduction. Remember that a comma is always placed after an introductory word or group of words.

> After you finish the dishes, you can begin washing the floor.

> Whenever you are in our city, please give me a call.

However, do not use a comma if the main thought appears first.

> You can begin washing the floor after you finish the dishes.

> Please give me a call whenever you are in our city.

● EXERCISE 5.20

Add commas to the following sentences.

✓**1.** In the first year of the civil engineering program, math and physics subjects are closely related.

2. One of these days,I think I'll hitchhike to Vancouver.

3. When he got home,he found that his pet Tamagochi had died.

✓**4.** Once upon a time,a princess kissed a toad and got warts.

5. Now,where shall we go next?

6. Even though they had won a large sum of money, they did not plan to change their simple lifestyle.

7. As a result of good study habits,Regine obtained 90 percent on her last test.

✓**8.** Taking a deep breath, the nervous contestant walked hesitantly up to the podium.

9. Unfortunately, the picnic was postponed because of rain.

10. After you have finished this exercise,you should recognize an introductory group of words.

Check your answers with those in the Answer section at the end of the book.

● EXERCISE 5.21—REVIEW

Complete the following exercise by adding necessary commas. If a sentence is correctly punctuated, mark it *"Correct."*

1. He made a very good salary, but he was still unhappy. X

2. Pencils, erasers, paperclips, etc., covered his desk. *Correct* X

3. Jogging along the trail, she felt exhilarated. ✓

4. After the storm passed, the forest took on a fresh appearance. ✓

5. Fundamental accounting principles, business statistics, and microeconomics were subjects ✓ included in his first semester business course.

6. It has been proven by medical researchers that smoking is hazardous to one's health, but ✓ many people continue this habit in spite of the warnings.

7. The real estate agents were advised to point out the scenic view and the picturesque cliff ✓ and the romantic setting of the newly developed area to all potential buyers. *Correct*

8. The couple invested in that property because they thought that the old building could be ✓ converted into apartments or offices or a sports facility. *Correct*

9. When he finally woke the people in the house, he found he had the wrong address. ✓

10. If you order your new barbecue before June 15, you will receive a free cookbook, shish kebab ✓ skewers, and oven mitts from the company.

11. There was a steady flow of traffic on the highway, as people were returning home after the X long weekend.

12. Because of the accident on the highway, traffic had to be rerouted. ✓

13. Your necklace could be in my jewellery box or on my dresser or in the top drawer of my ✓ night table. *Correct*

14. The park area was littered with cans, papers, plastic cups, etc., after the fireworks display. X

15. After a great deal of thought, Linda decided to accept the job offer in Alaska. ✓

16. Raising our glasses in the air, we all toasted the bride. ✓

17. The conservation officer explained the value and procedures for spraying trees in the ✓ bug-infested area, but many campers were reluctant to agree to this very expensive method of eliminating the problem.

18. Unfortunately, we had to leave before the party was over. ✓

19. Not satisfied with Sven's answer, the teacher asked someone else to respond to the question. ✓

20. The bright, colourful, intricate design, caught everyone's attention. X

Check your answers with those in the Answer section at the end of the book.

THE NEXT STEP

If you feel you understand the principles of comma usage, proceed to "Outlining" on the following page.

OUTLINING–THE THINKING AND PLANNING STAGE

There is **no** Pretest for this section. You will learn how to organize and plan, in proper outline format, a piece of writing on an assigned topic. Now is the time for you to learn how to be an effective communicator. As you know, it is easier to interpret another person's writing if it is well organized and conveys a clear message. After studying Units Two and Three, you should have an understanding of the outline format. While working on this section, you may want to review "Organizational Patterns in Reading" in Unit Two. Since you are now the author of what someone else will read, it is important for you to understand basic structure and organization.

Whether you are writing a paragraph, an answer to an exam question, or an essay, you will require two skills: the ability to organize facts in a logical order and the ability to explain them clearly. This section on writing skills will demonstrate the importance of limiting your topic and mapping out a plan as a preliminary stage in the writing process.

Using a writing plan or an outline helps you to structure the relationship and order of your facts and determine the relevance of each. By generating a "skeleton of ideas," you are able to visualize your overall message, rearrange points to create a better flow of ideas, add new examples, consider better wording—all before you actually begin to write. It is much easier to edit ideas at this preliminary stage than to tear up pages of written work in frustration and face the task of beginning again. This is the "thinking and planning" step.

These organizational steps are essential if you wish to help your readers understand your thoughts, and they are the same as those you used to interpret and comprehend passages in textbooks and articles—the focus of Units Two, Three, and Four.

I. CHOOSING AND LIMITING THE TOPIC

Before you begin your writing, consider the answers to the following questions:

1. What topic are you planning to discuss? It may be a given topic or one that you have chosen.

2. What specific aspect of this topic do you want to focus on? You need to narrow your topic to ensure your content will have specific value and/or interest to the reader.

If what you write is to interest the reader, your message must contain useful, meaningful data. Therefore, once you have determined your general topic or the subject matter, take a realistic look at the limits of your chosen topic as compared to the proposed length of the piece of writing. For example, hundreds of books have been written on every type of sports activity. Discussing "sports" in a single paragraph would not really be appropriate; the material would be so vague that it would have little or no value to the reader. It is preferable to focus instead on one small aspect of one particular sport.

Condense a topic as illustrated in the following examples. Stop condensing when your topic is suitable for discussion.

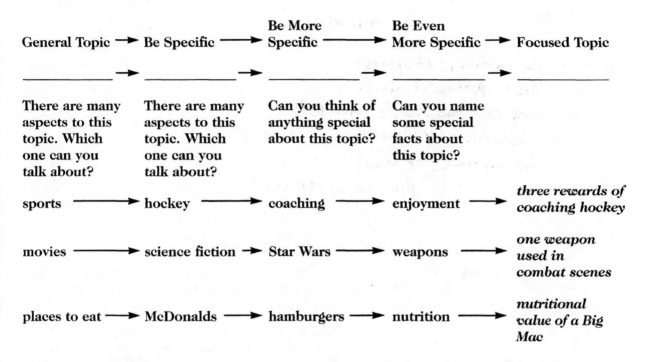

General Topic →	Be Specific →	Be More Specific →	Be Even More Specific →	Focused Topic
_____ →	_____ →	_____ →	_____ →	_____
There are many aspects to this topic. Which one can you talk about?	There are many aspects to this topic. Which one can you talk about?	Can you think of anything special about this topic?	Can you name some special facts about this topic?	
sports →	hockey →	coaching →	enjoyment →	*three rewards of coaching hockey*
movies →	science fiction →	Star Wars →	weapons →	*one weapon used in combat scenes*
places to eat →	McDonalds →	hamburgers →	nutrition →	*nutritional value of a Big Mac*

● EXERCISE 5.22

Read the following list of topics. Place a check mark (✔) next to those that are focused enough for a one-paragraph composition. Place an **x** next to those that are too general.

1. devices for exploring the sea X ✔
2. how to iron a shirt properly ✔ ✔
3. my study routines ✔ ✔
4. education systems in this country X ✔
5. implications of censorship laws X ✔
6. three reasons why students should stay in school ✔ ✔
7. differences in skiing on snow and on water ✔ ✔
8. history of the Olympic Games X ✔
9. benefits of taking vitamin C in cold seasons ✔ ✔
10. advantages of mandatory school uniforms for high school students X X
11. tips for buying a new car X X
12. the effects of the media on politics X ✔

13. a simple plan for keeping physically fit
14. the importance of coffee breaks for employees
15. why everyone should have a hobby X

Check your answers with those in the Answer section at the end of the book.

● **EXERCISE 5.23**   *no Answer section*

Condense each of the following subjects to a focused topic suitable for a one-paragraph discussion.

1. sports   *the importance of sports*
2. habits   *the importance of habits*
3. pets   *why everyone should have pets*
4. pollution   *benifits of pollution*
5. music   *the importance of music*
6. a topic of your own choice   *picking a topic*

II. BRAINSTORMING AND CHOOSING RELATED FACTS

Brainstorming a topic means that you write down everything you can think of that is related to your topic. It is important to have as specific a topic as possible so that your brainstorming produces some good support for your theme.

1. What details can you think of that are related to your focused topic? At this point, you need to brainstorm all the facts that you know about your topic. There are two ways to approach this step.

   a) You can use the freewriting method to exhaust your knowledge about a specific topic. Write non-stop for ten to fifteen minutes. Do not allow yourself to stop writing. Talk to yourself on paper and include all thoughts—even rambling ones or frustrations—that come to mind. Try to stay focused on what you know about the topic. At the end of that time, reread what you have written and identify specific points of view you expressed. Underline or highlight details that you could develop and look at the patterns of development listed in point 2.

   Computers are particularly useful for freewriting activities and for writing first drafts. Your fingers can input information much faster than they can write it, so you are more likely to keep up with your thinking processes.

   b) The second method is to use a "brainstorm circle." Write the title of your focused topic in the centre of the page and, in a circle around the topic, write all the ideas you have about your chosen topic. Do not be concerned about the order of your details.

2. When you have finished listing details, identify those that follow one pattern of development; for example, do some of the details represent

   a) **a sequence of events or instructions?** The main idea in this type of paragraph development should be followed by details arranged in some logical order, either chronological (by date or time) or procedural (step by step).

   b) **reasons, benefits, or negative results?**

Brainstorm Circle

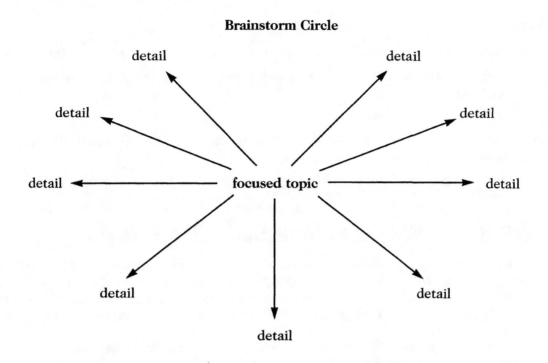

c) **examples or illustrations that explain the main topic**? If you plan to use examples to develop your main-idea sentence, then consider arranging your ideas in order of importance, that is, from least important to most important or from most important to least important. Ensure that your explanation has enough details to make your message clear.

d) **points of comparison or contrast to some other comparable topic**? The main idea can be developed in one of two ways. One approach is to discuss factors of one point and then factors of the other; for example, if you were comparing two types of programs, you might first discuss the requirements, course of study, and employment opportunities for Program A, and then turn to an examination of the requirements, course of study, and employment opportunities for program B. Thus, the pattern following the main idea is XXX YYY. On the other hand, you might choose to discuss the requirements for both Program A and Program B; then the course of study for both programs; and finally the employment opportunities for both. The pattern following the main idea is XY XY XY. This pattern is better suited to longer comparisons of two or three paragraphs.

Choose the pattern of development that best suits both the topic and the piece of writing. Cross out unrelated details and identify any details that support one of the major facts in your chosen development pattern. Now re-examine your topic and the details. Number the details according to importance, order, or natural flow of information; identify those that are related to major details of support, and add other related ideas that will enhance the value of what you intend to say. Some major points may require additional explanation; add the necessary details to make your message clear, complete, and exact. You should plan a minimum of three major details of support for your theme, with at least one major detail expanded by minor points.

● EXERCISE 5.24

1. Refer to your freewriting exercises from the first three units. Highlight, underline, or circle.

   a) Choose one exercise and identify a focused topic and specific details. Arrange these in a brainstorm circle.

   c) Identify a pattern of development.

   b) Choose the related supporting details and number them. Add any details that would complete this discussion.

2. Using either a brainstorm circle or freewriting, brainstorm the focused topics from Exercise 5.23.

III. WRITING A WORKING MAIN-IDEA STATEMENT

After you have established your focused topic, write a main-idea sentence that identifies this focus. Consider composing a "working main idea," one that may not be perfect but is a complete sentence that expresses your overall point of view and gets you started. Identify this statement with the Roman numeral "I." Later in the writing process, you will re-examine the effectiveness of this statement and decide whether to revise it.

Try to make your sentence specific. As you will recall in Unit Two, main-idea sentences frequently suggest how the paragraph will be developed. Review the following explanations.

1. Plural words—such as *many, several, numerous,* etc.—used in the main-idea statement usually suggest that examples or reasons will follow. For example,

   > Most people are aware of the *three basic advantages* of becoming physically fit.

   > Some very interesting *facts* were revealed during the trial.

   > Unfortunately, we encountered a *few problems* during our trip.

2. Clue words such as *story, history, stages, development, steps, process,* and *procedure* all indicate that a particular order or sequence will follow.

   > To appeal a grade, one must follow a specific *procedure.*

   > Performance appraisal is a *four-step process.*

   > The *life history* of the butterfly shows some remarkable changes in this insect.

3. To compare two topics meaningfully, there must be some basis for thinking of them as different. Take, for example, teaching and acting. These professions are very different, but there are some comparable aspects that could be developed into a paragraph or an essay.

4. To contrast two topics meaningfully, there must be some basis for thinking of them as similar. For example, think about business management styles in Canada and Japan. There are common aspects but there are many differences that could be discussed.

5. Comparisons or contrasts are suggested in the main-idea sentence by clue words such as *similar, alike, equal, the same,* or *dissimilar, unalike, opposite, different from,* etc. Make sure your statement is focused; the two topics must have comparable aspects and must be limited to facts that could be meaningfully discussed in one paragraph. There must be common factors between the two topics you have chosen, even if you plan to discuss differences.

   > **Incorrect:** Cook and police officer are different types of careers.

   This topic is too general. With this statement, there is no basis for argument; therefore, with no common elements, you cannot develop ideas for meaningful paragraph development. To arrive at a good main idea for this type of paragraph discussion, ask yourself the following questions:

- Why would the reader need to know the differences or similarities?
- Are there common factors for discussing either comparisons or differences?

Here are some examples of main-idea sentences that suggest that a useful comparison will follow.

To understand the complexity of the situation, the committee listened to *main points of argument* from the two opposing members.

Being a teacher in a class is *similar in many ways* to being a performer in front of an audience.

Parents' and teenagers' viewpoints about present-day issues often *differ*.

6. An explanation may be suggested if you give a definition or use singular terminology; the paagraph development that follows the main idea is a single illustration or story.

Stress is a condition that is characterized by emotional strain or physical discomfort.

To successful business owners, intuition is a natural trait.

7. Try to use specific clue words to identify your pattern of development. However, do not at any time announce your topic by using wordy expressions, such as

I am going to tell you ...

This paragraph is about ...

I am writing to tell you ...

The outlining process so far is as follows:

General Topic ⟶ **Be Specific** ⟶ **Be More Specific** ⟶ **Be Even More Specific** ⟶ **Focused Topic**

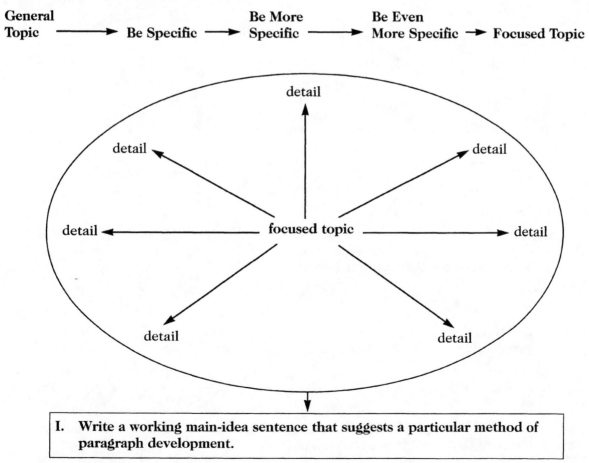

I. **Write a working main-idea sentence that suggests a particular method of paragraph development.**

● **EXERCISE 5.25**

Write a working main-idea sentence for five of your focused topics from Exercise 5.23.

IV. DEVELOPING THE WRITING PLAN

Select your supporting ideas and arrange them in a logical order. Which one should be mentioned first, second, third, etc., to create the best flow of information? You should use point form, not sentences, for these details. Use capital letters to identify each main point, and indent these under your main idea.

Look at the following example of a brainstorm circle:

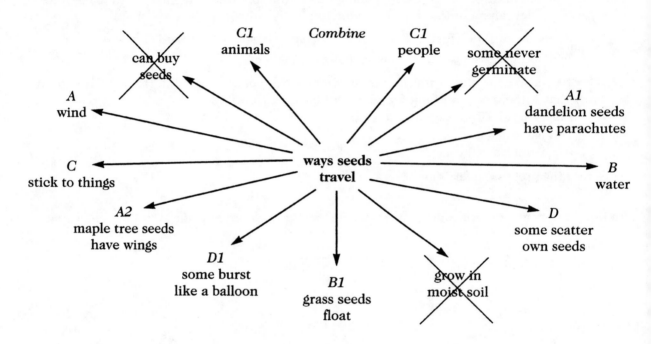

Now, look at the outline plan for this brainstorm circle:

I. There are many ways seeds travel.

    A. wind
       1. dandelion seeds have parachutes
       2. maple tree seeds have wings attached

    B. water
       1. grass seeds float

    C. stick to things
       1. people and animals carry seeds on clothing and fur

    D. some scatter own seeds
       1. seed pods ripen and burst like a balloon

 The special command for "Outline" on your word processor will automatically set up the correct format for your paragraph plan.

V. THE IMPORTANCE OF A CONCLUDING SENTENCE

Although you are still in the planning stage, considering your conclusion, at this point, is just as important as identifying and writing the main-idea statement. All pieces of writing end with a conclusion. Therefore, even if your intended message is only one paragraph, that composition must end with a concluding sentence.

A good concluding sentence relates to the main idea—it does not introduce a new topic. This statement might be advice, a result, a prediction, or a summary that will reinforce your message. Reread your outline and answer the following questions:

1. With all the facts you have given, what advice would you give to someone?

2. What is the outcome of all the given facts?

3. What will happen because of these facts?

4. What can you say after all the points you have made?

Use some of the following clue words to prompt you to formulate good concluding statements:

Therefore,	Because ...
As a result,	Even though ...
And so,	If ...
When ...	Since ...

Since you began this stage with a working main-idea sentence, it is a good idea to write two or three different concluding sentences. Respond to any of the above questions that are appropriate to your discussion.

Here is the sample outline with three possible conclusions:

    I. There are many ways seeds travel. (weak sentence—replace)

        A. wind
            1. dandelion seeds have parachutes
            2. maple tree seeds have wings attached

        B. water
            1. grass seeds float

        C. stick to things
            1. people and animals carry seeds on clothing and fur

        D. some scatter own seeds
            1. seed pods ripen and burst like a balloon

Conclusion 1: Therefore, Mother Nature has interesting ways for seeds to regenerate.

Conclusion 2: And so, if a plant is growing in an unusual place, there are many ways it could have been planted there.

Conclusion 3: Because of their unique methods of reproduction, trees and plants will continue to beautify the earth.

Choose the best two statements from the three concluding statements and your working main idea. Use one for the main-idea sentence (omit words such as *therefore, as a result*, etc.) and the other for the conclusion. Make sure your developing points still follow logically from your new main-idea sentence.

In the seed example, the working main idea is very weak. It should be replaced with any one of the three concluding sentences.

● EXERCISE 5.26

Complete your paragraph plan by composing three possible concluding sentences. Choose the best two for your main-idea and concluding sentences. Recheck your developing points to ensure they still provide the same good flow of ideas, and, if necessary, make appropriate revisions.

● EXERCISE 5.27

This exercise presents four different scrambled paragraph ideas. Follow the directions to create a paragraph plan for each.

a) Choose the topic from the list and number the other details in the most effective order.

b) Add any related facts you can think of or expand on the given ones to make your proposed paragraph interesting to your reader.

c) Compose a working main-idea sentence and arrange the details in an outline format.

d) Compose three possible conclusions for each paragraph plan.

e) For each topic, identify which statement would be the best main idea and which would be the best conclusion.

1. — knock on wood
    — throw salt over shoulder
    — believe in superstitions
    — avoid walking under ladders
    — walk around chair

2. — sitting in the driver's seat
    — getting a beginner's licence
    — taking one of the first steps into the adult world
    — feelings of maturity when driving past friends
    — learning to park the car
    — stopping at the first stoplight
    — being in traffic

3. — close to neighbours
   — likely to be "couch potatoes" once the working day is over
   — differences between urban and rural living
   — family life is often weakened by constant activity and opportunities for individuals to act independently
   — space between neighbours
   — families tend to act as a unit that works and plays together
   — outdoor living is the normal way of life

4. — breathe deeply and relax
   — take lots of showers
   — make the decision to quit
   — eat carrots or celery and chew gum
   — plan what to do with your savings
   — read your list of reasons whenever tempted to smoke
   — ways to quit smoking
   — exercise to relax
   — tell others about your intention to quit
   — replace usual smoking times with another activity
   — throw away lighters and matches
   — put ashtrays away or throw them out
   — save and keep a record of your usual daily cigarette expenses

Check your answers with those in the Answer section at the end of the book.

COLLABORATIVE EXERCISE 5.28

With a partner, decide upon a general topic that you both agree to or choose one of the following topics:

> sports, habits, pets, pollution, health, music

1. Focus the topic for a one-paragraph outline.

2. Brainstorm the topic together. Be sure to include a minimum of three major details with at least one of them developed through minor-point support. (One of your freewriting exercises could serve as the basis of your outline.)

3. Decide the best pattern of development and cross out the details that do not relate to that pattern. Check Section II, "Brainstorming and Choosing Related Facts."

4. Write a working main-idea sentence.

5. Add other major and/or minor details to your brainstorm circle to improve your proposed content.

6. Record this information in outline form so that you can easily see the importance and relevance of the content; your computer may automatically format this information.

   I. Making an outline plan of your proposed paragraph will help you organize your ideas more effectively and make the writing process easier.

      A. write your working main idea as a complete sentence

      B. arrange your details in a clear pattern of development that follows the suggestion of your main idea

      C. review your content and decide if other details should be added

         1. some major details may require additional explanation

         2. these could be expanded into one or more minor details

      D. reread the information as you have recorded it and decide the final arrangement

   Concluding Sentence:

   _____

7. Once you are satisfied with the above results, then, following the suggestions given in this unit, write three possible concluding sentences for this paragraph.

8. Decide upon your final choices for the main idea and conclusion; then check the content to see that the information still flows logically from the beginning to the end.

● EXERCISE 5.29

Now, using the same procedure as given in Exercise 5.28, work individually and compose a suitable outline plan for a topic from the General Topics given below. Remember to write three possible concluding sentences and then make the most effective choices for the main idea and conclusion.

General Topics

- an action or process—indicate a sequence of events or steps
- attitudes—indicate a contrast between your feelings about a certain topic when you were younger and now

- post-secondary education/secondary school education—indicate that certain aspects can be compared
- post-secondary education/secondary school education—indicate that certain aspects can be contrasted
- an irritation—explain a specific one
- an enjoyable recreation—give reasons for liking it
- a procedure for filling out forms or doing a task
- the latest craze—explain a specific one
- an embarrassing moment—describe a specific one

Do not write the paragraph in full! This is only the thinking and planning stage. All that is required is a formal outline of this preliminary step in the writing process.

When you have completed your outline, use the following checklist to ensure that you have the correct format.

❏ The topic is clear and focused.

❏ The main-idea sentence is a complete thought and contains one fact or presents one point of view about the topic. This statement has been identified by a Roman numeral placed at the left-hand margin and not by words.

❏ Major details, written in point form, have been indented under the main idea and identified by capital letters.

❏ Minor points, also written in point form, have been indented under each major detail and identified by Arabic numbers.

❏ The outline ends with a concluding statement (a complete sentence) that can be interchanged with the main idea.

❏ Your work is not only neat and legible but also easy to read for content.

Now discuss your outline with your instructor, who will review your ideas, discuss the organization of your plan, and comment on the quality of your work. With this guidance, make any necessary revisions or improvements.

THE NEXT STEP

If you feel confident about the skills presented in this unit, write the Unit Five Post-Test that follows.

▶ POST-TEST FOR UNIT FIVE

If you feel confident about the skills presented in this unit, complete the following Post-Test. **Do not attempt this test if you have not completed the required work.**

Once you have completed the whole test, check your answers with the suggested ones at the end of this unit. A marking scheme has been provided to give you a realistic idea of your ability in this area. Your goal should be to have no more than two minor errors in each of the spelling and punctuation categories and no more than two major errors in subject-verb agreement.

I. Correct any spelling errors contained in the following paragraph by writing the correction above the misspelled word. Your purpose is to recognize errors in plural forms or confusing pairs of words; therefore, you may use your dictionary as a reference text.

The doctors in the emergency departments of hospitals are often unsung heros [*heroes*] as they deal with many crisises [*crises*] in a single hour; their patience [*patients*] are usually seriously ill or very upset about any one of the tradgedys [*tragedies*], even minor ailmentes [*ailments*], that have caused them to seek assistants [*assistance*]. These physicianes [*physicians*], therefore, must treat both the physical and psychological illness [*illnesses*] of the peoples [*people*] they see and remain "professional" in their attitude, particularly in cases with mans [*men*], womans [*women*], or childs [*children*] requiring only everyday remedys [*remedies*] such as two teaspoonsful of cough medicine. After all, the medical oathes [*oaths*] that the doctors have taken indicate that curing the sicks and caring for mans [*men*] and women are the top prioritys [*priorities*] in their professional careeres [*careers*].

(Deduct one mark for each spelling error.)

TOTAL MARKS FOR SPELLING _____ 4 _____ /10

II.   In each of the following sentences, change the form of the verb to agree in number with the subject. If a sentence is correct, mark it *"Correct."*

  ✓ 1.   Lee and Kim, who are planning to return to school in the fall, has [*have*] applied to several local companies for summer employment opportunities.

  ✗ 2.   Has [*Have*] either of the clerks in the office told you about the changes in the company's dental plan?

  ✗ 3.   What criteria is [*are*] being used to assess the applicants? *Correct*

  ✓ 4.   Because of the fascinating experiment, neither the teacher nor the students was [*were*] aware that it was past four o'clock.

  ✓ 5.   A list of students' names were [*was*] issued to the teacher on the first day of class.

  ✓ 6.   Where is [*are*] the tape and scissors that you borrowed?

  ✓ 7.   The bracelets in the jewellery box belong to Marla and Monica. *Correct*

  ✓ 8.   The colour and style of the couch doesn't [*don't*] suit the living room.

  ✓ 9.   Several hectares of forest was [*were*] destroyed by the fire.

  ✓ 10. Fifty cents or a dollar is all I need to borrow for my coffee break. *Correct*

  ✓ 11. Physics in high school were [*was*] always one of my most difficult subjects because I neither understood nor liked anything to do with science.

  ✓ 12. Are [*Is*] measles prevalent in the elementary school system currently?

  ✓ 13. Is there any correspondence today? *Correct*

  ✓ 14. All I have time for in the morning is [*are*] coffee and a muffin.

  ✓ 15. Each person in the class were [*was*] responsible for presenting two oral presentations during the fall term.

(Deduct one mark for each error.)

TOTAL MARKS FOR GRAMMAR _____ 13 _____ /15

III. Correct the following sentences by adding any necessary commas. If a sentence is correct, mark it "*Correct.*"

1. Wherever Mary went, he was sure to follow!

2. Hoping to get a summer job, Harry made personal calls to several local businesses, applied to all the advertisements in the newspapers, and let everyone know that he was seeking seasonal employment.

3. Nadia had apologized to the members of her committee for her rude behaviour at the meeting, but it did not appear that she was sincere as she acted in the same manner at the next session.

4. If any person wants to be assured of a successful career, all he or she has to do is establish a business that helps people make a lot of money with no risk or shows them how to live longer or teaches them how to appear more attractive and more acceptable to others.

5. Many people strive to live up to someone else's expectations, and never realize that the only person they have to satisfy is themselves and their own personal goals.

6. Andy's wit, charm, good nature, and intelligence made him a popular person and one whom everyone liked and admired.

7. Unfortunately, Eva left her wallet credit cards and driver's licence at home and could not, therefore, pay the bill at the restaurant.

(Deduct one mark for each punctuation error.)

TOTAL MARKS FOR PUNCTUATION _____ 8 /10

IV. The following paragraph contains errors in spelling, grammar, and punctuation discussed in this unit. Proofread the passage and correct the following errors:

3 spelling errors—sp   4 commas needed—p,
4 subject-verb errors—s/v

Music is an integral part of our lives. From the time we are babies, the sounds of melodies, rhythms, and melodious tones ~~has~~ *have* lulled us to sleep or kept us entertained or put us in touch with our feelings. As years pass, music plays a more dominant role in our ~~lifes~~ *lives*. Teenagers' whole world ~~seem~~ *seems* to revolve around this subject, and the focus of their daily actions ~~are~~ *is* usually directed to listening to their musical ~~heros~~ *heroes* on portable radios. Music is just as important to us as adults. Most ceremonies and gatherings are made more meaningful and expressive with the addition of music. A wedding would not be complete without the strains of the bridal ~~marchs~~ *marches*, and even teams in sports ~~is~~ *are* encouraged to victory with the blast from a bugle or the musical chants from an organist's well-timed tunes. Therefore, it would seem that music is an art form that continually satisfies some innate need in every part of our daily existence.

(Deduct one mark for each spelling and punctuation error; deduct two marks for each subject-verb agreement error.)

TOTAL MARKS FOR PROOFREADING _____14_____ /15

V. The following questions are based on the composition skills introduced in this unit.

1. Using the clue words or patterns given in this unit, write main-idea statements that imply the paragraph development for each of the following situations.

Topic—A teacher I have had

a) Write a main-idea sentence that suggests he or she had a particular routine. (sequence or order) *Many times, in the early morning he would be avalible, so that people could get help with there work*

b) Write a main-idea sentence that introduces a description of that person. (explanation)
Despite his rough apperance, he was a nice person.

c) Write a main-idea sentence that compares two teachers who had similar classroom habits. (comparison) *Mr. Blank and Mr. Blank allways taught straight from the textbook.*

d) Write a main-idea sentence that contrasts two teachers who had different classroom habits. (contrast) *Even though Mr. Blank allway taught straight from the text book, Mr. Doe prepared his own material.*

e) Write a main-idea statement that suggests your paragraph will include reasons for your like or dislike of a particular teacher. (examples)
I liked Mr. Blank, he was allways friendly, helpful, and really cared about his students education.

(Deduct two marks for each error.)

TOTAL MARKS FOR MAIN-IDEA STATEMENTS _____ /10

2. Choose the best main-idea sentence from the ones you have written in the previous question; in the space below, construct a one-paragraph outline as instructed:

 a) Use the format presented in this unit.
 b) Use a Roman numeral to indicate the main-idea statement, capital letters to indicate the major details, and Arabic numbers to indicate minor details. (At least one major detail should be developed through minor points.)
 c) End with three possible concluding statements and indicate your choices for the main idea and the conclusion.

I. I liked Mr. Blank, he was allways friendly, helpful, and really cared about his students education

  A. friendly
   1. had a smile every day
   2. told jokes
  B. helpful
  C. carring

Conclusion 1. Therefore, he was a good teacher
   2. And so, he was a good teacher
   3. Because of his characteristics, students will learn from him better.

TOTAL MARKS FOR OUTLINE FORMAT AND CONTENT _____ /15

ANSWERS FOR UNIT FIVE POST-TEST

I. The doctors in the emergency departments of hospitals are often unsung *heroes* as they deal with many *crises* in a single hour; their *patients* are usually seriously ill or very upset about any one of the *tragedies,* even minor *ailments,* that have caused them to seek *assistance.* These *physicians,* therefore, must treat both the physical and psychological *illnesses* of the *people* they see and remain "professional" in their attitude, particularly in cases with *men, women,* or *children* requiring only everyday *remedies* such as two *teaspoonfuls* of cough medicine. After all, the medical *oaths* that the doctors have taken indicate that curing the *sick* and caring for *men* and women are the top *priorities* in their professional *careers.*

II. 1. Lee and Kim, who are planning to return to school in the fall, *have* applied to several local companies for summer employment opportunities.

 2. Has either of the clerks in the office told you about the changes in the company's dental plan? *Correct*

 3. What criteria *are* being used to assess the applicants?

 4. Because of the fascinating experiment, neither the teacher nor the students *were* aware that it was past four o'clock.

5. A list of students' names *was* issued to the teacher on the first day of class.

6. Where *are* the tape and scissors that you borrowed?

7. The bracelets in the jewellery box belong to Marla and Monica. *Correct*

8. The colour and style of the couch *don't* suit the living room.

9. Several hectares of forest *were* destroyed by the fire.

10. Fifty cents or a dollar is all I need to borrow for my coffee break. *Correct*

11. Physics in high school *was* always one of my most difficult subjects because I neither understood nor liked anything to do with science.

12. *Is* measles prevalent in the elementary school system at the present time?

13. Is there any correspondence today? *Correct*

14. All I have time for in the morning *are* coffee and a muffin.

15. Each person in the class *was* responsible for presenting two oral presentations during the fall term.

III. 1. Wherever Mary went, he was sure to follow!

2. Hoping to get a summer job, Harry made personal calls to several local businesses, applied to all the advertisements in the newspapers, and let everyone know that he was seeking seasonal employment.

3. Nadia had apologized to the members of her committee for her rude behaviour at the meeting, but it did not appear that she was sincere as she acted in the same manner at the next session!

4. If any person wants to be assured of a successful career, all he or she has to do is establish a business that helps people make a lot of money with no risk or shows them how to live longer or teaches them how to appear more attractive and more acceptable to others.

5. Many people strive to live up to someone else's expectations and never realize that the only person they have to satisfy is themselves and their own personal goals. *Correct*

6. Andy's wit, charm, good nature, and intelligence made him a popular person and one whom everyone liked and admired.

7. Unfortunately, Eva left her wallet, credit cards, and driver's licence at home and could not, therefore, pay the bill at the restaurant.

IV. Music is an integral part of our lives. From the time we are babies, the sounds of melodies, rhythms, and melodious tones *have* lulled us to sleep **p, s/v** or kept us entertained or put us in touch with our feelings. As years pass, music plays a more dominant role in our *lives.* Teenagers' whole world **sp** *seems* to revolve around this subject, and the focus of their daily actions **s/v p,** *is* usually directed to listening to their musical *heroes* on portable radios. **s/v sp** Music is just as important to us as adults. Most ceremonies and gatherings are made more meaningful and expressive with the addition of music. A wedding would not be complete without the strains of the bridal *marches,* and even teams in sports *are* encouraged to victory with the blast from a **sp p, s/v** bugle or the musical chants from an organist's well-timed tunes. Therefore, it would seem that music is an art form that continually satis- **p,** fies some innate need in every part of our daily existence.

V. You would be wise to have a teacher review your answers to ensure that all the items you have suggested are on topic and in the best order; however, your outline should have the appearance illustrated below.

   I. The main-idea sentence should be identified with a Roman numeral and should discuss the one point of view you are making about your given topic.

      A. first major detail

      B. second major detail

         1. minor point
         2. minor point

      C. third major detail

         1. minor point
         2. minor point

The concluding sentence is in a similar position to that of the main idea, does not mimic the words of your initial statement, and can be interchanged with the main idea.

You may elaborate any or all major details using minor points; the format above is just one of several acceptable patterns.

COMMUNICATING CORRECTLY

 ## OVERVIEW

The *ie* or *ei* principle and confusing words are reviewed in the spelling section of this unit. In the English language, there are so many homonyms, or words that sound very similar, that it is important for you to review all their meanings and spellings. Many will be simple words—but these are the ones most commonly misused or misspelled.

A review of verbs and their uses is presented in the grammar portion of Unit Six. This very important kind of word or word group controls the whole meaning of a sentence. An incorrect verb conveys an incorrect or confusing message. Because verbs and their forms can be complex, you should rely on the dictionary for any necessary information regarding correct spellings and forms. It is necessary for the verb to be correct so that your thoughts will be expressed exactly as you mean them to be.

The next section, on punctuation, involves one additional use of the comma as well as the more common uses of the semicolon. The instruction and practice provided give you the opportunity to build on your knowledge of commas from the previous unit.

Although outlining is reviewed in this section, the main emphasis is upon writing a single paragraph from an approved outline. This organizational task involves most of the skills presented thus far: effective, correct, and varied sentence structure; use of a dictionary and thesaurus to ensure correct spelling and wording; and proofreading skills for spelling, grammar, and punctuation.

LEARNING OBJECTIVES FOR UNIT SIX

Upon completion of this unit, you should be able to:

1. Apply the *ie* or *ei* rule in spelling.

2. Distinguish between and use common homonyms or confusing pairs of words listed in this section.

3. Identify the verb or verb phrase in a sentence.

4. Recall the four main parts of a verb and use them correctly in sentences.

5. Use verb forms and tenses to reflect the correct time frame and the intended message in the sentence.

6. Distinguish between the active and passive voice of verbs and use the appropriate forms in sentences.

7. Correct errors in verb consistency in sentences and paragraphs.

8. Use the correct forms of the confusing verb forms *lie* and *lay*.

9. Apply the following punctuation rules:

    a) Place commas around "extra" information.
    b) Use a semicolon to connect related sentences.
    c) Use a semicolon in a compound sentence when other commas have already been used.

10. Define the terms *unity* and *cohesiveness* as applied to paragraphs.

11. Using focusing, brainstorming techniques, and a writing plan, compose a unified and cohesive paragraph of seven to eleven sentences.

12. Using a dictionary, thesaurus, and cumulative grammar skills, proofread and refine written paragraphs.

Check Internet resources for grammar and composition (see pages 469–70).

PRETEST: SPELLING—WORDS WITH *EI* OR *IE* AND CONFUSING WORDS

Correct any spelling errors in the following sentences. Pay particular attention to words containing *ei* or *ie* and to confusing words. Use a dictionary if in doubt.

1. Because my ~~neice~~ *niece* had been outstanding in her ~~feild~~ *field* of studies, she was chosen to ~~recieve~~ *receive* ~~too sceince~~ *two science* awards.

2. I ~~here~~ *hear* that the ~~personal~~ *personnel* department is planning to ~~precede~~ *proceed* with the hiring of two new ~~prin-ciples~~ *principals* for the vacant positions.

3. ~~Thier~~ **There** was ~~descent~~ **dissent** among the ~~nieghbourhood~~ **neighbourhood** groups about the ~~affects~~ **effects** of the new ~~proceedure~~ **Procedure** to reduce the number of speeders in the suburban area. The construction of speed bumps was to start in the early spring. However, because those living in the small community would be travelling on these roads more often ~~then~~ **than** the late-night speedsters, many people felt that the raised portions of the roads would be more damaging to ~~thier~~ **their** own vehicles.

4. I ~~beleive~~ **believe** that the new legislation has been ~~past~~ **passed**, and there will be workshops and self-paced ~~lessen~~ **Lesson** books in the near future for community members to learn about the new laws.

5. The city ~~counsel~~ **Counsil** members ~~disgust~~ **discussed** the proposed ~~sight~~ **site** for the new casino. ~~They're~~ **There** was a great deal of debating as many didn't ~~no~~ **Know** ~~weather~~ **whether** the downtown area would be preferable to the out-of-town location ~~formally~~ **formerly** ~~choosen~~ **chosen** by the planning committee.

Check your answers with those in the Answer section at the end of the book.

If you made no more than two errors, go on to the Pretest for "Verbs." If you made more than two errors, complete the lessons on the following pages.

SPELLING—WORDS WITH *EI* OR *IE* AND CONFUSING WORDS

I. WORDS WITH *EI* OR *IE*

Nobody can spell perfectly; all of us have some words we have to look up. The trick, of course, is to learn what those words are. If you can't keep the *ei-ie* question straight, just accept the situation, but plan to use your dictionary for all of these words. Sometimes spelling tricks or jingles will help you to remember a correct spelling. For example, this jingle might help you to remember whether to use *ei* or *ie*:

> When said like *me,*
> it's I before E, except after C.

Examples:

believe
field } the sound is like *me*
niece } therefore, it's *i* before *e*

ceiling
receive } the sound is like *me*
conceit } *but* the sound comes after *c*

freight
weight } the sound is not like *me*
forfeit } therefore, it's *not i* before *e*

Exceptions: As with most rules, there are exceptions; but perhaps this little saying will help you to remember these exceptions:

Neither (either) friend seized weird leisure.

● EXERCISE 6.1

Correctly spell the following words by adding *ie* or *ei*.

1. dec _ei_ ve
2. v _ie_ l _ei_
3. h _ie_ r _ei_
4. rec _ei_ pt
5. gr _ie_ f
6. l _ei_ sure
7. sl _ie_ gh _ei_

8. pr _ie_ st
9. bel _ie_ ve
10. _ei_ ght
11. y _ie_ ld
12. n _ei_ ghbour
13. w _ei_ rd
14. p _ie_ rce

15. cash _ie_ r
16. conc _ei_ ted
17. gr _ie_ vous
18. s _ie_ ze _ei_
19. counterf _ei_ t
20. h _ei_ ght

Correct *ie-ei* spelling errors in the following sentences:

21. What a conc _ei_ ted person she is!
22. Th _ei_ r receipts were not in order.
23. Our l _ei_ sure time has greatly increased in the past eight years.
24. My n _ei_ ghbour came from a foreign country.
25. Looking down from such a h _ei_ ght gave me a weird feeling.

Check your answers with those in the Answer section at the end of the book.

II. CONFUSING WORDS

Some words in English are frequently confused because they are similar both in sound and in spelling. A few of the more common words are listed below. To circumvent this kind of spelling problem, review their differences and their uses in each of the examples that follow.

1. **accept, except**
   Accept means to receive something.
   Except means to exclude.

   > She *accepted* the award for best athlete of the year.
   > Everyone, *except* Rod, is planning to attend the meeting.

2. **affect, effect**
   Affect means to influence.
   Effect means the result of an action.

   > The recent problems with nuclear reactors will *affect* the world's energy plans for the future.
   > The *effects* of the radiation leaks on the people in that area will not be known for decades.

   Affected means influenced but can also mean pretentious, or artificial.

   > We were all *affected* by the amount of smoke in the room.
   > Since her trip abroad, she speaks in a very *affected* manner.

   Affective means to do with feelings or emotions.

   > It was an *affective* painting. It appealed strongly to one's emotions.

   Effective means impressive, competent, or effectual.

   > Her presentation was very *effective*; most of the audience showed their interest by asking many questions and requesting further information about her investment proposals.

3. **coarse, course**
   Coarse means rough or crude.
   Course means a direction taken or a series of studies.

   > Using *coarse* language is not an acceptable means of communication.
   > What *course* are you studying at college?

4. **council, counsel, consul**
   Council is a group chosen or elected to act in an advisory capacity.
   Counsel can mean advice or to give advice.
   Consul is a representative or official of a foreign country.

   > The city *council* was often in disagreement about the proposed arts complex.
   > The professor *counselled* the student.
   > When John was wrongly accused in Mexico, the Canadian *consul* assisted him in his efforts to return to Canada.

5. **chose, choose, lose, loose**
   The problem many students have with these words is their pronunciation.
   Chose—rhymes with goes
   Choose—sounds like chews
   Lose—rhymes with booze (It means to mislay or to be defeated.)
   Loose—rhymes with moose (It means free or not tight.)

   > She finally *chose* her wardrobe for the trip.
   > *Choose* your partner for the next dance.
   > Did you *lose* your ticket?
   > Lindsay has a *loose* tooth.

6. **decent, dissent, descent**
   Decent means respectable or proper and right.
   Dissent means disagreement.
   Descent means the act of going down.

   > He had not had a *decent* meal for a week.
   > The *descent* of the cliff was very dangerous.
   > *Dissent* arose among the committee members when some wanted to spend money on the urban renewal plan and others did not.

7. **device, devise, advice, advise, practice, practise**
   The *ice* words are nouns and indicate things:
   Device means apparatus.
   Advice means an opinion.
   Practice means a habitual performance.

   The *ise* words are verbs and indicate action:
   Devise means to plan.
   Advise means to give counsel.
   Practise means to perform.

   > The telephone is a *device* that most people cannot do without!
   > We will have to *devise* a wake-up system for you so you will be on time for class.
   > The police officer *advised* the prisoner of her rights.
   > It is not always easy to follow your parents' *advice*.
   > The choir *practice* will be held every Monday evening.
   > To be a good athlete, you must *practise* every day.

8. **discuss, disgust**
   Discuss means to talk.
   Disgust means to feel or cause one to feel dislike.

   > Because she was politically naive, she did not like to *discuss* politics.
   > His slovenly appearance and poor manners *disgusted* her.

9. **formerly, formally**
   Formerly means previously.
   Formally means properly or ceremoniously.

   > Sara had *formerly* lived in British Columbia.
   > Attendants at a wedding are usually *formally* attired.

10. **fourth, forth**
    Fourth is next after third.
    Forth means forward or onward.

    > On the *fourth* day of Christmas, my true love gave to me four calling birds.
    > You are required to put *forth* a sincere effort this semester.

11. **hear, here**
    Hear means to listen.
    Here means in this place (the opposite of there).

    > I didn't *hear* you come in *here.*

12. **know, no**
    Know means to have information about.
    No is a word used to deny or refuse.

    > I don't *know* the answer to your question.
    > *No,* I won't go.

13. **lesson, lessen**
    Lesson means something learned or studied.
    Lessen means to decrease.

    > Which *lesson* did Marion assign for homework?
    > To *lessen* his discomfort, he took a pain killer.

14. **past, passed**
    Past refers to a time gone by or indicates something is beyond in time, space, amount, or number.
    Passed is one form of the verb *pass* meaning to go beyond or forward or to complete successfully.

    > You cannot change events of the *past.*
    > It is now ten minutes *past* nine.
    > We slowly drove *past* the scene of the accident.
    > That car *passed* me at an excessive rate of speed!
    > Hurray! I *passed* my test.

15. **personal, personnel**
    Personal means private or belonging to oneself.
    Personnel refers to the employees of a company or office.

    > All my *personal* belongings are in my room.
    > I sent my job application to the *personnel* department of the company.

16. **precede, proceed, procedure, proceeds**
    Precede means to go or come before.
    Proceed means to carry on or continue any action.
    Procedure is a particular course of action or business.
    Proceeds are the total amount or the profits derived from a sale or other transaction.

    > Many hours of practice must *precede* the opening night's performance of any opera.
    > If you pass a Pretest, you may *proceed* to the next section.
    > Perhaps he is not following the correct *procedure* in applying for a job?
    > The *proceeds* from the school's fundraising projects were used to help finance the students' educational field trip.

17. **principal, principle**
    Principal means the first or highest in importance, a person of authority, or a capital sum of money.
    Principle is a belief or fundamental rule.

    > My *principal* concern is the economic situation in Canada.
    > In *principle,* his conclusions seem sound.
    > The *principal* of the school was very strict about punctuality and issued detentions to every student who did not have a valid excuse for being late.

18. **right, write, rite**
    Right means correct.
    Write means to record in words.
    Rite means a ceremony.

    > It is not always easy to do the *right* thing.
    > *Write* your compositions legibly.
    > Each society has its own *rites* for special occasions.

19. **sight, site, cite**
    Sight means a view, something worth seeing; ability to see.
    Site means a piece of land or a location.
    Cite means to quote or refer to someone else's work.

    > Travellers who want a carefree holiday usually join a group tour, as they know they will see the important *sights* of foreign places with an expert tour guide.
    > Because of the accident, he lost the *sight* in his left eye.
    > Before construction begins on any *site* in Japan, the owners and builders have a special goodwill ceremony on the property.
    > If you require more instruction or practice with any skill, you can access the recommended web *sites* listed in this text.
    > Writers must be careful to identify others' works that they have *cited* in their essays.

20. **stationary, stationery**
    Stationary means in a fixed position.
    Stationery refers to paper. (Hint: The *er* in paper should remind you of the *er* in stationery.)

    > We could move all the components except the *stationary* ones.
    > Would you reorder *stationery* supplies for our office?

21. **than, then**
    Than is used in comparisons.
    Then means next in order of time or place (it answers the question "When?") and can also mean "as a result."

    > I saw the movie; *then* I read the book to see if the plot and characters were similar.
    > Our English class, *then,* will have to be rescheduled for another day.
    > Allan is taller *than* Dan.

22. **their, there, they're**
    Their indicates ownership.
    There means to or at a place (the opposite of here).
    They're is the abbreviated form of "they are."

    > Bring *their* books over *there.*
    > *They're* busy with their homework.

23. **to, two, too**
    To means in the direction of or can be used with a verb to express its basic form or action (to work, to play, to have, to be).
    Too means also or excessive.
    Two is the number 2.

    > I can drive *to* the college in fifteen minutes.
    > She planned *to go* home after work.
    > I have *too* much homework!
    > Can I come, *too*?
    > *Two* books were missing from my desk.

24. **whether, weather**
    Whether is used to introduce an alternative and could be replaced with *if.*
    Weather refers to climate.

    > I don't know *whether* I'll go or not.
    > People in northwestern Alberta enjoy the sunny summer *weather* for four months of the year.

● EXERCISE 6.2

Make corrections where necessary in the sentences below.

1. My high school ~~principle~~ was a person of ~~principals~~.
2. Of ~~coarse~~, I will need ~~advise~~ on which historic ~~sites~~ I should see on my trip to Singapore.
3. You may ~~precede~~ to the next chapter only after you have ~~past~~ the test for this section.
4. Officials appreciate those who demonstrate ~~dissent~~ manners and follow the accepted ~~precedures~~ when they are ~~formerly~~ introduced at public events.
5. The city ~~counsel~~ met with members of the ~~personal~~ department and ~~disgust~~ the current staffing problems.
6. Often times we can learn valuable ~~lessens~~ from examining the ~~passed~~.
7. Many small companies can be negatively ~~effected~~ by the bad business ~~practises~~ of one major company.
8. Climbers use a special ~~devise~~ to lessen the dangers of coming down a steep ~~decent~~.
9. The mayor, who was ~~formally~~ a high school principal, was very ~~affective~~ in managing city business.

10. You must ~~except~~ [accept] and practice [practise] all the company's ~~principals~~ [principles] if you hope to~~o~~ be promoted.

11. Once the rain had ~~lessoned~~ [lessened], we knew that the worst part of the storm had ~~past~~ [passed]. ✓

12. If you have difficulties in a foreign country, the ~~counsel~~ [consul] for your country will provide you with free advice and assistance. ✓

13. Did you ~~here~~ [hear] if our representative was forth or fifth in the contest?

14. I am not sure ~~weather~~ [whether] this new medicine has the long-lasting ~~affects~~ [effects] I need ~~rite~~ [right] now; perhaps I should ~~chose~~ [choose] the brand that I formerly used. ✓

15. I often end up with more ~~lose~~ [loose] change then I ~~no~~ [know] what to do with. ✓

Check your answers with those in the Answer section at the end of the book.

THE NEXT STEP

If you feel confident about this section, proceed to the Pretest for "Verbs" that follows.

▶ PRETEST: VERBS

This exercise tests your ability to use verbs correctly in sentences; use the dictionary to find the correct verb forms if in doubt. Correct any verb errors in the following sentences.

✓1. I have never ~~rode~~ [ridden] in a smoother riding car than Anton's new Cadillac.

2. If you have a headache, take two aspirins and lie down for a while.

3. Anna has ~~wrote~~ [written] a book about her experiences in the Arctic.

4. During the past week I ~~seen~~ [saw] fifteen reruns on television!

5. He still ~~made~~ [makes] mistakes even though he knows better.

6. ~~Lie~~ [Lay] those books on my desk.

7. I ~~freezed~~ [froze] my fingers trying to get that key into the lock.

8. Ahmed said that he ~~give~~ [gave] you those tickets last Saturday.

9. Ken ran quickly to the end of the dock and ~~jumps~~ [jumped] into the water.

10. Everything Leta told me about the college I [had] heard before.

Check your answers with those in the Answer section at the end of the book.

If you had eight or more sentences correct, proceed to the Pretest for "The Comma and the Semicolon." If you had fewer than eight sentences correct, complete the lessons on the following pages.

VERBS

Three essential parts combine to create a sentence: a **subject, a predicate,** and a **complete message** for the reader. All are important; however, the most important word in the predicate is the **verb.** As you will recall, command sentences are complete with only the verb:

> Listen.

> Stop.

or with only the predicate:

> Watch this experiment.

> Write your name on your test paper.

A command sentence is created by leaving out the subject ("You"), but all sentences must have a complete verb. Without it, the group of words becomes a sentence fragment.

I. IDENTIFYING VERBS

There are basically two kinds of verbs: one describes an action—either physical or mental—and the other describes a state of existence or condition.

A. ACTION AND NON-ACTION VERBS

Action verbs are self-explanatory because they name the activity, either physical or mental, that is happening or has happened.

> Every day, she *runs* for thirty minutes before breakfast.

> I *laughed* at his story.

> I *knew* the answer to your question.

A non-action verb relates the subject to the word or word group that follows the verb. This "linking" verb names or describes the subject.

> We *are* students.

> The sky *is* blue today.

The following are the most common non-action verbs:

- all forms of the verb *to be*:

     am, is, are, was, were, be, being

- any verb that can be replaced by a form of the verb *to be* without changing the meaning of the sentence, such as:

     appear, seem, become, remain, look, taste, smell, sound, feel

In the following examples, each of the verbs could be replaced by *is* or *are* without changing the meaning of the sentence.

     She *appeared* happy to see us.

     The students *became* quiet when the teacher entered the room.

● EXERCISE 6.3

Underline all the verbs in the following exercise and describe them as ACTION or NON-ACTION.

1. She biked to the station and then caught the train.
2. Our team played very well but it lost the game.
3. Because Janice wrote the best essay, she won the contest.
4. Black coffee tastes bitter; I put sugar and cream in mine.
5. He became the class president because most students believed that he was the best leader and they voted for him.

Check your answers with those in the Answer section at the end of the book.

B. VERB PHRASES

Often, the main verb requires additional helping verbs to convey the correct intent or time (present, past, future) of the sentence.

     Rosa *should have arrived* early this morning.

(The verb indicates the possibility of a past action.)

     Rosa *will arrive* early tomorrow morning.

(The verb indicates that the action will happen in the future.)

The group of words that describes the time and/or the intent of the whole verb is called a *verb phrase*. All the words in the verb phrase are necessary to convey the correct meaning but the last verb in the phrase is the main verb.

Following is a list of the most common *helping verbs*:

am	shall	might	can
is	will	could	do
are	has	would	does
was	have	should	did
were	had	may	
be		must	
been			

You will note that some of the verbs listed as helpers can also be used as main verbs. To determine the function of the verb, look at its position. It is the main verb if it is used alone or if it is the last verb in the group.

Look at the following examples:

helpers   main

You *should be spending* more time on your assignments.

helpers   main

I *should have called* you earlier.

helper   main

They *must be* on time for that appointment.

● EXERCISE 6.4

Underline the helping verb in each of the following sentences. Put two lines under the main verb.

1. You must have met Franco before you left the party.

2. I could have been here earlier but I woke up late this morning.

3. I may leave before you arrive at the office because I feel ill.

4. I think Ann might have gone to the movies, but you can ask her best friend if she knows where Ann has gone.

5. If I had known you were coming here, I would have prepared something special.

Check your answers with those in the Answer section at the end of the book.

Verb phrases can be interrupted by other words. If your sentence is in mixed order, other parts of the subject or predicate may divide the verb phrase. If you cannot identify the verb, mentally place the sentence in natural order to make the verb phrase come together.

subject

helper │ main

When *will* you *learn* the rules of the game?

subject

helpers ╱ main

Have you *been going* to aerobics classes for a long time?

Descriptive words can also divide the words in the verb phrase. Look at the following examples:

descriptive word

helper │ main

I *will* never *finish* this book.

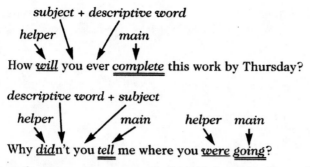

How *will* you ever *complete* this work by Thursday?

Why *did*n't you *tell* me where you *were going*?

Words such as *not, never, ever, always* describe a condition and are not part of the verb phrase. *Not* in its abbreviated form is often attached to the verb, such as did*n't* (did not), does*n't* (does not), could*n't* (could not), etc.

● EXERCISE 6.5

Underline the verb or verb phrase in each of the following sentences. Put two lines under the main verb.

1. You might have met Juan before.
2. Why do you bite your nails?
3. With luck, I will have finished this project by the end of the month.
4. Were you studying in the library last night?
5. I am not leaving until four o'clock.
6. May I go home now?
7. Why don't you ever listen to instructions?
8. You shouldn't have asked her for money.
9. You must have been working very late last night.
10. Students are always complaining about their homework.

Check your answers with those in the Answer section at the end of the book.

II. VERB TENSES

Verbs, as you know, are used alone or in combination to express various times or actions. Note the different messages conveyed by altering only the verb in the following statements in the "verb time line."

Each verb has four main parts to help express these various time changes. You can easily find these forms in your dictionary under the "root verb" (to + verb identifies the root verb—to laugh, to swim, to drive).

THE VERB TIME LINE

Past		
	I had walked home.	This action is not only over but it preceded another action in the past.
	I walked home.	This action has taken place and was completed sometime in the past.
	I have walked home.	1. This action may have just been completed. *OR* 2. The action may have begun in the past but is continuing. I have walked home from work for the last ten days.

Present		
	I am walking home.	This action is currently taking place or will take place soon.
	I walk home.	This action is a fact of the present time.

Future		
	I will be walking home.	This action is about to take place sometime in the near future.
	I will walk home.	This action will take place sometime in the future.

Regular verbs have few changes in their various forms and really do not cause too many problems. Following are the four main parts of a verb:

Present (the form of the verb used in the present tense)	Past (the form used to indicate simple past)	Past Participle (one form of the verb that requires a helper)	Present Participle (the "root verb" + *ing* always requires a helper)
no helper used	no helper used	form used with helper	form used with helper
walk	walked	walked	walking
call	called	called	calling

As you can see, regular verbs have the same past form and past participle form.

Irregular verbs are often used incorrectly because their forms change in each tense. Note the following examples:

Present	Past	Past Participle	Present Participle
no helper used	no helper used	form used with helper	form used with helper
sing	sang	sung	singing
drive	drove	driven	driving
go	went	gone	going
have	had	had	having

As you use each irregular verb, confirm the spelling or form you are using by consulting your dictionary.

According to the dictionary, the four principal parts of the verb *to write* are as follows:

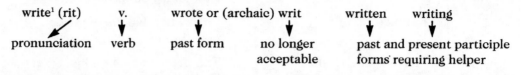

Therefore, the four principal parts of the verb *to write* are *write, wrote, written, writing*. Remember that, if two forms are given for either the past or the past participle, the first form stated is the preferred form.

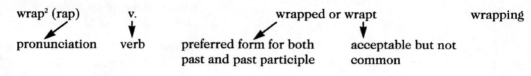

● EXERCISE 6.6

Write the four principal parts of the following verbs. (Use a dictionary if necessary.)

1. bite
2. forget
3. bring
4. drink
5. drown
6. sweep
7. swear
8. break
9. freeze
10. choose

Check your answers with those in the Answer section at the end of the book.

On the following page is a list of some of the irregular verbs you should master.

Present	Past	Past Participle	Present Participle
no helper used	no helper used	as a verb, always preceded by helper(s)	as a verb, always preceded by helper(s)
become	became	become	becoming
begin	began	begun	beginning
break	broke	broken	breaking
buy	bought	bought	buying
catch	caught	caught	catching
choose	chose	chosen	choosing
come	came	come	coming
do	did	done	doing
draw	drew	drawn	drawing
drink	drank	drunk	drinking
drive	drove	driven	driving
eat	ate	eaten	eating
fall	fell	fallen	falling
fight	fought	fought	fighting
fly	flew	flown	flying
get	got	got/gotten	getting
give	gave	given	giving
go	went	gone	going
grow	grew	grown	growing
have/has	had	had	having
hear	heard	heard	hearing
know	knew	known	knowing
lead	led	led	leading
lend	lent	lent	lending
lose	lost	lost	losing
make	made	made	making
pay	paid	paid	paying
ride	rode	ridden	riding
run	ran	run	running
say	said	said	saying
see	saw	seen	seeing
sing	sang	sung	singing
speak	spoke	spoken	speaking
spend	spent	spent	spending
steal	stole	stolen	stealing
take	took	taken	taking
teach	taught	taught	teaching
think	thought	thought	thinking
throw	threw	thrown	throwing
wear	wore	worn	wearing
write	wrote	written	writing

In its function as a main verb, the verb *to be* presents the most changes in form:

am/is/are	was/were	been	being

● EXERCISE 6.7

Use the correct form of the verb to suit the meaning of the sentence. If necessary, use your dictionary.

1. When I was young, I (drink) ___drank___ four glasses of milk a day.

2. Last week, we (make) ___made___ our vacation plans, (choose) ___chose___ our destination, and (pay) ___payld___ for our airline tickets.

3. We had (begin) ___begyan___ to worry about Rita because she was so late getting home from school.

4. It was reported in the paper that the police had (catch) ___caught___ the person who had (steal) ___stolen___ the car.

5. Last Christmas, we (buy) ___bought___ too many gifts and (spend) ___spent___ too much money.

6. What the secretary had (do) ___done___ with the documents no one (know) ___~~knows~~ knew___, but we all remembered that the manager had (bring) ___brought___ them to the office and had (give) ___given___ them to her.

7. The student (say) ___said___ that she had (forget) ___forgotten___ her report at home.

8. Yesterday, we (drive) ___drove___ to the site of the accident and (see) ___saw___ _____ where the bus had (run) ___rahn run___ off the road.

9. He (become) ___became___ a teacher many years ago and has always (teach) ___taught___ at that school.

Check your answers with those in the Answer section at the end of the book.

Note the obvious verb errors in the following examples:

Example 1:

incorrect verb
↓
Ajay has ate the whole pie!

The verb is incorrect because the simple past form of the verb has been used with a helper. If you intend to indicate the simple past, then no helper is required. However, if you intend a different time (past, present, or future), you must use the proper past participle form.

Corrected versions:

simple past
↙
Ajay ate the whole pie!

OR

Ajay has eaten the whole pie!
↗
correct past participle form

Example 2:

no such word

Anthea brung all her books to class.

There is no such word as "brung." Check the root verb in the dictionary (to bring); there you will find *bring, brought, bringing*. Therefore, the correct verb is *brought* for either the simple past or the past participle form.

Corrected versions:

simple past

Anthea brought all her books to class.

OR

Anthea has brought all her books to class.

correct past participle form

● EXERCISE 6.8

Correct verb errors in the following sentences. (Use a dictionary if necessary.) Keep verbs in the past tenses.

1. Maria ~~begun~~ began to wonder if she would ever finish this course.

2. Last year Jake and Andy had done a lot to improve school spirit.

3. Have you ever ~~drove~~ driven on the super expressway?

4. Have you ever ~~ate~~ eaten in the cafeteria on the second floor?

5. I opened the door and two wasps ~~flied~~ flew in.

6. The train had just ~~went~~ gone before I arrived at the station.

7. Barb ~~seen~~ saw that movie last Saturday.

8. Mr. West has often ~~spoke~~ spoken to the students about their tardiness.

9. She ~~sweared~~ swore that she wasn't guilty.

10. Have you ~~wrote~~ written to your parents yet?

11. By mid-term, Sam knew he had ~~choosen~~ chosen the wrong program.

12. I ~~seen~~ saw a full moon last night.

13. We had never ~~ate~~ eaten such a big meal!

14. Mika ~~brang~~ brought her lunch to school every day.

15. Unfortunately, their mother had ~~forgot~~ forgotten her cheque book at home.

Check your answers with those in the Answer section at the end of the book.

III. ACTIVE VOICE/PASSIVE VOICE

Some sentences can be written in two ways—in the **active voice** or in the **passive voice**. Active voice means that a sentence has been worded in a direct way and the subject is performing the action of the verb.

> I baked a cake yesterday.

The subject (I) is performing an action (baked) which is received by an object (a cake).

Writers use the active voice to convey clearly worded messages. There are fewer misunderstandings with this kind of sentence structure. The passive voice, on the other hand, means that the writer has changed the sentence pattern.

> The cake was baked (by me) yesterday.

Here, the subject (The cake) is the recipient of the action (was baked). The actual doer of the action (me) is placed in a phrase after the verb, or is dropped altogether.

The passive voice is a useful form of sentence if identifying the actual doer of the statement is not of great importance.

> **Passive:** This house has not been sold yet.
>
> **Active:** (The agent) has not sold this house yet.

This is a statement of fact, and it is not necessary to identify *who* has not sold the house. Notice that the verb in the passive voice always requires helpers to communicate whether the action takes place in the past, the present, or the future.

The passive voice is also useful if you want to emphasize the object of the action by placing it first.

> **Passive:** The movie *Gone With the Wind* has been acclaimed by millions over the years as a masterpiece.
>
> **Active:** Over the years, millions have acclaimed the movie *Gone With the Wind* as a masterpiece.

It is obvious in the first sentence that the writer wants to emphasize the movie. Therefore, the passive voice is appropriate, although the active voice could also be used.

However, the passive voice structure often creates awkward, vague, or grammatically incorrect sentences. Avoid the following kinds of errors:

> **Passive (awkward):** Scholarships were awarded by various organizations to worthy students.
>
> **Active (improved):** Various organizations awarded scholarships to worthy students.
>
> **Passive (vague):** Efforts to reduce pollution in the lakes have been increased.

Note that no subject has been specified; we do not know who will carry out the stated activity.

> **Active (clearer):** Factories surrounding the lake have increased their efforts to reduce pollution.
>
> **Passive (incorrect):** By studying the committee's recommendations, new policies were established by the board members.

The use of the passive voice in this sentence has created a grammatical error called a *dangling modifier*; that is, there is no word close by for the introductory word group (*By studying the committee's recommendations*) to describe. The structure makes it sound as if the *new policies* did the studying instead of the board members. This is a major grammatical error!

> **Active (corrected):** By studying the committee's recommendations, the board members established new policies.

Note that *studying* is now closer to the group who performed that action.

● EXERCISE 6.9

Improve the quality and clarity of each of the following sentences by rewriting them and changing the verbs from passive to active voice. If necessary, add an appropriate "doer" of the action.

1. The red fox was being chased across the field by the dog.
   The dog chased the red fox across the field.

2. Approval was given for us to add an attached apartment to our suburban home.
   Approval was given by city hall for us to add an attached apartment to our suburban home.

3. After examining the tiny holes in the ceiling of our cottage, a squirrel was discovered to be the culprit who had resided in our summer home during the winter.
   I discovered that a squirrel was the culprit

4. By placing butterfly appliqués over the holes, the ceiling was cleverly and inexpensively repaired.
   By placing butterfly appliques over the holes, we cleverly and inexpensively repaired the ceiling

5. The assignments were completed by the students.
   The students completed the assignments.

6. Permission was given to the student to delay payment of his tuition fees.
   The student got permission to delay his tuition fees payments

7. An error has obviously been made in calculating your grade for the mid-term test.
   I made an error in calculating your grade for the mid-term test.

8. In readiness for the tournament, the broken benches were repaired by the maintenance crew.
   In readiness for the tournament, the maintenance crew repaired the broken benches

9. Information about the new divorce laws will be circulated to all lawyers in the near future.
   I will circulate information about the new divorce laws to all lawyers in the near future

10. After a harried day of housework, shopping, and cranky kids, the children were put to bed early.
    After a harried day of housework, shopping, and cranky kids, I put the children to bed early

Check your answers with those in the Answer section at the end of the book.

It is important for you to recognize sentences written in the passive voice. Because of the number of errors that can easily be committed with this type of sentence structure, use it only when you know that

1. the subject is clearly understood or is not important, or

2. the emphasis in the sentence needs to be on the result rather than on the subject.

● EXERCISE 6.10

Correct or improve the quality of the sentences in the following exercise by rewriting them and changing verbs to either active or passive voice. You may need to combine some sentences; others may be correct as they are. If a sentence is correct, mark it "*Correct.*"

1. We were informed by the chairperson that the meeting would be postponed to next Monday.

2. Everyone had already begun to prepare for the major convention to be held next year.

3. Several homes were broken into during the summer and many valuable articles and pieces of jewellery were taken. It is suspected by the police that these crimes were committed by the same group of thieves.

4. The tragic explosion of the *Challenger* space shuttle was witnessed by millions who were watching the launch on television.

5. By recognizing your most common errors and correcting them, your written work can be improved.

6. Many buildings in the city were built at the turn of the century.

7. In the fall, recommendations for new and exciting activities will be submitted to the student council for the upcoming school year.

8. The answers to the test questions were given to the students by the professor.

9. Tired and frustrated, the student's project was finally completed at four o'clock in the morning.

10. Unfortunately, an error has been made in your bank statement and the matter will be investigated and corrected as soon as possible.

Check your answers with those in the Answer section at the end of the book.

IV. CONSISTENCY IN TENSE

To be consistent and correct in your written work, don't shift tenses in your sentences or in your paragraphs without good reason.

NOTE: Remember that singular verbs in the present tense end with s—she writes.

Incorrect:

He sat down at his desk and begins to write.

past tense   *present tense*

Correct this sentence in either of the following ways:

He sits down at his desk and begins to write.

both verbs in the present

OR

He sat down at his desk and began to write.

both verbs in the past

● EXERCISE 6.11

Correct the verb tense errors in the following sentences.

1. He smokes cigarettes even though he ~~knows~~ *knew* they weren't healthy for him. ✓

2. Terry says that he ~~needed~~ *needs* more time to think about his answer. ✓

3. When I stepped off the curb yesterday, I ~~twist~~ *twisted* my ankle and fell on the pavement.

4. Mr. Marco glared at me for a while before he ~~reprimands~~ *reprimanded* me.

5. Marina always consults a dictionary when she ~~didn't~~ *doesn't* know how to spell a word.

6. Occasionally our family prefers to go out for Sunday brunch at a nice restaurant because the prices ~~were~~ *are* usually reasonable and the food selection is excellent.

7. After the holiday weekend, traffic usually is very heavy; as a result, there ~~were~~ *are* several accidents.

8. Yesterday Joe left quickly and ~~drives~~ *drove* home.

9. After the teacher had scolded little Johnny, he ~~runned~~ *ran* home.

10. The roof leaks so he ~~repaired~~ *repairs* it.

The roof leaked so he repaired it

11. Last summer, we often sat around our camp fires and ~~sing~~ *sang* songs.

12. I planned to leave as soon as I'~~am~~ *was* ready.

13. As soon as the sun shines, the children ~~ran~~ *run* outside to play.

14. Amina found that working after school is difficult, but she made the extra money because she ~~needs~~ *needed* it to continue her studies.

15. Rosa was nervous every time she writes an exam; but as soon as she reads the paper over and ~~jotted~~ *jots* down a few notes, she usually gains her confidence and ~~lost~~ *loses* her jitters.

Check your answers with those in the Answer section at the end of the book.

V. "3-D" VERBS

We usually write about events that have already happened. To indicate that two events have occurred in the past but that one has happened before the other, use *had* and the past participle form of the verb to describe the first event. The following sentence is incorrect:

> She suddenly *realized* that she *locked* her keys in the car.

Two events have occurred in the past; however, she locked the car first and *realized* second. Therefore, the corrected sentence should read:

> She suddenly *realized* that she *had locked* her keys in the car.

This principle gives the correct "3-D" interpretation to your expression.

● EXERCISE 6.12

Correct the verb tenses (create the "3-D effect") in the following sentences.

1. I realized I ~~was~~ wrong.
   had been

2. Miguel knew he met Catrin somewhere before.
   had

3. By the time the police arrived, the vandals disappeared.
   had

4. Johanna phoned home to find out if her parcel arrived.
   had

5. I answered the phone but the caller hung up.
   had

6. They drove past the place where the accident happened.
   had

7. When all the lights went out, we thought that we blew a fuse.
   blown / had

8. We heard on the radio that the rock concert ~~was~~ cancelled.
   had been

9. Because Ricardo ~~drank~~ too much, his friend drove him home.
   had drunk

10. I was sure that he heard that story before.
    had

11. They ~~drove~~ for miles before they finally found a gas station.
    had driven   had

12. What she did in the past ~~was~~ soon forgotten.
    had done   had   been

13. After Mike carefully considered his answer, he wrote down his response to the question.
    had

14. Robin left as soon as she completed her work. /
had

15. We just finished dinner when we received the news.
had   had

Check your answers with those in the Answer section at the end of the book.

VI. CONFUSING VERBS—*LIE* AND *LAY*

Lie and lay are two verbs that have similar verb forms but very different meanings. Locate these verbs in your dictionary and record their principal parts. Read and record the usage note given with the verb *to lie*.

Root Verb	Present	Past	Past Participle	Present Participle
to lie v. (meaning to rest or recline)				
to lay v. (meaning to place or put an object)				

An easy way of determining the proper form to use in a sentence is to replace lie or lay with the suitable dictionary definition: *rest* or *recline* for *lie*, and *place* or *put* for *lay*.

> Marga had a headache so she decided to _____ down for awhile.
> (recline—the verb is *lie*)

> Zoe had _____ the keys on the table before she left.
> (placed—the correct verb is *laid*—past participle form)

● EXERCISE 6.13

Write the correct form of *lie* or *lay* in each of the following sentences. You may wish to mentally substitute the dictionary definitions to help you make the correct choice.

1. You should not have _____ your junk by the door.

2. Because he enjoys the "soaps," he _____ on the chesterfield every afternoon to watch them.

3. Who has _____ that rotten apple on my desk?

4. The village _____ to the north of Tokyo.

5. Christian was really tanned because he had been _____ on the beaches of Florida for the past two weeks.

6. Roberta said that she had _____ her report on your desk.

7. The installers were really efficient; they _____ the living room carpet in an hour.

8. Those clothes have _____ on the floor for a whole week!

9. The chairperson _____ great emphasis on the need for complete cooperation from all the committee members.

10. When I last saw Yvonne, she was _____ on the sundeck trying to get a tan.

Check your answers with those in the Answer section at the end of the book.

THE NEXT STEP

If you feel confident about this section of work, proceed to the Pretest for "The Comma and the Semicolon."

PRETEST: THE COMMA AND THE SEMICOLON

This exercise tests your ability to use commas to set off "extra" information and to use a semicolon correctly between separate related sentences and in compound sentences. Insert commas and semicolons where necessary in the following sentences.

1. The amount of time a lawyer must spend on your case of course determines his or her fee.

2. If you are going to Spain, take only the necessary items leave all your heavy clothing at home.

3. After trying to contact the sales representative all morning I left a message with his secretary he would she assured me return my call before closing time.

4. All those who are interested in drama should plan to attend the Drama Festival in May.

5. Poor organizational ability incidentally is almost always revealed in your essays poorly written essays however are not always the result of poor organization.

6. Our representative Mr. Pierre Dionne will call on you tomorrow.

7. Nicole a very good friend of mine wants me to go to Paris next spring but I am hesitant about committing myself because of the devalued dollar.

8. Marina was thrilled with her birthday gift a diamond dinner ring!

9. I hate to think of that embarrassing incident I just wish everyone would forget it!

10. Javed spent his last loonie on a cup of coffee as a result he had to walk home.

Check your answers with those in the Answer section at the end of the book.

If you had eight or more sentences correct, write the Unit Six Post-Test. If you had fewer than eight sentences correct, complete the lessons on the following pages.

The Comma and the Semicolon

I. Additional Use of the Comma

In the previous unit, you learned that commas are used

1. before a joining word in a compound sentence,

2. after an introductory word or group of words, and

3. between elements of a series.

There is one more use of a comma that you should know:

4. Use commas around "extra" information in a sentence. What is extra information? Any word or group of words that can be omitted from a sentence without destroying its basic meaning is extra. Some examples follow:

> Ganesh, *the boy next door,* graduated from high school last year.

Note the commas around the words *the boy next door.* These words give extra information about Ganesh and could be omitted without destroying the basic message of the sentence.

> Have you met Mr. Smith, *our new English teacher?*

Our new English teacher is added information to the question; therefore, use a comma before that group of words. No comma is required at the end because the question mark acts as the end punctuation.

> Their house, *which overlooks the lake,* is completely modern.

Which overlooks the lake is added information to the main sentence and could be omitted without destroying the basic meaning of the sentence.

> Some of the contestants, *unaccustomed to running long distances,* fell behind in the race.

Unaccustomed to running long distances is added information.

> This is, *in my opinion,* an excellent book.

In my opinion is an added comment and could be omitted.

How can you distinguish between relevant and extra information in a sentence? The following examples show the difference.

> Anyone wishing to join the Theatre Arts Club should go to Room 176 at 4:00 p.m.

The phrase *wishing to join the Theatre Arts Club* is essential to the meaning of the sentence and cannot be omitted without changing the meaning; therefore, do not use commas.

> All peaches that are bruised should be thrown in the garbage.

The words *that are bruised* cannot be omitted from the sentence without changing the meaning; therefore, do not use commas.

> Any plant that is well nourished and cared for will bloom for years.

All plants will not bloom for years; therefore, the clause is relevant.

> All passengers with children under the age of twelve will board the aircraft first.

Everyone will not board first; therefore, the clause is relevant.

● Exercise 6.14

Use commas around extra information in the following sentences.

1. Our manager, who has just returned from a month-long vacation, plans to hire two new sales representatives.

2. Niagara Falls, a famous tourist attraction, was one of the places we planned to visit.

3. Sylvie would be surprised, as a matter of fact, to learn that her birthday present has been in her closet for a month.

4. For dinner, we are having cheesecake, my favourite dessert.

5. Anyone who doesn't follow these instructions, will probably make a mistake.

6. Shanthi's office, the one at the end of the hall, contains most of the books you are looking for.

7. Most students, who plan their work carefully, have no problems completing assignments on schedule.

8. Maggie and Kirise, who are bridge fanatics, will compete in the International Bridge Tournament.

9. We must, on the other hand, consider an alternative solution to that problem.

10. Carlo, who used to work in this department, is now a pilot for a wealthy business owner.

11. The old bank building, which had been built in 1910, was demolished this year as part of the city's renovation program.

12. This new plan, however, will not be implemented until the new year.

13. Police have the right to remove the licence plates from all vehicles that do not pass the safety check.

14. The winner of the lottery, we were surprised to learn, had also won a sizable amount of money just three months ago!

15. Students who concentrate on their studies usually get excellent grades.

Check your answers with those in the Answer section at the end of the book.

II. THE SEMICOLON (;)

The semicolon has three uses.

A. It is used between related sentences that are not joined by a conjunction such as *and, but, or.*

> The telephone rang continually; no one answered it.
>
> The travel plans were made; our suitcases were packed; we were finally on our way to Hawaii.

The second sentence will often begin with an introductory word such as *however, consequently, nevertheless, unfortunately, therefore,* etc. In such cases, you must use a semicolon at the end of the first sentence and a comma after the introductory word.

> Her assignment was turned in on time; however, it was very poorly prepared.
>
> He missed several weeks of classes; consequently, he did not qualify for a time extension in that course.

The semicolon is similar to a period, but it has the added advantage of allowing a flow of thought between the sentences. Notice how the examples seem easier to read without the sudden interruption of a period and a capital letter between the related sentences.

● EXERCISE 6.15

Using the above rules for semicolons, punctuate the following sentences.

1. I was really impressed by that production of *Carmen*; however, I thought that some of the sets could have been improved.

2. Skiing can be a very dangerous sport; during our winter season; the hospitals report more incidents of broken bones and torn ligaments than at any other time of year.

3. Honestly, I just don't know how I am going to cope with this problem; I hope you can give me some advice.

4. In Canada, we travelled to Vancouver by train; travelling through the Prairie provinces and the Rocky Mountains was an unforgettable experience.

5. When you finish your assignment, you may leave; however, don't forget to proofread your work before submitting it to me for marking.

Check your answers with those in the Answer section at the end of the book.

B. The semicolon may also be used in a compound sentence if commas have been used in other parts of the sentence.

NOTE: A compound sentence is two or more complete thoughts joined by *and, but, or.* (See Unit Four for review.)

> Although we had taken every precaution against any invaders, the skunks found their way under our cottage; and in their own special way, the little critters let us know that they were there!
>
> When you leave, please lock both the front and back doors; and don't forget to take your keys with you.
>
> The design of the Toronto SkyDome is hard to explain; but if you can visualize a large eye open to the sky with a sectional eyelid that opens and closes, you will have a general idea of its appearance.

C. **The semicolon is also used to separate major items in a series that already contains other commas.**

> The newly elected officers for the coming year are Joan Brown, president; Roger Smith, vice-president; and Jacob Wojtecka, secretary-treasurer.

> If you are considering a trip to a foreign country, you must plan ahead by checking any visa requirements; ensuring your passport is in order; and, if necessary, having the required vaccinations.

● EXERCISE 6.16

Note the commas in the following sentences and add semicolons where needed.

1. When he was younger, he always made excuses for being late but those excuses are just not acceptable today.

2. They had no immediate plans to sell their home but if someone offered them a good price, I am sure they would not hesitate to move.

3. What you do with your time is your own business but if your plans interfere with mine, then I will complain.

4. Her new job as marketing representative for the company involved her travelling twice a year to Tokyo, Japan Seoul, Korea Brisbane, Australia and Hong Kong.

5. When financial cutbacks were announced, the manager quickly called a meeting of all the department heads and together they explored various ways to readjust the budget for the coming year.

Check your answers with those in the Answer section at the end of the book.

● EXERCISE 6.17—REVIEW

Using all the rules for the use of commas and semicolons presented in this chapter, punctuate the following sentences.

1. She finished her dinner quickly then she left the room without saying a word to anyone.

2. Many novels today unfortunately have boring story lines after reading a few chapters the average reader can recognize the same old plot because just the characters and the location have been changed.

3. When the rains came the planned events for the day had to be cancelled however the committee rescheduled them for the following Sunday.

4. In my spare time I like watching movies especially the classics listening to music in the winter skiing and in the summer playing tennis.

5. Some people welcome opportunities others are afraid to risk the chance of change.

Check your answers with those in the Answer section at the end of the book.

THE NEXT STEP

If you feel confident about this section, write the Unit Six Post-Test on the following pages.

POST-TEST FOR UNIT SIX

If you feel confident about the skills presented in this unit, complete the Post-Test that follows. **Do not attempt this test if you have not completed the required work.**

Once you have completed the whole test, check your answers with the suggested ones at the end of this unit. A marking scheme has been provided to give you a realistic idea of your ability in this area. Your goal should be to have no more than two minor errors in each of the spelling and punctuation categories and no more than two major errors in verbs or verb tenses.

I. Correct any spelling errors contained in the following sentences by writing the correction above the misspelled word. You may use your dictionary as a reference text.

1. I believe the ~~personal~~ *personnel* department has the right to ~~chose~~ *choose* between the two candidates. *(believe)*

2. An employee, who was ~~formally~~ *formerly* with our science department, developed a ~~devise~~ *device* that will reduce the amount of dust in the air.

3. See your student ~~councellor~~ *counsellor* for some good advice about which ~~coarses~~ *courses* are better for you to take then *(than)* others.

4. ~~Niether~~ *Neither* the cashier nor my ~~freind~~ *friend* saw the thief ~~sieze~~ *seize* the daily cash ~~reciepts~~ *receipts* that had been left on the side counter.

5. Some people's ~~practise~~ *practice* of using rude and ~~coarse~~ *course* language as a natural part of ~~thier~~ *their* daily communication with others really ~~disgusts~~ me. *(disgusts)*

(Deduct one mark for each spelling error.)

TOTAL MARKS FOR SPELLING _____8_____ /10

II. Correct any verb or verb form errors in the following sentences. If a sentence is correct as it appears, mark it "*Correct.*" There may be more than one verb error in a sentence or there may be an error with active or passive voice. Rewrite any sentence that cannot be corrected in the space above the error. You may use your dictionary as a reference text.

1. Omar says that he ~~seen~~ *saw* you in Ottawa just last week.

2. Kelly used both the school and the public libraries for her research projects, as she ~~needs~~ *needed* the different reference materials that both offer.

3. The patient was instructed by the psychiatrist to lay on the couch and talk.
   The psychiatrist instructed the patients to lay on the couch and talk.

4. If you had ~~went~~ *gone* downtown, you would have ~~sawn~~ *seen* the display of new cars along the main street.

5. The report will be brung to you as soon as I have wrote it.
   I will bring you the report as soon as I write it.

6. The teenager ~~sweared~~ *swore* that he had not ~~drank~~ *drunk* for several hours before he had ~~drove~~ *driven* his car.

7. If I had a chest cold, my grandmother would tell me to ~~lay~~ *lie* down and ~~lie~~ *lay* a hot mustard plaster on my chest. *Correct*

8. I called home to see if my mail ~~arrived~~ *had* yet.

(Deduct one mark for each verb error.)

TOTAL MARKS FOR GRAMMAR _____12_____ /15

III. Punctuate the following sentences correctly using commas and semicolons as they are discussed in this unit. If a sentence is correct as it appears, mark it *"Correct."*

1. Students who need special assistance should meet with the counsellors in the lecture hall at four o'clock.

2. Japanese tourists have recently discovered that Banff is a perfect location for a western holiday; in fact some couples travel to this city for their wedding ceremony and then honeymoon in the many beautiful surrounding areas.

3. During our final year in high school, Philip was the candidate voted most likely to succeed in his chosen career, and it was not surprising, therefore, to learn that he had become a self-made millionnaire before he had reached the age of thirty.

4. Pickering, a town about forty kilometres outside of Toronto, was the site that had been chosen for the new international airport; however, the public vetoed the idea because the plan would destroy thousands of hectares of valuable farmland in one of Canada's few remaining "green belts."

(Deduct one mark for each punctuation error.)

TOTAL MARKS FOR PUNCTUATION _____9_____ /10

IV. The following selection contains errors in spelling, grammar, and punctuation discussed in this unit. Proofread the passage, correct the listed errors, and make any additional changes resulting from your corrections.

3 spelling errors—sp   2 sets of commas needed—p,

4 verb errors—v   2 semicolons needed—p;

Terry Fox is a Canadian hero. When he was just a teenager, he lost a leg to cancer. However, he was extremely courageous and decided to raise money for cancer research by attempting to run across Canada, one of the biggest countries in the world.

Throughout his life, Terry Fox always fought to be the best at whatever he attempted. Even as a youngster, he played many sports and, as a result of his determination, excelled in all of them. This early trait of coarse, illustrates the strong will and motivation that were evident in Terry's "Marathon of Hope." Initially, most people did not know who he was or what he hoped to acheive by running across Canada but as his dream became publicized through the various media, gradually more support and financial backing was provided by the Canadian people in the provinces he had visited. Terry's main purposes were to make Canadians more aware of the need for cancer research and to raise the necessary money so that others could be spared the pain and hardships that he endured in passed years; these unselfish goals remained the same throughout his run. Although Terry's journey ended near Thunder Bay, he not only done what he had set out to do, but also became a hero and a legend in his short lifetime.

(Deduct one mark for each spelling and punctuation error; deduct two marks for each verb error)

TOTAL MARKS FOR PROOFREADING _____10_____ /15

Answers are on the following pages.

ANSWERS FOR UNIT SIX POST-TEST

I. 1. I *believe* the *personnel* department has the right to *choose* between the two candidates.

   2. An employee, who was *formerly* with our science department, developed a *device* that will reduce the amount of dust in the air.

   3. See your student *counsellor* for some good advice about which *courses* are better for you to take *than* others.

   4. *Neither* the cashier nor my *friend* saw the thief *seize* the daily cash *receipts* that had been left on the side counter.

   5. Some people's *practice* of using rude and *coarse* language as a natural part of *their* daily communication with others really *disgusts* me.

II. 1. a) Omar *said* that he *had seen* you in Ottawa just last week.

   b) Omar *says* that he *saw* you in Ottawa just last week.

   2. a) Kelly *used* both the school and the public libraries for her research projects, as she *needed* the different reference materials that both *offered*.

   b) Kelly *uses* both the school and the public libraries for her research projects, as she *needs* the different reference materials that both *offer*.

   3. REWRITE: The psychiatrist instructed the patient to lie on the couch and talk. (active voice required)

   4. If you had *gone* downtown, you would have *seen* the display of new cars along the main street.

   5. REWRITE: I will bring you the report as soon as I have written it. (active voice required)

   6. The teenager *swore* that he had not *drunk* for several hours before he had *driven* his car.

   7. If I had a chest cold, my grandmother would tell me to *lie* down and *lay* a hot mustard plaster on my chest.

   8. I called home to see if my mail *had arrived* yet.

III. 1. Students who need special assistance should meet with the counsellors in the lecture hall at four o'clock. *Correct*

   2. Japanese tourists have recently discovered that Banff is a perfect location for a western holiday; in fact, some couples travel to this city for their wedding ceremony and then honeymoon in the many beautiful surrounding areas.

   3. During our final year in high school, Philip was the candidate voted most likely to succeed in his chosen career; and it was not surprising, therefore, to learn that he had become a self-made millionnaire before he had reached the age of thirty.

   4. Pickering, a town about forty kilometres outside of Toronto, was the site that had been chosen for the new international airport; however, the public vetoed the idea because the plan would destroy thousands of hectares of valuable farmland in one of Canada's few remaining "green belts."

IV. Terry Fox is a Canadian hero. When he was just a teenager, he lost a leg to cancer. However, he was extremely courageous and decided to raise money for cancer research by attempting to run across Canada, one of the biggest countries in the world.

   Throughout his life, Terry Fox always fought to be the best at whatever   **p,**
he attempted. Even as a youngster, he played many sports and, as a result of   **p, p, sp p, v**
his determination, excelled in all of them. This early trait, of *course, illus-*
trated the strong will and motivation that were evident in Terry's "Marathon
of Hope." Initially, most people did not know who he was or what he hoped
to *achieve* by running across Canada; but as his dream became publicized   **sp p;**
through the various media, *gradually the Canadian people in the provinces*   **v**
he had visited provided more support and financial backing. Terry's main
purposes were to make Canadians more aware of the need for cancer
research and to raise the necessary money so that others could be spared
the pain and hardships that he *had endured* in *past* years; these unselfish   **v sp p;**
goals remained the same throughout his run. Although Terry's journey
ended near Thunder Bay, he not only *did* what he had set out to do but also   **v**
became a hero and a legend in his short lifetime.

Proceed to the composition section of this unit, "Writing a Single Paragraph."

UNIT SIX COMPOSITION SKILLS:
WRITING A SINGLE PARAGRAPH

In this section, you will learn how to write a unified and cohesive paragraph from an approved outline. There is **no** Pretest. This is a separate assignment that you can complete before or after the Unit Six Post-Test.

Unity and coherence are the two essential elements of a good paragraph. If you keep these words in mind and apply the word construction skills you learned in Unit One, you should have a clear understanding of what is expected of you in this section.

I. PARAGRAPH UNITY

A paragraph must be unified. Unified begins with the prefix *uni*, meaning one; therefore, your paragraph must contain a main-idea sentence and supporting details that discuss *one* point of view. If you have focused your topic and developed an outline using the method suggested in Unit Five, then you have already taken the first step towards making your paragraph unified.

A paragraph can be compared to an ordinary sandwich. The main-idea sentence and the concluding sentence have the same functions as the two pieces of bread; they must hold the paragraph together. The supporting details, on the other hand, are the filling; they should be substantial enough to create a complete and satisfying "meal" for your reader. Study the following example:

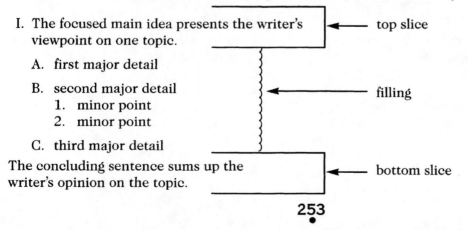

I. The focused main idea presents the writer's viewpoint on one topic. ←— top slice

   A. first major detail

   B. second major detail
      1. minor point ←— filling
      2. minor point

   C. third major detail

The concluding sentence sums up the writer's opinion on the topic. ←— bottom slice

Two slices of bread are required to make a sandwich; similarly, both a main-idea sentence and a concluding sentence are required to convey a complete message. The main idea must state the fact or opinion you are planning to discuss; the concluding statement should summarize your information or give advice or re-emphasize the purpose expressed in the main idea. Often these two statements can be interchanged.

When you are preparing a sandwich, fillings must be carefully considered; only ingredients that blend well together will produce an edible meal. Supporting details must be given the same consideration; a sufficient number of relevant ideas must be logically arranged to create a unified and complete paragraph.

Because this one paragraph is complete in itself, it needs an ending to let your readers know that "this is all there is!" Your conclusion is the "bottom slice of bread" that holds the paragraph together. If you have difficulty ending your work, use one of the following clue words to help you think of the most appropriate ending.

Therefore ..., As a result ..., And so ..., When ..., Because ..., Even though ..., If ..., Since ...

TEST FOR UNITY

Once you have established your paragraph plan with all the required elements, then test your ideas for unity by interchanging the main-idea and concluding sentences. Do all your details still logically follow?

Look at the following example from Unit Five.

I. If a plant is growing in an unusual place, there are many ways it could have been planted there.

  A. wind
    1. dandelion seeds have parachutes
    2. maple tree seeds have wings attached

  B. water
    1. grass seeds float

  C. stick to things
    1. people and animals carry seeds on clothing and fur

  D. some scatter own seeds
    1. seed pods ripen and burst like a balloon

Therefore, Mother Nature has some interesting ways for seeds to regenerate.

OR

Because of these unique methods of reproduction, trees and plants will continue to beautify the earth.

I. Mother Nature has some interesting ways for seeds to regenerate.

  A. wind
    1. dandelion seeds have parachutes
    2. maple tree seeds have wings attached

  B. water
    1. grass seeds float

  C. stick to things
    1. people and animals carry seeds on clothing and fur

  D. some scatter own seeds
    1. seed pods ripen and burst like a balloon

And so, if a plant is growing in an unusual place, there are many ways it could have been planted there.

EXERCISE 6.18

Unscramble the following details into one-paragraph outlines.

a) In each question, choose the one detail that would make a focused main idea and write an initial statement.

b) Eliminate two irrelevant details that would disrupt paragraph unity.

c) In a logical order, arrange the remaining details into major and minor points of your outline.

d) Write three concluding sentences for each outline plan and choose the two most effective ones for the main-idea and concluding statements of your final draft.

1. — additional frustrations of learning mathematics
   — learn another's culture and values
   — expand your mental capacity
   — history and geography
   — requires too much study time
   — people and traditions
   — educational value of studying a foreign language
   — can communicate with others
   — often a basis for vocabulary in your own language
   — better understand your own language
   — learn grammar and sentence patterns
   — learn about another country

2.   — wear eye-catching clothes
     — study and imitate the winning characteristics of popular sports broadcasters
     — be humble
     — be argumentative
     — show favouritism
     — speak in a monotone
     — loud sports jackets
     — cultivate a distinctive way of speaking
     — wear unusual ties
     — nasal whine
     — wear conservative suits
     — odd colour combinations
     — have strong opinions
     — use sports "lingo"
     — use aggressive voice

Check your answers with those in the Answer section at the end of the book.

II. PARAGRAPH COHERENCE

A paragraph must be coherent. The term *coherent* contains the prefix *co-*, meaning *together*, and the Latin word *haerere* meaning *stick*; therefore, the term coherent indicates that the sentences in your paragraph must "stick together." To achieve this, you must use transitional (linking) words to connect ideas together to indicate the relevance of and relationship between one point and another or between a point and the main idea. Using these guide words will help the reader follow your message.

TRANSITIONAL EXPRESSIONS

1. *To indicate an additional point*, you could use

      also, in addition, equally important, another, as well as, not only ... but also, besides, in addition to, furthermore, together with

2. *To indicate an example*, you could use

> for instance, for example, to illustrate, some, other, one, another

3. *To indicate a sequence*, you could use

> first, second, next, last, finally, then, currently, now, in the past, in the future, after a few days/hours/minutes, etc., before, after, soon

4. *To indicate a similar idea*, you could use

> similarly, in the same manner, in comparison, likewise, identical/identically, equal/equally, equivalent

5. *To indicate a contrasting idea*, you could use

> however, on the other hand, but, on the contrary, although this may be true ..., conversely, not the same, different, opposite, the reverse, unequal, in spite of, differ from

Be careful not to rely solely on these words to create the flow of ideas; varied sentence structure is equally important. To check your writing for effective and varied sentence structure, look for the following signals that indicate your writing needs revision:

- short, choppy sentences
- repetitious sentence patterns (e.g., a series of sentences that follow the subject/predicate pattern)
- vague terms such as *it* and *this*
- word repetition

Another element in paragraph cohesiveness is sentence variety. Varied sentence patterns and lengths often make the difference between a simplistic message and one that sounds professional. Look at the following paragraph, taken from the Unit Four Post-Test. Although the writer has included many good ideas, they are not effectively presented and do not have the professional tone expected of a college or university graduate.

> Leukemia is a cancer. It affects the blood-forming organs of the body. It can affect people of different ethnic groups and people of all ages. There is no cure for this disease. Treatments prolong life expectancy. There are many drugs and doses to treat leukemia. Persons are usually hospitalized for initial assessment and treatment. Once remission is achieved, they can usually live comfortably at home. They should be careful to avoid persons who may transmit infections. Infections are the prime cause of death in leukemia victims.

Now read the revised edition of this same paragraph. Although the vocabulary has remained almost the same, sentences have been combined in varied lengths and patterns. This simple editing has made the difference between a weakly worded passage that might be acceptable in junior high school and one that could be part of a college or university term paper.

> Leukemia, a cancer which affects the blood-forming organs of the body, can affect people of different ages and ethnic groups. Even though there is no cure for this dreaded disease, the life expectancy of diagnosed victims can be prolonged by medication. Those afflicted are usually hospitalized for initial assessment and treatment; however, once remission occurs, they can usually live comfortably at home. Because infections are the prime cause of death, leukemia victims should be careful to avoid persons who may transmit any viruses.

THE IMPORTANCE OF REVISION

You will probably not achieve perfect unity and cohesiveness in your first draft of a paragraph. In fact, most writers must produce more than one draft before they are satisfied with the final product. Be prepared to spend more time revising and polishing your work than you do in getting the first draft written. If possible, it is a good idea to set your work aside, at least overnight, before you begin to revise. When you look at it again, you will be better able to judge the quality of the writing.

If the first draft of your paragraph contains vague terms such as *it* or *this*, short, choppy sentences, or repetitious sentence patterns, use underlining and sentence combining skills to improve the tone and quality of your work. Also look for words or word phrases that could be replaced with more suitable choices. As you will recall from Unit Four, the thesaurus is an excellent reference text that contains hundreds of synonyms and antonyms to help you avoid word repetition, simplistic vocabulary, unnecessary negative words, or colloquial expressions. Use this book to improve your wording in any writing assignment; however, be sure that the replacement word you choose is one that you are familiar with. Remember that not all of the listed words given for a particular meaning will suit the context of your message.

● EXERCISE 6.19

1. Use your thesaurus to replace the italicized words with more effective ones.

2. Rewrite the following paragraph and make it more coherent by following the directions given in the margin. Use the most appropriate transitional phrases or the sentence-refining techniques discussed in Unit Four.

(1) Jobs are *hard to find.* (2) There is limited room for people to drift from one employer to another until they land in a position they like.

> Join sentences (1) and (2) to create a main idea that focuses on the limited room for people to move from job to job.

(3) *Learning on the job* may be the only exception. (4) It is essentially a form of education in a working environment. (5) On-the-job training alone is rarely *enough* for one to *get* a well-paying job offering scope for personal growth.

> Use a transition to join sentences (3), (4), (5), and relate this combined statement to the main idea.

(6) Employers are now demanding prior schooling. (7) Child care workers, ambulance attendants, retail clerks are all expected to have completed a course in a community college before they start work.

> Use a transition to relate sentence (7) to sentence (6).

(8) Even where on-the-job training is *okay,* employers tend to prefer the *person who applies for the job* with the better general education.

> Note the pattern of the paragraph and use a suitable transition to link sentence (8) to the paragraph.

(9) Recruits for most Canadian police forces are required to have completed Grade Twelve. (10) Fire departments require recruits to have Grade Twelve too.

> Combine sentences (9) and (10) and use a transition to relate this combined idea to the paragraph.

(11) Employers quite logically assume that a person who has 12 years or more of schooling is a harder and more intelligent worker than one who has only 10 years or fewer.

> Use a transition to show that sentence (11) is the concluding sentence.

Check your answer with the one suggested in the Answer section at the end of the book.

● EXERCISE 6.20

Use the editing skills you learned above to improve the quality and coherence of the following first draft of a composition.

> Many people believe that dreams have hidden meanings. Dream books provide interpretations. They are one source that people use to decode dreams. These books tell what dreams mean by attaching meanings to the occurrences in dreams. They also may give meanings to the symbols involved in dreams. A trip on a bus may mean that the "dreamer" is trying to fit in with a group. This person might secretly want to be accepted. A mountain may mean that the dreamer is exaggerating problems. Different books, however, may provide different answers. There is no guarantee of the trustworthiness of the books. Perhaps, then, dream interpretation is purely wishful thinking. It may also just be a justification for an action that the dreamer wants to take.

III. WRITING FROM AN OUTLINE

Study the following sample outlines and corresponding written paragraphs. In each case, note the use of transitional expressions, varied sentence structure, and appropriate words.

A. BASIC OUTLINE

Topic — Planning a report (developed by examples)

I.   In planning a report, one must give serious thought and consideration to the needs and temperament of the person for whom it is being prepared.
    A. all details included
    B. only concise well-documented deductions
    C. supportive statistical data
    D. no tables, graphs, or statistics

Therefore, considering the audience's needs is an integral part of any report writer's task and is often just as important as gathering the facts.

       In planning a report, one must give serious thought to the needs and temperament of the person for whom it is being prepared. *Some* people want all details carefully and completely explained. *Others, however,* prefer concise well-documented deductions. *On the other hand, many* employers demand tables and graphs that clearly and succinctly present all the information at a glance. *And still, there are those* who would "run a mile" from a report that contained any vestige of statistical data. *Therefore,* considering the audience's needs is an integral part of any report writer's task and is often just as important as gathering the facts.[1]

Notice the italicized clue words within the paragraph that help the reader follow the writer's plan. They clearly identify the four details the writer wants to communicate.

    Often, you will need to provide additional information to make your message exact, clear, and complete. Note how the basic outline given above can be expanded by providing necessary information for some of the major details.

B. Expanded Outline

In the expanded outline that follows, note that each major detail has been developed with additional points the writer wants to include in the message. By taking time to further explain or describe each major detail, the author makes the message crystal clear.

I. In planning a report, one must give serious thought to the needs and temperament of the person for whom it is being prepared.

   A. all details included
      1. essential background information
      2. facts as well as figures
      3. all evidence and research

   B. only concise well-documented deductions
      1. no patience with lengthy, wordy reports
      2. recommendations first
      3. evidence in appendices

   C. supportive statistical data
      1. "a picture is worth a thousand words"
      2. figures more meaningful

   D. no tables, graphs, or statistics
      1. impatience with confusing data
      2. misinterpretations

Therefore, considering the audience's needs is an integral part of any report writer's task and is often just as important as gathering the facts.

Read the suggested written version that follows. You should still clearly see the four major details; however, you should also have a clearer understanding of the topic.

> In planning a report, one must give serious thought to the needs and temperament of the person for whom it is being prepared. Some people want all details carefully and completely explained. Because they insist on knowing all the circumstances surrounding the issue, background information is essential. Not only do they expect to see facts and figures detailed for every aspect of the report, they also want the option of examining all the evidence and research. Others, however, prefer concise well-documented deductions. These employers lose patience if they are presented with lengthy and wordy reports. They want clear-cut conclusions and recommendations placed at the beginning of the report and do not wish to wade through obvious data. If evidence is part of the document, they expect to see that data in the appendices contained at the back of the report. On the other hand, many employers demand tables and graphs that clearly and succinctly present all information at a glance. To them, "a picture is worth a thousand words." Figures offer a more meaningful and relevant description of a situation than the clutter of words. And still, there are others who would "run a mile" from a report that contained any vestige of statistical data. They find numbers confusing and also claim that figures can be manipulated to support a viewpoint, even one that is inaccurate! Therefore, considering the audience is an integral part of any report writer's task and is often just as important as gathering the facts.[2]

C. Narrative Outline

Topic—Buffy, our family dog (developed by examples)

I Buffy, our family dog, is almost human in her behaviour.   **main-idea sentence**

  A. hides and sulks if spoken to crossly
     1. refuses to acknowledge you

  B. likes to be the centre of attention   **major details give examples**
     1. chases her tail   **of human activities**
     2. throws her ball in the air

  C. is very possessive   **minor details demonstrate**
     1. well-hidden bones   **specific situations**
     2. favourite chair

  D. receives mail addressed to her (from vet)
     1. looks at us intently, perks up ears, and understands
     2. begins to quiver in anticipated fear

And so, Buffy plays a very convincing role and has at least some people believing that she is a person and not just a canine!

The final draft of the above outline might look as follows:

Buffy, our family dog, is almost human in her behaviour. *For instance,* if you speak crossly to her, she runs to her bed and sulks.   ◄——— **Indent first sentence.**

She refuses even to look at you until she knows you are no longer   ◄——— **Use suitable linking words**

angry. *Also,* she likes to be the centre of attention. If no one   **to add more meaning.**

notices her, she chases her tail or throws her ball until, once again,   ◄——— **Use linking words to**

she has recaptured her audience. Her possessiveness is her worst   **help reader see your**

fault. She growls *ferociously* and bares her teeth if anyone tries to   **organization.**

take her well-hidden bones or attempts to sit in her favourite chair.   ◄——— **Use dictionary to spell**

She even receives letters from the veterinarian reminding her that   **words correctly.**

it is time to get her vaccination. As we read the letter addressed to

"Dear Buffy," she looks at us intently, perks up her ears in under-

standing, and begins to quiver in anticipated fear. And so, Buffy   **Recopy concluding state-**

plays a very convincing role and has at least some people believing   **ment as last sentence.**

that she is a person and not just a *canine*!   ◄——— **Use thesaurus to avoid**
                                             simple word repetition.

 ## Collaborative Exercise 6.21

Work in groups of three or four to develop a common outline for a one-paragraph composition. Choose one of the topics listed below.

Fears or phobias	Book/books	Bad habit/habits
Diets	Mistakes	Television
Friends	Family customs	Tradition/traditions
Hobbies	Values	A routine/process/procedure
Music	Stress	Recreation

1. After the group members agree on the common topic, then each member is responsible for contributing to and recording the group's suggestions for content in the appropriate format (e.g., focused topic, brainstorm circle, and outline).

2. Once the group has generated sufficient ideas, then decide the best pattern of development and eliminate details that do not relate to that focus.

3. Add any other major and minor details to improve the proposed content.

4. Together, write a working main-idea sentence.

5. Together, organize the details in correct outline format.

6. Together, review proposed content and add any other needed major or minor details to complete the ideas.

7. Together, write three concluding sentences and decide on the best choices for the main idea and concluding sentences.

8. Now, each member should have a copy of the suggested outline from the group's efforts.

9. The group should split up; and each member, working individually, should write his or her own unified and cohesive paragraph based on this one common outline.

10. Once all have completed the writing task, the group should reconvene, compare their written paragraphs, and exchange ideas on the effectiveness and cohesiveness of each other's work.

● EXERCISE 6.22

Now, using the same procedure, choose another topic from the ones listed in Exercise 6.21 and work individually to write a unified and cohesive paragraph based on a developed outline.

Use the following instructions to complete the planning stages in the writing process.

1. Consider these different methods of paragraph development for your chosen topic.

   a) Describe a sequence of events or routine. *(sequence)*
   b) Write a description or explanation. *(explanation)*
   c) Compare the topic to something similar. *(comparison)*
   d) Present a contrast between two different things. *(contrast)*
   e) Give reasons or examples. *(examples or reasons)*

2. Since each of these topics is much too general for meaningful discussion, focus the topic to suit a specific theme you want to develop as well as to correspond to the length of your assignment, in this case, one paragraph of seven to eleven sentences. If necessary, refer to Unit Five, "Outlining," for the correct method.

3. Brainstorm your chosen topic by freewriting or by using a brainstorm circle. Write down all the related facts you can think of about your focused topic.

4. Consider the best theme to follow and the most effective type of paragraph development.

5. Write a working main-idea sentence that encompasses all aspects of your theme. Identify this statement with a Roman numeral.

6. Look at your list of brainstorming facts. Cross out the irrelevant ones; choose the major facts and number them in logical order; indicate any minor points that would provide additional support for any of your chosen major details. Finally, add any other details—either major or minor—that would improve your message.

7. Arrange your chosen details in outline style. Use capital letters (A, B, C) to identify the major details and Arabic numbers (1, 2, 3) to indicate minor ones. Use the outline format; if necessary, refer to the sample outlines.

8. Reread your theme and your supporting evidence. Write three concluding sentences; choose the two strongest statements to replace the working main idea (if that expressed statement is weak) and to conclude your message. You should write these three statements after you have written your outline. Consider the following points:

   a) What advice could you give someone?
   b) What prediction can you make?
   c) What can you conclude or what is the result?
   d) What can you restate (using different wording) or summarize?

9. Test paragraph unity by replacing the working main idea with each of your concluding statements. Information will flow naturally if the statement and the details have the same focus. Choose the two strongest statements from all the ones you have written (including the working main idea) and use one for the main-idea sentence and one for the conclusion.

10. Make any necessary revisions in the order and content of your proposed paragraph. Your message should have a logical and natural flow of meaningful information.

Now, write your paragraph using the outline as your guide. If you follow your outline plan, then you can be fairly sure that your paragraph will demonstrate unity, and that all facts are relevant to the main idea of the paragraph. However, to ensure that your paragraph is coherent (that there is a "good flow" to your message), bear these considerations in mind as you write:

1. Use varied sentence lengths and patterns.

2. Use meaningful and varied linking words to join your major details or to indicate minor points.

3. Use the thesaurus to improve the vocabulary level and tone.

Using the online thesaurus is very convenient and may provide the variety of synonyms or antonyms that you need. Check for this feature under the heading "Tools."

4. Edit your work for coherence; revise by combining sentences, avoiding word repetition, and choosing effective vocabulary words. (Refer to Unit Four for directions on sentence-combining skills and on using the thesaurus.)

5. Proofread your work for mechanical errors.

Most computers have an online grammar check program that is useful in pointing out the kinds of errors that can slip past a spell-checker because the misspelled word happens to be in the dictionary. It also alerts you to mistakes or typing errors that have created run-on sentences, subject-verb errors, overuse of words and phrases, etc. Check for this feature under the heading "Tools."

For any composition you are submitting for marking, you must clearly indent the paragraph and double-space your final draft.

Your completed paragraph should be seven to eleven sentences long. When this assignment is completed, you may follow the same procedure with a different method of development for the same topic or another one from the list.

When you have completed the required number of assignments, you may proceed to Unit Seven. Use the evaluation form on the following page to assess your paragraph.

IV. PARAGRAPH EVALUATION

Critically assess both the strong and weak characteristics of your writing by placing a check mark in the appropriate column of the following evaluation form.

I. CONTENT MERIT

Excellent	Good	Weak	
			UNITY
_____	_____	_____	1. clearly focused and effectively worded main idea
_____	_____	_____	2. details follow one pattern of development
_____	_____	_____	3. logical order of content
_____	_____	_____	4. details are specific as opposed to vague or too general
_____	_____	_____	5. adequate coverage of topic
_____	_____	_____	6. irrelevant details excluded
_____	_____	_____	7. sound and effectively worded concluding sentence
			COHERENCE
_____	_____	_____	8. effective transition phrases used to create good flow of ideas
_____	_____	_____	9. good sentence variety (length and pattern)
_____	_____	_____	10. effective word usage
			STRUCTURE
_____	_____	_____	11. appropriate length
_____	_____	_____	12. correct paragraph format

MERIT SCORE: Circle the most appropriate score for your written work.

100   95   90   85   80   75   70   65   60   55   50   45   40   less than 40

II. TECHNICAL ERRORS

Mechanical errors reduce the quality of your writing. Your paragraph is considered weak if you have made more than two major errors and/or more than two minor errors in the same category.

1. Proofread for and correct the following types of major errors in your paragraph. (Deduct two marks from your merit score for each error made in this category.)

_____	sentence fragments (frag)	_____	faulty verb tenses (vt)
_____	run-on sentences (ro)	_____	sentence structure (ss)
_____	subject-verb agreement (sv)	_____	other

2. Proofread for and correct the following types of minor errors in your paragraph. (Deduct one mark from your merit score for each error made in this category.)

_____	incorrect spelling (sp)	_____	semicolon error (p;)
_____	misuse of words (m/w)	_____	comma error (p,)
_____	word omission (w/o)	_____	unnecessary punctuation (p)
_____	faulty end punctuation(p?)	_____	other

NET WORTH OF WRITTEN ASSIGNMENT = Merit score – Technical errors = _____

If you have excellent content and relatively few errors, you have made a communication link with your reader. Your written message has effectively and efficiently transmitted your thought processes. This is a valuable skill—one that all employers search for in their prospective employees. Therefore, strive for perfection in this area. Note your areas of weakness and try to make improvements in your next writing activity.

WRITING MORE SKILLFULLY

 ## OVERVIEW

Unit Seven reviews spelling rules regarding the doubling of a final consonant before a suffix. Once again, the dictionary is recommended as a main reference text.

To avoid word repetition, writers must use pronouns to refer to people, places, things, or ideas they wish to discuss. Although many technical rules govern the uses of these words, the logical and nongrammatical explanations presented in this unit should help you to use pronouns correctly by applying simple reasoning as well as by relying on grammar learned in previous units. In addition, prepositions are reviewed. Included are confusing pairs as well as specific commonly misused prepositional words.

The punctuation section deals with using apostrophes for possessive forms and contractions.

The composition section focuses on a two-paragraph theme and outline. Emphasis is placed on thesis statements, transitional expressions, paragraph development, and concluding statements. Skills already presented—effective, correct, and varied sentence structure; using a dictionary and thesaurus for correct spelling and wording; proofreading skills for spelling, grammar, and punctuation—are reinforced.

LEARNING OBJECTIVES FOR UNIT SEVEN

Upon completion of this unit, you should be able to:

1. Apply rules for doubling or not doubling the final consonant of a word before adding a suffix.

2. Correct errors in pronoun usage and reference.

3. Determine the correct use of confusing pairs of prepositions and of commonly misused prepositional terms.

4. Use apostrophes correctly in the following circumstances:

   a) to indicate ownership
   b) to form a contraction

5. Compose a thesis statement and an introductory sentence for a two-paragraph composition.

6. Construct a two-paragraph outline using both the composition skills presented in Units Five and Six and the following new skills:

   a) writing a main-idea sentence as the second sentence of a paragraph
   b) using appropriate transitional words within and between paragraphs
   c) editing for consistent pronoun focus
   d) composing effective concluding sentences for a two-paragraph composition

7. Using the above skills, write a unified and coherent composition of two paragraphs.

8. Use the Fog Index to assess the readability and suitability of your composition for an intended audience.

9. Using a dictionary, thesaurus, and cumulative grammar skills, proofread and refine your written work.

Check Internet resources for further help with grammar and composition (see pages 469–70).

PRETEST: SPELLING—
FINAL CONSONANTS

Add the suggested suffixes to the words in parentheses. This exercise tests your knowledge of when to double final consonants.

1. What is your (prefer + ence)—tea or coffee?
   preference

2. We planned to attend the (confer + ence) and discuss the (recur + ing) problem that faced us every year. *conference* *recurring*

3. The (plan + ing) (commit + ee) (develop + ed) the policy for (admit + ions).
   ✗ *planning* *committee* *developed* ~~admittions~~ *admissions*

4. I am (begin + ing) to understand this work.
   beginning

5. The employer (prefer + ed) to check the applicants' (refer + ences).
   preferred *references*

6. The two leaders (concur + ed) that both (govern + ments) would have to set aside their (differ + ences) and work together to control any future (develop + ment) of nuclear arms in order to reduce the danger of nuclear warfare that would destroy the world.
   concurred, governments differences, development

7. My request for new (equip + ment) was (refer + ed) to the purchase officer who (control + ed) all business expenses.
   ✗ *equipment, ~~refered~~, controlled, referred*

8. (Cancel + tions) for our banquet reservations will not be (accept + ed) on the day of the event; therefore, money has to be (budget + ed) for people who may not honour their (commit + ments).
   cancellations, accepted, budgeted, commitments

Check your answers with those in the Answer section at the end of the book.

If you had eighteen or more words spelled correctly, proceed to the Pretest for "Pronouns and Prepositions." If you had fewer than eighteen words spelled correctly, complete the lessons on the following pages.

SPELLING–
FINAL CONSONANTS

Many people have difficulty determining if a word has double letters or not (two "t's" or one, two "r's" or one, etc.). The following rule is rather lengthy, but it is worth memorizing if you have trouble with double consonants. When adding a suffix to a root word, the final consonant is doubled if **all** the following conditions exist:

1. the suffix begins with a vowel, such as *-ed, -ing, -ent, -ant, -ence, -ance*

2. the word ends with a single vowel followed by a single consonant

3. the last syllable of the word is accented

If these three conditions are present, then double the final consonant before adding the suffix; if any one of these conditions is not present, do not double.

Example 1: commit + -ing
- the suffix begins with the vowel *i*
- *commit* ends with the single vowel *i* followed by the single consonant *t*
- the last syllable *mit* is accented

Therefore, double the consonant and add -ing (*committing*).

Example 2: credit + -ed
- the suffix begins with the vowel *e*
- *credit* ends with the single vowel *i* followed by the single consonant *t*
- however, you do *not* stress the last syllable *it* when saying the word; you stress the first syllable *cred*

Therefore, do not double the consonant; just add the suffix (*credited*).

Example 3: commit + -ment
- the suffix does not begin with a vowel

Therefore, do not double the final consonant (*commitment*).

NOTE: One-syllable words that end with a single consonant preceded by a single vowel take a double consonant before suffixes beginning with vowels.

plan—planner
run—running
drop—dropped

● EXERCISE 7.1

Add suffixes to each of the following words. Note that not all suffixes apply to all words; some words may change or require other letters to make them easier to pronounce as well — for example, admit + ion = admission. (The *t*'s change to *s*'s.) Consult your dictionary if you have any doubts.

	-ed	-ing	-ence/ -ance	-ment	-ion
1. accept					
2. acquit					
3. admit					
4. allot					
5. audit					
6. benefit					
7. begin					
8. budget					
9. cancel					
10. canvass					
11. commit					
12. compel					
13. concur					
14. control					
15. equip					
16. occur					
17. omit					
18. plan					
19. remit					
20. run					

Check your answers with those in the Answer section at the end of the book.

● EXERCISE 7.2

Add suffixes to each of the following words. Some words change their accented portions when different suffixes are added. Listen to the sound of each word before you double the letter and add the suffix; for example, we stress *fer* in the words *infer´*, *infer´red*, and *infer´ring*, but in *in´ference*, the emphasis changes to the first syllable. Consult your dictionary if you have any doubts.

	-ed	-ing	-ence	ment	-able
1. adjourn					
2. confer					
3. comfort					
4. credit					
5. debit					
6. defer					
7. develop					
8. deter					
9. differ					
10. govern					
11. infer					
12. offer					
13. prefer					
14. refer					
15. transfer					

Check your answers with those in the Answer section at the end of the book.

THE NEXT STEP

If you feel confident about this section, proceed to the Pretest for "Pronouns and Prepositions."

PRETEST: PRONOUNS AND PREPOSITIONS

In the following sentences, correct any errors in pronoun and preposition usage.

1. The group interviewed for the job included Bill, George, and ~~myself~~. *me*

2. Our pay raises were retroactive ~~from~~ last January. *to*

3. ~~Who~~ did the college appoint as admissions officer? *Whom*

4. Pauline has more artistic talent than ~~me~~. *I*

5. Each girl prepared ~~their~~ own report. *her*

6. Either the architect or the engineer made an error in ~~their~~ calculations. *his*

7. A bad job is preferable ~~than~~ no job at all. *to*

8. Your opinions are quite different ~~than~~ hers. *to / from*

9. The people who received notices were my cousin, my brother, and ~~myself~~. *I*

10. Nobody works harder for her marks than ~~her~~. *she*

Check your answers with those in the Answer section at the end of the book.

If you had eight or more sentences correct, proceed to the Pretest for "The Apostrophe and Its Uses." If you had fewer than eight sentences correct, complete the lessons on the following pages.

PRONOUNS AND PREPOSITIONS

I. PRONOUNS

Before we can discuss pronouns, we must review what a noun is. A **noun** is a naming word—the name given to any person, place, object, or idea.

1. persons—woman, man, student, child, baby, etc.
2. places—city, park, lake, desert, etc.
3. objects—chair, desk, car, sky, hill, etc.
4. ideas—faith, love, hate, jealousy, happiness, etc.

However, our reading, writing, and speaking would become very repetitive and confusing if we used only nouns to refer to such things.

> Rod wondered where Rod put Rod's cheque as Rod wanted to deposit the cheque into Rod's chequing account.

To eliminate this repetition and confusion, we use pronouns. **Pronouns** take the place of nouns.

> Rod wondered where *he* put *his* cheque as *he* wanted to deposit *it* into *his* chequing account.

In this text, you do not have to know the names of the different types of pronouns or their specific purposes; you must, however, know how to use pronouns correctly.

There are two sets of pronouns: those used in the subjective form and those used in the objective form.

	Subjective Pronouns	Objective Pronouns
Singular		
First person	I	me
Second person	you	you
Third person	he / she / it	him / her / it
Plural		
First person	we	us
Second person	you	you
Third person	they	them

NOTE: *You* remains the same for both subjective and objective forms, and has no special plural form. (There is no such word as *youse*!)

274

II. Two Uses of the Subjective Pronoun

To make the correct use of pronouns easier to remember, learn only the two uses of the subjective pronoun. If neither of these two uses applies to the situation, use the objective form and don't worry about the technical reasons.

Rule 1: **Use the subjective pronoun if the word being replaced is the subject of the sentence.** If the sentence is in its natural order—and most sentences are—the subject will be at the beginning.

> *We* tried to get tickets for the play.

The subjective pronoun is used, as *We* is the subject.

> Clara or *I* will try to attend.

The subjective pronoun is used, as *I* is part of the subject. (You can test the usage in a compound structure by mentally saying *Clara will try to attend* and *I will try to attend*. Therefore, the correct version must be *Clara or I will try to attend*.)

> Do you think that John or *he* would be willing to do that task?

The subjective pronoun is used, as *he* is part of the subject. (You can test the usage by mentally saying *John would be willing to do that task* and *he would be willing to do that task*. Therefore, *John or he would be willing to do that task*.)

● Exercise 7.3

Fill in the correct pronoun by using the preceding rule.

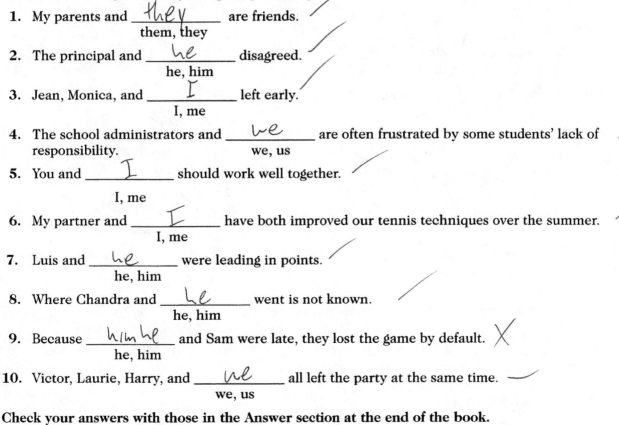

1. My parents and ___they___ are friends.
    them, they

2. The principal and ___he___ disagreed.
    he, him

3. Jean, Monica, and ___I___ left early.
    I, me

4. The school administrators and ___we___ are often frustrated by some students' lack of responsibility.
    we, us

5. You and ___I___ should work well together.
    I, me

6. My partner and ___I___ have both improved our tennis techniques over the summer.
    I, me

7. Luis and ___he___ were leading in points.
    he, him

8. Where Chandra and ___he___ went is not known.
    he, him

9. Because ___him he___ and Sam were late, they lost the game by default.
    he, him

10. Victor, Laurie, Harry, and ___we___ all left the party at the same time.
    we, us

Check your answers with those in the Answer section at the end of the book.

Many of you will think the sentences in these exercises sound odd; perhaps you are in the habit of using pronouns incorrectly. Be conscious of this fact and think about and use Rule 1. Continuous practice will help you correct this common pronoun error.

Rule 2:   **Use the subjective pronoun directly after the words *am, is, are, was, were, be, being, been*. These are all forms of the verb *to be*.**

That may be *she* at the door.

The subjective pronoun is used directly after *be*.

My best friends are Linda and *she*.

The subjective pronoun is used in a compound structure that directly follows *are*. (You can test the usage by mentally saying "My best friend is Linda," and "My best friend is she." Therefore, "My best friends are Linda and she.")

● EXERCISE 7.4

Fill in the correct pronouns by using Rule 2.

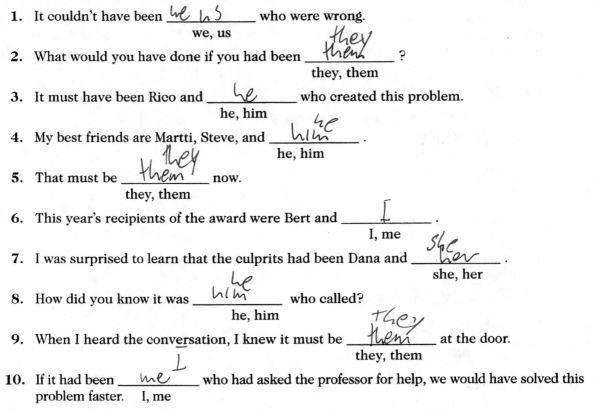

1.   It couldn't have been _____we us_____ who were wrong.
     we, us

2.   What would you have done if you had been _____they them_____ ?
     they, them

3.   It must have been Rico and _____he_____ who created this problem.
     he, him

4.   My best friends are Martti, Steve, and _____him he_____ .
     he, him

5.   That must be _____them they_____ now.
     they, them

6.   This year's recipients of the award were Bert and _____I_____ .
     I, me

7.   I was surprised to learn that the culprits had been Dana and _____she her_____ .
     she, her

8.   How did you know it was _____him he_____ who called?
     he, him

9.   When I heard the conversation, I knew it must be _____them they_____ at the door.
     they, them

10. If it had been _____me I_____ who had asked the professor for help, we would have solved this problem faster.   I, me

Check your answers with those in the Answer section at the end of the book.

Most of you will say or think, "This sounds crazy—nobody talks like this." Well, perhaps we don't all talk this way but we must write this way to be grammatically correct. Be extremely conscious of Rule 2 and practise, practise, practise.

Those are the two uses to remember. If a pronoun is not the subject or does not directly follow any form of the verb *to be*, then use the other form of the pronoun—the objective form—and don't worry about the many technical reasons why. The important fact for now is that you write correctly.

● EXERCISE 7.5

Using Rules 1 and 2, fill in the correct form of the pronoun in the following sentences. Remember—if Rules 1 and 2 do not apply, use the objective form.

1. The Bakers or ____they____ will drive to the meeting.
    they, them

2. The reporter snapped a picture of ____her____ .
    she, her

3. Mrs. Maki said that you and ____I____ were not paying attention.
    I, me

4. Among those at the party were Arjan and ____she____ .
    she, her

5. The college presented ____him____ with the award.
    he, him

6. I was suspicious of the man who sat beside Cathy and ____me____ .
    I, me

7. I sent ____him____ and ____her____ cards at Christmas time.
    he, him   she, her

8. They wrote ____me____ a letter.
    I, me

9. Neither ____her/she____ nor ____I____ like to walk home late at night. ✗
    she, her   I, me

10. Rod, Ira, and ____I____ waited for ____them____ after the meeting.
    I, me   they, them

11. No one had the solution to the problem except André and ____he____ .
    I, me

12. This agreement is just between you and ____me I____ . ✗
    I, me

13. In a local contest, the Smiths and ____they____ both won trips to the Bahamas.
    they, them

14. Celine and ____she____ invested their money in a furniture store.
    she, her

15. The announced winners of this year's trophies were Sophia, Moira, Helen, and ____I____ .
    I, me

Check your answers with those in the Answer section at the end of the book.

III. Other Pronoun Problems

A. The Comparative Pronoun

In the English language, we always try to avoid repetition or unnecessary wordiness so that our main message is clearly understood. We would probably avoid repetitious items such as the following:

> I can run faster than he can run.
>
> She has longer hair than I have.
>
> Dean Westcott praised you more than he praised me.
>
> *OR*
>
> Dean Westcott praised you more than I praised you.

(whichever meaning you intend)

You would probably say "I can run faster than *him*." "She has longer hair than *me*." These choices of pronouns are incorrect. To make sure that you use the correct form in these incomplete or understood portions of the sentences, mentally fill in the missing words as is done in the following examples.

> Very few people can speak as eloquently as he (*can*) in front of such a large audience.
>
> I can tell that Alex likes you better than (*he likes*) me!
>
> We were very frustrated to learn that the car salesperson had given them a better deal than (*he gave*) us.
>
> We should listen to our parents' advice because they are usually much wiser about life than we (*are*).
>
> That news will upset Beth more than (*it will upset*) them.

● Exercise 7.6

Write the correct pronoun by mentally filling in the "understood" portion of each sentence.

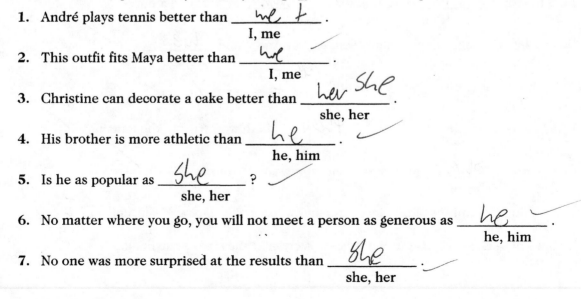

1. André plays tennis better than ___we t___ .
    I, me

2. This outfit fits Maya better than ___we___ .
    I, me

3. Christine can decorate a cake better than ___her she___ .
    she, her

4. His brother is more athletic than ___he___ .
    he, him

5. Is he as popular as ___she___ ?
    she, her

6. No matter where you go, you will not meet a person as generous as ___he___ .
    he, him

7. No one was more surprised at the results than ___she___ .
    she, her

8. The teacher gave Joan more marks than _____we_____ for the very same question!
   I, me

9. Because we ordered our tickets early in the season, we got better seats for the concert
   than _____they_____ .
   they, them

10. That company did not have a fair salary plan. They paid any relatives of management more
    per hour than _____us_____ .
    we, us

Check your answers with those in the Answer section at the end of the book.

B. THE REFLEXIVE PRONOUN

There are other pronouns in use, of course, and one of them is the "self" pronoun.

myself

yourself

himself   (There is no such word as hisself!)

herself

itself

ourselves

yourselves

themselves   (There is no such word as theirself or theirselves!)

These pronouns are called reflexive pronouns. "Reflexive" suggests that the pronoun makes a direct reference to a word previously stated. Therefore, only use this reflexive form when you can readily see the noun or pronoun that this form is "bouncing back to."

Ivan accidentally burned *himself* on the barbecue.

I *myself* would not have made that response.

They tried to build the house by *themselves*.

In the following examples, note how the meaning of the sentence changes when the non-reflexive pronoun is replaced by the reflexive pronoun:

Monica was angry at *her* for being so stupid.

Monica was angry at *herself* for being so stupid.

When troubled, Ron always talks to *him*.

When troubled, Ron always talks to *himself*.

Diana bought *her* a new outfit for the holidays.

Diana bought *herself* a new outfit for the holidays.

● EXERCISE 7.7—REVIEW

Correct any pronoun errors in the following sentences. Make sure to use Rules 1 and 2 to determine the correct usage. (Some sentences may be correct as they are.)

1. Sven, Fritz, and ~~myself~~ would represent our group at the meeting. ✓

2. Choi and ~~me~~ [I] went to the movies last night to see *The Titanic* with Leonardo DiCaprio.

3. Are you sure it wasn't Isabella and ~~they~~ [them] who left early?

4. Benazir arrived at the meeting earlier than ~~us~~. [we]

5. The fastest runners in the race were ~~him~~ [he] and Matthew.

6. She gave advice to Ramona and me.

7. He makes lasagna better than ~~me~~. [I]

8. Paul and ~~him~~ [he] met we associates in the bar.

9. They could probably do that job by ~~theirselves~~. [themselves]

10. He'd probably rather go with you than ~~I~~. [me]

11. How did you know it was ~~me~~? [I]

12. She has more experience at typing than ~~me~~. [I]

13. You should return the key to Lee or ~~myself~~. [me]

14. It might have been ~~her~~ [she] who made the long distance phone call.

15. If it were ~~him~~, [he] why didn't you say so?

Check your answers with those in the Answer section at the end of the book.

C. THE WHO/WHOM QUESTION

Another common pronoun problem is the use of **who** or **whom**. To decide which pronoun is correct, try this quick trick.

1. Omit the pronoun *who* or *whom* from the sentence. (Cover it up!)

2. Substitute *he* or *him* for the missing pronoun.

If you substitute *he,* the correct pronoun to use is *who.* If you substitute *him,* the correct pronoun to use is *whom.*

Example 1:
(Who, Whom) did you go with?
_____ did you go with?
Did you go with *him?*
(Use the word *whom.*)
CORRECT: *Whom* did you go with?

Example 2:
(Who, Whom) sent the flowers?
_____ sent the flowers?
He sent the flowers.
Use the word *who.*
CORRECT: *Who* sent the flowers?

● EXERCISE 7.8

Using the above method, write *who* or *whom* in each sentence.

1. _____who_____ do you think will answer the door?

2. _____Whom_____ were you waving at?

3. _____Who_____ do you think will apply for that position?

4. _____Whom_____ is the parcel for?

5. _____Whom_____ do you expect to do the dishes?

6. _____Who_____ was there when you called?

7. _____who_____ do the police suspect broke into your house?

8. _____Who_____ is responsible for this mess?

9. _____Whom_____ would you consider a worthy candidate for the position?

10. _____Who_____ could be phoning us at this time of night?

Check your answers with those in the Answer section at the end of the book.

One other kind of sentence involving the use of *who* or *whom* does not necessarily ask a question.

He was an old friend (who, whom) I had not seen for years.

There is a group of words in this sentence that begins with *who* or *whom.* Isolate this group of words and then apply the formula.

(who, whom) I had not seen for years.

I had not seen _____ for years.
I had not seen *him* for years.

(Use the word *whom.*)
CORRECT: He was an old friend whom I had not seen for years.

● **EXERCISE 7.9**

Using this formula, write *who* or *whom* in each sentence.

1. The men ___Who___ had been building the house went on strike.

2. Do you know ___who___ she is?

3. This is the man ___who___ will be our new premier.

4. Guess ___whom___ I met today?

5. ___Whom___ did she mention in her talk?

6. They asked me ___Whom___ I had invited to the party.

7. The elderly woman ___Whom___ they helped cross the street was very grateful.

8. We will cooperate with the person ___who___ is in charge of the project.

9. Mr. Rivera is a teacher ___who___ I know would be glad to help you with your assignment.

10. ___Whom___ did they choose to represent us on the negotiating committee?

Check your answers with those in the Answer section at the end of the book.

IV. USING OTHER FORMS OF PRONOUNS CORRECTLY

A pronoun must agree in gender and in number with the word it refers to. For example,

> Martha has done *her* share. (The pronoun must be feminine and singular.)

> The dog hurt *its* paw. (The pronoun must be neutral and singular.)

> The others are invited if *they* pay for *themselves*.

These examples illustrate the simplest reference form and are easy to understand. There are, however, some trouble spots that you should be alerted to.

1. When the words *each, either, neither, one, everyone, everybody, no one, nobody, anyone, anybody, someone, somebody* are used in a sentence, they are singular and require a singular pronoun reference. For example,

> Nobody is so perfect that *he* or *she* can criticize others.
> One of those girls is president of *her* class.

2. Two or more singular words joined by *and* should be referred to by a plural pronoun.

> If June and Jo call, tell *them* that I have left.
> Hilda, Linda, and Clara left *their* keys at home.

3. Two singular words joined by *or* or *nor* should be referred to by a singular pronoun.

> Either Yolanda or Sally will read *her* paper to the class.
> Lois or Jane will give you *her* key.
> Neither Mario nor Paul would reveal *his* plans.

● EXERCISE 7.10

Fill in each blank with an appropriate pronoun, making sure it agrees with its antecedent.

1. Each student reviewed _____ own timetable.

2. One of the robins built _____ nest in the eave of our porch.

3. Both Julie and Frieda added _____ contributions to the fund.

4. If anyone else wishes to go, tell _____ to notify the office.

5. Several of the boys have curled _____ hair.

6. Not one of the students turned in _____ paper late.

7. Neither Tom nor Dick has submitted _____ expense account on time.

8. Either the dean or the chairperson must give _____ permission.

9. Each of the members must pay _____ dues by the end of September.

10. Neither Betty nor Susan would tell what _____ had bought at the sale.

Check your answers with those in the Answer section at the end of the book.

V. PREPOSITIONS

A **preposition** relates one word in a sentence to another word. This connecting word links ideas and words to give meaning to your message.

> She walked *into* the glass door.

Into links *walked* with *glass door*.

Consider how difficult it would be to understand messages without these linking devices.

> Raoul threw the papers the table.
> The morning, she went the store groceries.

With prepositions linking the related words, the message becomes clear.

> Raoul threw the papers *on* the table.
> *In* the morning, she went *to* the store *for* groceries.

Since many prepositions express the relationship between two words or ideas, be sure to choose the correct one for your intended meaning.

Raoul threw the papers
{
under
beneath
below
over
above
beside   the table.
on
near
off
behind
across
}

Following is a list of common prepositions. Most will not cause you any problems; however, some have been identified so that you can review their usage.

about	*between	*off
above	but	on
after	by	over
against	except	to
*among	for	under
at	*from	until
before	*in	up
below	*into	upon
*beside	*like	with
*besides	of	

*These words are often used incorrectly. Note the usage lessons below:

among—used to discuss more than two
between—used to discuss two

> Who among us is not guilty of speeding?
> She overheard the conversation between Walter and Doris.

beside—next to
besides—in addition

> Roy sat beside me.
> Who is going besides Brenda?

from—links the idea of receiving to a person
off—gives the idea of removing

> I received a telegram from Marjorie.
> She took off her sweater.

NOTE: There is no such term as *off of*. Use *off*, or the preposition *from*, in its place.

in—gives the impression of remaining at the same level
into—gives the impression of going from one place to another

> He walked around in circles. (same place)
> She walked into the room. (from one place to another)

like—similar
like—to care or to enjoy or to prefer (verb)

> She looks like her mother.
> I like tea better than coffee.

NOTE: Occasionally *like* is used incorrectly in place of the words *as if*. See the following example:

> **Incorrect:** It looks like it's going to rain.
> **Correct:** It looks as if it's going to rain.

● EXERCISE 7.11

Correct prepositional errors in the following sentences.

1. ~~Beside~~ Barbara, who else is absent?
   Besides

2. We had ten dollars ~~between~~ the five of us.
   among

3. It seems ~~like~~ I always have to cook dinner.
   as if

4. Did you buy your tickets ~~off of~~ Cathy?
   from

5. She reached ~~in~~ her purse for her wallet.
   into

6. I got that idea ~~off~~ Emma!
   from

7. It seems ~~like~~ winter is never going to end.
   as if

8. The car crashed through the barrier and went ~~in~~ the ditch.
   into

9. The book fell ~~from~~ the desk.
   off

10. ~~Among~~ the two of us, we are sure to come up with the right answer.
    between

Check your answers with those in the Answer section at the end of the book.

COMMON PREPOSITIONAL ERRORS

Some words must be used with specific prepositions. Learn the following examples so you will use them correctly in your writing and daily speech. Many dictionaries include this information as a "usage note" after the listed word; if so, you would be wise to include it on the same page as the definition.

Inferior and **superior** are always followed by **to**.

> This brand is inferior to the others on the market.
> She won the contest because her writing was judged superior to the other contestants' entries.

Different is always followed by **from**.

> Your answers were different from mine.
> Her tastes in decorating were quite different from her husband's.

Retroactive is always followed by **to**.

> Her pay increase would be retroactive to last January.

Preferable is always followed by **to.**

> Rewriting the test is preferable to getting a failing grade in the course.

In regard is always followed by **to.**   (Note that there is no *s* on regard.)
With regard is also always followed by **to.**
As regards is the only term in which both words in the phrase end with *s*.

> I would like to talk to you for a few minutes in my office in regard to your vacation time.
> I would like to talk to you for a few minutes in my office with regard to your vacation time.
> As regards your vacation time, I would like to talk to you for a few minutes in my office.

(Usually *as regards* is written at the beginning of a statement.)

● EXERCISE 7.12

Correct any preposition errors in the following sentences. Occasionally you will have to rewrite a portion of the sentence to make it correct. Some sentences may be correct as they are.

1. Why isn't our salary increase retroactive ~~from~~ last June?
   to

2. Some types of jobs are often considered more inferior ~~than~~ others.
   inferior to

3. Cooking in a microwave oven is certainly different ~~than~~ cooking in a conventional one.
   from

4. I would like to see you in regards to the proposal you submitted.

5. I received that information ~~off of~~ a very reliable source.
   from

6. It seems ~~like~~ I am never right!
   as if

7. After many years, I had the opportunity to tour my old high school again, but all the familiar rooms and places seemed different ~~than~~ I had remembered them to be.
   from the way

8. Everyone became quiet when the tall, impressive-looking man stepped ~~in~~ the room.
   into

9. With more memory and built-in printers, this year's portable computers are considered to be much superior to last year's models.

10. Some people feel that being ignored is preferable ~~than~~ being seen as different ~~than~~ others.
    to   *from*

Check your answers with those in the Answer section at the end of the book.

THE NEXT STEP

If you feel confident about this section of work, proceed to the Pretest for "The Apostrophe and Its Uses."

PRETEST:
THE APOSTROPHE AND ITS USES

In the following sentences, insert any apostrophe or apostrophe and *s* where necessary. This exercise tests your ability to use apostrophes correctly to show possession or to indicate a shortened word phrase.

1. My brother-in-laws office doesnt contain much furniture.
   brother-in-law's   doesn't

2. Youre late for your appointment.
   you're

3. Tomorrows meeting will have to be cancelled, as were planning to be out of town.
   tomorrow's   we've

4. In everyones opinion, Banff is a skiers paradise.
   everyone's

5. Its been two weeks since I ordered Jim and Mario's jackets.
   It's   Jim's

X 6. Several students'cars were parked in the staffs parking lot.
   student's   staff's

7. The Walkers and the Robinsons boats were tied up at their docks when the storm struck.
   walkers' and Robinsons'

X 8. Several dollars worth of merchandise was missing from the supermarkets shelves but the police believed that, rather than one thief, many regular customers had shoplifted the goods during the day.
   supermarket's
   dollar's — dollars'

X 9. Because Mr. Fernandos firm is a proven and reliable one, you would be wise to transfer your mother-in-laws business to that company.
   fernandos'   mother-in-law's
   Mr. Fernando's

X 10. Theyre not interested in travelling to the Orient for two weeks vacation.
   They're   weeks'   week's

Check your answers with those in the Answer section at the end of the book.

If you made no more than two errors, you are ready to write the Unit Seven Post-Test on the spelling, grammar, and punctuation discussed in this unit. If you made more than two errors, complete the lessons on the following pages.

THE APOSTROPHE AND ITS USES

Apostrophes can be used to indicate ownership or to indicate that letters have been omitted in an abbreviated form of a word.

I. OWNERSHIP—POSSESSIVE CASE

Ownership is always indicated at the end of the word. To form the possessive case of a singular noun—that is, to show ownership—add an apostrophe and *s* to the word.

> the student's car—the car belonging to the student (add an apostrophe and *s* to indicate ownership)
>
> the child's book—the book belonging to the child (add an apostrophe and *s* to indicate ownership)
>
> Mr. Thompson's cottage—the cottage belonging to Mr. Thompson (add an apostrophe and *s* to indicate ownership)

To form the possessive case of a plural noun, pluralize the word. If the plural form ends with *s*, just add an apostrophe.

> several students' cars—the cars belonging to several students (the plural form ends with *s*; just add an apostrophe)
>
> the Thompsons' cottage—the cottage belonging to the Thompsons (the family) (the plural form ends with *s*; just add an apostrophe)

If the plural form does not end with *s*, add an apostrophe and *s*.

> the children's books—the books belonging to the children (the plural form does not end with *s*; therefore, add *'s*)

These principles are all correct, but may often seem confusing—there are so many rules and exceptions to remember! To help you to make this task easier, try the following suggestion. By reversing the ownership phrase, as illustrated in the explanatory words above, you can quickly determine if the word requiring an apostrophe is singular or plural and if it requires just an apostrophe or an apostrophe and *s*.

the student's *car*—the car belonging to the *student* (singular): add the apostrophe in the indicated place. (Read the above reversed phrase and use your pen or finger to follow the arrow.)

several students' *cars*—the cars belonging to the *students* (plural): add the apostrophe in the indicated place. (Read the reversed phrase and use your pen or finger to follow the arrow.)

men's *clothing*—clothing belonging to *men*: add the apostrophe in the indicated place.

my mother-in-law's *house*—house belonging to my *mother-in-law*: add the apostrophe in the indicated place.

Jack's *plants*—plants belonging to *Jack*: add the apostrophe in the indicated place.

my two sisters-in-law's *children*—children belonging to my two *sisters-in-law*: add the apostrophe in the indicated place. **Remember— ownership is always shown at the end of the word.**

Some singular words already end with *s*. If you say the extra *s* sound, add *'s* to the written version.

the boss's *secretary*—you must add an extra sound—add *'s*

the bus's *back wheel*—you must add an extra sound—add *'s*

Mr. Cortez's *car*—you must add an extra sound—add *'s*

Charles' *opinion*—extra sound is awkward—just add apostrophe

Mr. Greaves' *position*—extra sound is awkward—just add apostrophe

Their plural forms would indicate ownership in the following way:

several bosses' *secretaries*—secretaries belonging to several bosses (the plural form)

several buses' *back wheels*—back wheels belonging to several buses (the plural form adds *es*)

the Cortezes' *car*—car belonging to the Cortezes (the family) (the plural form adds *es*)

the Greaves' *home*—home belonging to the Greaves (family) (the extra sound would be awkward; just add the apostrophe)

● EXERCISE 7.13

Add apostrophes where needed in the following sentences.

1. We had to listen to several customers' complaints.

2. My two brothers-in-law's boats were tied up at our dock.

3. The manager's decision was final.

4. Mrs. Davies' bookstore is closed on Saturday.

5. The Curtis' home is in Academy Heights.

6. In the court case, many witnesses' testimonies supported Mr. Jones' alibi.

7. You will find both the women's and girls' fashions on the fifth floor of the department store.

8. Charles' European trip included visits to London, Paris, and Rome.

9. The company's new policies had been established by past practices, employees' recommendations, and customers' suggestions.

10. Our country's economy is steadily improving in spite of the government's decline in popularity.

Check your answers with those in the Answer section at the end of the book.

Some words require the possessive case even though we do not consider them to own anything.

yesterday's *paper*—paper from yesterday

fifty cents' *worth* of candy—worth of fifty cents

two weeks' *vacation*—vacation of two weeks

a moment's *delay*—delay of a moment

● EXERCISE 7.14

Add apostrophes where needed in the following sentences.

1. Tuesdays meeting has been cancelled.
   Tuesday's

2. The capital city is just a days journey from here.
   day's

3. There was two hours delay in air traffic.
   hours'

4. She took three weeks vacation in Spain.
   weeks'

5. Where did you put last nights paper?
   night's

6. You should proceed without a moments delay.
   moment's

7. Yesterdays news is history.
   yesterday's

8. A months vacation sounds sufficient; and it usually is, until the last two days of your holidays.
   month's

9. The shiftless son inherited thousands of dollars worth of stocks and bonds in his fathers will.
   dollars'   *father's*

10. Because of last nights snow storm, roads were closed and many residents homes were without electrical services.
    the night's   *residents'*

Check your answers with those in the Answer section at the end of the book.

Occasionally, you must distinguish between joint ownership and individual ownership. To indicate joint ownership, add the possessive case to just the last word.

Tom and Pat's *farm*—one farm shared by Tom and Pat

Marks and Spencer's annual *sale*—sale of one firm

To indicate individual ownership, add the possessive case to each word.

Vanessa's and Stewart's *cottages*—cottages (more than one) belonging to Vanessa and to Stewart

● EXERCISE 7.15

Add the possessive case ('s or just ') in the following sentences.

1. Anita and Junes office is on the second floor.

2. Both Eatons and Sears department stores are having sales next week.
   Eaton's

3. Kareem and Ahmed problem would not be easy to resolve.

4. Did you see Sue and Andrea notebooks in this room?
   Sue's

5. Marilyn and Jasons home is on Mary Street.

6. The date of the spring break was determined on the basis of students and teachers opinion polls.

7. Both local residents and campers assistance was requested in the search for the missing child.

8. The bride and grooms honeymoon destination was Hawaii.

9. The ladies and gentlemens restrooms are on opposite sides of the mezzanine in the concert hall.   *gentlemen's*

10. Todd and Dale collie won a blue ribbon in the dog show.

Check your answers with those in the Answer section at the end of the book.

NOTE: Possession can also be indicated in a phrase beginning with the words *of* or *belonging to*; however, in these cases no apostrophes are required, as the word group itself indicates ownership and does not require further identification. For example,

> the names of the authors
> the light of the moon
> the letters of the applicants

POSSESSIVE PRONOUNS

The possessive pronouns are:

> his
>
> hers
>
> its
>
> ours
>
> yours
>
> whose
>
> theirs

Possessive pronouns do not require an apostrophe, because these words already indicate ownership.

> That book is *hers.*
> *Whose* cup is this?
> The fault was *ours.*

II. CONTRACTIONS

Apostrophes are also used to indicate that letters have been omitted in an abbreviated form of two words.

don't	=	do not	I've	= I have
it's	=	it is	doesn't	= does not
I'm	=	I am	where's	= where is
we'll	=	we will	who's	= who is
we're	=	we are	they're	= they are
can't	=	can not	there's	= there is
we've	=	we have	you're	= you are

Some of these contracted forms are often confused with possessive pronouns which, as we have seen, need no additional sign for ownership, as their meanings imply this condition. Therefore, remember that **any pronoun that contains an apostrophe must be the abbreviation of two words.**
   Note the following examples:

its   The committee submitted *its* recommendations. (possessive)
it's   *It's* too late to go downtown. (it's = it is)

whose	Do you know *whose* books are on the desk? (possessive)
who's	I don't know *who's* planning to go. (who's = who is)
your	Did you leave *your* shoes by the door? (possessive)
you're	*You're* late again! (you're = you are)
theirs	Thank goodness those problems are *theirs*. (possessive)
there's	*There's* a hole in my shoe. (there's = there is)
their	Have you seen *their* new house? (possessive)
they're	*They're* not speaking to each other. (they're = they are)
there	I didn't see you sitting *there*. (there—the opposite of here)

Other confusing pairs of words:

were	There *were* six boats in the harbour. (were—verb form)
we're	*We're* not ready. (we're = we are)
are	What *are* you doing with your spare time? (are—verb form)
our	We have done *our* part in the project. (our—possessive)
well	I don't feel very *well*. (well—descriptive word)
we'll	*We'll* leave immediately. (we'll = we will)

Although all of the above groups of words are commonly misspelled or mispunctuated, probably the most serious ones are **its** to illustrate ownership and **it's** to form the contraction for *it is*. Pay particular attention to this confusing pair.

● EXERCISE 7.16

Correct any errors in the often misused words **its** indicating ownership and **it's** representing the contraction for *it is*.

1. Its said that the abacus, which has been used by the Chinese for hundreds of years, is the basis of all present-day computers; however, despite it's effectiveness, it was not widely adopted in any country outside the Orient.

2. While its recognized that the problem is in the abuse of alcohol and not in its use, alcoholism is one of the most subtle diseases that has ever confronted humankind.

3. Its now mandatory for everyone suspected of driving while under the influence of liquor to have a breathalizer test; and its now possible to convict a person on the basis of the results.

4. Its the committee's responsibility to submit it's report on time.

5. Its a long way to drive to the next town; therefore, have your car checked to ensure that its in good repair.

Check your answers with those in the Answer section at the end of the book.

● EXERCISE 7.17

Use apostrophes or corrected forms of words where necessary in the following sentences.

1. Im bored because theirs nothing to do.

2. Were not very well prepared for are test.

3. Whose responsible for that dent in the fender of our car?

4. Its a shame that your leaving so soon.

5. Do'nt there parents know their they're?

6. Jon dosent know who's books were left in our classroom.

7. As the saying goes, "Where theres smoke, theirs usually fire!"

8. I dont know why Im so tired; Ive been sleeping all afternoon.

9. That company also submitted its proposal for the renovations, but weve not made a decision about whose offer well accept.

10. Is that Corvette parked in the driveway hers' or their's?

Check your answers with those in the Answer section at the end of the book.

● EXERCISE 7.18—REVIEW

Correct errors in the following sentences by supplying apostrophes and making any necessary changes in incorrect word usage.

1. The Jones car was stalled in they're driveway.

2. Were planning to visit Nancy and Marilyn families in Toronto and Ottawa on are trip east this summer.

3. Whose sweater is this in Camerons closet?

4. Theirs only one week left until Christmas and weve still not purchased Tom and Harrys presents.

5. Were having are meeting in Mr. Curtis office.

Check your answers with those in the Answer section at the end of the book.

THE NEXT STEP

If you feel confident about this section, you are ready to write the Unit Seven Post-Test on the following page.

POST-TEST FOR UNIT SEVEN

If you feel confident about the skills presented in this unit, complete the Post-Test that follows. **Do not attempt this test if you have not completed the required work.**

Once you have completed the whole test, check your answers with the suggested ones at the end of this unit. A marking scheme has been provided to give you a realistic idea of your ability in this area. Your goal should be to have no more than two minor errors in each category of spelling or punctuation and no more than two major errors in the use of either pronouns or prepositions.

I. Add the suggested suffixes to the words in parentheses. Rewrite the combined version above or below the word. Use your dictionary, if necessary.

1. Because of the (differ + ences) *differences* of opinions among the (commit + ee) *committee* members, the issue concerning the (allot + ment) *allotment* of monies for new (equip + ment) *equipment* was (defer + ed) *deferred* to the next meeting.

2. Although the bank had (credit + ed) *credited* our account for the amount of the error, we (transfer + ed) *transferred* our business to another branch.

3. The staff members requested (permit + ion) *permission* to attend the (confer + ence) *conference* that was (plan + ed) *planned* for the fall.

(Deduct one mark for each spelling error.)

TOTAL MARKS FOR SPELLING _____10_____ /10

II. Circle the correct pronoun or preposition in the following sentences.

1. (Youse, **You**) guys may find this topic preferable (than, **to**) your old one.

2. It could have been (**she**, her) (**who**, whom) phoned while you were out.

3. Sonja did not have the same qualifications as (**I**, me) for that job, but the interviewer seemed to favour her more than (I, **me**).

4. (**Among**, Between) the three of them, the mischievous kids always seemed to get (**theirselves**, himself, hisself, themselves) into trouble.

5. (**Who**, Whom) did you say got (**off**, off of, from) the train at the last station?

6. At the end of the day, return the key to Eric or (**me**, **I**, myself). ✗

7. If it seems (like, **as if**) we will have to work overtime, everyone will be responsible for making (**his or her**, their) arrangements for a dinner break.

8. Both Karen and Edna walked (in, **into**) the manager's office to discuss (her, **their**) vacation plans.

(Deduct one mark for each error.)

TOTAL MARKS FOR GRAMMAR _____14_____ /15

III. In the following sentences, use apostrophes to indicate ownership or contractions, or use the correct form of the possessive pronoun. (Make any necessary changes resulting from your corrections.)

1. Now that you have voiced your opinion, ~~its~~ *It's* too late to worry about others' feelings.

2. I ~~dont~~ *don't* know whose going to the Jones' party.

3. ~~Tomorrows~~ *Tomorrow's* meeting will have to be postponed because the ~~companys~~ *company's* vice-president from Calgary will be visiting our office.

4. Well have to wait for Ms. King and Mr. Rogers responses before we plan the meeting.
Ms. King's and Mr. Rogers' responses

(Deduct one mark for each error.)

TOTAL MARKS FOR PUNCTUATION ____8____ /10

IV. The following selection contains errors in spelling, grammar, and punctuation discussed in this unit. Proofread the passage, correct the listed errors, and make any additional changes resulting from your corrections.

3 spelling errors—sp   ~~4 apostrophe errors—p'~~
~~3 pronoun errors—pron~~   ~~1 preposition error—prep~~

Who   among   doesn't
~~Whom between~~ us ~~does'nt~~ dream of being successful? This common goal, however, can have many different meanings, For some, success is mea-sured in dollars; while for others, *it's* ~~its~~ measured by the number of friends *they have* ~~he has.~~ Real success, however, is a matter of attaining a lifestyle in which one is comfortable with ~~themself~~ *oneself*. If, for example, a wealthy man lives his life hating the world and everyone in it, including himself, could he be looked upon as being successful? And what of a poor man who always appears happy and has countless friends? Is he not more successful than the wealthy man? The poor man is comfortable with himself and has an *acceptance* ~~acceptance~~ of his lifestyle; therefore, he can be *credited* ~~creditted~~ with leading a very successful life. Although success is *everyone's preferred* ~~everyones prefered~~ goal, ~~they're~~ *there* are many different viewpoints about how one achieves this desired state.

(Deduct one mark for each spelling and punctuation error; deduct two marks for each pronoun or preposition error.)

TOTAL MARKS FOR PROOFREADING ____12____ /15

Answers are on the following pages.

ANSWERS FOR UNIT SEVEN POST-TEST

I. 1. Because of the *differences* of opinions among the *committee* members, the issue concerning the *allotment* of monies for new *equipment* was *deferred* to the next meeting.

   2. Although the bank had *credited* our account for the amount of the error, we *transferred* our business to another branch.

   3. The staff members requested *permission* to attend the *conference* that was *planned* for the fall.

II. 1. *You* guys may find this topic *preferable to* your old one.

   2. It could have been *she who* phoned while you were out.

   3. Sonja did not have the same qualifications as *I* for that job, but the interviewer seemed to favour her more than *me*.

   4. *Among* the three of them, the mischievous kids always seemed to get *themselves* into trouble.

   5. *Who* did you say got *off* the train at the last station?

   6. At the end of the day, return the key to Eric or *me*.

   7. If it seems *as if* we will have to work overtime, everyone will be responsible for making *his or her* arrangements for a dinner break.

   8. Both Karen and Edna walked *into* the manager's office to discuss *their* vacation plans.

III. 1. Now that you have voiced your opinion, *it's* too late to worry about *others'* feelings.

   2. I *don't* know *who's* going to the *Joneses'* party.

   3. *Tomorrow's* meeting will have to be postponed because the *company's* vice-president from Calgary will be visiting our office.

   4. *We'll* have to wait for *Ms. King's* and *Mr. Rogers'* responses before we plan the meeting.

IV. *Who among* us *doesn't* dream of being successful? This common goal,   **pron prep p'**
however, can have many different meanings. For some, success is measured in dollars; while for others, *it's* measured by the number of friends   **p'**
they have. Real success, however, is a matter of attaining a lifestyle in   **pron**
which one is comfortable with *oneself*. If, for example, a wealthy man lives   **pron**
his life hating the world and everyone in it, including himself, could he be
looked upon as being successful? And what of a poor man who always
appears happy and has countless friends? Is he not more successful than
the wealthy man? The poor man is comfortable with himself and has an
acceptance of his lifestyle; therefore, he can be *credited* with leading a   **sp sp**
very successful life. Although success is *everyone's preferred* goal, *there*   **p' sp p'**
are many different viewpoints about how one achieves this desired state.

Proceed to the composition section of this unit, "Writing a Two-Paragraph Composition."

UNIT SEVEN COMPOSITION SKILLS:
WRITING A TWO-PARAGRAPH COMPOSITION

All writing must be directed to an intended audience. In every piece of writing, you need to consider the pronoun focus and the appropriateness of your message for your reader.

As you have learned, a single paragraph is a group of sentences developing one fact or viewpoint on a topic; two paragraphs, then, will develop two facts or two viewpoints about a single topic. This type of discussion requires a **topic sentence,** or thesis statement, to introduce the two aspects of your composition as well as an appropriate transitional word(s), phrase(s), or sentence to link the two paragraphs and create the continuing flow of discussion. In this composition section, you will produce a two-paragraph composition directed to an intended audience.

I. WRITING FOR A SPECIFIC AUDIENCE

Too often, writers forget to check their pronoun focus and to adjust the level of their writing to suit their intended audience. As you expand your thoughts and produce longer compositions, these factors become more and more important.

A. PRONOUN FOCUS

It is absolutely essential to present your ideas from a consistent point of view. Once you have established the pronoun reference in your writing, try to be consistent in both person and number. Only switch pronoun focus when the sentence seems awkward or doesn't make sense. Note the confusion created by the continual shift in pronoun usage in the following paragraph.

> Today, *everyone* relies on credit cards to purchase anything from an inexpensive book to an entire trip. *We* have learned that "buy now; pay later" can bring immediate satisfaction of *our* whims. However, *people* must be cautious with this type of easy credit for *you* can quickly end up with a bigger financial burden than *your* monthly salary can accommodate. Therefore, *I* try to think twice before *I* say, "Charge it!"

Whom is this message directed to? The writer begins with the reference *everyone,* an anonymous singular focus, then uses the pronouns *we* and *our*—words which imply the author is part of the group referred to. The writer then uses the word *people,* an anonymous plural focus. The next reference is *you*, the pronoun used to identify the reader; and last, the focus is *I*. With such inconsistency, the poor readers will have a difficult time interpreting whom the message is for!

Study the following pronoun patterns. Once you decide on the one pattern that seems most appropriate for your piece of writing, be as consistent as possible with that reference throughout your written passage.

First Person Singular and Plural

Singular	Plural
I, me, my, mine	*we, us, our, ours*

If you decide to use either the first person singular or the first person plural (not both), your message will suggest that you are writing from your own personal experience. Note that your pronoun choices are restricted, as you may use references from only one of the above lists.

> *I rely*
> Today, ~~we rely~~ on credit cards to purchase anything from an inexpensive book to an entire
> *I*   *my*
> trip. ~~We~~ have learned that "buy now; pay later" can bring immediate satisfaction of ~~our~~
>   *I*   *I*
> whims. However, ~~we~~ must be cautious with this type of easy credit for ~~we~~ can quickly end
>   *my*   *I*
> up with a bigger financial burden than ~~our~~ monthly salary can accommodate. Therefore, ~~we~~
>   *I*
> try to think twice before ~~we~~ say, "Charge it!"

Second Person Singular and Plural

> *you, your, yours*

If the second person pronoun is the most appropriate form to use, your message will tend to be instructional. Note the very limited choice of reference words. The writer who chooses this type of format will have to rely on a refined sentence structure to create an interesting passage and to avoid the lecture tone illustrated in the following revision.

> Today, *you rely* on credit cards to purchase anything from an inexpensive book to an entire trip. *You* have learned that "buy now; pay later" can bring immediate satisfaction of *your* whims. However, *you* must be cautious with this type of easy credit for *you* can quickly end up with a bigger financial burden than *your* monthly salary can accommodate. Therefore, *you should* try to think twice before *you* say, "Charge it!"

Third Person Singular

> (Masculine gender)—*he, him, his, individual, person, student, everyone*, etc., *OR* the name of, or reference to, any singular masculine person
>
> (Feminine gender)—*she, her, hers, individual, person, student, everyone*, etc., *OR* the name of, or reference to, any singular feminine person

NOTE: To avoid having to choose between male and female references in your writing, try to use the third person plural, which is the same for both genders.

Third Person Plural

> *they, them, their, theirs, individuals, people, students, all*, etc., *OR* the names of, or reference to, more than one person.

Because of the many and varied choices of both pronoun and alternate word references they offer, the third person singular and third person plural are the two most common focuses in writing. If one of these (not both) is the most suitable approach for your written work, then be consistent with your chosen list. One advantage of this option is that, in addition to the pronouns listed, the writer can use the thesaurus to locate other suitable reference words. However, read the following version of the sample paragraph and note the awkwardness caused by the use of the third person singular. For this message, the latter would be the *poorest* choice.

> *all people rely*
> Today, *the average person relies* on credit cards to purchase anything from an inexpensive
> *They have*
> book to an entire trip. *He or she has* learned that "buy now; pay later" can bring immediate
> *their* *buyers*
> satisfaction to *his or her* whims. However, *the individual* must be cautious with this type of
> *they* *their*
> easy credit for *he or she* can quickly end up with a bigger financial burden than *his or her*
> *shoppers should think* *they say,*
> monthly salary can accommodate. Therefore, *he or she should think* twice before *he or she*
>
> *says,* "Charge it!"

Depending on the author's purpose, any of the points of view we have discussed could be used in the preceding passage; however, the wordiness produced by the use of the third person singular should encourage the writer to try the first person, second person, or third person plural instead. Note, however, that the tone of the message changes with each version.

● EXERCISE 7.19

Eliminate the incorrect shifts of pronoun reference in the following paragraphs.

1. Even in the case of what seems to be an emergency, one should be cautious about allowing strangers to enter their homes. Because of the increase in crime rates, unfortunately, we cannot assume that a person making a simple request to use the telephone is someone you can trust!

2. Procrastination is one of my worst faults. Our tendency to put off things we dislike doing creates feelings of guilt and causes unnecessary worry. Those unwritten letters and unsavory tasks usually plague one's mind; in fact, they may even cause you sleepless nights! I know that, if we spent as much time completing the things that needed to be done as we did thinking and worrying about them, there would be no problem of getting behind. As a result, I am attempting to overcome my bad habit by "not putting off until tomorrow what you should have done yesterday." I hope this revised motto helps!

Check your answers with those in the Answer section at the end of the book.

B. ASSESSING YOUR WRITING

In order to improve your work, you must have some gauge with which to measure the effectiveness of what you have written. Using a "readability formula" will help you determine if your writing is acceptable for your intended audience and will also identify what type of revision is necessary to make your work more appropriate.

Gunning's Fog Index[1]

Sometimes it is useful to check your work using a readability formula. The Fog Index is one such formula. It can help you to determine whether you are using appropriate vocabulary and sentence structure for your intended audience.

Use a calculator for accurate and speedy results.

1. a) Select a passage of approximately 100 to 125 words, containing a number of consecutive sentences. Write down the number of words in each sentence, like this:

    8 - 14 - 28 - 16 - 5 - 22 - 10

    TOTAL: 103 words in 7 sentences

    Treat independent clauses as separate sentences; for example, "In school we studied; we learned; we improved," would count as three sentences.

    b) Find the average sentence length by dividing the length of the passage (103 words) by the number of sentences (7).

    $$\frac{103 \text{ words}}{7 \text{ sentences}} = (14.7) = 15 \text{ (rounded to the nearest whole number)}$$

    Average sentence length = 15

2. a) Read the selected passage and place a check mark (✔) above all words that contain three syllables or more.

    DO NOT include   i)   capitalized words
                      ii)   combinations of short easy words like *bookkeeper* or *nevertheless*
                    iii)   verbs made into three syllables by the addition of *-es* or *-ed* such as *trespasses* or *created*.

    b) Now, count the number of check marks, divide your count by the number of words in the passage (103 words), and multiply by 100 to get the percentage of long words. Round to the nearest whole number.

    For example:

    $$\frac{12 \text{ long words}}{103 \text{ words}} = .1165 \times 100 = 11.65\% \text{ or } 12\% \text{ (rounded to the nearest whole number)}$$

    Percentage of long words = 12

3. Calculate the Fog Index by adding the results of step 1 (average sentence length) and step 2 (percentage of long words). Multiply this sum by the constant factor of 0.4. *Ignore the digits following the decimal point.* For example:

    (Average sentence length   +   Percentage of long words)   ×   .4 = Fog Index
              (15   +   12)   ×   .4 = 10

Note the application of the Fog Index to the following announcement of a new policy by a major manufacturing company:

For some time, there has been under consideration a policy of adopting a practice to alleviate the adverse effect on employees of long trips overseas. One way to solve this problem, at least partially, would be to permit returning travellers a brief period of adjustment before full resumption of their duties. Therefore, the following policy is established, effective the first of next month.

As soon as possible after a trip of one month or longer, employees are allowed three days' paid leave of absence. The employee will arrange this leave with his or her supervisor in conformity with this policy.

1. a) The sentence pattern:
            25 - 26 - 12 - 21 - 16
                TOTAL: 100 words in 5 sentences

   b) Average sentence length = $\dfrac{100}{5}$ = 20

2. Percentage of long words = $\dfrac{20}{100} \times 100$ = 20%

3. Fog Index = (20 + 20) $\times$ .4 = 16

Use the following guidelines to evaluate your writing:

Fog Index: 12 and above—very good; acceptable
              10-11—good (perhaps consider minor revisions)
              9—definitely consider revisions
              8 or below—very weak; consider major revisions

Warning: This formula cannot help you recognize errors in your writing or judge the relevance of the content. Therefore, if your composition contains misspellings, word repetition, incorrect sentence structure, or grammar/punctuation errors, the calculations will be invalid. Furthermore, this formula assesses the words and sentence patterns that you have identified as meaningful content; if what you have written is irrelevant, vague, disorganized, etc., then the calculated index will again be invalid.

Also, remember that the Fog Index provides a method for personal assessment and indicates the need for revision. As there are many other measurable factors that only the reader can assess, this calculation does not reflect an absolute, accurate grade level for your work.

The following are assessments of a weak piece of writing and then the same piece improved.

Weak writing — An excerpt from the first draft of a student essay:

Leukemia is a cancer. It affects the blood-forming organs of the body. It can affect people of all kinds of ethnic groups and people of all ages. There is no cure for this disease. Treatments will help people live longer. There are many drugs and doses to treat leukemia. Persons are usually put in a hospital for an initial assessment and treatment. Once remission is achieved, they can usually live comfortably at home. They should be careful to avoid persons who may transmit infections. Infections are the prime cause of death in leukemia victims.

Assessment calculation:

$$\frac{94}{10} \frac{\text{(number of words)}}{\text{(number of complete sentences)}} = \overset{9}{\cancel{9.4}} \text{ (average number of words per sentence)}$$

$$\frac{10}{94} \frac{\text{(number of challenging words)}}{\text{(total number of words)}} \times 100 = \overset{11}{\cancel{10.6}} \text{ (percentage of long words)}$$

(Average sentence length + Percentage of long words) $\times$ .4 = Fog Index
(9 + 11) $\times$ .4 = 8 *Weak* assessment

Improved writing — After initial assessment and revision:

Leukemia, a cancer which affects the blood-forming organs of the body, can affect people of different ages and ethnic groups. Even though there is no cure for this dreaded disease, the life expectancy of diagnosed victims can be prolonged by medication. Those afflicted are usually hospitalized for initial assessment and treatment. However, once remission occurs, they can usually live comfortably at home. Because infections are the prime cause of death, leukemia victims should be careful to avoid persons who may transmit any viruses.

Assessment calculation:

$$\frac{84}{5} \frac{\text{(number of words)}}{\text{(number of complete sentences)}} = \overset{17}{\cancel{16.8}} \text{ (average number of words per sentence)}$$

$$\frac{14}{84} \frac{\text{(number of challenging words)}}{\text{(total number of words)}} \times 100 = \overset{17}{\cancel{16.6}} \text{ (percentage of long words)}$$

(Average sentence length + Percentage of long words) $\times$ .4 = Fog Index
(17 + 17) $\times$ .4 = 13.6 *Acceptable* assessment

● EXERCISE 7.20

Apply the formula to the paragraphs you wrote in Unit Six. What does it tell you about your writing? Don't forget that, in using this formula, you must also critique your work for effective content, word repetition, grammatical errors, spelling, and punctuation.

II. WRITING A TWO-PARAGRAPH COMPOSITION

As you will remember from your outlining practice in Unit Two, main ideas can be located in various places in a paragraph. For example, the main idea can be the first sentence or it can be in mid-paragraph with a question or topic sentence preceding it. In this composition, you will write a main-idea sentence after the topic sentence.

A. CHOOSING AND LIMITING A TOPIC

The focus for this writing assignment is *two*. You will write *two* paragraphs on *two* discussion points of a topic; therefore, to work on the step-by-step procedures in this section, choose *two* different topics from those listed below:

two members of a family

two important lessons you have learned through experience

advantages and disadvantages of _____

two advantages of _____

two disadvantages of _____

two effects of television/a particular show on _____

work and leisure times

two emotions that can be confused

two aspects of one emotion

two major reasons for _____

two steps required to _____

your feelings now compared to your feelings before about _____

two major attractions at a tourist sight

● EXERCISE 7.21

Look at the example and then write your chosen topics in the spaces provided; condense your topics as illustrated. **Stop when each of your topics is suitable for discussion.**

General Topic → Be Specific ⟶ Be More Specific ⟶ Be Even More Specific → Focused Topic

There are many aspects to this topic. Which one can you talk about?	There are many aspects to this topic. Which one can you talk about?	Can you think of anything special about this topic?	Can you name some special facts about this topic?

Sample Topic:

men and women	media portrayals of men and women	gender in advertising	stereotyped roles in ads

Your Topics:

1. _____ _____ _____ _____

2. _____ _____ _____ _____

B. BRAINSTORMING AND WRITING A WORKING THESIS STATEMENT

One aspect of this composition that is different from your last writing effort is the initial sentence. Note that this statement presents the topic and identifies the two points of view. Because this introductory sentence gives an overview of both points to be discussed, it is called the **thesis statement.** Look at the following illustration:

Topic with two discussion points—Women's and men's roles in advertising

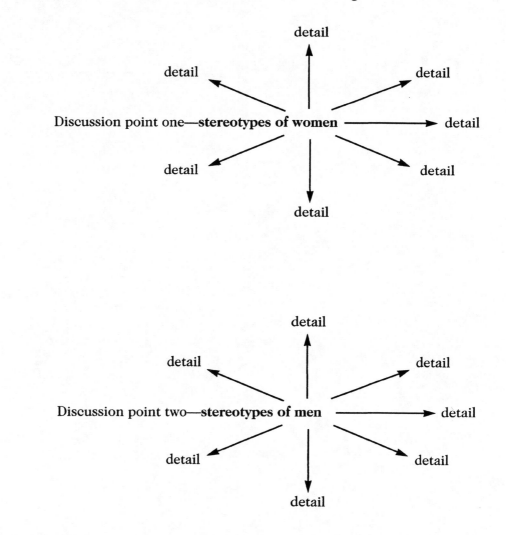

Working thesis statement—Women and men are stereotyped in advertisements.

● EXERCISE 7.22

In the space provided, write your focused topic for a two-paragraph composition and then identify your two discussion points. Brainstorm your two thesis points separately and look for a pattern of development that will produce a meaningful written discussion.

Once you have decided on your theme, write a working thesis statement to introduce both aspects of your composition. This statement does not have to be perfect, as you will re-examine it when you have completed your paragraph plan.

1. **Topic with two discussion points**_____

Discussion point one _____

Discussion point two _____

Working thesis statement_____

_____

2. Topic with two discussion points_____

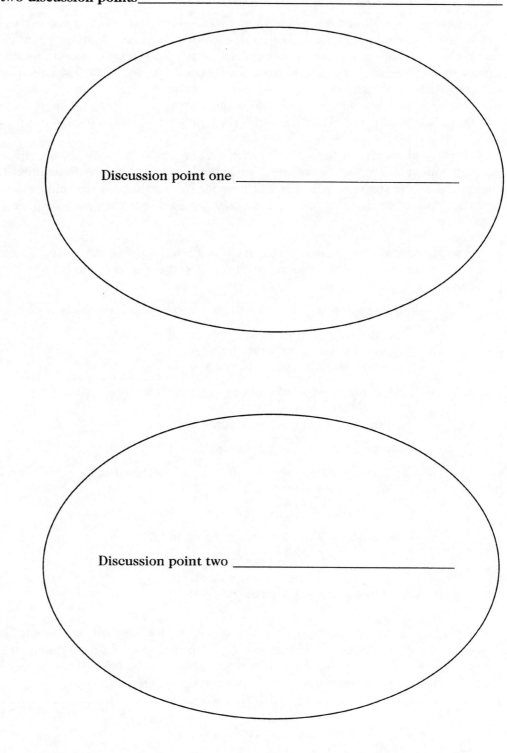

Discussion point one _____

Discussion point two _____

Working thesis statement_____

_____

C. DEVELOPING EACH DISCUSSION POINT

Once you have developed a working thesis statement, you are ready to expand each discussion point into a separate paragraph. For each of your discussion points, review your brainstorming facts; choose and/or complete the necessary details for the two separate paragraphs. **Each paragraph should begin with a clearly worded, focused main-idea statement supported by logically developed facts.**

The working thesis statement should begin your first paragraph, followed by the main idea for the first discussion point. Write the supporting major and minor details in proper outline fashion to complete the plan for the first paragraph.

The second paragraph should begin with a main-idea statement that identifies your second thesis point. Major and minor supporting points should follow as before. Remember that the number of major and minor supporting details will vary for each paragraph depending on your topic choice and the depth of your explanation. The following model summarizes the proper outline format.

Thesis statement: A sentence that introduces both aspects of your topic and suggests your method of discussion. This sentence begins the first paragraph and is immediately followed by the main-idea statement about the first thesis point.

I. Main-idea sentence gives the writer's viewpoint on just the first discussion point.

   A. first major detail of support for main idea
      1. minor point to elaborate point A
      2. minor point to elaborate point A

   B. second major detail of support for main idea
      1. minor point to elaborate point B
      2. minor point to elaborate point B

   C. third major detail of support for main idea

II. Transitional word, phrase, or sentence in combination with the main idea of the second discussion point.

   A. first major detail of support for main idea

   B. second major detail of support for main idea

   C. third major detail of support for main idea
      1. minor point to elaborate point C
      2. minor point to elaborate point C

Concluding sentence: A sentence that gives advice, a prediction, or a result of your discussion about the two thesis points. If your writing is unified, you can interchange this sentence with the thesis statement. It is a good idea to write three concluding statements so that you can choose the two strongest ones for your beginning and ending.

● EXERCISE 7.23

Record the discussion points for your two proposed compositions in outline form. Follow the instructions for outlining a two-paragraph composition given in this section.

D. Using Transitional Expressions to Link the Paragraphs

To connect the two paragraphs, use transitional (linking) words to show the relevance of, and relationship between, the two paragraphs. Using guide words will help the reader follow your message. Choose the most appropriate ones from the following list:

Transitional Expressions

1. **To indicate an additional point,** you could use
    also, in addition, equally important, another, as well as, not only ... but also, besides ...,
    in addition to ..., furthermore, together with

2. **To indicate an example,** you could use
    for instance, for example, to illustrate ..., some ..., other ..., one ..., another ...

3. **To indicate a sequence,** you could use
    first, second, next, last, finally, then, currently, now, in the past, in the future,
    after a few days/hours/minutes, etc., before ..., after ..., soon

4. **To indicate a similar idea,** you could use
    similarly, in the same manner, in comparison, likewise, identical/identically,
    equal/equally, equivalent

5. **To indicate a contrasting idea,** you could use
    however, on the other hand, but, on the contrary, although this may be true..., conversely,
    not the same, different ..., opposite ..., the reverse ..., unequal, in spite of ..., differs from ...

Transitional expressions are used to connect ideas from one paragraph to another as well as to relate one sentence to another within a given paragraph. Therefore, choose your words carefully. Do not overuse any one of these expressions, and connect your paragraphs and your paragraph ideas thoughtfully.

E. Composing an Effective Concluding Sentence

Remember that your concluding sentence is just as important as your initial one. This statement will not only unite your ideas, but will also give a prediction, a result, advice, or a summary of what you have stated in your two-paragraph discussion. In a two-paragraph composition, your concluding statement must address both aspects you have discussed; therefore, generate two or three concluding sentences, as you did before, in response to the various resolutions of your discussion.

1. Reread your theme and your supporting evidence. Now write three concluding sentences. You should write these three statements after you have written your outlined points. Consider the following questions:

    a) What advice could you give someone about both viewpoints?
    b) What prediction about these two issues can you make?
    c) What can you conclude about or what is the result of these two points of view?
    d) What can you restate (using different wording) or summarize from both aspects of your topic?

2. Test paragraph unity by replacing the working thesis statement with each of your concluding sentences. There should be a natural flow of content support if the thesis statements and the details have the same focus. Choose the two strongest statements from all the ones you have written (including the working thesis) and use one for the topic sentence to introduce both aspects of your theme and one for the conclusion.

3. Make any necessary revisions to the order and content of your proposed paragraphs. Your message should have a logical and natural flow of meaningful information.

If you have difficulty ending your composition, use one of the following words or phrases to prompt you to write a conclusion. As you discover more appropriate words of this nature, add them to the list.

Therefore, ...	Because ...
As a result, ...	Even though ...
Although ...	And so ...
If ...	Since ...
In the future ...	

F. SAMPLE OUTLINE AND COMPOSITION

Here is a sample outline and two-paragraph composition about gender roles in advertising.

Topic—two viewpoints about a single topic: Roles in advertising

Thesis statement—Advertisers still rely heavily on the traditional female and male roles to appeal to their consumers. ◄—— **Thesis statement that introduces both aspects of the topic**

   I. Women in most commercials are still cast as the weaker sex. ◄—— **Main idea that introduces a focused comment on the first thesis point**

      A. portrayed as boring housewives for household products
         1. incapable of making a decision

      B. used as sex objects in car advertisements   **Major and minor points to support the first main-idea statement**
         1. silent and sensuous
         2. materialistic and unintelligent

      C. shown as helpless in life insurance ads

  II. On the other hand, men are continually presented as the dominant gender. ◄—— **Transition expression plus the main idea that introduces the focused comment on the second thesis point**

      A. apparent strength
         1. drink beer
         2. test-drive trucks

      B. capable of knowing what is right and wrong   **Major and minor points to support this main idea**
         1. decision-making emphasized with sounds
         2. subtle evidence of natural dominance

Concluding sentence—And so, even with today's emphasis on equal status for both sexes, in the eyes of many advertisers, women and men are still typecast with the chauvinistic beliefs of yesteryear. ◄—— **Concluding statement that sums up both thesis points; if this sentence is interchangeable with the thesis statement, it verifies the unity of the content.**

Read the following draft based on the given writing outline.

Advertisers still rely heavily on the traditional female ← **Thesis statement introduces**
and male roles to appeal to their consumers. Women in ← **two aspects**
most commercials are still cast as the weaker sex. For → **Main idea for the first**
example, many females are portrayed as boring homemak- **thesis point**
ers whose greatest problem is to discover which product **Transition phrase to indicate**
produces whiter clothes or cleaner dishes. These house- **paragraph development**
wives often need the approval of other family members to
arrive at a decision about which is the best detergent to
use. In a majority of car commercials, beautiful, sexy models silently slink invitingly into the velvet upholstered seat.
They say not a word, but their sensuous actions suggest ← **Spell words correctly**
that women, particularly beautiful ones, are materialistic
and blindly attracted to men who own and drive that particular model of car. Even life insurance advertisements
depict the helplessness of a woman who cannot exist with- ← **Use thesaurus for effective**
out the protective arm of her spouse or his thoughtful **word choices**
planning for her future.

On the other hand, men are continually presented as ← **Transition phrase to link**
the dominant gender. Their strength is apparent in most **paragraphs plus the main idea for**
commercials. Strong men drink beer after a tedious task or **the second paragraph**
stupendous feat. Tough men test-drive trucks over the **Use sentence patterns to create**
most incredibly rocky terrain. A man, it seems, is always **desired effect**
capable of knowing what is right and how to make a deci-
sion. Have you ever noticed the loud sounds—a fist crash- ← **Use varied sentence patterns**
ing on a table, doors being slammed, the resonant tones of
trumpets—that accompany his decision-making? All these
factors are subtle evidence of his natural dominance and
intelligence. And so, even with today's emphasis on equal ← **Concluding statement that sums**
status for both sexes, in the eyes of many advertisers, **up both thesis points and is**
women and men are still typecast in the chauvinistic styles **interchangeable with the thesis**
of yesteryear. **statement**

COLLABORATIVE EXERCISE 7.24

Prepare an outline for a two-paragraph composition based on one of the topics you developed in earlier exercises.

1. Exchange outlines with another class member. Each student should read the other's outline and critique it using the criteria given below. (This kind of exercise is called a peer review.) Use or photocopy the checklist for your evaluations.

2. If you believe your partner has satisfactorily completed an item in the checklist, then place a check mark in the "Okay" column; but if you feel that some parts need to be improved, then write your recommendations in the suggested column. Try to be helpful in your suggestions for improvement.

Checklist	Okay	Recommendations
Paragraph 1		
a) effective thesis statement for composition	_____	
b) main-idea statement for 1st paragraph	_____	
c) relevance and effectiveness of details	_____	
d) sufficient support for main idea	_____	
Paragraph 2		
a) good choice of transitional word(s) or sentence	_____	
b) main-idea statement for 2nd paragraph	_____	
c) relevance and effectiveness of details	_____	
d) sufficient support for main idea	_____	
e) concluding statement for whole composition	_____	
Overall proposed content	_____	
Overall organization	_____	
Content appears unified	_____	

Outline has been reviewed by _____ for _____'s proposed two-paragraph composition.

G. Writing from the Outline

If you follow your outline plan, then you can be fairly sure that your paragraphs will demonstrate unity; that is, all facts are relevant to the main issue of each paragraph. However, to ensure that your paragraphs are coherent—that is, that there is a good flow to your message—take care to do the following:

1. Use varied sentence lengths and patterns.

2. Use meaningful and varied linking words to join your major details or to indicate minor points.

3. Use the thesaurus to improve the vocabulary level and tone.

 Using the online thesaurus is very convenient and may provide the variety of synonyms or antonyms that you need. Check for this feature under the heading "Tools."

4. Avoid using vague words such as *it* or *this* unless absolutely necessary.

5. Ensure clear and correct pronoun focus.

6. Proofread your work for mechanical errors.

 Most computers have an online grammar check program that is useful in pointing out the kinds of errors that can slip past a spell-checker because the misspelled word happens to be in the dictionary. It also alerts you to mistakes or typing errors that have created run-on sentences, subject-verb errors, overuse of words and phrases, etc. Check for this feature under the heading "Tools."

7. Calculate the level of your written work using Gunning's Fog Index.

8. Revise.

9. Recalculate the readability level of your work.

● EXERCISE 7.25

Once you are satisfied with the outline you prepared in Exercise 7.24, write the corresponding two-paragraph composition. Make sure to indent each paragraph clearly and double-space your final draft. Your completed assignment should be 150 to 200 words long. Use the evaluation sheet at the end of this unit to assess your work.

THE NEXT STEP

When you have completed this assignment, follow the same procedure using a different topic from those listed earlier and a different method of development. When you have completed the required number of assignments for this unit, proceed to Unit Eight.

III. A QUICK REVIEW OF THE PROCEDURE FOR WRITING A TWO-PARAGRAPH COMPOSITION

1. Choose a topic with two discussion points.

2. Focus the topic to suit a specific theme you can develop.

3. Brainstorm your chosen topic.

4. Consider the best theme to follow and choose the most effective type of paragraph development.

5. Write a working thesis sentence that encompasses both aspects of your theme.

6. Write the main-idea sentence for your first discussion point. Identify this statement with a Roman numeral.

7. Look at your list of brainstorming facts. Cross out the irrelevant ones; choose the major facts and number them in logical order; indicate any minor points that provide additional support for any of your chosen major details; and, finally, add any other details—major or minor—that improve your message.

8. Choose a suitable transitional expression and write the main idea to introduce your second discussion point.

9. Arrange your chosen details in outline format; use Roman numerals to mark your main ideas, capital letters to identify the major details, and Arabic numbers to indicate minor ones.

10. Reread your thesis, your main-idea sentences, and your supporting evidence. Now write three concluding sentences. You should write these three statements after you have written your outlined points; the statements should address both discussion points.

11. Test paragraph unity by replacing the working thesis with each concluding statement. There should be a natural flow of content support if the statement and the details have the same focus. Choose the two strongest statements from all the ones you have written (including the working thesis) and use one for the beginning and one for the conclusion.

12. Make any necessary revisions to the order and content of your proposed paragraph. The information in your message should be meaningful and have a logical and natural flow.

IV. TWO-PARAGRAPH EVALUATION

Critically assess both the strong and weak characteristics of your writing by placing a check mark in the appropriate column of the following evaluation form.

I. CONTENT MERIT

Excellent	Good	Weak	
			UNITY
_____	_____	_____	1. clearly focused and effectively worded thesis statement
_____	_____	_____	2. clearly focused and effectively worded main ideas
_____	_____	_____	3. details follow specific patterns
_____	_____	_____	4. logical order of content
_____	_____	_____	5. details are specific as opposed to vague or too general
_____	_____	_____	6. adequate coverage of topic
_____	_____	_____	7. irrelevant details excluded
_____	_____	_____	8. sound and effectively worded concluding sentence
			COHERENCE
_____	_____	_____	9. effective transition phrases used to create good flow of ideas within and between paragraphs
_____	_____	_____	10. good sentence variety (length and pattern)
_____	_____	_____	11. effective word usage
			STRUCTURE
_____	_____	_____	12. appropriate length
_____	_____	_____	13. correct paragraph format

MERIT SCORE: Circle the most appropriate score for your written work.

100   95   90   85   80   75   70   65   60   55   50   45   40   less than 40

II. TECHNICAL ERRORS

Mechanical errors reduce the quality of your writing. Your paragraph is considered weak if you have made more than two major errors and/or more than two minor errors in the same category.

1. Proofread for and correct the following types of major errors in your paragraph. (Deduct two marks from your merit score for each error made in this category.)

_____ sentence fragments (frag)	_____ sentence structure (ss)	_____ faulty verb
_____ run-on sentences (ro)	_____ incorrect pronoun (pron)	tenses (vt)
_____ subject-verb agreement (sv)	_____ incorrect preposition (prep)	_____ other

2. Proofread for and correct the following types of minor errors in your paragraph. (Deduct one mark from your merit score for each error made in this category.)

_____ incorrect spelling (sp)	_____ semicolon error (p;)	_____ other
_____ misuse of words (m/w)	_____ comma error (p,)	_____ other
_____ word omission (w/o)	_____ unnecessary punctuation (p)	
_____ faulty end punctuation(p?)	_____ apostrophe error (p')	

NET WORTH OF WRITTEN ASSIGNMENT = Merit score – Technical errors = _____

If you have excellent content and relatively few errors, you have made a communication link with your reader. Your written message has effectively and efficiently transmitted your thought processes. This is a valuable skill—one that all employers search for in their prospective employees. Therefore, strive for perfection in this area. Note your areas of weakness and try to make improvements in your next writing activity.

COMPLETING THE CIRCUIT

 ## OVERVIEW

In Unit Eight, the principles governing the use of the suffixes *-ible* and *-able* and of suffixes added to words ending with *y* are reviewed.

Description and explanation are absolutely essential in any written work. Imprecise use of descriptive words or ambiguous sentence structure can mislead and confuse the reader. The three major errors discussed here are the ones most commonly made. The lessons and exercises in this unit should help you avoid these weaknesses in your own work.

Students rarely have the opportunity to have their papers professionally printed; most often, they either input assignments themselves or have someone else prepare them. In the punctuation section, rules and exercises for using underlining or italics are reviewed. Since most students are not involved in writing narratives, the focus on quotation marks is directed to their use in academic papers and reports only.

The section on writing an expository essay completes the assignments in this program. The essay's organization, sentence structure, use of grammar and punctuation, spelling, and choice of words challenge you to use all the skills presented in the writing portion of this text. In turn, this exercise also provides a challenge for the reader who must interpret your message. If both goals are reached, congratulations—the communication circuit has been successfully completed.

You now have the necessary tools to study and write effective essay exams. Following the advice and study techniques suggested in this section will help you put all the communication skills together. If you are a skillful reader, listener, note-taker, and writer and continue to practise these skills, you will achieve success in all future communication activities.

LEARNING OBJECTIVES FOR UNIT EIGHT

Upon completion of this unit, you should be able to:

1. Apply the rules for adding the suffixes *ible* and *able* to root words.

2. Apply the rules for adding suffixes to words ending with *y*.

3. Demonstrate the correct use and placement of descriptive words or groups of words: for example,

   a) adjective and adverb usage
   b) comparative, superlative, and non-comparative forms of adjectives and adverbs
   c) the correct use of *fewer* and *less*
   d) correction of double negatives
   e) correction of dangling or misplaced modifiers

4. Correct errors in parallel structure.

5. Apply the rules for underlining and using quotation marks in titles and excerpts from printed sources.

6. Limit and focus the topic for an expository essay.

7. Compose a precise and unified thesis statement.

8. Using cumulative composition skills from previous chapters, construct an outline for an expository essay of four or more paragraphs.

9. Compose an appropriate introduction for your composition from among the many types suggested.

10. Using a writing plan, compose a unified and cohesive expository essay.

11. Use the Fog Index to assess the readability and suitability of your essay for your intended audience.

12. Using a dictionary, thesaurus, and your cumulative grammar skills, proofread and refine your written work.

13. Apply the accumulated study and writing skills presented in this text to prepare for and write essay exams.

 Check Internet resources for help with grammar and composition (see pages 469–70).

PRETEST: SPELLING—WORDS WITH *IBLE* OR *ABLE* AND THE FINAL *Y*

This exercise tests your ability to add the *ible/able* suffixes correctly and to change the ending of words ending with *y*. Use a dictionary if you have doubts. In the following pairs of words, circle the word that is spelled correctly.

1. receivable   receivible
2. credible   credable
3. changable   changeable
4. negligible   negligable
5. valuable   valueable
6. despicable   despicible
7. delayed   delaid
8. relys   relies
9. appling   applying
10. said   sayed
11. applys   applies
12. noticeable   noticable
13. laid   layed
14. multiplys   multiplies
15. desirable   desireable
16. usable   useable
17. complying   compling
18. terrible   terrable
19. predictible   predictable
20. possable   possible

Check your answers with those in the Answer section at the end of the book.

If you made no more than two errors, proceed to the Pretest for "Modifiers and Parallel Structure." If you made more than two errors, complete the lessons on the following pages.

SPELLING–WORDS WITH *IBLE* OR *ABLE* AND THE FINAL *Y*

I. *IBLE* OR *ABLE*?

Many rules govern the use of -able or -ible at the end of a word; there are also many exceptions to these rules. Therefore, try to follow these guidelines, but if you have any doubts, *consult the dictionary.*

Rule 1: For most words, add *-able* if the root word is a complete word; add *-ible* if the root word is not a complete word.

Exceptions: If the root ends with *c* or *g*, add *-ible* to make the consonant soft; and *-able* to make it hard.

● EXERCISE 8.1

Add *-able* or *-ible* to the following root words:

1.	mail	11.	terr
2.	agree	12.	cred
3.	perish	13.	feas
4.	accept	14.	poss
5.	profit	15.	aud
6.	adjust	16.	comprehens
7.	tax	17.	horr
8.	predict	18.	plaus
9.	reason	19.	indel
10.	understand	20.	ed

● EXERCISE 8.2

Add *-ible* or *-able* to each of the following words:

1. amic   6. intellig
2. neglig   7. despic
3. invinc   8. tang
4. reduc   9. leg
5 indefat   10. forc

Rule 2: If the word ends with silent *e*, drop the *e* and add *-able* to form the new word.

Exceptions: If the word ends with *g* or *c* plus a silent *e*, retain the *e* and add *-able*.

● EXERCISE 8.3

Add *-able* to each of the following words, dropping the final *e* if necessary.

1. compare   6. marriage
2. change   7. value
3. notice   8. service
4. use   9. advise
5. receive   10. conceive

● EXERCISE 8.4

Fill in the missing letters.

1. It is poss_ible_ that the valu_able_ necklace was misplaced rather than stolen.
2. There was tang_ible_ evidence that this despic_able_ practice had been carried on for years.
3. There was an amic_able_ relationship between the two families.
4. He was inelig_ible_ for the printing course because his writing was illeg_ible_.
5. She is a reason_able_ woman who is also indefatig_able_ in her efforts to keep her family a happy and healthy unit.
6. Forc_ible_ entry into the home was gained through the basement window.
7. The amount of his tax_able_ income was unbeliev_able_.
8. It is advis_able_ to teach your children how to save before they reach a marriage_able_ age.
9. Every accept_able_ solution to the problem was carefully assessed.
10. Because of the many exceptions, spelling rules are not always applic_ible_ to every situation; therefore, to make a notice_able_ improvement in your written work, double-check your spelling!

Check your answers with those in the Answer section at the end of the book.

II. THE FINAL Y

Rule 1: If the final *y* is preceded by a consonant and the ending begins with a vowel change the *y* to *i*.

Exception: When adding the ending *-ing*, retain the final *y* and add the ending (*relying*).

> rely + es = relies
> rely + ing = relying

NOTE: If the ending you plan to add begins with a consonant (e.g., *-tion*), you may have to add an extra syllable for pronunciation purposes (certify + tion = certification).

● EXERCISE 8.5

Add the following suffixes to the root words listed below. Not all suffixes will apply to all words. Check your dictionary if you have any doubts.

	-es	-ed	-ing	-ic	-able	-al	-tion
1. amplify							
2. apply							
3. clarify							
4. certify							
5. comply							
6. deny							
7. electrify							
8. horrify							
9. justify							
10. magnify							
11. multiply							
12. notify							
13. occupy							
14. ratify							
15. rely							
16. reply							
17. specify							
18. supply							
19. terrify							
20. verify							

Check your answers with those in the Answer section at the end of the book.

Rule 2: If the final *y* is preceded by a vowel, just add the endings.

Exceptions: The words *pay, lay, say,* and *repay* change the *y* to *i* before the addition of just *d*.

	-ing	-ed
stay	staying	stayed
obey	obeying	obeyed
survey	surveying	surveyed
pay	paying	**paid**
lay	laying	**laid**
say	saying	**said**
repay	repaying	**repaid**

● EXERCISE 8.6

Add the following suffixes to the root words listed below. Not all suffixes will apply to all words. Check your dictionary if you have any doubts.

	-ed	-ing	-or/-er	-ance
1. allay				
2. buy				
3. convey				
4. defray				
5. delay				
6. lay				
7. obey				
8. pay				
9. pray				
10. relay				
11. repay				
12. say				
13. stay				
14. stray				
15. survey				

Check your answers with those in the Answer section at the end of the book.

● EXERCISE 8.7

Correct spelling errors in the following sentences. If you have any doubts about the spelling of any word, please consult your dictionary.

1. Aisha always ~~trys~~ [tries] to please her teachers by being polite and ~~compling~~ [complying] with their rules and regulations.
2. Were you notified about the ~~unpayed~~ [unpaid] balance of your account?
3. The ~~supplyer~~ [supplier] ~~sayed~~ [said] that he had ~~tryed~~ [tried] to obtain those materials as promised, but the continual strikes in the area were the main reason all his shipments had been ~~delaid~~ [delayed].

4. Is Reno applying for a job as a surveyor?

5. He ~~sayed~~ said that his bill had been ~~payed.~~ paid ✓

Check your answers with those in the Answer section at the end of the book.

THE NEXT STEP

If you feel confident about this section, proceed to the Pretest for "Modifiers and Parallel Structure" on the following page.

PRETEST: MODIFIERS AND PARALLEL STRUCTURE

This exercise tests your ability to correct errors in descriptive words or groups of words, and to recognize and correct parallel structure errors in sentences. The following sentences may contain errors in adjective/adverb confusion, dangling or misplaced modifiers, or faulty parallel sentence structure. If a sentence is incorrect, rewrite it correctly in the space provided.

1. Swimming in a pool is more fun than ~~to swim~~ in a lake.
   Swimming

2. Do you think he presented that information report ~~proper~~?
   properly

3. Being an old-fashioned family, ~~a formal dinner was serv~~ed in the dining room every evening at precisely six o'clock.   *we served a formal dinner*

4. I felt ~~real~~ bad about what I had said in my moment of anger.
   really

5. She was responsible not only for designing the house but ~~constructed~~ it too.
   for constructing

6. Some children get ~~more~~ funnier as they grow older.

7. Flying overhead we saw the flight team of the Canadian Snowbirds.
   We saw the flight team of the Canadian Snowbirds flying overhead

8. I am so pleased that, as I progress through this program, I have ~~less~~ *fewer* grammatical errors in my written work.

9. The police officer charged the youth with resisting arrest and ~~because he assaulted~~ an officer.
   assaulting

10. When *one is* travelling in a strange city, a local map is an absolute necessity.

Check your answers with those in the Answer section at the end of the book.

If you had eight or more sentences correct, proceed to the Pretest for "Underlining, Italics, and Quotation Marks." If you had fewer than eight sentences correct, complete the lessons on the following pages.

MODIFIERS AND PARALLEL STRUCTURE

I. MODIFIERS

Modifers are additional words, phrases, or clauses used with nouns and verbs to create a better description or to clarify the message. For the most part, modifiers describe nouns and verbs. In addition to making your writing more precise, modifiers also allow you to create varied sentence structures and improve your sentence style.

A. ADJECTIVE/ADVERB CONFUSION

What Is an Adjective?

An **adjective** is a word that describes a noun (the name given to a person, place, thing, or idea). Usually this descriptive word is placed in front of the noun it describes.

> *Several important* people attended the meeting.
> A *tall, good-looking* man sat down beside me.

However, an adjective can also follow certain verbs, including all forms of the verb *to be* (*is, are, was, were*), as well as verbs such as *appear, seem, feel, smell, taste, remain,* when they do not express an action. In these cases, the adjective refers back to the subject.

The grass is *greener* on the other side of the street.

The gift was *appropriate.*

The pie tastes *delicious.* (no action to *taste*)

Ben remained *silent.* (no action to *remained*)

Adjectives can express three degrees of a quality: positive, comparative, and superlative. The positive degree is the basic form of the adjective and does not indicate a comparison (e.g., *clear*); the comparative is used to compare two objects (*clearer*); and the superlative is used to compare more than two (*clearest*).

To form the comparative and superlative of **one-syllable adjectives**, add *-er* and *-est.*

Positive	Comparative	Superlative
tall	taller	tallest
short	shorter	shortest

For adjectives of **three or more syllables**, use *more* and *most*.

Positive	Comparative	Superlative
beautiful	more beautiful	most beautiful
difficult	more difficult	most difficult

Two-syllable adjectives vary; some use the *-er* and *-est* forms, while others use *more* and *most*. If you are unsure which form to use, locate the positive form of the word in the dictionary. If no comparative or superlative forms are listed, use *more* and *most*.

Positive	Comparative	Superlative
early	earlier	earliest
pretty	prettier	prettiest

(These forms are listed in the dictionary under *early* and *pretty*.)

Positive	Comparative	Superlative
evil	more evil	most evil
famous	more famous	most famous

(No forms are listed in the dictionary under *evil* and *famous*, therefore, use *more* and *most*.)

● EXERCISE 8.8

Using your dictionary, find and record the various degrees for the following words:

Positive (basic form)	Comparative (form used to compare two)	Superlative (form used with more than two)

1. strong
2. efficient
3. friendly
4. far
5. many
6. fast
7. important
8. kind
9. ambitious
10. fine

Check your answers with those in the Answer section at the end of the book.

Avoid making double comparisons such as "more smarter" or "most smartest." Use just one acceptable form.

Some words are absolute and cannot be compared. Consider the following examples:

genuine	black	fatal	fundamental	wrong
round	white	perfect	complete	impossible
square	dead	unique	right	full

Each of these descriptive words states the extreme limit of the word's meaning, and it is illogical to state that "something is deader than dead" or "more fatal" or "whiter than white."

If you want to express the idea that one is close to the limit of the word, you may use the comparative terms "more nearly" and "most nearly."

> Carla's answer was *more nearly right* than mine.
> That blouse is the *most nearly white* of the three you have selected.

This usage, however, is not common, and, if possible, you should avoid comparing absolute adjectives.

● EXERCISE 8.9

Correct any errors in the positive, comparative, or superlative uses of adjectives. If a sentence is correct, mark it "*Correct.*"

1. Of the two types of pain relievers, I believe Tylenol is the ~~best~~ one for headaches. *betta*

2. Charles Atlas was at one time considered to be the ~~stronger~~ man in the world. *strongest*

3. We received many submissions to the contest; however, the committee thought your ideas were the most unique.

4. Of the three apartments, we chose the one that was ~~closer~~ to the school. *closest*

5. Alex felt that he was the ~~most~~ luckiest man in the world!

6. Your answer is more nearly right than mine.

7. Among the three of us, Mom liked me ~~better~~. *best*

8. Being second means that you will have to try ~~hard~~ next time. *harder*

9. Since his illness, Mr. Spock says he is feeling ~~more~~ stronger each day.

10. I have travelled by train just as frequently as I have by plane; but I have to admit that I like the train trip ~~best~~. *better*

Check your answers with those in the Answer section at the end of the book.

Fewer and **less** are two adjectives in the comparative degree that are often used incorrectly. *Fewer* should be used to compare numbers of people or objects (things that can be counted). *Less* is used to compare amounts (things that can be measured).

> You have *fewer* bills in your wallet than I do.
> (*Fewer* refers to the number of bills.)

> You have *less* money in your wallet than I do.
> (*Less* refers to an amount.)

● EXERCISE 8.10

Use the correct adjective (*fewer* or *less*) in the blank spaces in the following sentences.

1. _____ people are travelling today because they have _____ money to spend on luxuries.

2. Because there was _____ rain this summer, farmers had _____ vegetables to take to market.

3. There are _____ job opportunities today for anyone seeking a teaching position.

4. Because Tina was trying to maintain a full-time job and attend school at the same time, she had _____ time to devote to her studies.

5. Because there are _____ cars travelling on that particular highway, there are _____ accidents.

Check your answers with those in the Answer section at the end of the book.

What Is an Adverb?

Adverbs describe action words, adjectives, or other adverbs. Most of these descriptive words can be placed anywhere in the sentence. They answer the questions *how, where, when, why, how much,* or *to what extent.* Although not all adverbs end with the suffix *-ly,* those *-ly* words that describe an action will be adverbs.

> The crowd moved *quickly.* (how?)
> The crowd moved *forward.* (where?)
> *Immediately* the crowd moved. (when?)

Most adverbs express the three degrees of quality—positive, comparative, and superlative—by using the terms *more* and *most* with the basic adverb.

Positive	Comparative	Superlative
dangerously	more dangerously	most dangerously
carefully	more carefully	most carefully

Remember, you must use the comparative degree of both adjectives and adverbs to compare two persons, places, objects, or ideas. The superlative degree is used to compare more than two.

> Dan works *more diligently* on projects than Steve does.
> (Two boys are compared.)
>
> In fact, he works the *most diligently* of all the students in the class.
> (More than two are being compared.)

● EXERCISE 8.11

Correct any errors in the positive, comparative, or superlative uses of adjectives and adverbs.

1. To ensure that you make ~~less~~ errors on this test than you did on the last one, proofread your work ~~most~~ carefully.

2. Of all the lawyers who work in this office building, Clara dresses ~~more~~ conservatively.

3. Because my car operates ~~most~~ efficiently in the summer than it does in the winter, I have less car expenses during the months of May to September.

4. Although the new bank is ~~most~~ conveniently located to my workplace, I still prefer the other branch because the staff there is ~~the friendliest~~.

5. Raoul is one of the ~~more~~ healthier *healthiest* looking members of our team.

Check your answers with those in the Answer section at the end of the book.

How Are Adjectives and Adverbs Confused?

Some words (such as *feel, taste, smell, look, sound*) can be used as action words or non-action words. Since most *-ly* words that describe actions are adverbs, try this quick trick: **If the verb expresses action, add *-ly*; no action, no *-ly*.**

no action   no -ly

The accused remained silent.

action   add -ly

In spite of all the repairs, my car still runs poorly.

no action   no -ly

He felt bad about his remarks.

add -ly   action

In the dark, I cautiously felt my way across the room.

action   add -ly

The critics looked at my material carefully.

no action   no -ly

The results looked bad.

Good and **well** are easily confused. *Good* is an adjective and is used if no action is expressed. *Well* is an adverb and is used with actions. An exception is when *well* is used as an adjective to describe a state of health.

action   adverb

He works well on his own.

action   adverb

That motor runs well.

action   adverb

She did well on her test.

no action   adjective

Tran is good at sports.

no action   adjective describing health

John looks well now.

● EXERCISE 8.12

Underline the correct choice of words in the parentheses. (Hint: No action means no *-ly*.)

1. We felt (<u>bad</u>, badly) about the news.

2. The coffee tasted a little (<u>strong</u>, strongly).

3. Things were looking (<u>bad</u>, badly) for our hometown baseball team.

4. Drive (slow, <u>slowly</u>) as you approach the crosswalk.

5. I felt my way (careful, <u>carefully</u>) along the darkened hallway.

6. The actor performed (poor, <u>poorly</u>) because he was ill.

7. Do those flowers smell (<u>sweet</u>, sweetly) to you?

8. Eat your lunch (quick, <u>quickly</u>) so we may leave.

9. She tasted the hot beverage (cautious, <u>cautiously</u>).

10. The accused remained (<u>silent</u>, silently) when questioned about the crime.

11. Wayne Gretzky (consistent, <u>consistently</u>) played (good, <u>well</u>) for his team.

12. Celia is looking very (good, <u>well</u>) since her surgery.

13. I felt (<u>good</u>, well) about the interview I had last week.

14. After Allan had eaten four hamburgers, he said he didn't feel very (good, <u>well</u>).

15. She can play the piano really (good, <u>well</u>).

Check your answers with those in the Answer section at the end of the book.

What Are "Power" Adverbs?

Some adverbs give special emphasis to the words they describe. Note the emphatic adverbs in the following examples.

> Pierre dresses *very* conservatively.
> Mia is a *really* good pianist.
> Debbie works *too* hard.
> She left *rather* suddenly.

These "power" words usually do not cause problems; however, review the usage of this one pair of easily confused words:

real is an adjective
really is an adverb—a power or emphatic adverb

> Is that a *real* diamond? (adjective describing diamond)
> That is a *really* beautiful diamond! (emphatic adverb)

To help you avoid this confusion, try substituting the words *very* or *certainly* for *really*. If the substitution sounds illogical, then use the adjective *real*.

● EXERCISE 8.13

Underline the correct descriptive word in each of the following sentences:

1. Helen is a (real, <u>really</u>) good friend of mine.

2. Preena has always had (real, <u>really</u>) good marks.

3. My school ring is made of (<u>real</u>, really) gold.

4. I was (real, <u>really</u>) disappointed to learn that our trip had been cancelled.

5. The (<u>real</u>, really) test was (real, <u>really</u>) difficult.

Check your answers with those in the Answer section at the end of the book.

Double Negatives—No-No's!

Do not use two or more negative words (*not, never, hardly, scarcely,* or the abbreviated form of not, *n't*) with one verb. This grammatical error is called a double negative and is definitely a "no-no"!

> not: We do*n't* have *no* milk. (a "no-no")
> but: We do*n't* have any milk.   *OR*   We have no milk.
>
> not: I could*n't* hard*ly* move after my exercise class. (a "no-no")
> but: I could *hardly* move after my exercise class.   *OR*   I could*n't* move after my exercise class.

● EXERCISE 8.14

Correct double negative errors ("no-no's") in the following sentences.

1. Haven't you never been to London?
2. I don't never want to see you no more!
3. Because I was sitting at the back of the auditorium, I couldn't hardly hear the speaker.
4. We don't get no satisfaction from that restaurant so we aren't going there no more.
5. Our committee had discussed that issue for two hours and still couldn't reach no decision.
6. The employee claimed that he had never received no notice about the changes in regulations.
7. The suspect said that she didn't know nothing about the break-in.
8. I am not going nowhere tonight; I am staying home for a change.
9. I couldn't scarcely see the road in the dense fog.
10. Some people never take no advice; they prefer to learn through life's experience.

Check your answers with those in the Answer section at the end of the book.

B. DANGLING OR MISPLACED MODIFIERS

A modifier is a word or group of words that provides extra information to make the writer's message clearer. Note the descriptions in the following sentences (in parentheses) and the words these modifiers quite clearly describe.

> (Sitting at my living-room window,) I like to watch the ships in the harbour.
>
> (At the age of twelve,) I went on a (two-month) trip to Australia with my family.
>
> (To keep the party simple,) we plan to serve our guests hot dogs (covered with Coney Island
>
> sauce) (which is now available from the new restaurant on Main Street.)

Often, however, careless writers do not place their descriptive phrasing close to the appropriate word. This situation can create confusing, and sometimes humorous, sentences. Note what happens to the clearly worded sentences from the above examples when word groups are misplaced:

> I like to watch the ships in the harbour sitting at my living-room window.
> (Who is where?)
>
> At the age of twelve, my family took me on a two-month trip to Australia.
> (Who is twelve?)

To keep the party simple, hot dogs were served to our guests covered in Coney Island sauce which is now available from the new restaurant on Main Street.
(Who is keeping the party simple? Who or what is covered with sauce? At least, however, by reading this sentence, you should clearly understand where you can purchase the sauce!)

Dangling Modifiers

If a descriptive group of words is placed in a sentence with no reference word to indicate who or what is being described, this error is referred to as a dangling modifier. This type of common mistake is most often made if you use the passive voice of the verb in your sentences. (This topic was thoroughly presented in Unit Six grammar. If you require more understanding of, or practice with, dangling modifiers, please review that section.) Note the dangling modifiers in the following examples, as well as the suggested corrections.

Incorrect: Standing at the top of the mountain, the whole city can be seen.
("Standing at the top of the mountain" seems to refer to *city*—impossible!)

Revised: Standing at the top of the mountain, *you* can see the whole city.
(The modifier now correctly describes the word closest to it—"you.")

Incorrect: After making up my mind, my decision was submitted to the president.
("After making up my mind" seems to refer to *my decision*—impossible!)

Revised: After making up my mind, *I* submitted my decision to the president.
(The modifier now correctly describes the person *I*.)

Incorrect: When only ten years old, my parents took me to England.
("When only ten years old" seems to refer to *my parents*—impossible!)

Revised: When *I* was only ten years old, my parents took me to England.
(The modifier has been clarified.)

To correct a dangling modifier, you must rewrite the sentence completely. Read the sentence that follows and identify the portion that is dangling.

Incorrect: After listening to the evidence, a verdict of guilty was arrived at by the jury.

There are two ways to correct this error.

Method 1. a) After careful consideration, decide who or what is being described in the modifier. In this case, *the jury* is the implied subject.

b) Change the verb in the dominant (main) clause to the active voice, so that the subject of the main clause is the same as the implied subject of the modifier (*the jury*).

Revised: [After listening to the evidence,] the jury arrived at the verdict of guilty.

OR

The jury, [after listening to the evidence,] arrived at the verdict of guilty.

Method 2. a) Clarify the meaning of the dangling modifier by adding the subject to the modifier itself and by changing the verb form to agree with the subject.

b) To avoid repetition, substitute a pronoun for the subject in the main clause.

Revised: After *the jury had listened* to the evidence, *they* arrived at the verdict of guilty.

OR

The jury arrived at the verdict of guilty after *they* had listened to the evidence.

Whichever method you use, remember that the key to correcting dangling modifiers is to determine the implied subject of the modifier. Once you have this vital information, you can decide how best to clarify the sentence for your readers.

● EXERCISE 8.15

Each of the following sentences contains a dangling modifier. In the space provided, write a corrected version of each sentence. Add or change words as you find necessary.

1. After completing his homework, the assignment was turned in by the student.
   After completing his homework, the student turned in his assignment

2. To achieve a better grade, more studying should be done before you write a test.
   To achieve a better grade, you should study more before you write a test
   do more studying

3. Not seeing the police car following, the car was driven down the street at an excessive rate of speed. *The driver not seeing the police car following, was driving down the street at an excessive rate of speed.*

4. After being late every day this week, the teacher gave the student a severe scolding. *a severe sc*
   Because the student was late everyday this week, the teacher gave him

5. Being a little tired today, my meeting was postponed until tomorrow.
   Because I'm a little tired today, my meeting was postponed until tomorrow

6. After graduating from high school, Jawal's parents bought him a car.
   After Jawal graduated from high school, his parents bought him a car

7. We enjoy watching the birds with our binoculars building their nests.
   we enjoy watching the birds build their nest with our binoculars.

8. After having a bird bath, Angela fed her canary some lettuce.
   After her canary had its bird bath, Angela fed it some lettuce.

9. I saw several moving vans walking home in front of the new house.
   I saw several moving vans in front of the new house, while walking home.

10. To get to know the students better, their names and faces were memorized by the teacher during the first week of classes.
    To get to know the students better during the first week of classes the teacher memorized the students names and faces.

Check your answers with those in the Answer section at the end of the book.

Misplaced Modifiers

Modifiers should be placed close to the word or words they describe—or placed so that the meaning of your sentence will be interpreted clearly.

Note how the following suggestions for rearranging these modifiers help to clarify or even change the meaning of each sentence.

> *Only* he looked at the new sports car.
> (No one else looked.)
>
> He *only* looked at the new sports car.
> (He didn't buy it!)
>
> He looked *only* at the new sports car.
> (He didn't look at any other cars.)

He looked at the *only* new sports car.
(There was just one new sports car to look at.)

In the following examples, the misplacement of the modifiers makes for some incorrect, and sometimes humorous, results!

Ed found his wallet *in the snow* that he had lost.
(Ed didn't lose the snow!)

We huddled in front of the roaring fire *chilled by the cold wintry night.*
(The fire was not chilled; we were!)

● EXERCISE 8.16

Correct the following sentences by placing the modifiers in their correct places.

1. I noticed that my book was on the chair turning on the light.

   Turning on the light, I noticed that my book was on the chair. ✓

2. I phone my sister who lives in Texas every Sunday.

   Every Sunday I phone my sister who lives in Texas. ✓

3. I always give Lara a kiss before she goes to school on her cheek.

   I always give Lara a kiss on her cheek before she goes to school. ✓

4. The photographer focused the camera as we all smiled and snapped our picture.

   As we all smiled, the photographer focused the camera and snapped our picture. ✓

5. The members of the comedy team kept the audience ~~nearly laughing for two hours~~.

   laughing for nearly two hours ✓

6. We planned to serve our guests steak and lobster who were arriving at seven for dinner.

   We planned to serve steak and lobster to our guests who were arriving at seven for dinner. ✓

7. Last night, a pedestrian was struck by a car wearing dark-coloured clothes.

   Last night, a pedestrian wearing dark-coloured clothes was struck by a car. ✓

8. The lecturer will be speaking about the dangers of drinking and driving in the school auditorium at three o'clock.

   ✗ *The lecturer in the the school auditorium at three o'clock will be speaking about the dangers of drinking and driving.*

9. I was kept only after class; everyone else was allowed to leave.

   ✓ *I was the only one kept after class; everyone else was allowed to leave*

10. The bucket slipped out of my hands which was fortunately empty.

    The bucket, which was fortunately empty, slipped out of my hands.

Check your answers with those in the Answer section at the end of the book.

II. PARALLEL STRUCTURE

As you will recall from Unit Four, the coordinating conjunctions—*and, but, or*—join two or more similar words, actions, word groups, or sentences if they are equal in structure. For example, examine the equal portions in the following sentences:

Lisa completed the math question *quickly* and *accurately.*	**Two adverbs**
Krista or *Curt* will represent us.	**Two people**
Connie *completed* the math question and then *left* the room.	**Two actions**
Shelley *put on* her record, *sat* in a comfortable chair, *relaxed* with a cup of tea, and *let* the worries of the day fade away.	**A series of actions**
Clean up your room or *suffer the consequences.*	**Two complete sentences**
Charles arrived at the office early this morning but *he was late for our nine o'clock meeting.*	**Two complete sentences**
Walking stealthily down the corridor and *pausing in each alcove,* the detective carefully followed the suspect.	**Two similar modifying word groups**

Note that, in each of the examples, the portions joined are equal in construction. This grammatical sentence arrangement is called **parallel structure.**

In this grammar section, you must examine and correct sentences that contain faulty parallel structure and apply this proofreading skill to your own work. Note the following common errors and their suggested corrections:

Incorrect: In this program, you will learn how to organize your thoughts and writing them down effectively.

The two portions joined by *and* are not equal in structure and must be corrected. Perhaps seeing the sentence divided will make this point clearer.

In this program, you will learn how to
{
organize your thoughts

writing them down effectively
}

You can easily see that the two portions are different. Correct the error by making both the same:

In this program, you will learn how to
{
organize your thoughts

write them down effectively
}

In this program, you will learn how to *organize your thoughts* and *write them down effectively.*

There is more than one way to correct errors in parallel structure; some, of course, are more effective than others. Make sure you include enough of the common portion of the sentence to make your meaning clear, but not so much that you make your sentences unnecessarily wordy. For example:

items are not parallel

Incorrect: In my spare time I like reading, biking, and to play tennis.
Correct but wordy: In my spare time I like to read, to bike, and to play tennis.
Better: In my spare time I like to read, bike, and play tennis.

OR

My favourite pastimes are reading, biking, and playing tennis.

● EXERCISE 8.17

Correct errors in parallel structure in the following sentences. Avoid unnecessary wordiness.

1. She promised to read a book and that she would turn in her report by Monday.
   She promised to read a book and turn in her report by monday

2. I often like to go for a stroll along the beach and looking for interesting shells.

3. Arvo was wearing a black suit, a white shirt, a bow tie, and had on brown shoes.

4. Antonio found that the best way to get to the Queen Charlotte Islands was to drive to Prince Rupert and flying the rest of the way.
   to fly

5. Your letter of application should include relevant details about your education, you should give information about your past work experience, and give the names of three references.
   your

6. Before we move into our summer cottage we have to remove all traces of "little critters," washing the floors thoroughly and to clean all cupboards.

7. You should proofread your written work for errors in punctuation, grammar, and look for spelling mistakes too.

8. When Marga completes high school, she wants to work for a year and then planning a trip to Europe with the money she will have saved.

9. To keep proper balance in your life, make sure you allow equal time for work, play, and save time for relaxation too.

10. To get along in life, one needs purpose, determination, and it helps if you have a good sense of humour too.

Check your answers with those in the Answer section at the end of the book.

Some joining words are used in pairs: for example, *either ... or; neither ... nor; not only ... but; both ... and*. The words placed between these conjunctions must be the same in structure as those that follow the last word in the pair.

Not parallel:	Either you can bring a sandwich or buy your lunch in the cafeteria.
Parallel:	You can either *bring a sandwich* or *buy your lunch in the cafeteria.*
Not parallel:	I not only think that she will win the election but lead with a majority vote.
Parallel:	I think that she will not only *win the election* but *lead with a majority vote.*
Not parallel:	Anna enjoys concerts and seeing live theatre productions.
Parallel:	Anna enjoys seeing both *concerts* and *live theatre productions.*

● EXERCISE 8.18

Correct errors in parallel structure in the following sentences.

1. Golf is a popular sport that not only appeals to men but to women too.

2. Any evening during the summer, you can find Farzin attending either a ball game or watching one on television.

3. Either you must find my book or buy me a new one.

4. During my last term, I not only read the required books for English but also several novels.

5. We decided to cancel our plans for building a new home because both the labour costs are high and so are the materials.

6. Pierre accepted neither the first job offer he received nor did he accept the second.

7. The travellers were not only tired but they were hungry as well.

8. We had the choice of either renting a fifth-floor apartment or the main floor of a house.

9. Mrs. Hayashi's new home is not only decorated with fine furniture in every room, but she also has beautiful oil paintings on the walls.

10. On the first day of classes, students were asked both to bring their registration forms to every class and their books.

Check your answers with those in the Answer section at the end of the book.

● EXERCISE 8.19—REVIEW

In the following exercise, correct any errors in adjective/adverb confusion, in dangling or misplaced modifiers, or in parallel structure. If a sentence is correct, mark it "*Correct.*"

1. Students often earn extra money by working in local hotels or some clerk in stores.

2. The aroma of freshly baked bread smelled so deliciously that I had to stop and buy a loaf.

3. She has neither cleaned her room nor did she wash the dishes.

4. After studying for days, my exam did not seem so difficult.

5. I am real tired of seeing reruns on television.

6. Canadians are not only concerned about national unity but also about retaining their cultural differences.

7. If you take the time to collect and organize all your material, you won't have no problems writing an effective essay.

8. Your glass is fuller than mine.

9. Less people are attending the minor hockey league games than in previous years.

10. He was honest, helpful, and a good organizer.

Check your answers with those in the Answer section at the end of the book.

THE NEXT STEP

If you feel confident about your ability in this area, proceed to the Pretest for "Underlining, Italics, and Quotation Marks."

PRETEST: UNDERLINING, ITALICS, AND QUOTATION MARKS

This exercise tests your ability to use underlining and quotation marks correctly. Use underlining and/or quotation marks in each of the following sentences. Make any additional changes in capitalization and punctuation as required.

1. For Christmas, Steffie bought her sister a gift subscription to Châtelaine.

2. Winston Churchill, famous for his brilliant words of wisdom, is the one who said courage is what it takes to stand up and speak. Courage is also what it takes to sit down and listen!

3. In the dictionary, the term bibliophile is defined as a person who loves or collects books.

4. Joni Mitchell's album Ladies of the Canyon is still one of my favourites; I particularly like hearing the song Big Yellow Taxi.

5. My assignment included reading an article entitled Faith or Medicine in the latest issue of Maclean's.

6. Try to avoid overusing the words it and this in your writing.

7. When I was young, the Beatles were the grooviest musical group going!

8. The horse and buggy style of management is becoming an obsolete method for motivating workers.

9. Potential car buyers can now purchase a book called Lemon-Aid to help them avoid buying a costly lemon.

10. With the challenge of going where they are not supposed to go, many bright computer students use skill and luck to hack school computer systems and enter private protected files.

Check your answers with those in the Answer section at the end of the book.

If you made no more than two errors, then complete the Unit Eight Post-Test. If, however, you had more than two errors, complete the lessons on the following pages.

UNDERLINING, ITALICS, AND QUOTATION MARKS

In documenting or referring to the works of an author, you must give proper credit. In this section on punctuation, you will learn how to use underlining, italics, and quotation marks correctly. Since the two forms of identification are often misused or confused, carefully study each rule and the examples that follow.

I. UNDERLINING AND ITALICS

The titles of complete works, such as movies, magazines, newspapers, books, plays, recordings, and television shows, should be underlined in typed or handwritten work. If you are working on a computer, set these names in *italics*.

Movies:	I never tire of seeing <u>The Return of the Pink Panther</u>, starring Peter Sellers.
Magazines:	I subscribe to two magazines, <u>Equinox</u> and <u>Maclean's</u>.
Newspapers:	Yesterday's <u>Globe and Mail</u> had a review of the book called
Books:	<u>Our Changing Times</u> by Bill Brown.
Plays:	The play I enjoyed seeing most at our local dinner theatre was <u>Forever Plaid</u>.
Recordings:	When I want to relax, I play Oscar Peterson's <u>In the Key of Oscar</u>.
Television shows:	<u>The Beachcombers</u> was one of the best television shows ever produced.

II. QUOTATION MARKS

Although quotation marks are commonly used to indicate someone's exact words in conversation, our study of these punctuation marks will be limited to their use in written college papers and reports.

A. TITLES

Use quotation marks to identify portions of a larger work, such as titles of chapters, lessons, topics, sections, articles, essays, poems, short stories, or songs.

When you read Chapter Five, entitled "The Effective Business Letter," pay particular attention to the section headed "Writing Letters of Response."

She loves to read romantic poems such as "The Highwayman" and "The Listeners."

Did you read the article "Speak for Yourself" in last night's editorial?

NOTE: 1. The word *the* is capitalized and included in the underlined portion or within quotation marks if that word is used as part of the title.

2. Periods and commas are always placed inside quotation marks.

● EXERCISE 8.20

Use quotation marks and underlining where necessary in each of the following sentences.

1. Do you subscribe to the newspaper The Bulletin, or do you just buy a copy on the weekends?

2. Did you read the article Communications in the Future in the latest edition of Maclean's?

3. Underline the most important parts of the chapter Developing a Program in the text Introduction to Data Processing.

4. L.M. Montgomery's books Anne of Green Gables and Anne of Avonlea have both been made into television serials.

5. There are many great songs on Leonard Cohen's album The Future, but Closing Time is a real classic.

Check your answers with those in the Answer section at the end of the book.

B. WORDS OR PHRASES WITH SPECIAL SIGNIFICANCE

If you use technical terms, specific words, or symbols that may be unfamiliar or confusing to your reader, use quotation marks or italics to indicate their significance.

Those working in the hospitality industry should be educated to spell the word "accommdate" with two "c's" and two "m's."

The judge ordered a *"voir dire"* to determine if the witness's evidence would be admissible to the case.

Slang, colloquial expressions, sarcasm, or intentionally poor grammar should be used sparingly; however, if these words or phrases are necessary to your message, use quotation marks or italics to indicate your intentional use of this kind of terminology.

Unlike the flower children of the 1960s, so-called "Generation Xers" face bleak employment prospects.

Whenever you feel the urge to enclose an expression in quotation marks (unless it is a direct quotation or a title, as discussed earlier), you should search for a way to rephrase the expression. By doing so, you will avoid using too many clichés and overworked expressions, and your work will be clearer and more concise.

● EXERCISE 8.21

Use quotation marks to indicate words or symbols that have special significance in the following sentences.

1. Use the word and sparingly in your compositions.

2. In business jargon, downsizing means reducing the number of employees in a firm.

3. If you want to make an effective presentation, do not use terms such as gonna and youse!

4. Computers have added many expressions to our everyday language: we ask for feedback instead of a response; we interface with each other instead of discussing; and we all get upset when the coffee machine is down!

5. Low-grade bonds, known as junk bonds, are not usually very safe investments.

Check your answers with those in the Answer section at the end of the book.

C. QUOTATIONS FROM PRINTED SOURCES

Use quotation marks around phrases or statements that you have borrowed from someone else. Often, another writer or a notable authority will present an expression or theory that clearly states the point you wish to make. Using exact words is permissible if you use quotation marks to identify the quoted portion and if you cite your source of information. Some students feel that identifying another's work in their term papers somehow reduces the quality of their assignments; however, the opposite is true. Written assignments gain in credibility if the student attributes material to its rightful author.

If you are citing a long excerpt—that is, one that is more than four typed lines—indent the quoted portion. This method, plus the one that illustrates how you record and number the footnotes that identify your sources, is explained in the back section of your dictionary or in many English handbooks.

Use quotation marks around words, partial statements, or complete sentences if they are from another source.

> In his book <u>Trudeau</u>, George Radwanski described Pierre Trudeau as being "one of the most intriguing and least understood leaders on the public scene." However, as new leaders appear in the political field, that phrase seems to be applicable to all of them! Unfortunately, more of them are "least understood" and fewer of them are "intriguing."

> Stephen Leacock, a Canadian humorist, once wrote: "Advertising is the science of arresting the human intelligence long enough to get money from it."

NOTE: 1. A word or partial statement does not require a capital letter nor does it need any additional punctuation.

2. A complete statement begins with a capital letter and requires a comma or colon to separate it from the text.

3. If a quotation contains more than one sentence, use one set of quotation marks—one mark at the beginning and the other at the end.

● EXERCISE 8.22

Use quotation marks wherever necessary in the following sentences. Make changes in capitalization and punctuation as required.

1. Mark Twain once described golf as a good walk spoiled.

2. My own personal motto is practice makes perfect.

3. There are a number of sayings a person can use to get through difficult times. The ones I apply most are first things first and one day at a time. Using these simple clichés seems to put my problems into perspective and also helps me to tackle them in manageable portions rather than all at one time.

4. A true friend can be defined as one who knows you as you are, understands where you have been, accepts who you have become, and still invites you to grow.

5. In one of his articles, Mark Twain described his maturing years in the following way when I was a boy of fourteen, my father was so ignorant I could hardly stand to have the old man around. But when I got to be twenty-one, I was astonished at how much the old man had learned in seven years!

Check your answers with those in the Answer section at the end of the book.

● EXERCISE 8.23—REVIEW

Use underlining and quotation marks as needed in each of the following questions. Make any additional changes in capitalization and punctuation that are required.

1. One of my favourite songs from Fiddler on the Roof is If I Were a Rich Man.

2. The article entitled The Age of Communications and published by the Royal Bank points out the following fact: of the 550 million telephones in service today, three-quarters are confined to only eight of the world's 170-odd countries. The great bulk of the world's people live out their lives without what we Canadians regard as an indispensable communication device.

3. When questioned about her past, Mae West retorted I used to be Snow White but I drifted.

4. To say I ain't got none is a real reflection of one's command of the English language!

5. Although most employees work as team members, performance measures are written for individuals. The phrases the client will ..., the patient will ..., or the student will ... imply this directed focus and mean that each person will be evaluated individually in a group setting.

6. A few years ago, real estate agents noticed a back-to-the-country movement. More people seemed interested in relocating in some picturesque, quiet, rural area away from the hustle and bustle of the city.

7. Because of his film roles in such chillers as The House of Wax and Fall of the House of Usher, Vincent Price has become known as the master of the macabre.

8. In the article Walk Your Way to Good Health in the magazine Prevention, researchers from Stanford University reported the following findings: brisk walking can lower blood pressure, help people lose weight without dieting, improve blood-fat levels, reduce the need for insulin in adult diabetics, relieve back pain and headaches, even improve mood and thinking skills.

9. One of the researchers also reported we found that men who walked nine or more miles a week had a risk of death 21 percent lower than those who walked less than three miles a week. Since this report has been made public, there has been more interest in establishing a walk-a-mile-a-day campaign.

10. Some advertisements bug us. However, in a recent survey about commercials people best remember, it was discovered that among the top contenders were eight of the most irritating ones. The researchers made the following conclusive comment irritating commercials may be effective because they firmly establish a product name in your mind.

Check your answers with those in the Answer section at the end of the book.

THE NEXT STEP

If you feel confident about your ability in this area, write the Unit Eight Post-Test on the following pages.

▶ POST-TEST FOR UNIT EIGHT

If you feel confident about the skills presented in this unit, complete the Post-Test that follows. **Do not attempt this test if you have not completed the required work.**

Once you have completed the whole test, check your answers with the suggested ones at the end of this unit. A marking scheme has been provided to give you a realistic idea of your ability in this area. Your goal should be to have no more than two minor errors in each category of spelling or punctuation (quotation marks, italics, and underlining) and no more than two major errors in modifiers or parallel structure.

I. Add the suggested suffixes to the words in parentheses. Rewrite the combined version above the word. Use your dictionary, if necessary.

Note to my secretary:

As you may recall, (notify + tions) *notifications* for the annual meeting of (survey + ors) *surveyors* were to be (relay + ed) *relayed* to us by mail. It is an (undeny + ible/able) fact that our office has had an (unpredict + ible/able) amount of business recently, and I know the amount of paperwork has been barely (manage + ible/able); however, is it (poss + ible/able) that some of the written (reply + es) *replies* were (mislay + ed) *mislaid*? Would you mind (clarify + ing) *clarifying* this matter by checking your files or telephoning the members this afternoon to determine their intentions?

(Deduct one mark for each spelling error.)

TOTAL MARKS FOR SPELLING _____*10*_____ /10

II. In the following sentences, correct errors involving incorrect modifiers or improper parallel sentence structure. If a major revision is necessary, rewrite the corrected version in the space provided.

1. Of the two copies of the proposal, which do you like ~~best~~? *better?* ✓

2. ~~Only studying will help you learn the facts~~. It will not help you learn the theory that was presented in class.
   Studying will only help you learn the facts ✓

3. Getting an interview is easy but ~~to prepare~~ for it is difficult.
   Preparing ✓

4. Having expressed his opinion that the proposal would not work, ~~a quick vote was taken by the chairperson.~~ ✓
   the chairperson took a quick vote

5. This course can be completed by anyone who has taken high school English.~~in three months.~~
   in three months ✓

6. The teacher advised the students to improve their business vocabulary and ~~that they should~~ *to* keep a notebook of new terms. ✓

7. I felt ~~real~~ *really* bad about receiving such poor marks on the exam.

8. He was implicated not only in the crime itself but also *in the* attempted to cover it up.

9. It is my feeling that we would be taking ~~lesser~~ *fewer* risks if we bought our appliances from a major department store.

10. Because the baby had ~~nearly cried for an hour~~ *cried for nearly an hour*, her eyes were red and swollen.

11. Kamiel was hired to put in the wiring, nail up the panelling, and ~~as a~~ *to* painter.

12. Josef lost the gold watch somewhere in the plaza that he had always treasured.
Josef lost the gold watch he had always treasured somewhere in the plaza.

13. The holidays always seem the ~~most~~ busiest time of the whole year.

14. I don't need to take ~~no~~ *any* more English courses since I'm not ~~never~~ going to need to write grammar for ~~no~~ *any* one; besides there's nothing wrong with the way I put things on paper!

15. After slowly baking and basting for five hours, the cook removed the turkey from the oven and called us for dinner.
After slowly baking and basting the turkey for five hours, the cook removed it from the oven and called us for dinner

(Deduct one mark for each sentence error.)

TOTAL MARKS FOR GRAMMAR _____ 13 _____ /15

III. Use underlining and quotation marks in each of the following passages. Make any additional changes required in capitalization and punctuation.

1. Remington's president, Victor Kiam, has used novel ways to promote his products. Many television viewers will remember him for the commercial in which he proudly exclaimed, "I liked Remington so much I bought the company!" After this sales campaign, he wrote about his successful marketing techniques in a book entitled <u>Going For It! How to Succeed as an Entrepreneur</u>. He reinforced his methods by personally advertising the book in a similar manner. If his sincerity and personality continue to attract the public, both his book and his products will keep him "rolling in riches."

2. An article in a recent issue of <u>Psychology Today</u> described various executive management attitudes and pointed to what could be termed "ideacide" as being one of the most common negative attributes of busy executives. Hastily rejecting employees' innovative

ideas or suggestions with such comments as "send it to the committee" or "this would be too great a risk" or "oh, no!" Don't tell me you have another idea" or "we've always done it this way," destroys motivation and opportunities for expansion as well as fortifies what could be termed "stifling rigidity."

(Deduct one mark for each punctuation or underlining error.)

TOTAL MARKS FOR PUNCTUATION _____4_____ /10

IV. The following selection contains errors in spelling, grammar, and punctuation discussed in this unit. Proofread the passage, correct the listed errors, and make any additional changes resulting from your corrections. Mark the appropriate symbol in the margin.

3 spelling errors—sp //   3 parallel structure errors—//sm ///
1 set of quotation marks—p"/   2 modifier errors—mod //
1 underlining error—u /

For many years, the terms "alcoholic" and "drug addict" have caused feelings of fear, rage, and ~~some people feel~~ disgust. Only since the mid-fifties have study and research proven that chemical dependency, a word ~~both~~ both encompassing alcohol and other drug ~~dependencys~~ dependencies, is a chronic disease. This deduction, as well as the many resultant treatment opportunities, has clearly had an effect on attitudes toward those who suffer the ravaging effects of this disease.

Many myths, however, continue to be prevalent. Some still believe that alcohol and drug abuse are simply the result of the dependent's lack of will power, poor moral beliefs ~~is often cited as being the cause~~, or some other character defect. However, this disease has the same definitive description as other chronic life-threatening malad~~ys~~ies; that is, it is primary, progressive, chronic, and terminal! Also, as with diseases such as multiple sclerosis or diabetes, it can strike people of all ages, religions, cultures, and even those with the highest degree of moral fibre and strong will. But as society gains more knowledge and understanding of the real concept, this disease, now ranked as the second ~~most~~ more devastating illness in North America, is being approached with more realistic~~ally~~ and effective treatment processes. These new incentives have literally saved thousands of lives, both of those directly afflicted and of those whose lives have been seriously affected by the behaviour of the chemically dependent person.

Currently, North American leaders are making an admirable admireable attempt to combat this disease that has reached epidemic proportions. Although no one

is sure about the numbers involved, an article in a recent issue of <u>Maclean's</u>
provided a clue with the following stated fact "police estimate that of a
$10-million drug market it can be assumed that four million Canadians spend
$2500 each year on drugs." If one considered that this general estimate
includes only drug abusers, how many more would be added with the number
of alcohol abusers; and how many more would be added with the number of
friends, family, coworkers, employers, etc., indirectly affected?

(Deduct one mark for each spelling, quotation, or underlining error; deduct two marks for each modifier or parallel structure error.)

TOTAL MARKS FOR PROOFREADING ____14____ /15

Answers are on the following pages.

ANSWERS FOR UNIT EIGHT POST-TEST

I. Note to my secretary:

As you may recall, *notifications* for the annual meeting of *surveyors* were to be *relayed* to us by mail. It is an *undeniable* fact that our office has had an *unpredictable* amount of business recently, and I know the amount of paperwork has been barely *manageable;* however, is it *possible* that some of the written *replies* were *mislaid?* Would you mind *clarifying* this matter by checking your files or telephoning the members this afternoon to determine their intentions?

II.
1. Of the two copies of the proposal, which do you like *better?*

2. Studying will help you learn *only the facts.* It will not help you learn the theory that was presented in class.

3. a) Getting an interview is easy but *preparing for it is difficult.*
   b) *To get an interview is easy* but to prepare for it is difficult.

4. Having expressed his opinion that the proposal would not work, *the chairperson took a quick vote.* (active voice required so that the introductory expression will correctly describe the subject)

5. a) Anyone who has completed high school English can complete this course in three months. (to avoid awkward wording, use the active voice)
   b) This course can be completed in three months by anyone who has taken high school English. (awkward!—marginally correct)

6. The teacher advised the students to improve their business vocabulary and *to keep a notebook of new terms.*

7. I felt *really* bad about receiving such poor marks on the exam.

8. He was implicated *not only* in the crime itself *but also* in the attempt to cover it up.

9. It is my feeling that we would be taking *fewer* risks if we bought our appliances from a major department store.

10. Because the baby had cried *for nearly an hour,* her eyes were red and swollen.

11. Kamiel was hired to *put in the wiring, nail up the panelling,* and *paint.*

12. Somewhere in the plaza, Josef lost the gold watch that he had always treasured.

13. The holidays always seem the *busiest time* of the whole year.

14. I don't need to take *any* more English courses since I'm not going to write grammar for *anyone;* besides there's nothing wrong with the way I put things on paper!

15. After *the turkey had been* slowly baked and basted for five hours, the cook removed it from the oven and called us for dinner.

III.
1. Remington's president, Victor Kiam, has used novel ways to promote his products. Many television viewers will remember him for the commercial in which he proudly exclaimed: **"I liked Remington so much I bought the company!"** After this sales campaign, he wrote about his successful marketing techniques in a book entitled <u>**Going For It! How to Succeed as an Entrepreneur**</u>. He reinforced his methods by personally advertising the book in a similar manner. If his sincerity and personality continue to attract the public, both his book and his products will keep him **"rolling in riches."**

2. An article in a recent issue of <u>**Psychology Today**</u> described various executive management attitudes and pointed to what could be termed "**ideacide**" as being one of the most common negative attributes of busy executives. Hastily rejecting employees' innovative ideas or suggestions with such comments as "**Send it to the committee**" or "**This would be too great a risk**" or "**Oh, no! Don't tell me you have another idea**" or "**We've always done it this way**," destroys motivation and opportunities for expansion as well as fortifies what could be termed "**stifling rigidity**."

IV. For many years, the terms "alcoholic" and "drug addict" have caused feelings of fear, rage, and *disgust*. Only since the mid-fifties have study and research proven that chemical dependency, a word encompassing *both* alcohol and other drug *dependencies,* is a chronic disease. This deduction, as well as the many resultant treatment opportunities, has clearly had an effect on attitudes toward those who suffer the ravaging effects of this disease. //sm //sm sp

    Many myths, however, continue to be prevalent. Some still believe that alcohol and drug abuse are simply the result of the dependent's lack of will power, *poor moral beliefs*, or some other character defect. However, this disease has the same definitive description as other chronic life-threatening *maladies;* that is, it is primary, progressive, chronic, and terminal! Also, as with diseases such as multiple sclerosis or diabetes, it can strike people of all ages, religions, cultures, and even those with the highest degree of moral fibre and strong will. But as society gains more knowledge and understanding of the real concept, this disease, now ranked as the second *most* devastating illness in North America, is being approached with more *realistic* and effective treatment processes. These new incentives have literally saved thousands of lives, both of those directly afflicted and of those whose lives have been seriously affected by the behaviour of the chemically dependent person. //sm sp mod mod

    Currently, North American leaders are making an *admirable* attempt to combat this disease that has reached epidemic proportions. Although no one is sure about the numbers involved, an article in a recent issue of <u>Maclean's</u> provided a clue with the following stated fact: *"Police estimate that of a $10-million drug market it can be assumed that four million Canadians spend $2500 each year on drugs."* If one considered that this general estimate includes only drug abusers, how many more would be added with the number of alcohol abusers; and how many more would be added with the number of friends, family, coworkers, employers, etc., indirectly affected? sp u p"

Proceed to the Unit Eight composition section.

UNIT EIGHT COMPOSITION SKILLS:
WRITING A SHORT EXPOSITORY ESSAY

When you produce an extended piece of writing that supplies information, offers an explanation, or provides a complete answer to an examination question, you are using the expository style of writing. Although this type of essay is considerably longer, it follows the same structure and organization as a single paragraph. The length and depth of discussion are the only variables. An expository essay begins with an introduction and thesis statement. Each of the main supporting facts is thoroughly and separately discussed in the well-organized paragraphs that follow the thesis statement.

Following is a list of topics to get you started in the composition exercises and assignment for this unit.

adolescence	movies
astrology	music
astronomy	organizing
censorship	pollution
dreams	punctuality
drugs	soap operas
ecology	*Star Trek*
education	styles
English language	televised sports
flea markets	television
laughter	travelling
law enforcement officers	unions
learning a second language	violence
lotteries	your suggested topic
manners	

I. LIMITING THE TOPIC OF AN EXPOSITORY ESSAY

To ensure that your composition is clearly focused and provides details that are helpful and meaningful to the reader, begin by limiting the topic to a manageable size. There is no value in trying to discuss "good health" in a composition of four or five paragraphs. The content would be too general and vague to interest the reader. The topic must be more clearly focused.

   Use the same technique described in Unit Five; that is, reduce your general topic three or four times by continually being more specific until you are satisfied that the topic is focused enough for a 350- to 500-word essay of three to five paragraphs. Once your topic is focused, brainstorm ideas around it. Note the following method for focusing and brainstorming a general topic.

Topic ⟶ **Be Specific** ⟶ **Be More Specific** ⟶ **Be Even More Specific**

good health   being fit   exercising   benefits of regular exercise

Brainstorm Circle

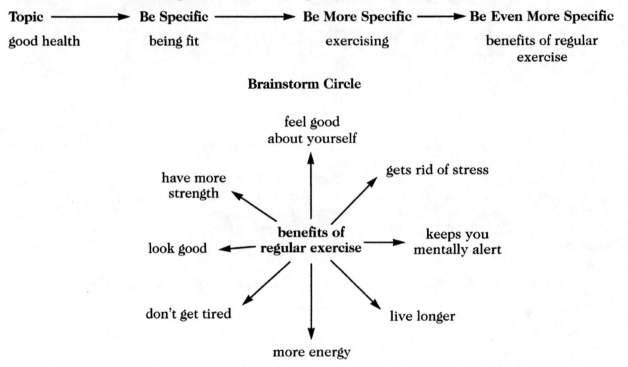

● EXERCISE 8.24

Choose two or more topics from the list of general topics given at the beginning of this section. Use the space provided to reduce the scope of each topic to suit a 350- to 500-word essay of three to five paragraphs.

Topic	Be Specific	Be More Specific	Be Even More Specific
1. _____	_____	_____	_____
2. _____	_____	_____	_____

Next, brainstorm to establish specific discussion points for your topics.

focused topic 1

focused topic 2

II. IDENTIFYING THE APPROPRIATE PATTERN OF DEVELOPMENT

Review your ideas and identify three related ways you could discuss your focused topics; for example, one of the following patterns might be appropriate:

- **Examples or reasons:** What three facts, examples, or reasons could you discuss about the topic?

- **Explanation:** What three details or points of description could you provide about the topic?

- **Sequence:** What three steps or stages are involved?

- **Comparison or Contrast:** What three ways are two items mentioned in your topic similar or dissimilar? For example, you could relate the differences between playing blackjack in Las Vegas and playing the game with your friends. (Use either comparison or contrast—not both!)

Now you have several ways to develop your focused topics. For instance, the three facts you might wish to make about the sample focused topic could be the following:

benefits of regular exercise	— live longer and better
	— relieves stress
	— good for mind and body

To make the discussion of your topics flow, consider the best order for developing these points. Would they be most effective if arranged in

1. **natural order:** arranging the facts from the most important one to the least important one?

2. **sequence:** arranging the points in chronological order or in logical steps or stages of development?

3. **persuasive order:** arranging facts from the least important one to the most important one so that the reader will be convinced?

To develop the topic "benefits of regular exercise," assess the listed points to determine if all are relevant and to decide the best order. In this case, natural order seems most appropriate; therefore, arrange the facts as follows:

benefits of regular exericise	a) good for mind and body
	b) relieves stress
	c) live longer and better

III. WRITING A WORKING THESIS STATEMENT

Once you have identified your three points of discussion, compose a working thesis statement to reflect your purpose. A thesis statement discusses what will be in your essay. This initial sentence should encompass all the issues you plan to write about and reflect your overall purpose. At this point, write a working thesis statement to get you started on the first draft of your writing plan. Look at the following examples.

> **Working thesis statement:** Regular exercise is good for the body, relieves stress, and promotes a longer and better life.

This focused statement prepares both you and your reader for the composition that will follow. It helps you keep track of your purpose and organization, and gives the reader an overview of what is to come. If your method of presenting your information is effective, then a communication circuit will be formed.

● EXERCISE 8.25

Using one of your two focused topics, write down the three discussion points you considered and arrange them in the most effective order. Make sure that your sentences are parallel in structure. Then:

a) Write a working thesis statement that reflects the overall concept and organization of your proposed essay.

b) Brainstorm each discussion point separately.

When you have completed the brainstorming for your first topic, repeat the process with the other focused topic.

1. **Focused topic:** _____

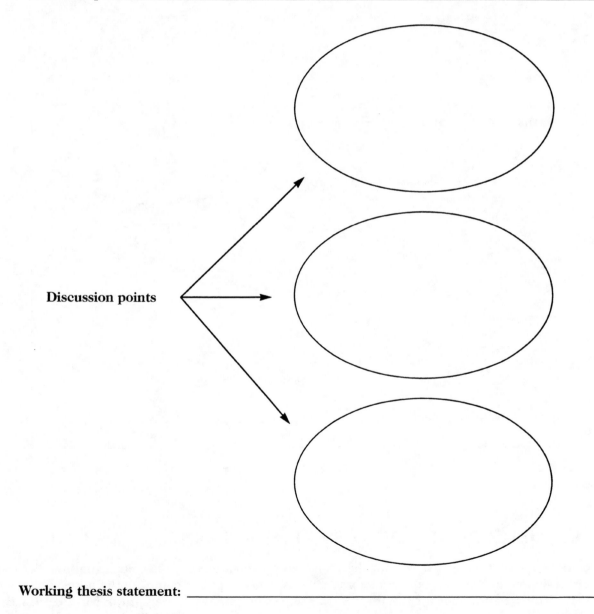

Discussion points

Working thesis statement: _____

_____

2. Focused topic: _____

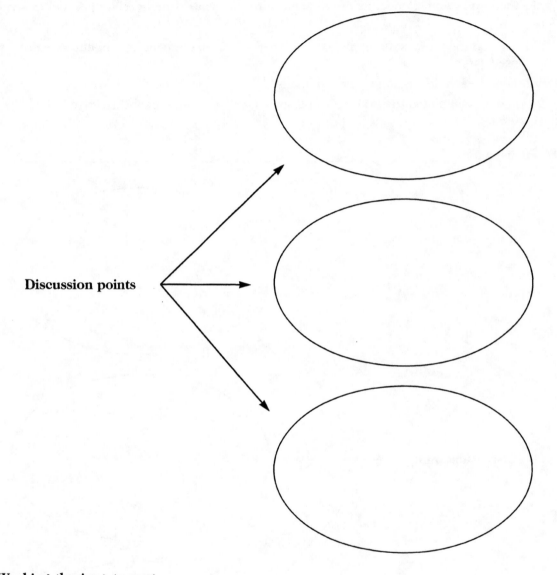

Discussion points

Working thesis statement: _____

_____

IV. DEVELOPING EACH DISCUSSION POINT

Once you have developed a working thesis statement, you are ready to create an outline. For each discussion point, review your brainstorming facts; choose and/or complete the necessary details that would be sufficient for the three separate paragraphs. **Each paragraph will begin with a clearly worded, focused main-idea statement supported by your logically developed facts.**

At this point, the working thesis statement should be the only sentence in the first section of your outline. The second section should discuss your first thesis point; the third section should present details about your second thesis point; and the fourth, the third thesis point. Remember that, even in the outline format, each paragraph must begin with a main-idea sentence that clearly identifies your viewpoint on this particular aspect of your overall topic. The following annotated outline summarizes the format and procedure for creating an outline for a short (four or five paragraph) essay.

Topic: _____

I. Thesis, or main-idea statement, *divided into three parts.* ◄—— **After you have completed your outline, add an introduction that ends with your thesis statement.**

II. Statement introducing the first part of your thesis statement.
   A. first major supporting detail
      1.
      } minor points as necessary
      2.
   B. second major supporting detail   ◄—— **You may include as many major and minor details as are necessary to support your main-idea statement.**
      1.
      } minor points as necessary
      2.

III. Using a suitable transition, introduce the second part of your original thesis statement.
   A. first major supporting detail   ◄—— **This statement must include a transition as well as present the main idea of the second portion of your thesis statement.**
      1.
      } minor points as necessary
      2.
   B. add a second major detail
      1.
      } minor points as necessary
      2.

         ◄—— **You may include as many major and minor details as are necessary.**

IV. Using a suitable transition, introduce the main idea of this paragraph. It will elaborate the third part of your thesis statement.
   A. first major supporting detail
      1.
      } minor points as necessary
      2.
   B. second major supporting detail
      1.
      } minor points as necessary
      2.

Concluding statement that is attached to your last paragraph ◄—— **If your conclusion is just one sentence, attach it to the last paragraph.**
and effectively ends your composition.

OR

V. Concluding paragraph that presents advice or results or ◄—— **However, if your conclusion consists of more than one sentence, form a separate concluding paragraph.**
restatements of the ideas you have presented in your composition.
   A. first major supporting detail

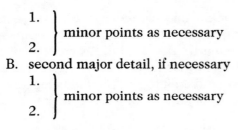

    B. second major detail, if necessary

● EXERCISE 8.26

Record in outline form the discussion points for each of your two proposed essays. If necessary, refer to the sample outline above.

V. WRITING THE CONCLUSION

In an essay, your concluding statement must address all the viewpoints you have discussed. To respond to the various resolutions of your discussion, generate two or three concluding sentences as you did in previous compositions. Consider the following questions:

a) What advice could you give someone about your viewpoints?

b) What prediction about these issues can you make?

c) What can you conclude about or what is the result of these points of view?

d) What can you restate (using different wording) or summarize from the aspects of your topic?

If you have difficulty ending your composition, use one of the words or phrases given in previous units to prompt you to write a conclusion.

In previous writing assignments, you concluded your compositions with a single concluding sentence. This assignment, however, is more complex than the others; you will have discussed your topic in greater detail, expressed more thoughts, and written many more words. A simple concluding sentence might be acceptable, but it might also end your lengthy discussion too abruptly. In this assignment, you should expand on that concluding sentence and give either details about your results or an explanation of your conclusion. Therefore, your concluding sentence and resulting explanation must be placed in a separate paragraph.

Now, test the unity of your essay by replacing the working thesis statement with each of your concluding sentences. There should be a natural flow of content support if the thesis, main-idea statements, and details have the same focus. Choose the two strongest statements from all the ones you have written (including the working thesis) and use one for the thesis sentence to introduce your theme and one for the conclusion.

Make any necessary revisions to the order and content of your proposed paragraphs. Your message should have a logical and natural flow of meaningful information.

VI. WRITING THE INTRODUCTION

Now that you have completed your outline plan for your essay, you are ready to begin arranging your ideas in effective sentence patterns to convey your message to your reader. However, one essential ingredient for an expository essay is missing—an introduction! All readers must be inspired to read; as a result, all writers must stimulate interest or set the stage for the focus of their compositions.

CHOOSING AN APPROACH

There are several kinds of moods you can establish by your introductory paragraph For example, you may wish to

- shock your readers,

- raise questions in your readers' minds,

- create a serious mood,

- create a mood of optimism, or

- create a relaxed mood.

Consider the following methods and choose the one that is best suited to your style and purpose.

1. Present necessary background information. Perhaps the readers will need to know what has happened or is happening that relates to the topic. Sometimes statistical data or figures create the right reason for reading. (Always identify your source of information.) What do the readers need to know to appreciate and understand the details of your essay? Your thesis statement would include these details.

2. Describe a scene or situation that builds up to your thesis. This description "paints a picture" for which *your thesis will be a result, a proposed solution, or an alternative.*

3. Use a quotation, a story, or startling facts related to your thesis. If you choose this method of development, remember to identify your source of information. Try to keep quotations and stories brief so they do not detract from your main purpose. *Your thesis will provide the reason for the story.*

4. Ask a relevant question or describe a problem. *Your thesis will provide the answer.*

5. Present a contrasting scene or situation. *Your thesis will offer a preferable solution or alternative.*

6. Make a prediction. Predicting the future requires some feasible or documented proof, but *your thesis will tell your readers that this proof will be forthcoming in your essay.*

This introductory paragraph promises the readers that the written material that follows will provide well-organized and relevant facts to support the thesis. Therefore, this first paragraph will begin with a suitable introduction and end with your thesis statement.

Your introductory paragraph must be a minimum of two sentences. Study each of the following sample introductions and accompanying thesis statements.

Example 1:

Mention exercise to some people and they think of sweating or painful straining of the body. They envision stiff muscles, pulled tendons, and physical exhaustion. To them, exercise is nothing but unnecessary punishment of the body. Others, however, think differently of exercise. For those who practise this activity regularly, exercise stimulates a new awakening of the mind and body, provides a release of tension and stress, and enhances the probability of a longer and healthier life.

← A negative description of exercise that builds up to the thesis statement

← Thesis statement divided into three parts

Example 2:

According to Jacques Cousteau, the famous oceanographer and marine biologist, "The oceans of the world have held the answers to all man's questions since the beginning of time. For me, it is a chance to be at peace with myself and mankind." Ever since I was a tot, I have been fascinated by the beauty, excitement, and mysteries of the oceans.

← Quotation that relates to the theme of the essay

← Thesis statement divided into three parts

Example 3:

There is no guarantee any more that people can or will be happy at their jobs. Changes in technology continue to dictate the kinds of employment needed in the future, and it will be up to individuals to derive as much satisfaction as possible from their work. Those who do find job satisfaction are likely to be people who, in their youth, have thought seriously about the kind of career they wanted to pursue, taken advantage of the educational resources available to them, and applied themselves to be the best in their fields.

← Necessary background information that leads up to your thesis statement

← Thesis statement divided into three parts

Example 4:

What qualities does one need to become a manager? It has been noted that most successful supervisors have profited by cultivating patience, modesty, and enjoyment of work.

A relevant question that prompts the thesis ← statement

← Thesis statement divided into three parts

● EXERCISE 8.27

Using the methods suggested in this section, write introductory paragraphs for the two essay outlines you have prepared. Use different methods of development and write more than one type of introduction for each topic. Choose the ones you like best. Remember that the introductory paragraph ends with the thesis statement and should spark the reader's interest.

1.

2.

Ask an instructor to review the effectiveness of these initial paragraphs.

VII. SAMPLE OUTLINE AND ESSAY

Read the following sample outline and final draft of the essay on "finding job satisfaction." Pay particular attention to the introductory and concluding paragraphs. Remember that the writer has written more than one draft to produce this quality of writing.

Topic: finding job satisfaction ◄──── **Topic**

I. Those who find job satisfaction are likely to be people who, ◄──── in their youth, have thought seriously about the kind of career they wanted to pursue, taken advantage of the educational resources available to them, and applied themselves to be the best in their field.

Thesis statement divides main idea into three parts and introduces theme of essay.

II. Determining a specific career is not an easy task. ◄────
   A. high school counselling
      1. learn about self
      2. directed by tests, questionnaires, interviews

Main idea of second paragraph gives information about first portion of the thesis statement.

   B. other career-seeking opportunities ◄────
      1. Career Week
      2. professional guest lecturers

Major and minor supporting details

III. In the next step, students should relate present activities to ◄──── future ones.
   A. in high school, importance of subject choices
      1. algebra for engineering
      2. sciences for nursing
      3. importance of doing well in these areas

Main idea of third paragraph gives information about second portion of the thesis statement (notice the transitional words).

   B. in college or university ◄────
      1. applying themselves
      2. getting best job opportunities

Major and minor supporting details

IV. Obtaining work in chosen career can be the end and also ← **Main idea of fourth para-graph gives information about the third portion of the thesis statement.**
the beginning.
   A. feeling of accomplishment

   B. importance of continued learning
     1. learn present job
     2. have cooperation, diligence, willingness, creativity

   C. involvement in extra-curricular activities ← **Major and minor supporting details**
     1. playing a sport
     2. working with an organization
     3. devoting time to a hobby
     4. taking a course

V. Unfortunately, for some, what a person does with his or her ← **Concluding paragraph gives a summary of what was said.**
life usually hinges on those crucial decisions made during the
difficult adolescent years.
   A. listen to parents and counsellors
   B. prepare for productive and personally rewarding work

Read the following written composition from the given writing plan and note the suggestions in the margin.

There is no guarantee anymore that people can or will be happy at ← **Introductory paragraph presents interesting, relevant background information that leads to thesis statement.**
their jobs. Changes in technology continue to dictate the kinds of
employment needed in the future, and it will be up to individuals to
derive as much satisfaction as possible from their work. Those who
do find job satisfaction are likely to be people who, in their youth,
have thought seriously about the kind of career they wanted to pursue, taken advantage of the educational resources available to them,
and applied themselves to be the best in their field. ← **Thesis statement**

    Choosing a career is not an easy task for young people. ← **Main idea develops first discussion point.**
However, high school counselling can help to direct them.
Guidance provides opportunities for students to find out more ← **Use varied sentence patterns.**
about themselves and become more aware of their strengths and
weaknesses. *Aptitude* tests, *questionnaires,* and interviews all ← **Spell words correctly.**
help the *counsellor* to point students towards satisfying careers.
In addition, there are opportunities for young people to discover
more about the various kinds of *occupations.* Career Week usually ← **Use thesaurus to avoid word repetition.**
involves excursions to local universities and colleges where stu-
dents can see for themselves the new and different programs that
are offered. Also, at this time, professionals are invited as guest
lecturers to provide information about their chosen career as well
as to answer many queries students might have.

    In the next step, students should relate present activities to ← **Main idea develops second discussion point.**
future ones. In high school, they must realize the importance of
their subject choices so that they do not close the door to their
chosen career. For example, students who plan to enter the engineering field must realize that algebra is essential; or those who
plan a nursing career must have a solid science background. Not
only should they ensure that these subjects are included in their ← **Use varied sentence patterns.**
curricula, but they should also plan to do their best in these key
areas. Once they have been accepted into college or university,

they must also realize how necessary it is to apply themselves. The best job opportunities are offered to the top students in the class.

Obtaining work in a chosen career can be the end and also the beginning. It is a great feeling of accomplishment to achieve goals that one has set; however, once these have been achieved, new goals appear. To adapt to future situations, people must continue to learn. First, they should learn everything they can about their present job. Then their cooperation, diligence, willingness, and creativity in their chosen field will provide opportunities for advancement as well as provide valuable learning experiences that could be directed to broader fields. Equally important is their learning or involvement in extra-curricular activities. Playing a sport, working with an organization, devoting time to a hobby, taking a course—any or all are important factors in rounding out a person.

◄—— **Main idea develops third discussion point.**

Unfortunately for some, what a person does with his or her life usually hinges on those crucial decisions made during the difficult adolescent years. The wise students listen to parents and teachers and prepare for a future of productive and personally rewarding work.

◄—— **Concluding paragraph gives a summary of what was said.**

VIII. A QUICK REVIEW OF THE PROCEDURE FOR WRITING EXPOSITORY ESSAYS

1. Choose a topic.

2. Focus the topic to suit your assignment and the specific theme you have chosen to develop.

3. Brainstorm your chosen topic by using either freewriting or brainstorm circles. Write down all the related facts you can think of about your focused topic.

4. Consider the best points to develop and choose the most effective type of paragraph development for each.

5. Write a working thesis statement that encompasses all aspects of your theme. Identify this statement with the Roman numeral I.

6. Write the main-idea sentence for your first discussion point. Identify this statement with the Roman numeral II.

7. Look at your list of brainstorming facts. Cross out the irrelevant ones; choose the major facts and number them in logical order; indicate any minor points that provide additional support for any of your chosen major details; and, finally, add any other details—either major or minor—that improve your message.

8. Choose a suitable transitional expression and write the main-idea sentence for your second thesis point. Remember that you need to make a smooth transition to link the ideas of the second paragraph to the first one.

9. Arrange your chosen details in outline format. Use Roman numerals to mark your main ideas, capital letters to identify the major details, and Arabic numbers to indicate minor ones. If necessary, refer to the sample outlines given in this section.

10. Develop your third thesis point in a similar fashion.

11. Reread your thesis, your main-idea sentences, and your supporting evidence. Now write three concluding sentences. You should write these three statements after you have written your outlined points; these sentences should address all of your thesis points.

12. Test paragraph unity by replacing the working thesis with each concluding statement. There should be a natural flow of content support if the statement and the details have the same focus. Choose the two strongest statements from all the ones you have written (including the working thesis) and use one for the thesis sentence and one for the conclusion.

13. Make any necessary revisions to the order and content of your proposed paragraph. Your message should have a logical and natural flow of meaningful information.

● EXERCISE 8.28

Using your outline and the introductory paragraph you prepared for one of the topics in earlier exercises, write a composition following the directions given in this unit. Indent each paragraph clearly and double-space your final copy. Your completed essay should be four to five paragraphs long and contain 350 to 500 words.

   As you write, consider the following to ensure that your paragraphs and your essay are coherent throughout.

1. Use varied sentence lengths and patterns.

2. Use meaningful and varied linking words to direct your readers. These words should relate points to the main idea or main ideas to the thesis.

3. Refer to the thesaurus to avoid the use of simplistic or repetitive language.

 Using the online thesaurus is very convenient and may provide the variety of synonyms or antonyms that you need. Check for this feature under "Tools."

4. Avoid using vague terms such as *it* and *this* unless absolutely necessary.

5. Ensure clear and correct pronoun focus.

6. Proofread your work for mechanical errors.

 Most computers have an online grammar check program that is useful in pointing out the kinds of errors that can slip past a spell-checker because the misspelled word happens to be in the dictionary. It also alerts you to mistakes or typing errors that have created run-on sentences, subject-verb errors, overuse of words and phrases, etc. Check for this feature under the heading "Tools."

7. Calculate the level of your completed essay by using the Fog Index.

8. Revise your essay. This step is even more important with a longer piece of writing, so do not rush. Take the time to read critically and make improvements in the flow of your sentences and your use of vocabulary. (Remember, revisions are sometimes easier to make if you take a rest period between the writing and revising processes.)

9. Recalculate the readability level of your revision.

COLLABORATIVE EXERCISE 8.29

Exchange essays with another class member. Each student should read the other's essay at least twice and then evaluate it using the criteria outlined in the composition evaluation form given at the end of this unit. You may use or photocopy this form.

a) Place a check mark to identify your assessment of each listed item under the headings Unity, Coherence, and Structure.

b) Then circle what you consider a fair mark (merit score) for the overall effectiveness of the content according to your assessment and your general impression of the essay.

c) Identify technical errors with symbols used in this text (see inside back cover). Place these identifying marks in the margin on the lines that correspond to the places of the perceived errors.

d) Score this section as suggested and subtract this number from the merit score you gave in (b).

e) On the back of the evaluation form, write your comments—write positively about the areas you liked and make suggestions for improving the areas you found weak. Try to be helpful in your suggestions for improvement.

You and your partner should now return one another's essay and assessment. Once this exchange has taken place, discuss the content and recommendations of both your papers.

Revise the content of your paper according to your partner's suggestions and your own beliefs about your original work. Correct any errors that you know have been correctly identified, and check, perhaps with your teacher, the correctness of the ones you dispute.

● EXERCISE 8.30

Follow the instructions for Exercise 8.28 for a second topic or the same topic. This time, choose a different type of development and a different method of introduction. Always consider the readability level of your work and direct the content to your intended readers. With each assignment, you should try to improve both the organization and quality of your written work and gain a better understanding of the communication circuit. This time, use the evaluation form as a checklist and guide for assessing your own completed work.

IX. Composition Evaluation

Critically assess both the strong and weak characteristics of this essay by placing a check mark in the appropriate column of the following evaluation form.

I. CONTENT MERIT

Excellent	Good	Weak	
			UNITY
_____	_____	_____	1. introduction appropriate to topic
_____	_____	_____	2. clearly focused and effectively worded thesis statement
_____	_____	_____	3. clearly focused and effectively worded main ideas
_____	_____	_____	4. details follow specific patterns
_____	_____	_____	5. logical order of content
_____	_____	_____	6. details are specific
_____	_____	_____	7. adequate coverage of topic
_____	_____	_____	8. irrelevant details excluded
_____	_____	_____	9. sound and effectively worded concluding sentences
_____	_____	_____	**COHERENCE**
_____	_____	_____	10. effective transition phrases used to create good flow of ideas within and between paragraphs
_____	_____	_____	11. good sentence variety (length and pattern)
_____	_____	_____	12. effective word usage
_____	_____	_____	**STRUCTURE**
_____	_____	_____	13. appropriate length
_____	_____	_____	14. correct paragraph format

MERIT SCORE: Circle the most appropriate score for the written work.

100   95   90   85   80   75   70   65   60   55   50   45   40   **less than 40**

II. TECHNICAL ERRORS

Mechanical errors reduce the quality of the writing. A paragraph is considered weak if there are more than two major errors and/or more than two minor errors in the same category.

A. Proofread for and correct the following types of major errors in the composition. (Deduct two marks from the merit score for each error made in this category.)

_____	1. sentence fragments (frag)	_____	7. incorrect preposition (prep)
_____	2. run-on sentences (ro)	_____	8. adjective/adverb error (a/a)
_____	3. subject-verb agreement (sv)	_____	9. incorrect modifier (mod)
_____	4. faulty verb tenses (vt)	_____	10. faulty parallelism (//sm)
_____	5. sentence structure (ss)	_____	11. other
_____	6. incorrect pronoun (pron)	_____	12. other

B. Proofread for and correct the following types of minor errors in the composition. (Deduct one mark from the merit score for each error made in this category.)

_____	1. incorrect spelling (sp)	_____ 7. unnecessary punctuation (p)
_____	2. misuse of words (m/w)	_____ 8. apostrophe error (p')
_____	3. word omission (w/o)	_____ 9. quotation error (p")
_____	4. faulty end punctuation (p?)	_____ 10. underlining error (u)
_____	5. semicolon error (p;)	_____ 11. _____
_____	6. comma error (p,)	_____ 12. _____

NET WORTH OF WRITTEN ASSIGNMENT = Merit score – Technical errors = _____

If you have excellent content and relatively few errors, you have made a communication link with your reader. Your written message has effectively and efficiently transmitted your thought processes. This is a valuable skill—one that all employers search for in their prospective employees. Therefore, strive for perfection in this area. Note your areas of weakness and try to make improvements in your future writing activities.

STUDY TECHNIQUES FOR WRITING ESSAY EXAMINATIONS

Does anyone like examinations? Not really. Most students don't look forward to all the pressures and work associated with exams. And many instructors have similar negative feelings about them. Nevertheless, these assessment times are extremely important for both these groups. With practice, you can begin to overcome your fears and concentrate on improving your marks. Here are some suggestions to make exams easier and less stressful.

I. WAYS TO OVERCOME STRESS AND FEAR

Since examination periods are a necessity in the education system, students need methods to overcome the stresses and fears that so often accompany the thoughts and realities of impending examinations. A simple remedy for students is to be prepared each day and keep focused on the specific reasons for being at school, in each course, and at each lecture.

- Be organized.
- Make the most of your time.
- Overlearn your course material.
- Think success!

A. BE ORGANIZED

Use good study skills during the whole semester. Take good lecture notes so that you can easily recall and reinforce this information for study purposes.

Obtain copies of previous examinations set by each of your professors. If this information is not provided, ask your professors about the kinds of questions that will be included on the upcoming exam. Will there be a certain percentage of multiple-choice questions, essay-choice questions, etc.? Seeing a professor's previous exams will help you understand his or her style of questioning, scope of content, marking scheme, and expectations. Look at the wording in the questions and the types of questions used most often. Become familiar with the meanings and expectations of the following key words:

Key words used in essay-exam questions	In your answer, you are expected to
1. analyze, relate, or discuss	explain each part and discuss the relationship and connections of various points to each other and/or to the main theme.
2. arrange, enumerate, or sequence	give and organize main facts in either time order or order of importance. (Do not use outline format.)
3. compare	state and explain how two topics are alike. You may also explain one or two differences, but there should be considerably more similarities than differences.
4. contrast, differentiate, or distinguish	state and explain ways two topics are different. Your answer may also contain one or two similarities, but there should be considerably more differences than similarities.
5. criticize or evaluate	give your and/or experts' opinions about a topic. Provide facts, evidence both for and against, any strengths and/or weaknesses in the theories or statements, any points of comparison and/or contrast, and/or discussion of comparative worth.
6. define	explain the meaning of a given topic. You may describe it, compare it to something known, give examples, and/or tell how it is used.
7. demonstrate, justify, or prove	by using logic, facts, and examples, demonstrate how a given statement or idea is either true or not true.
8. describe or discuss	give factual details of a topic, including any positive and negative factors.
9. explain, support, or illustrate	give reasons and/or examples for a specific viewpoint.

10. list, identify, or name

give the main facts of a specific topic; categorize your information, if appropriate.

11. summarize or outline

give a condensed version of the main points of a topic; include major factors and conclusions.

Some examiners will use two or more of these key words in their questions; in such cases, follow the instructions for both key words in your written discussion.

B. Make the Most of Your Time

Begin your study review three or four weeks before the exam. It is better to have too much time than to face the pressures of not having enough. Realize that cramming the day or night before an exam is a natural habit. However, if you are well prepared, this cram session will be more of a review of the content you have learned and studied, and not the frightening experience of trying to learn, comprehend, and memorize all the required information at once … an almost impossible task! This approach could be referred to as "Russian roulette" studying; unless you just happen to study the exact materials that will be tested, you will not perform well on the exam.

Make a well-planned and spaced-out study timetable. See the example below. Post it in places that will remind you of your intended commitments. Then stick to the schedule! Be organized both before and after each session. Don't postpone studying because of your mood; even if you don't feel like studying, **do it anyway!**

	Sunday	Monday	Tuesday	Wednesday	Thursday	Friday	Saturday
Sample Schedule **Overall One-Month Study Plan** **Proposed Daily Study Times**							
Week 1							
Week 2							
Week 3							
Week 4							

Make an individual study schedule for each of your subjects. Use or copy the examples of a Study Schedule by Topic presented below.

Have a good, quiet study area with all your materials close at hand. After each study session, refer to your overall study plan; then organize all your notes and study materials and place them on your desk for your next planned study session. As you do this pre-study activity, make a list of any new ideas, questions, or things you hope to accomplish for the upcoming session.

Sometimes it helps to have a study partner to share the study tasks, but be sure that your chosen study partner will be a help to this process and not a hindrance. Find someone who will work as hard as you will and who is compatible in study habits. Teaching each other is a good way to learn.

Study Schedule by Topic		
1. Subject:	**Exam Date:**	**Time:**
	Examination Place:	

Date	Accomplished	Next Session Reminders

2. Subject:	**Exam Date:**	**Time:**
	Examination Place:	

Date	Accomplished	Next Session Reminders

3. Subject:	Exam Date: Time: Examination Place:	
Date	Accomplished	Next Session Reminders

4. Subject:	Exam Date: Time: Examination Place:	
Date	Accomplished	Next Session Reminders

C. OVERLEARN YOUR COURSE MATERIAL

Good study notes require a lot of work and effort, but they guarantee that you will gain the most from the course content. If you have already kept good lecture and textbook notes, this task will be much easier for you.

1. Read, summarize, and condense your notes and related reading materials in an easy-to-read and indented format (similar to an outline but not necessarily with the numbers and letters). Write on only one side of the paper, and leave lots of space in your notes so that you can add comments, questions, or other information as you reread, review, reassess, and re-analyze each section of your study notes.

2. Write legibly and use meaningful headings and indented subheadings to identify information. Include supporting evidence and arrange this information in an easy-to-comprehend fashion.

3. Use effective numbering, lettering, pictures, diagrams, graphs, or shortened writing to identify related facts in whatever pattern of development your notes follow. Include formulas, given or devised diagrams, graphs, pictures, or any other study aid that will help you to digest the material in memorable bites.

4. Once your study notes are complete, reread them. Write questions in the margins that would prompt you to write a short essay response. Prepare the answers to your questions.

5. To prepare for a longer essay-style exam, and to gain a more thorough comprehension of your course material, review the content again. This time, try to anticipate more difficult examination questions that would cover several sections of your study notes. Prepare answers to your essay questions.

6. To help you remember important facts about your anticipated responses, you could use any or all of the following memory gems:

    a) Use diagrams or outlines to create a memorable image in your mind.
    b) Memorize the key words in the development of a topic that would prompt you to remember the content.
    c) Use the first letter of each of the key words in your anticipated response and memorize the series of letters to prompt your recall of the content. Write them several times until you have mastered the series of letters.
    d) Use the reverse study procedure. Using only your chosen method for remembering content—either (a), (b), or (c) above—write your anticipated answer from your diagrams or codes.

    Practise whichever method works best for you and try to visualize these responses in your mind as you reread your questions.

7. Before the exam, review your anticipated questions and your memory codes for recall and review of the content. Visualize your codes and responses in paragraph form.

8. Your review study notes could follow this suggested format:

Examination Review Notes			
Exam Subject: **Examination Place:**		**Date of Exam:** **Time:**	
Anticipated Questions	Outline of Answer	Memory Gems or Reminders	Notes to Self

9. All written examination answers, except for one-word or single-phrase answers to questions, require the same characteristics as any written paragraph or composition:

   a) They should have a thesis paragraph and/or main-idea sentence, well-organized support-ing evidence for that idea, and a concluding statement or paragraph.

   b) Your answer should address the requested information in the exam question and be clearly organized. Always use specific examples to support your thesis. Use specific ref-erences to information from lectures, texts, other study materials, experiments, etc.

   c) You should use formal—but natural—structure, vocabulary, and style.

D. THINK SUCCESS!

The following advice should help to relieve those feelings of stress that often accompany examinations.

The Day and Night before the Exam ...

1. Go to the exact location of your examination room; check the schedule to ensure there have been no last-minute changes. Look into the room, if possible, so you can become acquainted with the atmosphere.

2. Review your questions and responses plus your memory gems from your study notes. (This is the cramming method for achievers.)

3. Go to bed early. The best method for putting all your hard work to the test is to have a good night's sleep and be refreshed on the day of your exam. Remember that being exhausted from late-night study will be detrimental to your mental performance on an exam.

4. Have a relaxing bath before you go to bed and listen to some quiet, soothing music.

5. Be confident and know that you have done the best you could do. You have followed the pattern for success:

   a) You have prepared.
   b) You have been organized throughout the semester and particularly during the intense study times.
   c) You have made the most of your study time.
   d) You have overlearned the material.
   e) Now, you must think success!

For the Day of the Exam ...

1. Allow plenty of time for all your routine activities.

2. Review any specific sections of your notes that you feel the need to reread.

3. Make sure that you have all the necessary materials you will need to write the exam.

4. Plan to arrive at the exam site a little early but not too early. Re-check the schedule and go to the room location.

5. Avoid too much idle chatter.

6. Think success ... Relax ... Breathe easily and deeply.

When You Get Your Examination Paper

1. Before you read any of the examination questions, jot down formulas and/or memory gems on the top or back of the exam page or on a scrap sheet. (Make sure that you ask for and receive scrap paper from the exam supervisor. Do not use your own scrap paper unless the supervisor has approved its use!)

2. Next, read all the questions and underline the key words for each question. Also note the number of marks and/or time allotment suggested for each question. As you read each question, jot down any ideas, formulas, letter codes, or facts that you know beside each respective question.

3. Decide your approach to the exam.

   a) If you are given a choice, select the questions you will answer in each section of the exam.
   b) Estimate how much time you plan to spend answering each question. (Generally, the more a question is worth, the more time you should plan to spend on it.) Leave some time for rereading and revising.
   c) Decide in what order you will answer the questions. You do not need to answer questions in the order in which they are presented. Instead, start with the section you feel most confident you can do well in; however, make sure that you number each answer clearly and that the numbers coincide with the numbers on the exam questions.

4. For objective-type questions, such as true/false or multiple choice, read each question carefully and pay attention to wording. If there are penalties for guessing, do not guess ... unless you are making an educated guess.

5. Because of the time restrictions in examinations, it is extremely important for you to take a few minutes to sketch a brief outline of your answers before you begin. On the scrap paper, make a sketch outline of all your essay responses, with spaces so that you can add any other points as you think of them.

6. If you require clarification of any wording in a test question, ask the exam supervisor for clarification.

7. Do not share any materials, allowable reference texts, or anything else with another student. Do not talk to anyone other than the exam supervisor.

During the Examination ...

1. Budget your time; don't get so carried away with one response that you do not leave enough time to complete the whole exam.

2. Even though you may be in a hurry, remember that your instructor has many papers to mark. Therefore, double-space written answers and write very legibly; number your pages and examination booklets clearly; and ensure that your name, student number, and any other relevant information are clearly written on all examination booklets or papers.

3. Write in good essay style with well-constructed and organized paragraphs, clear explanations, and good wording.

4. As you write, you may think of other facts or supportive data for the present question or for others. Take a few moments to jot down the facts in your sketched outline for that question. Keep these facts very brief, just enough to act as reminders of your thoughts.

5. Focus on what you know and leave all unknown questions to the very end. When you don't know the answer and there are no penalties, use the "guess-method": write any and all facts you can recall about the topic. You just may be right!

6. When you have completed your test paper, reread the questions and your responses. If you have recalled additional information, add it at the appropriate place. If your added response is lengthy, rewrite the whole response at the end of your paper; or, if you are short of time, ask your examiner for advice about the placement of this added content.

CONGRATULATIONS!

YOU HAVE NOW COMPLETED THE COMMUNICATION CIRCUIT. YOUR ONE REMAINING TASK IS TO REINFORCE THESE SKILLS IN ALL YOUR FUTURE READING, LISTENING, WRITING, AND STUDY ACTIVITIES.

ANSWERS
TO EXERCISES

UNIT ONE: DISCOVERING VOCABULARY SKILLS

ANSWERS TO EXERCISE 1.1

1. biplane
2. quadrilateral
3. unison
4. century
5. tripod
6. semiconscious
7. monorail
8. millisecond
9. monotone
10. bifocals
11. trifoliate
12. unilateral
13. hemisphere
14. binary
15. quadrant

ANSWERS TO EXERCISE 1.2

1. submarine
2. circumvent
3. contravene
4. precede
5. postscript
6. interscholastic
7. antipathy
8. circumlocution
9. surplus
10. project
11. pro-abortion
12. substandard
13. post-operative
14. surfeit
15. transition

ANSWERS TO EXERCISE 1.3

1. multinational
2. pseudonym
3. retrospect
4. misconceive
5. unusual
6. indefatigable
7. micrometer
8. irrelevant
9. concur
10. resilient
11. pseudo-intellectual
12. microcosm
13. misconstrue
14. reiterate
15. multi-talented

ANSWERS TO EXERCISE 1.4

1. (c)
2. (b)
3. (b)
4. (a)
5. (c)
6. (a)
7. (b)
8. (b)
9. (c)
10. (b)
11. (a)
12. (b)
13. (c)
14. (b)
15. (a)

ANSWERS TO EXERCISE 1.5

Any two of the following suggested words will be acceptable. If the words you chose are not listed below, check them with your instructor.

1. *lingua*—linguistic, trilingual, language, "lingo," linguist
2. *cap, capit*—capital, decapitate, cap, caption, incapacitate
3. *pos, pon*—position, transpose, repose, depose, postpone, impose, expose
4. *duce, duct*—educate, deduce, produce, induct, seduce, introduce, product

5. *spec, spect, spic*—spectacle, spectacles, inspect, respect, despicable, introspective, retrospect
6. *aud, audit*—auditorium, audience, inaudible, audition
7. *tract*—retract, detract, protractor, abstract, subtract, traction, distract
8. *cred*—credentials, credible, incredulous, credit, credence, discredit
9. *rupt*—disrupt, bankrupt, erupt, corrupt, interrupt
10. *ject (action word)*—rejected, deject, object, subject, project, interject, inject
11. *dict*—predict, dictaphone, contradict, addiction, edict
12. *ped, pod*—pedestrian, peddler, pedestal, tripod, impede, moped, pedal, centipede, expedite, impediment
13. *scribe, script*—prescribe, subscription, transcript, scripture
14. *derm*—epidermis, dermatitis
15. *port*—transport, deport, import, reporter, portage
16. *phobia*—acrophobia (fear of high places), phobia (a fear), xenophobia (fear of strangers), hydrophobia (fear of water), agoraphobia (fear of open spaces), pyrophobia (fear of fire), zoophobia (fear of animals), astraphobia (fear of thunder and lightning), monophobia (fear of being alone,) hemaphobia (fear of blood), necrophobia (fear of death), algophobia (fear of pain)
17. *pathy, pathos*—sympathy, sympathetic, apathy, apathetic, empathic, pathetic, pathos, telepathy, antipathy, sympathize, empathize
18. *vent, vene*—intervene, contravene, venture, adventure, prevent, invent, venue, event, convenient, inventory, circumvent
19. *loqua, loqui, locu*—ventriloquist, soliloquy, colloquial, eloquent, elocution, circumlocution
20. *thesis, theses*—antithesis, thesis, prosthesis, hypothesis, synthesis

ANSWERS TO EXERCISE 1.6

1. *retract*—take or pull back
2. *unilingual*—one language
3. *centipede*—an insect with many legs (one hundred legs)
4. *retrospect*—a survey of past times or events; a looking back
5. *incredible*—not believable
6. *antithesis*—opposite or contrasting idea; against a set idea
7. *intervene*—come between
8. *circumlocution*—a roundabout way of talking
9. *antipathy*—a feeling against
10. *interrupt*—break between

ANSWERS TO EXERCISE 1.7

1. The *employer* hired the *employee* to begin work on Monday.
2. My *spacial* sense is not great, but even I could tell that the apartment was *spacious* enough for the two of us.
3. The victim cried for *mercy* but the assailant was *merciless* and refused to be *merciful* in his treatment.

4. The courageous soldier was *fearless* in the face of grave danger and showed no visible signs of *fear* even though all others in the company were *fearful* and shook and trembled as the enemy approached.

5. People are most *educable* when they are young. This is the time when most learning takes place. Therefore, to develop the mind and make full use of your potential, you should stay in school and take advantage of every *educational* opportunity.

ANSWERS TO EXERCISE 1.8

1. geno*cide*
2. pamph*let*
3. radio*logy*
4. derma*titis*
5. pass*ive*
6. gar*ish*
7. horticultur*ist*
8. hypno*tism*
9. vapor*ize*
10. real*ist*
11. pessim*ist*
12. socio*logy*
13. minim*ize*
14. styl*ish*
15. act*ive*
16. rivu*let*
17. tonsi*litis*
18. sui*cide*
19. optim*ism*
20. verbal*ize*

ANSWERS TO EXERCISE 1.9

1. *pugnacious* means quarrelsome
2. *inveigled* means enticed or persuaded by artful talk
3. *nemesis* means punishment for wrongdoings
4. *lethargic* means slow or sluggish; lacking energy
5. *pernicious* means causing great harm; injurious; fatal
6. *enervated* means weakened; lessen the vigour or strength
7. *facetious* means not to be taken seriously; said in fun
8. *amulet* means object worn as magic charm against evil
9. *kinesics* means gestures or facial expressions that accompany speech making
10. *acumen* means keen insight; quickness in seeing and understanding

ANSWERS TO EXERCISE 1.10

1. *apocalyptic* means prophesying events of great significance
2. *cacophonous* means harsh; unmelodious
3. *ingenuous* means honest; innocent; naive
4. *insatiable* means never satisfied
5. *indolence* means laziness; lack of effort
6. *nugatory* means ineffective; useless
7. *eclectic* means made up of selections from various sources
8. *amenable* means willing to listen and agree
9. *in tandem* means one following the other; following closely in cooperation with one another
10. *plagiarism* means the act of taking another writer's work and using it as one's own

ANSWERS TO EXERCISE 1.11

1. *garrulous* means <u>talkative</u>

2. *egotism* means <u>self-centredness</u>

3. *disseminate* means <u>spread</u>

4. *affable* means <u>friendly</u>

5. *strident* means <u>shrill; screeching; harsh</u>

6. *nepotism* means <u>showing favour to relatives</u>

7. *pedantic* means <u>impressively scholastic</u>

8. *vacillate* means <u>waver</u>

9. *acronym* means <u>accepted abbreviated form that is now considered a word</u>

10. *germane* means <u>related; relevant</u>

11. *succinct* means <u>expressed briefly and clearly; concise</u>

12. *integral* means <u>essential; necessary for the completeness of the whole</u>

13. *syntax* means <u>sentence structure; the arrangement of words to form sentences, clauses, or phrases</u>

14. *redundant* means <u>extra; not needed; wordy</u>

15. *deviate* means <u>to turn away from a way, course, rule, or truth</u>

ANSWERS TO EXERCISE 1.12

1. *mesmerized* means <u>fascinated; hypnotized</u>

2. *streetscape* means <u>scenery of the street</u>

3. *gargoyle* means <u>ugly statue that often projects from old buildings</u>

4. *grotesque* means <u>odd; unnatural in shape; ugly</u>

5. *kaleidoscope* means <u>a continuous change of patterns and colours; an optical tube with mirrors that reflect interesting patterns and colours</u>

6. *diverse* means <u>different; varied</u>

7. *unique* means <u>being the only one of its kind</u>

8. *palls* means <u>becomes tiresome; grows weary with</u>

9. *cognizant* means <u>aware</u>

10. *mediocrity* means <u>average or ordinary ability or accomplishment</u>

11. *herculean* means <u>great strength; very powerful; very hard to do</u>

12. *lucrative* means <u>profitable; bringing in money</u>

13. *entrepreneur* means <u>a person who manages a business and who attempts to make a profit but takes the risk of a loss</u>

14. *enterprise* means <u>project; plan; venture; an important undertaking</u>

15. *monetary* means <u>of or pertaining to money; financial</u>

ANSWERS TO EXERCISE 1.13

1. postscript
2. conference or convention
3. transmission
4. peddler
5. sociable

Unit Two: Reading for Comprehension

ANSWERS TO EXERCISE 2.1

1. a) Topic: *books as friends*
   b) Main idea: *Besides being great teachers, books can also be great comforters.*
   or
   Books are similar to friends; they are not only great teachers but also comforters in times of loneliness or trouble.

2. a) Topic: *Canadians*
   b) Main idea: *The majority of Canadians continue to enjoy the fruits of American culture without feeling any less Canadian for it.*

3. a) Topic: *making a decision*
   b) Main idea: *There are two ways of making a decision.*

4. a) Topic: *being grown up*
   b) Main idea: *Being grown up does not depend on your age but upon your emotional maturity.*

5. a) Topic: *choosing a career*
   b) Main idea: *Choosing a career is one of the most important challenges for a young person today.*

6. a) Topic: *maturity*
   b) Main idea: *Maturity is a state of mind, not a date on a calendar.*

7. a) Topic: *taking things for granted*
   b) Main idea: *People take many things for granted.*

8. a) Topic: *record of things to be recalled*
   b) Main idea: *The record of things to be recalled is contained in books, in the minds of parents, in universities and colleges, and in business files.*

9. a) Topic: *monogram "CSA"*
   b) Main idea: *Every CSA-approved product has been subjected to rigorous testing.*

10. a) Topic: *success*
    b) Main idea: *Real success is a matter of attaining a lifestyle in which one is comfortable with oneself.*

ANSWERS TO EXERCISE 2.2

1. a) Topic: *marriage*
   b) Main idea: *Marriage has changed throughout this century.*

2. a) Topic: *collecting*
   b) Main idea: *Collecting is an instinctive habit of many living creatures.*

3. a) Topic: *collecting genuine friends*
    b) Main idea: *To have a collection of genuine friends, consider the following basic rules.*

4. a) Topic: *young people of the 1960s*
    b) Main idea: *Young people of the 1960s began a rebellion against the middle-class establishment.*

5. a) Topic: *pride in appearance*
    b) Main idea: *One's appearance often is symbolic of one's pride or self-esteem.*

    or

    The way a person dresses or appears often indicates his or her feelings about self.

ANSWERS TO EXERCISE 2.3

The Practical Writer

1. Some writers deliberately muddy the meaning of their words, if indeed they meant anything to begin with. When most people write, however, it is to get a message across. This is especially so in business and institutions, where written words carry much of the load of communication. The written traffic of any well-ordered organization is thick and varied—letters, memos, reports, policy statements, manuals, sales literature, and what-have-you. <u>The purpose of it all is to use words in a way that serves the organization's aim</u>.

2. <u>Unfortunately, written communications often fail to accomplish this purpose.</u> Some organizational writing gives rise to confusion, inefficiency, and ill-will. This is almost always because the intended message did not get through to the receiving end. Why? The main reason usually is that the message was inadequately prepared.

3. <u>An irresistible comparison arises between writing and</u> another craft which most people have to practise sometimes, namely <u>cooking.</u> In both fields there is a wide range of competence, from the great chefs and authors to the occasional practitioners who must do the job whether they like it or not. In both, care in preparation is of the essence. Shakespeare wrote that it is an ill cook who does not lick [his or] her fingers; it is an ill writer who does not work at it hard enough to be reasonably satisfied with the results.

4. <u>In the working world, bad writing is not only bad manners; it is bad business.</u> The victim of an incomprehensible letter will at best be annoyed and at worst decide that people who can't say what they mean aren't worth doing business with. Write a sloppy letter, and it might rebound on you when the recipient calls for clarification. Where one carefully worded letter would have sufficed, you might have to write two or more.

5. <u>Muddled messages can cause havoc within an organization.</u> Instructions that are misunderstood can set people off in the wrong direction or put them to work in vain. Written policies that are open to misinterpretation can throw sand in the gears of an entire operation. Ill-considered language in communications with or between employees can torpedo morale.

Mysteries of Motivation

6. <u>To motivate people, the dictionaries tell us, is to cause them to act in a certain way.</u> This is done by furnishing them with a motive to do your bidding. By the strictest definition, the most elementary form of motivation would be if a hold-up man were to stick a pistol in your face and growl: "Your money or your life." He instantly arouses a motive in you for doing what he wants you to—the motive of staying alive.

Management uses the "carrot and stick" system to motivate workers to ultimate goals.

7. In the lexicon of management science, the system of reward and punishment is known as the "carrot and stick" approach, the carrot being dangled in front of a donkey's nose and the stick applied smartly to his hindquarters. In this fashion he is alternately enticed and impelled towards his master's goal. Whether the donkey ever gets to eat the carrot in this analogy is not made clear in management literature. We can be sure, however, that he gets to feel the stick.

8. <u>The modern worker clearly is motivated by much more than the carrot of pay and advancement and the stick of discipline and insecurity,</u> although it would be foolish to underestimate the continuing effectiveness of these devices. Money might not be everything—otherwise movie stars would be the happiest people on earth—but there is no evidence that the mass of humanity has ceased to have a strong desire for the comfort and possessions that money will buy. The "stick," at the very least, is what makes us get up in the morning and go to work even when we don't feel like it. It is part of normal human nature to stay clear of trouble and to want the assurance of a steady, well-paid job.

ANSWERS TO EXERCISE 2.4

1. As children *grow from infants to adolescents,* their attitudes towards their parents change.

   Developed by *sequence*

2. There are usually *many* different motives for reading.

   Developed by *example*

3. *A crowd is* a temporary grouping of people in physical proximity.

   Developed by *example*

4. From the *earliest times to the present,* humanity has believed in a form of higher power.

   Developed by *example*

5. Children are too *often* handy targets for adult frustrations.

   Developed by *example*

6. *Books* are good for us.

   Developed by *example*

7. Two books I have recently read, *Gone with the Wind* and *Ashes in the Wind,* are incredibly *alike.*

   Developed by *comparison*

8. *Jealousy is* an emotional response that fosters aggression.

   Developed by *example*

9. The function of one's eye is *similar to* the function of a camera.

    Developed by *comparison*

10. Effective speech making *means avoiding vague and clumsy words* that are often misinterpreted.

    Developed by *example*

ANSWERS TO EXERCISE 2.5

1. The average reader can read an average book at the rate of 300 words a minute. That means one would cover 4500 words in a quarter of an hour, or 1 642 500 words in a year. <u>If you spend just fifteen minutes a day you can read twenty average-length books between January 1 and December 31.</u>

    Developed by *example*

2. <u>There is a difference between politeness and courtesy.</u> According to Dr. Samuel Johnson, politeness is fictitious benevolence. Courtesy, on the other hand, has benevolence built in. One cannot be genuinely courteous without having a genuine regard for the feelings and general welfare of one's fellows. Politeness is a quality of the head; courtesy, of the heart.

    Developed by *contrast*

3. <u>A minority of the killers and mutilators of the road go beyond carelessness to wanton recklessness.</u> Some—not all of them young—get a thrill out of willfully breaking traffic laws. Some bully their fellow road users by racing down pedestrians, forcing their way into traffic flows, and cutting perilously close in front of other vehicles when passing. Some lose their tempers and employ their vehicles as weapons to threaten the objects of their anger. Terrifyingly enough, some persist in driving while under the influence of alcohol or drugs. Drivers like these are public menaces, and they should be publicly condemned as such.

    Developed by *example*

4. Trans Canada Airlines went to work in the 1930s to establish a route across the country. It added larger Lockheed 14s and, on April 1, 1939, inaugurated a transcontinental passenger service between Montreal and Vancouver. The flying time of the first east-west flight was 16 hours, 5 minutes, with five intermediate stops. As early as 1943, TCA spread its wings over the Atlantic, operating the Canadian Government Trans-Atlantic Air Service, which carried priority passengers and mail in Lancaster bombers to and from Britain. This war effort paved the way for routine postwar transatlantic crossings by North Stars, then Super Constellations, then DC-8s, and the present giant Boeing 747s and Lockheed L-1011s. In the meantime, <u>TCA, renamed Air Canada, has grown into one of the ten largest airlines in the world.</u>

    Developed by *sequence*

5. <u>Some people treat danger with greater equanimity than others.</u> For instance, it comes naturally to a man born into a warrior class in an Eastern country to fear being branded a coward more than the prospect of sudden death. Similarly, a person with a genuine faith that he or she will enter into a happier state through dying is apt to be less afraid of mortal peril than one who thinks of death as the ultimate extinction. Some societies place a relatively low premium on human life so that they pay less attention than others to physical risks.

    Developed by *example*

SUGGESTED ANSWERS TO EXERCISE 2.6

1. I. Money represents different things to different people. (Developed by *example*)

    A. survival and basic needs for the poor

    B. security for the middle class

    C. power symbol for the rich

2. I. The chief function of a family meeting is for members to discuss matters of common interest and to agree on what is to be done. (Developed by *reasons*)

    A. times when family must act as a unit

    B. necessity for all to have input on serious issues

    C. respect learned for individual's rights and opinions

    D. negotiations learned for harmonious living

    E. learned communication skills mean feelings of security within the family

SUGGESTED ANSWERS TO EXERCISE 2.7

1. I. Communication is a process of transmitting a message from the sender to the receiver. (Developed by *sequence*)

    A. considered and put into words

    B. conveyed to receiver
        1. by telephone
        2. by written letter, memo, or telegram
        3. by personal contact

    C. decoded and interpreted by recipient

2. I. Although this method appears to be a simple process, communicating effectively seems to be a major problem in today's society. (Developed by *reasons*)

    A. message inadequately prepared
        1. missing or incomplete information
        2. meaning clouded by ambiguity or errors

    B. manners negatively affect intent of sender
        1. tone of voice
        2. sloppiness of document
        3. inappropriate dress or manners

    C. recipient capable of reading and interpreting

    D. skillful messengers and recipients needed

3. I. In the early 1800s, phrenology, a medical theory that bumps and depressions on people's skulls indicated their ability and personality traits, was a popularly used practice. (Developed by *examples or reasons*)

    A. brain shaped according to its used and unused parts
        1. used portion grew and created a bump
        2. unused part formed indentation

    B. physicians studied people in jails and insane asylums
        1. thieves had bumps above ears
        2. destructive people had bumps behind their ears
        3. sex deviates had bumps at back of head

    C. theory short-lived but carried over to today
        1. meaning of "rocks in your head"

4. I. It takes a superhuman effort to throw out everything in a household that should be thrown out. (Developed by *examples*)

    A. homemakers' collections of paper products and attire

    B. children's collections of toys
      1. hold memories of the past
      2. part of every child's security

    C. family's collection of sports equipment
      1. skiing might be popular again
      2. needed in case owner decides to ski

    D. everyone's horde of personal treasures

SUGGESTED ANSWERS TO EXERCISE 2.8

An irresistible comparison arises between writing and another craft which most people have to practise sometimes, namely cooking. In both fields there is a wide range of competence, from the great chefs and authors to the occasional practitioners who must do the job whether they like it or not. In both, care in preparation is of the essence. Shakespeare wrote that it is an ill cook who does not lick [his or] her own fingers; it is an ill writer who does not work at it hard enough to be reasonably satisfied with the results.

IV. **An irresistible comparison arises between writing and cooking.**

    A. **wide range of competence**

    B. **care in preparation**

    C. **reasonably satisfied with results**

Unlike bachelor cooks, however, casual writers are rarely the sole consumers of their own offerings. Reclusive philosophers and [others] keeping diaries are about the only writers whose work is not intended for other eyes. If a piece of writing turns out to be an indigestible half-baked mess, those on the receiving end are usually the ones to suffer. The reader of a bad book can always toss it aside. But in organizations, where written communications command attention, it is up to the recipient of a sloppy writing job to figure out what it means.

V. **Writers are rarely the sole consumers of their own offerings.**

    A. **only private writers keep work hidden**

    B. **receiver suffers from poor writing**
      1. **in literature, reader can toss it aside**
      2. **in business, recipient must figure out what it means**

The reader is thus put in the position of doing the thinking the writer failed to do. To make others do your work for you is, of course, an uncivil act. In a recent magazine advertisement on the printed word, one of a commendable series published by the International Paper Company, novelist Kurt Vonnegut touched on the social aspect of writing: "Why should you examine your writing style with the idea of improving it? Do so as a mark of respect for your readers. If you scribble your thoughts any which way, your readers will surely feel that you care nothing for them."

VI. **The reader must do thinking writer failed to do.**

    A. **an uncivil act**

    B. **novelist Kurt Vonnegut's advice on writing**
      1. **examine writing as a mark of respect for your reader**
      2. **if you scribble your thoughts, readers feel you don't care**

In the working world, bad writing is not only bad manners, it is bad business. The victim of an incomprehensible letter will at best be annoyed and at worst decide that people who can't say what they mean aren't worth doing business with. Write a sloppy letter, and it might rebound on you when the recipient calls for clarification. Where one carefully worded letter would have sufficed, you might have to write two or more.

VII. **Bad writing is bad business.**

    A. **victim annoyed**

    B. **letter might rebound**
      1. **might have to write two or more**

Muddled messages can cause havoc within an organization. Instructions that are misunderstood can set people off in the wrong direction or put them to work in vain. Written policies that are open to misinterpretation can throw sand in the gears of an entire operation. Ill-considered language in communications with employees can torpedo morale.

VIII. Muddled messages can cause havoc within an organization.

    A. misunderstood instructions set people off in wrong direction

    B. misinterpreted written policies can destroy operation

    C. ill-considered language can torpedo morale

ANSWERS TO EXERCISE 2.9

1. MAIN IDEA

Source:	K.P.D. Broekhuizen, the deputy director of the Anne Frank Foundation
Where:	Amsterdam
When:	"yesterday" (check dateline)
Who	Anne Frank and her family
What:	the secret annex where they hid from the Nazis during World War II has been restored
Why:	for a documentary film on the teenage diarist's life

SUPPORTING DETAILS

— small wing maintained as a museum

— filming begins next week

— portrays boy reading her diary

— includes superimposed images of photos of the Frank family

— researchers restored annex using Anne's descriptions in her diary, her father's notes, and Miep Gies's recollections

— Anne's hiding began in July 1942

— Anne described her surroundings

— the Franks were betrayed in the fall of 1944

— Anne and her sister are believed to have died in February or March 1945, in Nazi extermination camps

— her father was the only survivor

2. MAIN IDEA

Source:	Coca-Cola Company
Where:	(not stated)
When:	(not stated — check dateline)
Who:	Coca-Cola, the world's biggest soft-drink company
What:	entering the fast-growing bottled water business with its own brand of purified water from tap or wells with some added minerals
Why:	market for such products is increasing

SUPPORTING DETAILS

— already has brand name, Dasani

— has hesitated to diversify because the company's success has been based on simplicity by selling concentrates to bottlers who then add water and carbonation before distributing product

— previously thought that sale of bottled water might undercut soft-drink sales

— can no longer ignore the increased market sales for bottled water

— archrival PepsiCo. now has top-selling brand of water called Aquafina

— bottled water sales have increased from $2.65 million to $4 billion a year and are continuing to rise

— biggest competitors are Perrier, Poland Springs, and Arrowhead brands, and French owner of Evian and Dannon is expanding by buying AquaPenn Spring Water, which is the 10th largest firm in the U.S.

Unit Three: Developing Good Study Skills

SUGGESTED ANSWERS TO EXERCISE 3.1

It takes a superhuman effort to throw out everything in a household that should be thrown out, and most people prove to be only too human when the moment of decision arrives. Almost all homemakers have a collection of supermarket bags, old magazines, last year's telephone directory, or boxes of out-dated clothes and footwear that just might be useful some day in the distant future. Children are often reluctant to part with favourite, old, ragged toys that are no longer a part of their everyday lives. How could they part with these priceless treasures that hold such memories of the past and are an important part of every child's security? Other members of the family insist on keeping sports equipment, even when these articles are just collecting dust in the basement. One never knows when skiing will once again be the sport of the year, and those old skis will be there, waiting for the owner to strap them on again. Regardless of how organized and tidy one is, everyone will likely have a horde of personal treasures that just might come in handy some day.

SUGGESTED ANSWERS TO EXERCISE 3.2

Title is already a question, so no change.

What Use Is Education?

[*A student once wrote to the editor of the* Monthly Letter, *Royal Bank of Canada, and questioned why young people should continue in school and get an education. The following letter was the response.*]

The commonplace thing to do would be to enlarge upon the material aspects of a good education, and to tell you that the principal benefit is in helping you to get a good job, etc. We are sure you already know about that. A young person who does not make the best of all the learning opportunities of school years will be at a disadvantage in competition with others in later life.

We are not going to suggest to you that you should fill yourself chock-full of information, for the real benefit of your education will be knowledge and understanding and not a long list of memorized facts. The main purpose of education, as we see it, is to teach one to think.

How does education help us learn to think?

Learning to Think

It is only by learning how to think, and by learning how to sift out things worth thinking about, that you can put yourself in the best position for enjoying a happy life. This is a very important reason for wishing to continue at school and get an education. <u>Education,</u> when of the right sort, <u>helps you to see things clearly, to distinguish between</u> the <u>essential and</u> the (trivial) and <u>to give you</u> a frame of mind and system of <u>thought and judgement that will fit you into your place in life.</u> Without education (1) you <u>could never</u> hope to really <u>understand the world or its people or what goes on in it;</u> (2) you <u>could not handle yourself graciously</u> and with ease in an environment that is not always so well disposed towards you as your home and your school; (3) you <u>could never relate</u> yourself properly <u>to the problems of others or achieve the peace of mind and understanding</u> which one must have <u>to support one through the crises</u> that come to try all of us.

We believe it is very much worthwhile for you to study and we hope that you will pursue your education so successfully that you will have a very happy life. You will realize, we are sure, that <u>everyone faces problems</u> and difficulties <u>at some time or other</u> and everyone suffers distress and sorrow. These seem to be inescapable. But <u>the educated person</u> is in a much <u>better position to cope</u> with these things, <u>to solve</u> these problems, and <u>to master</u> some of the <u>difficulties,</u> and <u>thus</u> in the end to be <u>less disturbed and grieved by it all.</u> An educated individual is, we think, <u>entitled</u> to count upon life holding out <u>prospects of achievement and security</u>—not the kind of security that is dependent upon one's ideals, capability and understanding.

What we are trying to say is that <u>education is absolutely essential</u> but we are not referring to a mass of what, in an old-fashioned way, we called "book learning" and nothing else. What we are after is the education that will teach you to think and reason, which will <u>improve your material</u> prospects, which will add to your poise and (deportment,) which will develop your judgement and which, all in all, <u>will round you out for a fully successful and happy life.</u> That is the kind of life we wish for you.

What sense of values do we get from an education?

A Sense of Values

<u>One of the most frightening things</u> in our world <u>is ignorance;</u> not merely lack of knowledge, but more than anything else the ignorance that consists in not knowing that there are better things, better ways of doing things, and a social responsibility to try to see and do these better things.

<u>Education will help you</u> to think clearly and <u>reach good judgements about</u> the relative importance of the various <u>kinds of activity that make up human life.</u> What are these activities? There are some that minister directly to <u>self-preservation,</u> like obtaining food and keeping healthy; others are concerned with the raising of offspring; some have to do with <u>social and political relations; and</u> there are activities associated with the <u>leisure part of life.</u> All of these (clamour) for attention, effort and time. The <u>value</u> of any of them <u>exists</u> for you <u>in relation to the values you give the others.</u>

An ancient <u>Greek philosopher</u> said the <u>purpose of education</u> is to <u>persuade you to like what you ought to like,</u> and to <u>dislike what you ought to dislike.</u> Education will <u>open up</u> to you the <u>opportunity to follow the true, the beautiful and the good,</u> to avoid vulgarity and false sentiments by providing you with standards by which to judge values. It will <u>enable you to decide what will contribute toward your happiness in life.</u> Without education, how can you (discern) what is good for you? what is right or wrong? what is true or false? what is lovely or ugly?

trivial—slight importance; not essential
deportment—proper behaviour
clamour—cry out
discern—perceive; recognize

SUGGESTED ANSWERS TO EXERCISE 3.3

Your answer may be slightly different from the one that follows; however, what you have underlined should make sense and should not be overdone. If you have doubts about the correctness of your work, ask your instructor to check your answer.

How does an education affect this changing world?

This Changing World

We in Canada are very conscious of our natural resources, because our economy is founded on them—our forests and our farmlands, our minerals and our waterpower, our fisheries and our wildlife. But all these resources are useless without two others: the intelligence and the initiative of our people.

And where do we get these personal qualities? From the accumulated intellectual talent of our people given to us through the discipline of education.

We need knowledge and enterprise more than people ever before needed them, because we are living in a period of the most profound social and cultural transition. Young people of today do not realize it, for this is the only sort of world they know, but during the past sixty years our world has become increasingly strange and frightening.

Less than two generations ago, the life of ordinary people was fairly routine. Crisis was something that came only once in ten years, like an earthquake or a political joust about tariffs or a spot of sabre-rattling—and these were handled with dexterity and aplomb by experts.

Today, we live with crises at home and abroad, and not only the catastrophe-relief people, the politicians and the military are involved: we are all in it. That is why we need education, to gain knowledge and attain wisdom.

We cannot estimate with any certainty what changes may be brought about in the lifetime of you who are now young: changes due to medical science, interplanetary communication, atomic energy, increasing population, exhaustion of certain natural resources, conquest of the polar and tropical regions, aggression by despotic powers. You cannot face these prospective changes with intelligence or serenity if you have only the education that was adequate a half century ago.

Young people have more and more to learn as our culture grows more complex. Education gives us the tools with which to deal with material forces that were once our enemies, and turn them into slaves to do our bidding, but education must go on to teach us how to live and behave in this new society.

Scientific technology has broken up the placid life familiar to our grandparents. It has converted the person of general competence into a specialist.

Our ancestors had to be content so long as they were just one potato row ahead of starvation; tomorrow, science will have moved forward another step, machines will run machines, labour will be upgraded in terms of skill, and there will then be no appeal from the judgement that will be pronounced on the uneducated person.

profound—intense; great
transition—gradual change to something different; phase
joust—battle; conflict
dexterity—competence; expertness
aplomb—poise; assurance; confidence
interplanetary—between planets
despotic—tyrannical; oppressive

Title is already a question, so no change.

What Is Education?

<u>Education should be useful.</u> We don't mean useful in the sense of making us (adept) in manipulating gadgets. Every young person reading this letter wants something better than that. You wish to be fit to perform justly, skilfully, (magnanimously) and with personal satisfaction, all the offices of life.

<u>Learning sheer fact is not all of education.</u> The three R's do not constitute education, any more than a knife, fork and spoon constitute a dinner. Some of the greatest bores are people who have memorized a great deal of information and love to talk about it.

The <u>aim of an educational institution</u> is to <u>give students</u> a living <u>fund of knowledge from which</u> they <u>may generate ideas. When you</u> can <u>bring relevant background</u> to bear on a problem, <u>assemble pertinent data, grasp relationships,</u> appraise <u>the values</u> involved, and <u>make a judgement;</u> when you can do that <u>you are an educated person.</u>

<u>Then</u> you need <u>not fear becoming bewildered by change</u> or thrown into a panic by misfortune, because you will be able to determine three vital things: where you are, where you are headed, and what you had better do under these circumstances.

<u>In seeking that education, be imaginative.</u> The <u>first ten or twelve years</u> of your life were its <u>romantic stage.</u> When you looked through a telescope to study the stars you saw not lumps of matter floating in space but the glory of the sky. In <u>secondary school</u> you pass through the <u>age of precision.</u> You must learn things correctly, exactly and completely, because these things form the bank account on which you will be drawing all through your life. <u>After secondary school</u> you enter the <u>period of generalization.</u> You will <u>begin to apply what you have learned,</u> transferring particularities of knowledge to the problems of general living. As one peak is climbed, farther ranges will appear upon the horizon, beckoning to you. You cannot climb them until you reach them, but there they are, eternally luring you.

But, you may say, <u>"so-and-so made good</u> in life <u>without</u> having had <u>an extensive formal education."</u> Quite <u>true.</u> Many men and women <u>did not have the opportunity</u> that is open to every young person in Canada today. They left school and went to work before completing high school; some did not go any further than public school. But they <u>continued to learn while they worked.</u>

They <u>succeeded in spite of handicaps</u> and not because of them. They had a (daemon) in them <u>that prodded, and</u> a <u>vital energy that strengthened them</u> to attain education by home study, or in evening classes, or in other ways. <u>Sir Winston Churchill,</u> who contributed so greatly to the world in war and in peace, told an audience in Boston: "I have no technical and <u>no university education,</u> and have just <u>had to pick up</u> a <u>few things as I went along."</u>

<u>Young people</u> in Canada today <u>need not endure hardship and suffer delay.</u> So far as is in their power and so far as their knowledge carries them, people of the older generation have made it possible for young people to become educated to the utmost extent of their capability and their desire.

<u>Don't expect</u>—and don't desire—that <u>education</u> shall <u>be poured into you.</u> You will see more interesting and useful things when you look for them yourself. You can't profit by accepting facts without questioning, by accepting words instead of trying to understand ideas. You <u>need to explore the many sides</u> there may be to a question.

<u>If you walk all around</u> the <u>opinion of a famous [person], question it,</u> and then <u>embrace it,</u> the <u>opinion is no longer his [or hers] but yours.</u> When you learn how a danger occurs, you may take steps to avoid it; <u>if you want to escape being fooled, find out how the fooling is done;</u> go behind the puppet show to see with what skill the little figures are manipulated.

adept—skilled; expert
magnanimously—generously; heroically
daemon—demon

SUGGESTED ANSWERS TO EXERCISE 3.4

Marriage has changed throughout this century.

1. <u>In the early part of this century, marriage</u> between young people <u>was an arrangement</u> made between parents—or even nations—<u>to join two people for reasons other than love. As time progressed,</u> it did <u>become more acceptable for young people to choose</u> their <u>own lifetime partners.</u> The young man, however, had to declare his honorable intentions to his lady's parents before he was allowed to court her. Then, of course, it became more fashionable for young people to meet and date before they made the "big decision." <u>Up until the 1960s,</u> though, <u>a young man still</u> continued to <u>show formal respect for his date</u> and always saw her to and from her front door, bought her gifts of candy or flowers, and showed her every courtesy. <u>With today's young people, formal courtesies</u>—including dating—seem to <u>have disappeared;</u> and <u>marriage, if there is one,</u> has become <u>a legal agreement</u> in which both parties indicate their rights—<u>and,</u> in some cases, <u>state renewable dates for a renegotiated contract!</u>

Ways in which writing and cooking can be compared

2. An irresistible <u>comparison</u> arises <u>between writing and</u> another craft which most people have to practise sometimes, namely <u>cooking.</u> In both fields there is a <u>wide range of competence,</u> from the great chefs and authors to the occasional practitioners who must do the job whether they like it or not. In both, <u>care in preparation</u> is of the essence. Shakespeare wrote that it is an ill cook who does not lick her fingers; it is an ill writer who does not <u>work at it hard enough to be reasonably satisfied with</u> the <u>results.</u>

Poor writing skills cost time and money.

3. <u>In the working world, bad writing is</u> not only bad manners; it is <u>bad business.</u> The victim of an incomprehensible letter will at best be annoyed and at worst decide that people who can't say what they mean aren't worth doing business with. Write a sloppy letter, and it might rebound on you when the recipient calls for clarification. Where one carefully worded letter would have sufficed, you might have to write two or more.

Results of poorly written messages

4. <u>Muddled messages</u> can <u>cause havoc</u> within an organization. <u>Instructions</u> that are <u>misunderstood</u> can set <u>people</u> off in the wrong direction or put them to <u>work in vain. Written policies</u> that are open to <u>misinterpretation</u> can throw sand in the gears of an entire operation. <u>Ill-considered language</u> in communications with or between employees <u>can torpedo morale.</u>

Motivating people means encouraging them to follow your ideas.

5. To motivate people, the dictionaries tell us, is to cause them to act in a certain way. This is done by furnishing them with a motive to do your bidding. By the strictest definition, the most elementary form of motivation would be if a holdup man were to stick a pistol in your face and growl: "Your money or your life." He instantly arouses a motive in you for doing what he wants you to—the motive of staying alive.

Management may use a "reward and punishment" system to attempt to motivate their employees.

6. In the lexicon of management science, the system of reward and punishment is known as the "carrot and stick" approach, the carrot being dangled in front of a donkey's nose and the stick applied smartly to his hindquarters. In this fashion he is alternately enticed and impelled towards his master's goal. Whether the donkey ever gets to eat the carrot in this analogy is not made clear in management literature. We can be sure, however, that he gets to feel the stick.

SUGGESTED ANSWERS TO EXERCISE 3.5

If your answers are very different from the ones suggested below, ask an instructor to check your work. Try to underline meaningful word phrases.

What kinds of special training do we need?	**Special Training**
	<u>Choosing a career today</u> is <u>not</u> the (docile) <u>following in your parents' foot-steps</u> that was common a half century ago. There are <u>attractive professions and businesses</u> and crafts that were <u>not heard of,</u> some not even imagined, when today's university graduates were born.
Values of general education	It is <u>not desirable that you</u> should <u>pursue technical education to</u> the <u>exclusion of general or cultural education.</u> Supervisors will tell you that <u>workers who have had practice in learning at school</u> usually <u>turn out to be better at learning in a factory.</u> They <u>catch on</u> more quickly, not only <u>to the "how"</u> of the job but to the <u>"why" of it.</u> They <u>have</u> a <u>quicker and surer grasp of problems.</u> They are <u>more likely to think up time- and labour-saving ideas.</u> They have the <u>broad outlook and</u> the <u>capacity for straight thinking</u> that are <u>essential to promotion and advancement.</u>
Comparison to earthworm is rationale for learning general education.	The earthworm has not only digging skill but a sense of the principles involved in digging a good hole at the proper depth and in the right direction. We, on the higher (stratum) of the animal kingdom, need no less. <u>It is principles,</u> and <u>not mere data, we need</u> if we are to <u>find our way through the mazes of tomorrow.</u>
You cannot be single-minded in your learning. Best to have general knowledge for modern business world.	<u>If you</u> are <u>going in for commerce,</u> do not imagine for a moment that all you need is training in reading, writing and arithmetic. Even the addition of bookkeeping, shorthand and typing is not enough. You <u>need an intelligent knowledge of the realities of modern economic life.</u>
	<u>People in business believe</u> that <u>more attention</u> should be <u>given</u> in schools and colleges <u>to the art of communicating</u> ideas. There is <u>not much</u> prospect for <u>advancement</u> in commercial firms <u>unless you can express your thoughts competently.</u> You cannot buy or sell, give instructions to subordinates, make a report, win friends or influence people, unless you can say clearly and appealingly what it is in your mind to say.
You are what you learn!	If you are going to learn a trade, <u>don't be satisfied to become a specialist in "know-how" rather than in knowledge. The sort of person you are to be</u> is <u>more important</u> in the long run <u>than the sort of skills you acquire.</u>
	Really <u>useful training in a trade</u> will <u>provide</u> you with some <u>general principles</u> and a <u>thorough grounding</u> in their <u>application to certain concrete details.</u> It will <u>give you a base</u> on which you may build a bigger and better job. It will (habituate) you to <u>use all your brain instead of just the fragment that directs your fingers.</u>
	<u>Should you be going on to university,</u> you need to know that the <u>function of higher education is twofold: to</u> (disseminate) <u>knowledge already stored up,</u> and <u>to spur you to acquire new knowledge.</u> What training there is in a university is directed toward conditioning the mind to think; to pushing back the barriers of the past and extending the boundaries of what is known; to discovering problems to be solved.

docile—contented; inclined; voluntarily
stratum—level or layer
habituate—accustom; become a habit
disseminate—spread; circulate

SUGGESTED ANSWERS TO EXERCISE 3.6

1.

'GREEN' HOUSE WILL POWER ITSELF AND RECYCLE WASTE

TORONTO (CP)—<u>A Toronto architect is building a self-sufficient house that will generate its own electricity, compost its sewage, store rainwater for drinking and recycle dirty water.</u>

<u>The house,</u> designed by Martin Liefhebber Architect Inc., <u>will operate completely independent of basic public utilities or city services.</u>

"This is <u>the house of tomorrow,</u>" said Chris Ives, an engineer in the research division of the Canada Mortgage and Housing Corp.

The design was <u>one of two winners of CMHC's healthy housing design competition last year.</u> It was among the leading housing technology on display earlier this week as part of the Canadian Home Builders' Association's annual conference in Toronto.

"It may sound space-age and implausible to some," Ives said. "But <u>all of the technology used</u> in Martin (Liefhebber's) design <u>is already available on the market.</u>"

<u>The features of the house will include:</u>

—<u>Twelve roof-top solar panels</u> that <u>turn the heat of the sun into electrical currents</u> to be <u>stored in large batteries in the basement.</u> A device called <u>an inverter transforms the energy into 110 volts of power.</u>

—<u>A composting tank in the basement</u> that <u>processes sewage and</u> will <u>provide one cubic foot of fertilizer for the garden about every four years.</u>

—<u>A second tank in the basement</u> that <u>filters waste water from the kitchen sink and shower.</u> The water will <u>then be pumped up to a roof top greenhouse where plants indigenous to swamps will play the final role in cleansing it for re-use.</u>

—<u>Drinking water will be supplied by rain and snow caught by an external tank and stored in a larger one in the basement with a capacity of 20 000 litres.</u> The storage tank will contain lime to neutralize the acid caused by air pollution. "Drinking rainwater is a lot healthier than the stuff that comes out of Lake Ontario," Liefhebber said.

—<u>A masonry stove made from soapstone will provide additional heating for the house,</u> for <u>cooking,</u> and will <u>only require about $175 worth of wood for the winter season.</u>

<u>A first-floor solarium filled with plants will help clean the air, and thick walls and large windows facing south will help to retain heat.</u> A <u>solar-powered pump will provide cooling in the summer.</u>

"A design like this won't work if a family continues to use lots and lots of water and lots and lots of electricity," Ives said.

A <u>family</u> would <u>have to be willing to give up their clothes dryer and blow dryer.</u> But they <u>can keep the microwave, television and VCR.</u>

The <u>house</u> will be <u>equipped with</u> an <u>energy efficient refrigerator,</u> which uses about one-fifth as much power, Liefhebber said.

The <u>two-storey, 900-square-foot [83.6 square metres] house will cost about $100 000 to build,</u> he said. CMHC estimates it would likely <u>sell for</u> a market price <u>of about $160 000.</u>

Construction is set to begin in May, but <u>Liefhebber still has to complete a few stages of the municipal approval process.</u>

The <u>prototype is being built for an individual</u> who owns a piece of unserviced land <u>in Riverdale, an east end district of Toronto.</u>

<u>The lot has garages on either side</u> and it <u>would cost about $150 000 to establish connections to sewage and other city services,</u> Liefhebber said.

It <u>costs about $10 000 on average to hook up a new house to water, sewage, drainage and hydro</u> if the necessary <u>infrastructure is already in place,</u> he said.

2.

PEPSI TURNING BLUE TO LURE MARKETS

LONDON (Reuter) —Escalating its battle against soft drinks giant Coca-Cola Co. and others <u>for a stake in emerging markets</u>, <u>PepsiCo Tuesday unveiled "Project Blue,"</u> with <u>a new blue can and advertising campaign in 24 countries outside the United States</u>.

Running <u>a far second behind</u> giant <u>Coca-Cola in the world market</u>, <u>Pepsi</u> has <u>lacked a unified image</u>, critics say. <u>For example</u>, <u>in Germany</u>, a can of <u>Pepsi looks one way</u>, and <u>in Latin America</u>, <u>another</u>. <u>Some</u> of Pepsi's <u>billboards are more than 20 years old and</u>, critics say, <u>the soft drink tastes different wherever you are</u>.

But <u>PepsiCo said those days are over</u>.

<u>Launched in Britain</u>, "Project <u>Blue</u>" is a <u>$500 million project</u> to claw back market share from arch-rival Coke, senior executives said.

In a razzmatazz media launch here, <u>Pepsi introduced a new electric blue can</u>, scrapping the old red, white and blue. It <u>also flew in supermodels</u> Claudia Schiffer and Cindy Crawford <u>and tennis star Andre Agassi to publicize a series of</u> television <u>commercials</u> they were hired to make.

In <u>addition</u>, <u>Pepsi unveiled a $190,000</u> marketing exercise—<u>a Concorde supersonic airliner painted in Pepsi's new colours</u>.

<u>But</u> it was <u>unclear how Pepsi intended to use the blue Concorde because aviation experts said</u> the <u>plane could fly</u> at <u>supersonic speeds only if painted pure white</u> due to the heat generated at high speed.

"We have to be big in the new emerging markets, that's where the real battle is being fought," said John Swanhaus, senior vice president, international sales and marketing.

Swanhaus said that sales growth in emerging sectors was in excess of 20 percent a year compared with only 4 percent or 5 percent in the maturer drinks markets.

<u>Pepsi has moved into Asia</u>, <u>Eastern Europe</u> and the <u>Middle East</u> in recent years, <u>where growth in sales of soft drinks has spiked higher</u> from a very low base, he said.

<u>Swanhaus</u>, speaking at London Gatwick Airport where Pepsi unveiled its new blue cola can, <u>said Pepsi was actually outselling Coca-Cola in China</u> where it has already invested over $500 million.

<u>But</u> it's <u>still an uphill struggle</u>. <u>Outside the</u> United <u>States</u>, <u>Coke outsells Pepsi</u> about <u>three to one</u>.

Coke is the U.S. market leader, with about 43 percent to Pepsi's 31 percent, according to Beverage Marketing, a trade publication.

However, <u>Swanhaus said</u>, <u>Pepsi</u> has been <u>gaining share internationally</u>.

While Swanhaus <u>said</u> the <u>United States and Canada</u> were <u>expected to</u> follow suit and <u>change</u> their <u>brand designs</u> shortly, a <u>spokesperson for Pepsi International said</u> <u>this was news to him</u>.

Keith Hughes, a spokesperson for Pepsi International, based in Purchase, N.Y., said from London "that's not the way I would see it. We're very excited about it but I <u>don't think</u> there are <u>any</u> specific <u>plans</u> at this point" <u>to change</u> the <u>Pepsi cans in</u> the <u>United States and Canada</u>.

<u>Pepsi worked with</u> San Francisco-based <u>corporate image consultants</u> Landor Associates, <u>basing the new can on</u> the <u>success of Pepsi Max</u>, a popular diet <u>drink sold overseas in a blue can</u>.

<u>In British markets</u>, Swanhaus said <u>Pepsi</u> had been <u>squeezed</u> not only <u>by Coca-Cola</u>, but also <u>by supermarkets' own brands</u> of colas <u>and Richard Branson's Virgin Cola</u>.

"<u>To compete in the own-brand markets</u> you <u>have to be price-competitive, innovative and imaginative</u>. We're <u>trying to be more relevant to the teen market</u>, which is <u>not</u> an <u>easy</u> segment to get through to," he said.

As <u>part of Pepsi's</u> big <u>marketing</u> push, it <u>is</u> rolling out a <u>series of five new TV commercials in Europe</u>—TV takes the largest share of Pepsi's advertising budget—<u>and will increase its use of neon billboards in central London</u>'s Piccadilly Circus district.

Unit Four: Making the Connection

ANSWERS TO EXERCISE 4.1

1. accidently — (accidentally)
2. (acquire) — aquire
3. (accommodate) — accomodate
4. (across) — accross
5. adjurn — (adjourn)
6. alchol — (alcohol)
7. alright — (all right)
8. alot — (a lot) (the synonym *many* is the preferred word choice)
9. analysized — (analyzed)
10. apparant — (apparent)
11. (arguing) — argruing
12. asending — (ascending)
13. (association) — assosciation
14. atomsphere — (atmosphere)
15. (athletics) — atheletics
16. attitute — (attitude)
17. audiance — (audience)
18. basicly — (basically)
19. bilingal — (bilingual)
20. (boundary) — boundry
21. bussiness — (business)
22. canidate — (candidate)
23. caos — (chaos)
24. (children) — childern
25. choosen — (chosen)
26. (college) — collage (post-secondary institution)
27. (congratulations) — congradulations
28. (consensus) — concensus
29. consistant — (consistent)
30. (cruel) — crule
31. decidions — (decisions)
32. developement — (development)
33. differant — (different)
34. disasterous — (disastrous)
35. discus — (discuss)(talk)

36. drasticly   (drastically)
37. (embarrassing)   embarasing
38. (emotionally)   emotionly
39. esential   (essential)
40. (exaggerate)   exagerate
41. expecially   (especially)
42. excercise   (exercise)
43. (existence)   existance
44. (familiar)   familar
45. (February)   Febuary
46. (friends)   freinds
47. finial   (final)
48. fourty   (forty)
49. goverment   (government)
50. (gradual)   gradule
51. grammer   (grammar)
52. (grievous)   grievious
53. (guarantee)   garantee
54. heighth   (height)
55. hinderance   (hindrance)
56. hunerd   (hundred)
57. humors   (humorous) (funny)
58. ilegal   (illegal)
59. (incidentally)   incidently
60. inisiate   (initiate)
61. interduce   (introduce)
62. (interest)   intrest
63. knowlege   (knowledge)
64. liason   (liaison)
65. lisence   (licence)
66. (maintenance)   maintainance
67. (marijuana)   marjana
68. mediocer   (mediocre)
69. mischievious   (mischievous)
70. (misspell)   mispell
71. modren   (modern)
72. neccessary   (necessary)
73. (officially)   officialy
74. opinon   (opinion)

75.	pachients	(patients)
76.	payed	(paid) (received or spent money)
77.	preperation	(preparation)
78.	prespiration	(perspiration)
79.	possitive	(positive)
80.	posess	(possess)
81.	pratice	(practice)
82.	(prescribe)	perscribe
83.	priviledge	(privilege)
84.	(professional)	proffessional
85.	pernounce	(pronounce)
86.	(psychology)	phsycology
87.	(quantity)	quanity
88.	questionaire	(questionnaire)
89.	realisticly	(realistically)
90.	reconize	(recognize)
91.	refrences	(references)
92.	(registrar)	registrer (the person who admits students to a post-secondary school)
93.	(relevant)	relevent
94.	rememberance	(remembrance)
95.	sarcasticly	(sarcastically)
96.	secratery	(secretary)
97.	sence	(sense)
98.	(separate)	seperate
99.	(skiing)	sking
100.	speach	(speech)
101.	(strict)	strick (rigid or severe)
102.	submite	(submit)
103.	substancial	(substantial)
104.	sucess	(success)
105.	tangant	(tangent)
106.	(their)	thier
107.	tommorrow	(tomorrow)
108.	(tragedy)	tradgedy
109.	(until)	untill
110.	(writing)	writting

ANSWERS TO EXERCISE 4.2

1. What does it take today to be a *success?* Some people believe that if they graduate from *college* or university they will be *guaranteed* a well-paying job in the *profession* of *their choosing.* Even though a good education is *necessary,* it is not the only factor. *Possessing* a *positive attitude,* demonstrating a willingness to learn, and *especially* having *patience* to implement the *knowledge* they *sense* they have *acquired* are all *essential* elements in getting ahead. And so, if "opportunity knocks" but doesn't promise all that young people hoped it would, they should *recognize* that some of the simple tasks can be the first step in their career *development.* No one knows the meaning that today's actions will have on *tomorrow.* Being *successful* means making the best of present situations, being *interested* in the job (even if it is very boring), and being ready and watchful for new doors to open.

2. *Children* are well known for their *cruelty* to one another. Last *February,* one of the contenders in the *speech* contest continually *mispronounced* the words "relevant" and *"atmosphere." Apparently,* every time she made these *disastrous* mistakes, young schoolmates in the front row began to create a little bit of *chaos* with their whispering and giggling. Knowing their reactions must be directed at her, the poor *candidate* became *embarrassed* and forgot her lines. Even with prompting, she could not recover her composure. *Finally,* she left the stage in tears. All her *practice* and *preparation* were *ruined* because she had *paid* attention to her *mischievous friends* instead of concentrating on getting her information *across* to the *audience.* There were no *congratulations;* instead, her potential moment of glory had turned into an unforgettable *tragedy!*

ANSWERS TO EXERCISE 4.3

(Section numbers are included for those using the original version of the thesaurus.)

1. a) How much money did she plan to *put* into mutual funds?
    SECTION 787—*invest.*

    b) You cannot *make* me do anything I don't *want* to do.
    SECTION 744—*compel, force, coerce*
    SECTION 865—*desire, wish*

    c) That was a *good* meal!
    SECTION 394—*tasty, palatable, delectable, appetizing, delicious, luscious*

    d) Lisa felt that she *got* a better understanding of herself from her psychology classes.
    SECTION 775—*acquired, gained, obtained, secured, received*
    (Look up the original form of a word; for example, locate synonyms for "get" rather than "got.")

    e) The victim *told* in detail all the events that had happened the night of the crime.
    SECTION 594—*described, portrayed, narrated, related, recounted, reported*

2. a) Her reasoning is definitely *not right,* as she jumps to conclusions without having all the facts.
    SECTION 923—*wrong, bad, unjust, unfair, unreasonable, unwarrantable, objectionable, improper, unjustified*
    SECTION 495—*erroneous, untrue, false, faulty, erring, fallacious, inaccurate, incorrect*
    (Refer to a dictionary for the meaning of any listed word that you do not know; sometimes a given word will not suit the context of the sentence.)

    b) Some people are *not sensitive* to the needs of others.
    SECTION 376—*insensitive, unfeeling*
    SECTION 823—*insensitive, impassive, unfeeling, apathetic, unemotional, indifferent*
    (Choose only the words that will suit the context of the sentence.)

    c) I am *not* going to *continue* my subscription to that magazine.
    SECTION 142—*cease, discontinue*
    (Some choices given in the thesaurus are inappropriate for formal English usage; use good judgment in making your selections.)

    d) Her comments were *not related* to the topic being discussed.
    SECTION 10—*unrelated, extraneous, irrelevant*

(Do not supply another synonym that contains "not"; for example, the choice "not pertinent" contains the negative word you were asked to avoid.)

e) There was *no agreement* among the school board members on the choice of the new administrator.
SECTION 24—*disagreement, discord, dissonance, dissension*

3. a) Because the owners were renovating their business, customers were asked to *put up with* a few inconveniences.
SECTION 826—*endure, bear, tolerate*
(Some choices given in the thesaurus are inappropriate for formal English usage; use good judgment in making your selections.)

b) It was Evan's job to *weed out* the problems in the project.
SECTION 301—*eradicate, eliminate, remove*

c) Good employees *stick to* established company policies.
SECTION 143—*abide, uphold, maintain, preserve*
SECTION 604a.—*adhere to*

d) It is difficult at times to *make out* another person's handwriting.
SECTION 522—*interpret, decipher*

e) Did you *find out* how much you will have to pay for car insurance?
SECTION 480a.—*discover, determine*

SUGGESTED ANSWERS TO EXERCISE 4.4

1. I believe that high schools should place more emphasis on the fundamentals of English and mathematics.

2. Although high school students have a much better general education, presently their basic skills seem weak.

3. In the 1990s, many changes were made in the education system to improve the programs in communication and math skills.

4. Although all students cannot be at the same level in these basic skills, I believe that when these changes have been in effect for a few more years, students will demonstrate many improvements in their everyday work.

5. Then, more students may desire to remain in school and be better prepared for the work force.

6. My college English teacher has agreed to supply my prospective employer with the required report concerning my excellent written communication skills.

7. If potential college or university students can demonstrate the required job skills during their field placements, both the employers and the students will benefit from the results of an effective educational experience.

8. Today, new bank employees have many opportunities for advancement within this corporation's structure.

ANSWERS TO EXERCISE 4.5

1. Full-time jobs are becoming more and more difficult to find. C

2. Members of the ski team are planning to compete in the college races. C

3. The new residence is heated by solar energy. C

4. Take out the garbage. (You is understood) C

5. Everyone was looking forward to the holidays. C

6. That report was due last Friday. C

7. Go directly to the office after the meeting. (You is understood) C

8. A list of the prize winners was posted on the bulletin board. C

9. You should have a study plan for all courses. C

10. You need good communication skills in every kind of career today. C

ANSWERS TO EXERCISE 4.6

1. The old man walked slowly down the street. *Natural*

2. On the exam were several difficult questions. *Reversed*

3. What have you done with my report? *Mixed*

4. In the autumn all the leaves fall off the trees. *Mixed*

5. On the first page was a list of the candidates' names and addresses. *Reversed*

6. I was very tired by the end of the day. *Natural*

ANSWERS TO EXERCISE 4.7

1. Write sentence 1 in reversed order.
   Down the street slowly walked the old man.

2. Write sentence 1 in mixed order.
   Down the street the old man walked slowly.

3. Write sentence 2 in natural order.
   Several difficult questions were on the exam.

4. Write sentence 4 in natural order.
   All the leaves fall off the trees in the autumn.

5. Write sentence 6 in mixed order.
   By the end of the day I was very tired.

Your answers to the remaining exercises in Unit Four may not be identical to the ones listed here; however, they should follow the same kind of sentence pattern. Have your instructor check questionable answers.

SUGGESTED ANSWERS TO EXERCISE 4.8

1. The colour of the water. *Add a predicate or add a subject and partial predicate.*
   a) The colour of the water was sea green.
   b) Did you notice the colour of the water?

2. The workers who built the bridge. *Eliminate* who *or add a predicate.*
   a) The workers built the bridge.
   b) The workers who built the bridge won an award.

3. Plan to leave at three o'clock. *Add a subject.*
   I plan to leave at three o'clock.

4. Suyin finding an error in her work. *Change the form of the action verb or add a predicate.*
   a) Suyin found an error in her work.
   b) Suyin, finding an error in her work, rewrote her essay.

5. Was reading the sports section of the paper. *Add a subject.*
   Sam was reading the sports section of the paper.

6. Happy the storm was over. *Add a subject and a predicate or omit* happy.
   a) We were all happy the storm was over.
   b) The storm was over.

7. Sorry Fritz had to miss the party. *Add a subject and predicate.*
   They were sorry Fritz had to miss the party.

8. All cars that don't pass a safety check. *Omit* that *or add a predicate.*
   a) All cars don't pass a safety check.
   b) All cars that don't pass a safety check are towed to a garage for repair.

SUGGESTED ANSWERS TO EXERCISE 4.9

1. During the spring and summer seasons, we often go for long drives in the country.
   Attach the fragment to the sentence.

2. Because it rained. *Omit* because *or add a subject and a predicate.*
   a) It rained.
   b) Because it rained, we cancelled our plans.

3. Although I had been there before. *Omit* although *or add a subject and a predicate.*
   a) I had been there before.
   b) Although I had been there before, I still couldn't find my way.

4. If you plan to leave as soon as this class is over. *Add a subject and predicate.*
   If you plan to leave as soon as this class is over, I will go with you.

5. If you need some help, please telephone me at home or at work.
   Attach the fragment to the sentence.

6. Although I have had a driver's licence for six years and I have never had a speeding ticket. *Omit* and.
   Although I have had a driver's licence for six years, I have never had a speeding ticket.

7. I enjoy playing all sports because they are a lot of fun. *Attach the fragment to the sentence.*

8. Ali promised to meet us at the bus station, which is near the new post office building.
   Attach the fragment to the sentence.

SUGGESTED ANSWERS TO EXERCISE 4.10

1. After studying house designs and decorating techniques for two years, Sara decided to take a business management course. She felt this extra training would give her the skills she would need to open her own company. In the beginning, she had to work long hours doing the ordering, the accounts, deliveries, as well as decorating customers' homes because she couldn't afford to hire anyone to help her. Her work was excellent because she made sure that her customers were always satisfied. As more people learned about her talents, her company expanded and she had to hire some assistants. Today, Sara is one of the city's most successful businesswomen.

SUGGESTED ANSWERS TO EXERCISE 4.11

1. Will you leave the light on? I might be late.

2. Planning a trip is very easy. Paying for it is the difficult part.

3. Plastic materials cause pollution. They do not decompose as other waste products do.

4. When you answer the phone, don't use a different tone of voice. Try to speak naturally and just be yourself.

5. First you should consider all the benefits of travelling. Then you should decide if it is really worth the expense.

6. Olena was the one who did all the work. Why should others receive the credit for her efforts?

7. I have one serious fault. I am always late.

8. I have tried various solutions to solve this character defect. So far none of them have worked.

9. Psychologists say that it is not really difficult for people to overcome bad habits. All they require is the right attitude and the determination to change.

10. What have you done about your problems? If you haven't yet acknowledged their existence, how can you expect to change?

SUGGESTED ANSWERS TO EXERCISE 4.12

1. Maria had made a record number of real estate sales in the last month. *She* was given a promotion, *which* she really deserved.

2. If you finish your assignment by eleven, *you* should plan to meet me for lunch. *Perhaps* we could eat at the new restaurant downtown. I understand they have an excellent salad bar.

3. No matter what you decide to do, *you* should discuss your decision with a counsellor. *Why* don't you listen to his or her ideas *before* you actually make your plans? *Then* you can consider all the options available to you.

4. After all the work I put into writing that essay, *I received only a C grade.*

5. Shut all the windows before you leave. *It* might rain while we are away.

6. Skiing is a great way to meet people. *If* you excel at this sport, you can join a racing team, *compete* at all levels, and travel to other ski areas.

7. Hutoshi finally finished her project *which* had been very difficult and had taken up all of her free time. *She* now intended to celebrate!

8. Whenever we sit down to dinner, *the telephone rings.*

9. To begin a research paper, first jot down your purpose in one statement. *Next* write a few questions that you feel need to be asked. *Then* go to the library or other resource centres for the answers. *Finally,* sort your information to see what other data should be investigated. These are just the beginning steps of preparing a research project. *(Semicolons could also be used between the related sentences.)*

10. To my amazement, for each ticket I had purchased for the lottery, I won either a free ticket or two dollars. *I hoped* to be the big winner now that I had five free tickets and ten extra dollars in my pocket.

SUGGESTED ANSWERS TO EXERCISE 4.13

1. Be sure to take your key *and* lock the door behind you.

2. The speaker looked confident *but* he was really nervous.

3. Catrin had carefully cut all the savings coupons out of the newspaper *but* she forgot them at home.

4. Next year I may apply for the accounting program *or* the business administration course.

5. Mario is planning to leave as soon as this class is over, type up his late assignment, *and* submit it before five o'clock. *(Note the commas after each item in the series.)*

6. Dana stayed up all night studying for her midterm test, *but* the next day she was too drowsy to think clearly. (And *would also fit.*)

7. You should not dwell on your past mistakes or concentrate on problems that might occur in the future *but* only pay attention to what you can do about today.

8. We were sure the boy had committed the crime *and* was lying about his whereabouts, *but* we had no evidence to support our theory.

9. I tried to sleep *but* the thought of tomorrow's exam kept me awake.

10. Allan repaired his watchband with a paper clip *but* the clip broke *and* the watch slipped off his wrist.

If your answers differ from the ones above, have your instructor check them.

SUGGESTED ANSWERS TO EXERCISE 4.14

1. *If*
    Because   you haven't enough money for coffee, you will have to drink water.
    Since

2. *Even though*
    Although   I studied hard enough for the exam, I still didn't pass.

3. She stared at me
    even though
    as if   she didn't know me.
    although
    as though

4. We went for coffee
    after
    before   the concert was over.
    when

5. The recipe was a failure
    even though
    although   I followed the directions carefully.

6. I like to have a glass of wine
    after
    while
    when   I eat a gourmet dinner.
    as
    before

7. *Even though*
    Although   I was exhausted after a hard day at work, I could not sleep.
    Because

8. *After*
    Before   we had raced to the airport, we discovered that the plane would be late.

9. *Even though*
    Although   I had tickets for the concert, I could not go   *because*
                                                                  as   I was sick.

10. *Because*
    Since   I have known you for a while, I would like you to meet my family.
    After
    When

SUGGESTED ANSWERS TO EXERCISE 4.15

1. Although the accident victim has fully recovered, <u>his head injury had been very serious.</u>

2. Even though Syed had a speech impediment, <u>he was a popular dinner speaker.</u>

3. Even though the money was turned over to the authorities, <u>the boys had been tempted to keep it.</u>

4. <u>Chanda never missed an episode of her favourite soap opera</u> even though she had a very busy work schedule.

5. <u>I get nervous</u> whenever I drink coffee.

SUGGESTED ANSWERS TO EXERCISE 4.16

1. Al was at a party last night; *therefore (as a result, consequently),* he had difficulty concentrating on his work in the morning.

2. I really enjoy the sunny, warm, tropical weather; *however,* I don't enjoy the reptiles that also like that climate!

3. I set the clock fifteen minutes ahead of time; *therefore (as a result),* I am never late for any appointments.

4. It had been ten years since Anu had attended any school; *however (nevertheless),* her writing skills were excellent.

5. The lighting is poor in the bedroom; *consequently (therefore),* I cannot study there.

6. To me, the doctor's handwriting seemed almost illegible; *nevertheless (however),* the pharmacist had no problem deciphering the prescription.

7. Mahdi never did any homework in math; *consequently (as a result, therefore),* he failed the course.

8. Repairs were being made to the highway; *consequently (therefore, as a result),* traffic had to be rerouted.

9. The sun shone brightly; *however,* it was extremely cold. ·

10. The students encountered many problems learning the new computer program; *nevertheless (however),* after many frustrating hours, the majority finally mastered the technique.

SUGGESTED ANSWERS TO EXERCISE 4.17

1. It is good to take Vitamin C every day. It will prevent colds. Many people believe that.

    Many people believe that taking Vitamin C every day will prevent colds.

2. Today more women are participating in weight-training programs. It helps them keep their muscles toned. It helps them stay in good physical condition.

    Today more women are participating in weight-training programs to keep their muscles toned and to stay in good physical condition.

3. James Clavell is a very successful writer. He has written many interesting novels. These novels are about the history of Japan.

    James Clavell, a very successful writer, has written many interesting novels about the history of Japan.

4. Our friends have a new burglar alarm. This alarm is very sensitive. A leaf falling off a plant will set it off.

    Our friends have a new burglar alarm that is so sensitive that a leaf falling off a plant will set if off.

5. It is a good idea to preview your exams before you write them. This might help you to plan your time wisely. This might result in your achieving a better grade.

    Previewing your exams might help you to plan your time wisely and result in your achieving a better grade.

SUGGESTED ANSWERS TO EXERCISE 4.18

1. The weather at this time of year gives me a cozy feeling. On a cold winter day, I like to curl up in front of the fireplace with a good book and forget the freezing world outside.

2. Because his marks have been steadily improving since last September, I think he is going to surprise everyone and pass his year.

3. While I was biking to the park, my jeans got caught in my bicycle chain. As a result, I fell and badly scraped my arm.

4. Having a hobby teaches you to relax and gives you something to do with your leisure hours. You always get a sense of satisfaction to see a project completed.

5. Some drivers like to compete on the highway. For example, they use stoplights for racing signals, break speed limits, and swerve in front of other drivers. These public menaces, who often are the cause of many accidents, should receive stiff penalties for these kinds of infractions.

SUGGESTED ANSWERS TO EXERCISE 4.19

1. Currently, Canadians are unhappy about the high cost of living and wage restraints. According to many, the situation is grim. However, shopping plazas are crowded with people buying expensive luxury items such as microwave ovens, video games, and video players. Perhaps people should stop complaining and learn to live within their means. True happiness stems not from what you have but from who you are.

2. In my opinion, health insurance rates should be increased for people who indulge in self-destructive habits. Not only do drinkers develop many serious health problems but drinking drivers are the cause of most accidents. Smoking, another self-destructive habit, also causes serious illnesses such as lung cancer and emphysema. Because people with these habits require extra medical care, they should be the ones who pay higher insurance rates. They might even realize the dangers and quit their destructive habits. This solution might not only solve our present hospital bed shortage but also help people live longer and healthier lives.

SUGGESTED ANSWERS TO EXERCISE 4.20

Although your answers will probably not be identical to the ones suggested, the content should be approximately the same. Please note that the word count at the end of each summary is only a suggested number. Neither this number nor the wording need to be rigidly adhered to. Ask your instructor to check any answer you have doubts about.

1. A. **Use your reading skills.**

   If the family were to be swept away, the world would become a place of regimentation, chaos and desolation. Why? Because the family fulfils at least three vital functions: it provides sustenance and trains its members in the art of surviving; it provides the earliest group association, teaching the art of social living; and it is the primary place where the values and knowledge of culture are passed from generation to generation.

   (72 words)

   B. **Write your summary.**

   Without families   *harshness—austere (see thesaurus)*   *ing*   *gloomy*
   If the family disappeared, we would live in a place of inflexible rules, confusion, and gloom. The
                                      educates
   family is important for three reasons. It nurtures and trains members in survival skills, teaches
         sociability
   social skills within the family unit, and instills both traditional values and cultural knowledge.

   (46 words)

   C. **Condense your summary.** (24 to 28 words)

   Without families, our world would become austere, confusing, and gloomy. The family educates its members in survival skills, teaches sociability, and instills values and knowledge of traditions.

   (27 words)

2. A. **Use your reading skills.**

   democratic—governing by the people
   egalitarian—advocating equality for all
   In a democratic egalitarian society, dignity attaches itself not so much to social status as to conduct. Given the basic knowledge of manners taught in most homes and schools, a person may become as much of a gentleman or lady as he or she chooses to be. It is simple in theory but difficult in practice, because being a real gentleman or lady means running a continuous check on one's words and actions to ensure that they do not needlessly offend or disconcert anyone.

   (84 words)

B. Write your summary.

In society, dignity is ~~based more on conduct than~~ [*no longer determined by*] on one's social status. Because a person learns basic manners at ~~home and school,~~ [*developed*] [*educational years*] he or she can become as ~~gentlemanly~~ [*mannerly*] ~~or ladylike~~ as desired.

Although theoretically this seems easy, learning good manners is difficult. True dignity requires a continual monitoring of ~~one's behaviour~~ [*courtesy*] and ~~its effects on others.~~ [*sensitivity*]

(58 words)

C. Condense your summary. (28 to 32 words)

In society, dignity is no longer determined by social status. Mannerly behaviour can be developed during the educational years: however, it requires continual monitoring of one's courtesy and sensitivity to others.

(31 words)

3. A. Use your reading skills.

Bosses who make a serious effort to understand their subordinates become better motivated themselves, because they come closer to fulfilling their own ego and self-expression needs in the process. Motivation must, in fact, work two ways, because superiors must be open to their subordinates' influence if they expect the subordinates to be open to theirs. The cross-motivation that comes from healthy superior-subordinate relationships gives rise to an ideal working climate, not only for the people directly concerned, but for the organization as a whole.

(87 words)

B. Write your summary.

Bosses who strive to understand their employees improve their own motivation because, in the process, they satisfy their own egos and needs. However, motivation must ~~operate two~~ [*mutual*] ~~ways;~~ bosses and employees must be equal partners in interactive open communication. A healthy rela-~~tionship resulting~~ [*created by*] from cross-motivation ~~creates~~ [*generates*] an ideal working environment for ~~both parties~~ [*everyone within*] and for the organization.

(58 words)

C. Condense your summary. (30 to 35 words)

Bosses who strive to understand their employees improve their own motivation and satisfy their own egos. Mutual respect and communication created by cross-motivation generates a healthy working environment for everyone within the organization.

(34 words)

4. A. Use your reading skills.

submersion—a covering up (usually with water)
deference—respect
implicit—understood

"I don't give a damn about what other people think of me," a well-known rock star was recently quoted as saying. She might as well have said that she doesn't give a damn about other people, period; it amounts to the same thing. A certain degree of (submersion) of one's own will in (deference) to others is (implicit) in any effort to be kind and civil. If you insist on doing just what you want, you are liable to trespass on other people's sensibilities, if not their rights.

(91 words)

B. Write your summary.

>   *profess*   *immunity*   *opinions*   *unconcerned*
> Those who say that they don't care what other people think about them, often do not really care
>   *attempting*   *conceal personal viewpoints*
> about people. In any effort to be considerate of others, one must often cover up one's thoughts.
>   *feelings*   *and*
> Self-centred people tend to infringe on others' sensibilities as well as their rights.

(51 words)

C. Condense your summary. (30 to 35 words)

Those who profess immunity to others' opinions are generally unconcerned about people. In attempting to be considerate, one must often conceal personal viewpoints. Self-centred people tend to infringe on others' feelings and rights.

(34 words)

5. A. Use your reading skills.

The intellectual discipline required to make thoughts come through intelligibly on paper pays off in clarifying your thoughts in general. When you start writing about a subject, you will often find that your knowledge of it and your thinking about it leave something to be desired. The question that should be foremost in the writer's mind, "What am I really trying to say?" will raise the related questions, "What do I really know about this? What do I really think about it?" A careful writer has to be a careful thinker—and in the long run careful thinking saves time and trouble for the writer, the reader, and everybody else concerned.

(111 words)

B. Write your summary.

>   *produce*   *clearly written*
> The mental discipline needed to express you thoughts in writing helps you see all your ideas more
> *messages*
> clearly. When you begin writing on a topic, your initial information and impressions are often lacking.
>
> You should begin by considering your purpose, background information, and opinions. Good writing is
>   *results from*   *appreciated by recipients*
> the result of thorough thinking processes, a time-saver for all concerned with the information.

(62 words)

C. Condense your summary.

Mental discipline helps you produce more clearly written messages. Often your initial information and impressions about a topic are lacking. Begin by considering your purpose, background materials, and opinions. Good writing results from thorough thinking and is appreciated by the recipients.

(41 words)

SUGGESTED ANSWERS TO EXERCISE 4.21

Have your instructor check any answer that you are unsure of.

1. A. Read and underline.

In some cities the world is quite <u>literally</u> <u>represented.</u> Canadians are particularly favoured in this respect. <u>Thanks to immigration</u> and <u>the Canadian tradition</u> of <u>encouraging ethnic diversity,</u> few cities in the world are as <u>cosmopolitan</u> as our <u>three largest ones.</u> Smaller places such as Winnipeg and Hamilton are not far behind.
(51 words)

Within three blocks of a single street in Montreal, for instance, you will find <u>Russian,</u> <u>Creole, Japanese, Spanish, Italian, Chinese,</u> <u>French, Arab,</u> and <u>West Indian restaurants,</u> plus <u>American</u>-style <u>bars</u> and a <u>British</u>-style <u>pub</u> or two. <u>Nor is this street unique</u> for its variety in the cosmopolitan heart of Montreal. <u>Whole districts of our cities have</u> <u>assumed the character of the country of origin</u> of most of their <u>residents.</u> Hence there are <u>parts of Toronto</u> where you would <u>swear</u> <u>you were in Lisbon or Athens,</u> and <u>streets in</u> <u>Vancouver</u> that <u>might be in Hong Kong.</u>
(96 words)

<u>Ethnic diversity</u> is <u>only one of</u> the <u>reasons</u> <u>why Canadians should explore</u> their <u>own cities</u> <u>before looking farther afield.</u> If there is <u>variety</u> <u>within</u> Canadian cities, there is <u>also</u> great <u>variety among</u> them. A person from, say, <u>Calgary</u> will find a <u>world of difference from</u> what he or she is used to at home in the <u>salty old seaport</u> <u>and garrison atmosphere of Halifax.</u> And <u>vice</u> <u>versa:</u> for <u>someone from Halifax</u> to <u>visit Calgary</u> is to <u>sample</u> an entirely <u>unfamiliar air of cowboys and Indians, oil and cattle</u>—the air of both the <u>old and new West.</u>
(97 words)

Total—244 words

B. Write your summary.

In some Canadian cities, the world <u>is represented.</u> *[depicted]*

Immigration and the Canadian tradition of encouraging <u>ethnic diversity</u> have <u>made</u> our three largest cities very cosmopolitan. *[multicultural] [created]*
(25 words)

For example, within three blocks of one Montreal street, there are <u>Russian, Creole, Japanese, Spanish,</u> <u>Italian, French, Arab,</u> and <u>West Indian restaurants,</u> an <u>American</u> bar, and a few <u>British pubs.</u> However, this is not unusual. Whole <u>areas of our cities</u> have <u>assumed</u> the <u>character of the nations</u> of the residents. *[ten different] [nationalities] [eating and drinking establishments] [city sections] [depict] [residents'] [homelands]*
(68 words)

Areas in Toronto could be mistaken for Lisbon or Athens; streets in Vancouver could be in Hong Kong.
(68 words)

Ethnic diversity should encourage Canadians to explore <u>their own cities</u> before travelling to other countries. There is variety within and among Canadian cities. A <u>Calgarian</u> would discover a new world in a seaport and garrison city like Halifax. One from <u>Halifax</u> would enjoy the unfamiliar atmosphere of both the old and the new West in Calgary. *[Canada] [Westerners (plural form reduces number of words)] [Easterner]*
(56 words)

C. Condense your summary. (81 to 88 words)

Our Canadian tradition of encouraging multicultural immigration has created three very cosmopolitan cities. Within a three-block area of Montreal, ten different nationalities are represented in the eating and drinking establishments. In fact, whole city sections depict the residents' homeland. Areas in Toronto could be mistaken for Lisbon or Athens; some Vancouver streets could be in Hong Kong.

Diversity between cities and differences among them should encourage Canadians to explore Canada first. Both Westerners and Easterners would discover a new world in traditional features of each other's cities.
(88 words)

NOTE: Because the original first paragraph was condensed to one sentence, this statement was attached to the paragraph that followed.

2. A. Read and underline.

Since <u>most of us live in crowds,</u> we are <u>faced with</u> the <u>problem of having to establish</u> our <u>distinctive identities within an existing social framework.</u> <u>People who</u> insist on <u>doing precisely what they want</u> with <u>no self-discipline</u> and <u>no regard to</u> the impact of their actions on <u>those around them</u> are likely to <u>end up in jail,</u> where <u>individualism is not encouraged</u> at all. In his immortal work, <u>*On Liberty,*</u> John Stuart Mill struck the <u>balance between</u> the <u>individual and society</u> quite neatly. "The <u>liberty</u> of the individual <u>must be</u> thus far <u>limited; that he must not make a nuisance of himself to other people,"</u> he wrote.

(108 words)

Individualism, then, is <u>not antisocial;</u> rather the opposite. A <u>person's identity</u> is <u>not his or hers alone;</u> it is <u>only complete when</u> it is <u>rounded out by loved ones and friends.</u> <u>Individualism is strength,</u> so a true individualist is <u>strong enough to tolerate</u> the <u>habits and opinions of people</u> who <u>differ</u> from him or her. <u>A true individualist respects</u> the <u>individuality of everyone else.</u>

(65 words)

"This is my way; what is your way? The way doesn't exist," wrote the philosopher Friedrich Nietzsche. <u>In this perplexing world, finding one's own way and</u> then <u>sticking to it</u> is something that <u>comes</u> naturally only <u>to a lucky few. Most of us lose our way</u> from time to time, <u>straying</u> down the wrong streets and <u>going up blind alleys. It is all very exhausting.</u> It would be much <u>less trouble to take directions from those who assure us they know the way.</u> But wait! <u>"Most</u> of the greatest <u>evils</u> that man has inflicted upon man <u>have come through people</u> feeling <u>quite certain about something which,</u> in fact, <u>was false,"</u> Bertrand Russell <u>tells us.</u> Quite certainly, <u>what he says is true.</u>

(122 words)

Total—295 words

B. Write your summary.

Living in crowds *creates problems*
<u>Because most of us live in crowds,</u> we <u>have difficulty</u>

establishing our own identities in society. <u>People who</u>
Aggressive and *undisciplined people*
insist on doing what <u>they want with no self-discipline</u>
who ignore *consequences* *incarcerated*
and <u>no regard to the effects on others</u> can <u>end up in</u>

<u>jail</u> where there is no individualism. John Stuart Mill
limited freedom
said that balance in society means <u>one's liberty must</u>
unprovoking
<u>be limited</u> and one must <u>not be a nuisance to other</u>

<u>people.</u>

(72 words)

involves others
Individualism <u>is social</u> as a person's identity is

only complete with the help of family and friends. It

is strength, as one must be strong enough to tolerate
antagonists
<u>other people who are different.</u> A true individualist

respects individuality of everyone else.

(44 words)

In this <u>puzzling</u> world, it is exhausting and diffi-
remaining
cult to find our way and <u>stay with</u> it. It would be eas-
experienced people
ier to be guided by <u>those who say they know the way.</u>
states
However, Bertrand Russell <u>points out</u> that most evils
self-righteous people
have originated from <u>people who insist they are right,</u>

when, in fact, they are not. Certainly he is right.

(60 words)

C. **Condense your summary.** (97 to 106 words)

Living in crowds creates problems in establishing one's identity. Undisciplined, aggressive people who ignore consequences to others are incarcerated. Jail does not allow individualism. Social balance means one has limited freedom to provoke others.

(35 words)

Individualism involves others. One's identity is complete only with family's and friends' assistance. It involves strength, for one must tolerate antagonists. True individualists respect others.

(25 words)

In this puzzling world, one exhausting, difficult task is discovering and remaining on a path. It would be easier being guided by experienced people; however, Bertrand Russell states that most evils in life originate from self-righteous people who are wrong. Surely, he is right.

(45 words)

Total—105 words

SUGGESTED ANSWERS TO EXERCISE 4.22

1. Source: bankers and technology experts
   Where: in the United States
   When: ——
   Who: ——
   What: were optimistic about an electronic-cash card trial but are now questioning the use of these little cards embedded with silicon chips — known as smart cards
   Why: because they don't know why smart cards have not taken off and how they can be made more attractive

SUPPORTING DETAILS

— the trial sponsors, Citibank, Chase Manhattan Corp., Visa USA, and MasterCard USA, did not view the enterprise a failure as there was a lot of good learning in the process
— the main goal was to create a reader that could accept different types of cards that would recognize the individual technologies from the various sponsors
— but, card readers frequently broke
— merchants weren't happy about having another devise to use on their counters and many dropped out of the program
— of 600 initial trial merchants, fewer than 400 were involved a month before the end of the pilot and only about 200 were involved at the end of the trial period
— because smart cards were not popular with customers and represented only a fractional percentage of commercial sales, it was easy for merchants to decide to drop out of the project
— people already have plenty of payment choices today in the United States with a good telecommunication structure that allows for credit and debit cards to work effectively
— bankers and smart card experts say several things must fall into place before smart cards will be accepted here as they have been in Europe and parts of Asia and Latin America
— consumers need financial incentives such as loyalty or rewards programs or discounts
— cards must be more than an electronic purse
— in successful trials in controlled settings such as campuses and military bases, people have used smart cards to gain access to buildings and computer files as well as to buy food and borrow library books
— the vice president of marketing for smart cards at Schlumberger USA, a company that produced about 35 percent of the cards used in the Manhattan trial period, states that they require a critical mass of people, a well-defined set of applications, and a more controllable environment than the one used
— analysts state that the growth in electronic commerce will be a boost to smart cards, as they will be terrific enablers to secure Internet transactions

Suggested Summary:

Although U.S. bankers and technology experts were optimistic about an experimental electronic cash-card trial project, they are now questioning the reasons why these little silicon chip cards, known as smart cards, did not become popular in their trial project. They are also considering how smart cards can be made more appealing to consumers. However, in spite of the disappointing outcomes, the trial sponsors from major U.S. credit card companies and banks believe they learned a great deal in the process. The main objective had been to create a card reader that would recognize the individual technologies from the various participating sponsors.

But, there were many reasons for the failed project. Merchants weren't happy about having another device to use and the card readers frequently broke. Also, smart cards were only used for a fractional percentage of commercial sales and were not popular with their customers. As a result, many merchants dropped out of the project. Of the 600 initial participating merchants, only about 200 remained involved by the end of the experiment.

Because there are many ways for consumers to pay for goods and there is also a good telecommunication structure in place that allows them to use credit and debit cards effectively, bank and smart-card experts say that several positive changes will have to be made in order for smart cards to gain popularity as they have in Europe and in parts of Asia and Latin America. They are considering using financial incentives such as discounts or loyalty and rewards programs to encourage their popularity. Also, smart cards must have more than financial uses. In some successful trials in controlled places such as campuses and military bases, smart cards have been used to gain access to buildings and computer files, borrow library books, and purchase food in cafeterias. According to the vice president of marketing for smart cards, what is needed for the success of smart cards is well-defined applications, a more controlled environment, and a critical mass of people. But the continuing growth of electronic commerce and the ease with which users could also secure Internet transactions should help to increase the need for smart cards in the future.

Opinion paragraph should follow.

2. Source: U.N. climate summit
   Where: Buenos Aires
   When: in November 1998
   Who: developing nations led by China
   What: blocked efforts to add the discussion of voluntary quota for poorer nations to assert a bigger role in combating global warming to the conference agenda
   Why: their economies cannot afford the costs that the quotas would require; in addition, they believe the industrialized Northern nations initially filled the atmosphere with carbon dioxide gases

SUPPORTING DETAILS

— issue of poorer nations is one of the touchiest under the 1997 treaty
— U.S. negotiator Melinda Kimble is disappointed that countries will not have opportunity to explore this matter in detail but was encouraged by Argentina's act to advance the issue for discussion
— but she says the developing nations will be taking the first step towards a debate on issues
— the 163 nations are to debate several contentious issues to put the words of the treaty established at the Kyoto meeting into action
— last December, governments established 2012 as the deadline for cutting back on greenhouse gases in the U.S., Japan, the 15-nation European Union, and 15 other industrial nations
— currently, the cuts apply only to those 38 nations
— by 2015, India and China are expected to exceed the pollution levels of the present biggest polluter, the United States
— many scientists believe the Earth is gradually warming because of five gases, chiefly carbon dioxide from power plants and automobile consumption
— those opposing these beliefs say the facts about global warming are not proven and therefore don't call for the costly changes away from fossil fuels
— after the industrial nations' agreement in Kyoto to cut greenhouse gas emission, the U.S. was hopeful that this conference would encourage additional agreements on implementing the plan, thereby making the pact easier to sell to a critical U.S. Congress
— the U.S. is not one of the signing nations of the accord so far and its Republican Senate is skeptical because of the lack of greater efforts by the developing world
— many developing nations argue that their economies cannot assume costly greenhouse gas reductions that quotas would require
— they point out that the industrialized nations in the North filled the atmosphere with carbon dioxide to begin with

Suggested Summary:

At the U.N. summit meeting, held in Buenos Aires, the developing nations, led by China, blocked efforts to add the discussion of voluntary quotas for poorer nations that would require them to take a bigger role in combating greenhouse gases. Although the U.S. negotiator was encouraged by Argentina's attempt to advance this discussion, she was disappointed that the issue will not be explored at this time. However, the developing nations will be taking initial steps towards debate as the 163 nations will discuss several contentious issues in their attempts to implement the words of the treaty established at Kyoto last December into actions. Governments, at that time, set 2012 as the deadline for cutting back on greenhouse gases in the United States, Japan, the 15-nation European Union, and 15 other industrial nations. Currently, the cuts apply only to 38 nations. However, by 2015 India and China are predicted to surpass the pollution levels of the United States, which is presently the biggest polluter. Many scientists believe that the Earth is gradually warming because of five gases, mainly carbon dioxide produced by power plants and automobiles. But some oppose these beliefs, saying the causes of global warming have not been proven; therefore, they are against taking costly measures to move away from the present use of fossil fuels. After the industrial nations' agreement in Kyoto to cut greenhouse gas emissions, the U.S. had been hopeful that this conference would encourage additional agreements of cooperation for implementation and, thereby, make the pact easier to sell to a critical U.S. Congress. The U.S. is not one of the signing nations of the accord and its Republican Senate is skeptical because of the lack of greater efforts by the developing world. Many developing nations argue that their economies cannot afford the costly gas reductions that quotas would require. They further present the argument that the Northern industrialized nations were the ones who initially filled the atmosphere with carbon dioxide.

Opinion paragraph should follow.

SUGGESTED ANSWERS TO EXERCISE 4.23

1. Source: Members of the Hiroshima Peace Museum
  Where: Hiroshima
  When: recently
  Who: ———
  What: Panoramic pictures of Hiroshima after the nuclear bomb was dropped during World War II can now be viewed on the Internet
  Why: to appeal to people to realize the importance of peace

SUPPORTING DETAILS

— image created by computer-edited pictures taken about two months after the bombing
— it offers a previously unseen view of the city after the attack
— original photographs taken in October 1945 by a member who is now 80 years old.
— pictures were taken from the roof of a building that was about 320 metres north of the centre of the blast
— group hopes image would convey the full horror of the atomic bombing

Suggested Summary:

Recently, the members of the Hiroshima Peace Museum have created a Web site that includes panoramic pictures of Hiroshima after the nuclear bomb was dropped during World War II. These images, from pictures taken by an 80-year-old member of the committee, give viewers previously unseen views of the city after the attack. The pictures were taken from a roof of a building about 320 metres north of the centre of the blast about two months after the attack. The members of the civic group for establishing this Peace Museum hope that the Web site will inform people of the complete horror of atomic bombing and convince them of the importance of peace in the world.

Opinion paragraphs should follow.

SUGGESTED ANSWERS TO EXERCISE 4.24

On Reading Profitably

Abstract

A problem today is to use our accumulation of books on every topic. Because books help us evaluate, we need a system to utilize past experiences to resolve similar present issues. A book is good if it helps us discover or causes us to be inquisitive, pensive, inspired, or entertained. The classics are often topics of conversation. People must read their professional materials; however, the wise ones also read to improve their general knowledge. Reading not only builds self-confidence but also broadens our outlook. Reading materials inform about the past and often forewarn about the future. Books illustrate that history repeats itself.

Unit Five: Putting the Basics Together

ANSWERS TO EXERCISE 5.1

1. accidents
2. instruments
3. neighbours
4. residents
5. the Smiths (family)
6. mechanisms

ANSWERS TO EXERCISE 5.2

1. addresses
2. bosses
3. the Blatzes (family)
4. boxes
5. lunches
6. dishes

ANSWERS TO EXERCISE 5.3

1. attorneys
2. secretaries
3. inventories
4. Sallys
5. turkeys
6. the Murphys (family)

ANSWERS TO EXERCISE 5.4

1. heroes
2. dittos
3. banjos
4. autos
5. zeros or zeroes
6. innuendos or innuendoes

ANSWERS TO EXERCISE 5.5

1. loaves
2. wives
3. handkerchiefs
4. waifs
5. halves
6. leaves

ANSWERS TO EXERCISE 5.6

1. fathers-in-law
2. mouthfuls
3. library technicians
4. general managers
5. tablespoonfuls
6. cupfuls

ANSWERS TO EXERCISE 5.7

1. phenomena or phenomenons
2. analyses
3. alumni (masculine reference)
4. mice
5. news (no plural form)
6. criteria

ANSWERS TO EXERCISE 5.8

1. presence, attendance
2. patience
3. adolescence
4. residence
5. correspondence
6. residents
7. adolescents
8. attendants
9. patience
10. presents

ANSWERS TO EXERCISE 5.9

1.	countries	8.	women	15.	sopranos
2.	businesses	9.	handfuls	16.	athletics (no plural form)
3.	indexes or indices	10.	mumps (no plural form)	17.	residents
4.	sisters-in-law	11.	mosquitoes	18.	juries
5.	roofs	12.	secretaries	19.	the Curtises (family)
6.	the Makis (family)	13.	parentheses	20.	derbies
7.	data	14.	priorities		

ANSWERS TO EXERCISE 5.10

1. The coffee in the cafeteria/ is reasonably priced.

2. The applicants for the job/ were asked to fill out a special form.

3. Most first-year students at post-secondary institutions/ are required to take an English course.

4. Many new and exciting programs/ are being planned for the future.

5. People who live in glass houses/ shouldn't throw stones.

ANSWERS TO EXERCISE 5.11

1. Solar-heated houses, ~~which are still in the experimental stage~~,/ are ideally suited to sunny northwestern Ontario.

2. The problems ~~that she encountered~~/ were impossible to solve.

3. Mentally handicapped children ~~in our present society~~/ appear to have a better chance to live more rewarding and independent lives.

4. The person ~~responsible for that action~~/ was justifiably punished.

5. The boy ~~running up the stairs~~/ was the thief.

6. All the students ~~in the pie-eating contest~~/ were asked to wear aprons.

7. Textbooks/ are getting more and more expensive every year.

8. The water level ~~in the lake~~/ is high this year.

9. ~~Some grocery~~ stores/ stay open all night for the convenience of shift workers.

10. Sandi/ was thrilled to receive a special invitation to the gala event of the year.

ANSWERS TO EXERCISE 5.12

1. How well does he understand the French language?

2. What is Oksana planning to do after class?

3. Does Pascal or Rod know about your plans?

4. Into the room stomped the angry instructor.

5. During the night the thieves burglarized the house.

6. There could be more than one answer to that question.

7. Down the long aisle walked the bride with her father.

8. Where are you going for your vacation?
9. For some people, learning seems to be an easy task.
10. Across the lake sped the motor boat with a water-skier in tow.
11. After two days of rain usually comes a Monday.
12. Amongst the pile of debris, she found a valuable antique tray.

ANSWERS TO EXERCISE 5.13

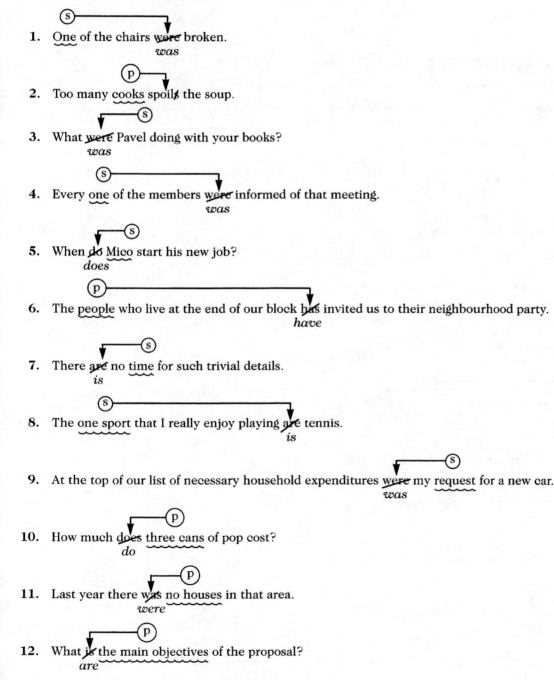

1. One of the chairs were broken.
   was

2. Too many cooks spoils the soup.

3. What were Pavel doing with your books?
   was

4. Every one of the members were informed of that meeting.
   was

5. When do Mico start his new job?
   does

6. The people who live at the end of our block has invited us to their neighbourhood party.
   have

7. There are no time for such trivial details.
   is

8. The one sport that I really enjoy playing are tennis.
   is

9. At the top of our list of necessary household expenditures were my request for a new car.
   was

10. How much does three cans of pop cost?
    do

11. Last year there was no houses in that area.
    were

12. What is the main objectives of the proposal?
    are

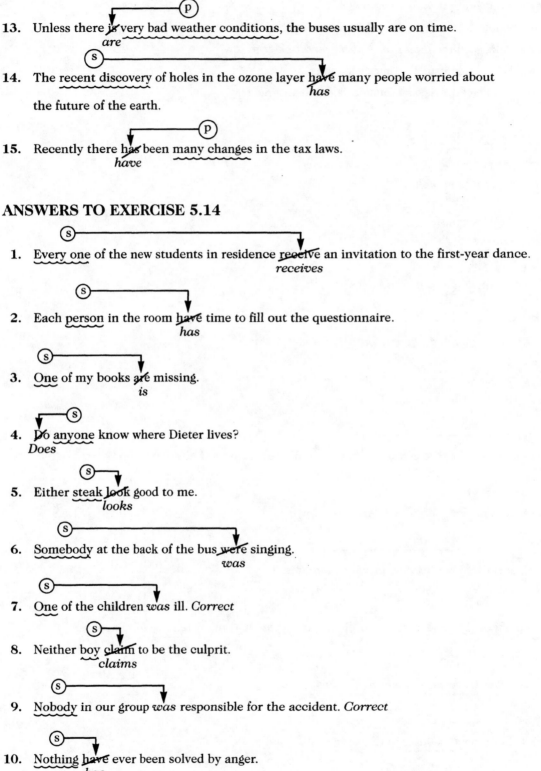

13. Unless there ~~is~~ very bad weather conditions, the buses usually are on time.
    are

14. The recent discovery of holes in the ozone layer ~~have~~ many people worried about
    has
    the future of the earth.

15. Recently there ~~has~~ been many changes in the tax laws.
    have

ANSWERS TO EXERCISE 5.14

1. Every one of the new students in residence ~~receive~~ an invitation to the first-year dance.
   receives

2. Each person in the room ~~have~~ time to fill out the questionnaire.
   has

3. One of my books ~~are~~ missing.
   is

4. ~~Do~~ anyone know where Dieter lives?
   Does

5. Either steak ~~look~~ good to me.
   looks

6. Somebody at the back of the bus ~~were~~ singing.
   was

7. One of the children *was* ill. *Correct*

8. Neither boy ~~claim~~ to be the culprit.
   claims

9. Nobody in our group *was* responsible for the accident. *Correct*

10. Nothing ~~have~~ ever been solved by anger.
    has

ANSWERS TO EXERCISE 5.15

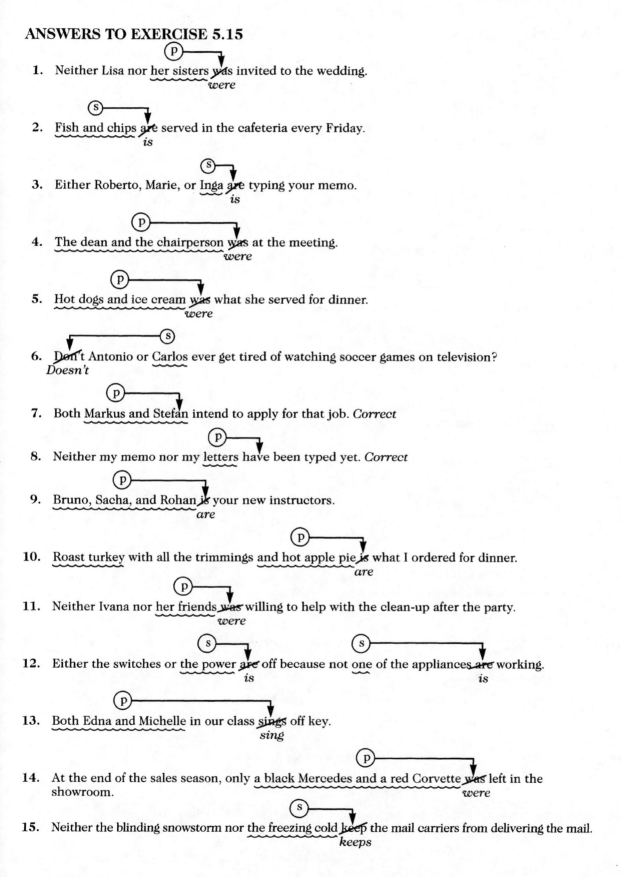

1. Neither Lisa nor her sisters ~~was~~ invited to the wedding.
    were

2. Fish and chips ~~are~~ served in the cafeteria every Friday.
    is

3. Either Roberto, Marie, or Inga ~~are~~ typing your memo.
    is

4. The dean and the chairperson ~~was~~ at the meeting.
    were

5. Hot dogs and ice cream ~~was~~ what she served for dinner.
    were

6. ~~Don't~~ Antonio or Carlos ever get tired of watching soccer games on television?
    Doesn't

7. Both Markus and Stefan intend to apply for that job. *Correct*

8. Neither my memo nor my letters have been typed yet. *Correct*

9. Bruno, Sacha, and Rohan ~~is~~ your new instructors.
    are

10. Roast turkey with all the trimmings and hot apple pie ~~is~~ what I ordered for dinner.
    are

11. Neither Ivana nor her friends ~~was~~ willing to help with the clean-up after the party.
    were

12. Either the switches or the power ~~are~~ off because not one of the appliances ~~are~~ working.
    is   *is*

13. Both Edna and Michelle in our class ~~sings~~ off key.
    sing

14. At the end of the sales season, only a black Mercedes and a red Corvette ~~was~~ left in the showroom.
    were

15. Neither the blinding snowstorm nor the freezing cold ~~keep~~ the mail carriers from delivering the mail.
    keeps

ANSWERS TO EXERCISE 5.16

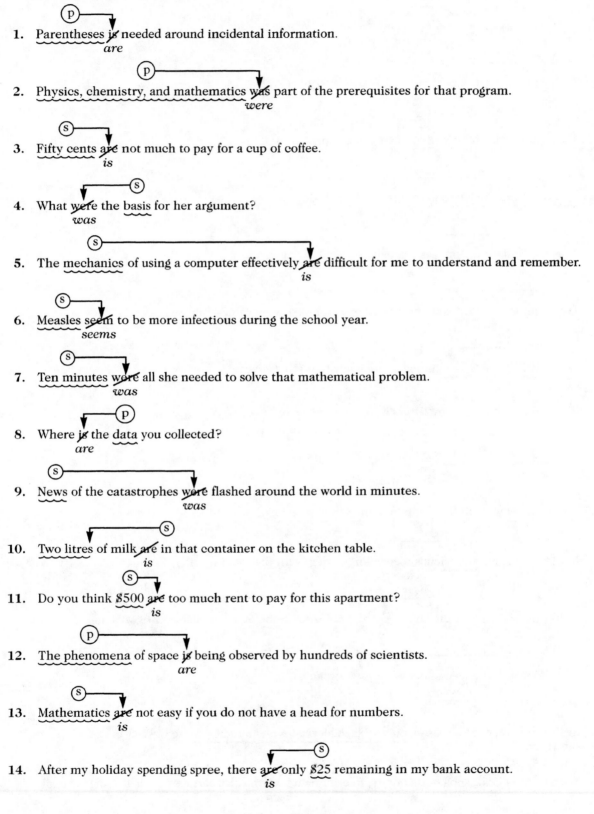

1. Parentheses is needed around incidental information.
   are

2. Physics, chemistry, and mathematics was part of the prerequisites for that program.
   were

3. Fifty cents are not much to pay for a cup of coffee.
   is

4. What were the basis for her argument?
   was

5. The mechanics of using a computer effectively are difficult for me to understand and remember.
   is

6. Measles seem to be more infectious during the school year.
   seems

7. Ten minutes were all she needed to solve that mathematical problem.
   was

8. Where is the data you collected?
   are

9. News of the catastrophes were flashed around the world in minutes.
   was

10. Two litres of milk are in that container on the kitchen table.
    is

11. Do you think $500 are too much rent to pay for this apartment?
    is

12. The phenomena of space is being observed by hundreds of scientists.
    are

13. Mathematics are not easy if you do not have a head for numbers.
    is

14. After my holiday spending spree, there are only $25 remaining in my bank account.
    is

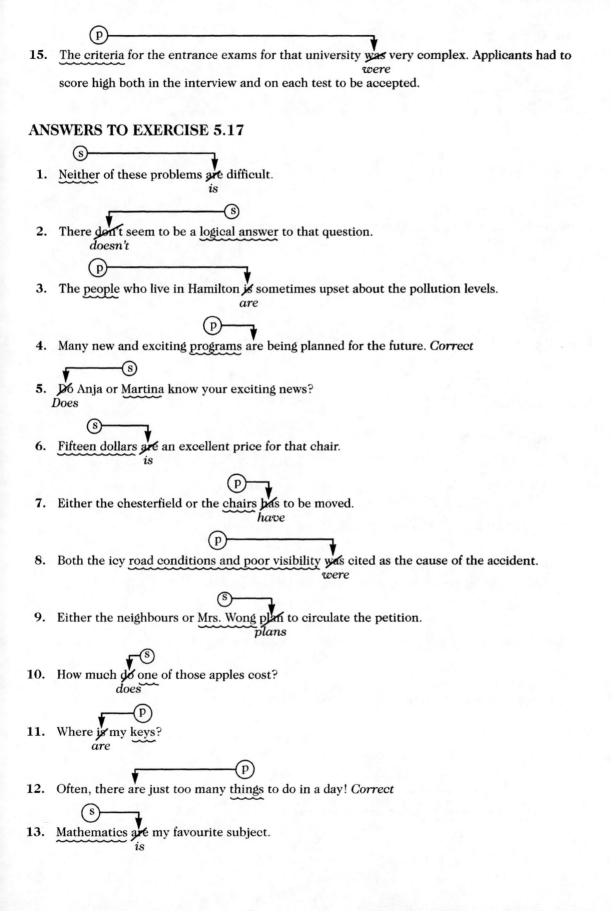

15. The criteria for the entrance exams for that university w̶a̶s̶ very complex. Applicants had to
    were

    score high both in the interview and on each test to be accepted.

ANSWERS TO EXERCISE 5.17

1. Neither of these problems a̶r̶e̶ difficult.
   is

2. There d̶o̶n̶'̶t̶ seem to be a logical answer to that question.
   doesn't

3. The people who live in Hamilton i̶s̶ sometimes upset about the pollution levels.
   are

4. Many new and exciting programs are being planned for the future. *Correct*

5. D̶o̶ Anja or Martina know your exciting news?
   Does

6. Fifteen dollars a̶r̶e̶ an excellent price for that chair.
   is

7. Either the chesterfield or the chairs h̶a̶s̶ to be moved.
   have

8. Both the icy road conditions and poor visibility w̶a̶s̶ cited as the cause of the accident.
   were

9. Either the neighbours or Mrs. Wong p̶l̶a̶n̶ to circulate the petition.
   plans

10. How much d̶o̶ one of those apples cost?
    does

11. Where i̶s̶ my keys?
    are

12. Often, there are just too many things to do in a day! *Correct*

13. Mathematics a̶r̶e̶ my favourite subject.
    is

14. Stefan and Marta was married in July of this year.
were

15. Someone at the game were blowing a bugle to encourage the home team on to victory.
was

16. Hamburgers and hot dogs is most commonly served at barbecues.
are

17. Hours flies by like minutes when I am working at the computer.
fly

18. Neither Willy nor Larry were able to be master of ceremonies at the reception.
was

19. Is the answers to these questions in the back of the book?
Are

20. Spaghetti and meatballs are one of our favourite family meals.
is

21. In essays, parentheses is needed around any added information; however, these marks
are
should be used sparingly.

22. Strawberries and cream were the only dessert choice.
was

23. Two metres of material are not enough for me to make that dress.
is

24. The doctor said that the cause of my sinus problems are dust and pollen.
is

25. Bacon and eggs are always a popular item on the breakfast menu.
is

26. For business-minded people, there is many ways to make money.
are

27. Both the conductor and his assistant was from Germany.
were

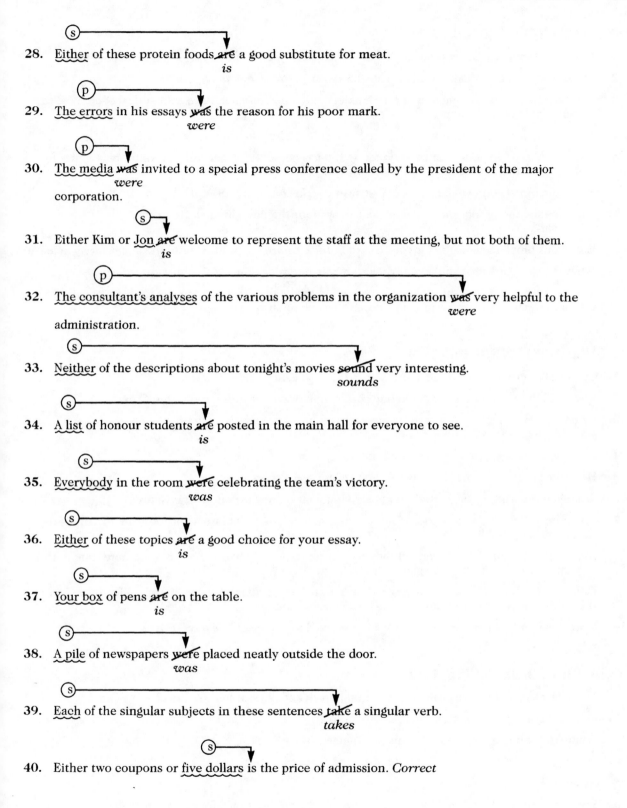

28. Ⓢ Either of these protein foods ~~are~~ a good substitute for meat.
is

29. Ⓟ The errors in his essays ~~was~~ the reason for his poor mark.
were

30. Ⓟ The media ~~was~~ invited to a special press conference called by the president of the major
were
corporation.

31. Ⓢ Either Kim or Jon ~~are~~ welcome to represent the staff at the meeting, but not both of them.
is

32. Ⓟ The consultant's analyses of the various problems in the organization ~~was~~ very helpful to the
were
administration.

33. Ⓢ Neither of the descriptions about tonight's movies ~~sound~~ very interesting.
sounds

34. Ⓢ A list of honour students ~~are~~ posted in the main hall for everyone to see.
is

35. Ⓢ Everybody in the room ~~were~~ celebrating the team's victory.
was

36. Ⓢ Either of these topics ~~are~~ a good choice for your essay.
is

37. Ⓢ Your box of pens ~~are~~ on the table.
is

38. Ⓢ A pile of newspapers ~~were~~ placed neatly outside the door.
was

39. Ⓢ Each of the singular subjects in these sentences ~~take~~ a singular verb.
takes

40. Ⓢ Either two coupons or five dollars is the price of admission. *Correct*

ANSWERS TO EXERCISE 5.18

1. I sent in my application as soon as I heard of the vacancy, but I have not yet received a reply.

2. She quickly ate her breakfast and rushed off to work. *(No commas required)*

3. "Hotdogging" is an exciting new sport for skiers, but a person must have a great deal of courage to attempt some of those stunts.

4. Today was nice but tomorrow is supposed to be nicer. *(No commas required)*

5. You should send in your confirmation fee as soon as possible, or you will lose your opportunity for admission to that program.

6. The phone rang and two of us raced to answer it. *(No commas required)*

7. You can take the supplies we have in stock or wait for the new shipment to arrive. *(No commas required)*

8. Have you completed packing for your trip to Europe, or are you waiting until the day before you leave?

9. What she says and what she actually does are two different things. *(No commas required)*

10. The heavy waves tossed the small craft around in the water like a toy, but the skilled crew finally managed to guide their boat into a protective bay along the coast.

ANSWERS TO EXERCISE 5.19

1. The little mouse ran down the stairs, around the table, and under the sofa.

2. The child didn't know if she should buy pop or gum or candy with her quarter. *Correct*

3. Tying strings around fingers, writing messages on mirrors, and leaving notes on doors are some of the ways people try to remember things.

4. Newspapers, books, toys, etc., littered the living room.

5. He rushed home, changed his clothes, and left for the airport.

6. What you do, where you go, and how you spend your money is your own business.

7. The proper placement of periods, commas, and semicolons is necessary for the reader to interpret the message correctly.

8. Students can achieve good marks if they have a consistent study program, devote more time to troublesome subjects, and develop good self-discipline.

9. Chico claimed that the alarm ringing in the morning, the clatter of dishes in the kitchen, the blare of the radio, etc., were the reasons for his cranky behaviour.

10. More wind and rain and cloud cover were predicted for the next five days. *Correct*

ANSWERS TO EXERCISE 5.20

1. In the first year of the civil engineering program, math and physics subjects are closely related.

2. One of these days, I think I'll hitchhike to Vancouver.

3. When he got home, he found that his pet Tamagochi had died.

4. Once upon a time, a princess kissed a toad and got warts.

5. Now, where shall we go next?

6. Even though they had won a large sum of money, they did not plan to change their simple lifestyle.

7. As a result of good study habits, Regine obtained 90 percent on her last test.

8. Taking a deep breath, the nervous contestant walked hesitantly up to the podium.

9. Unfortunately, the picnic was postponed because of rain.

10. After you have finished this exercise, you should recognize an introductory group of words.

ANSWERS TO EXERCISE 5.21

1. *Correct*

2. Pencils, erasers, paperclips, etc., covered his desk.

3. Jogging along the trail, she felt exhilarated.

4. After the storm passed, the forest took on a fresh appearance.

5. Fundamental accounting principles, business statistics, and microeconomics were subjects included in his first semester business course.

6. It has been proven by medical researchers that smoking is hazardous to one's health, but many people continue this habit in spite of the warnings.

7. *Correct*

8. *Correct*

9. When he finally woke the people in the house, he found he had the wrong address.

10. If you order your new barbecue before June 15, you will receive a free cookbook, shish kebab skewers, and oven mitts from the company.

11. *Correct*

12. Because of the accident on the highway, traffic had to be rerouted.

13. *Correct*

14. The park area was littered with cans, papers, plastic cups, etc., after the fireworks display.

15. After a great deal of thought, Linda decided to accept the job offer in Alaska.

16. Raising our glasses in the air, we all toasted the bride.

17. The conservation officer explained the value and procedures for spraying trees in the bug-infested area, but many campers were reluctant to agree to this very expensive method for eliminating the problem.

18. Unfortunately, we had to leave before the party was over.

19. Not satisfied with Sven's answer, the teacher asked someone else to respond to the question.

20. The bright, colourful, intricate design caught everyone's attention.

ANSWERS TO EXERCISE 5.22

Too general	1.	devices for exploring the sea
Focused	2.	how to iron a shirt properly
Focused	3.	my study routine
Too general	4.	educational systems in this country
Too general	5.	implications of censorship laws
Focused	6.	three reasons why students should stay in school
Focused	7.	differences in skiing on snow and on water

Too general	8.	history of the Olympic Games
Focused	9.	benefits of taking Vitamin C in cold seasons
Focused	10.	advantages of mandatory school uniforms for high school students
Focused	11.	tips for buying a new car
Too general	12.	the effects of the media on politics
Focused	13.	a simple plan for keeping physically fit
Focused	14.	the importance of coffee breaks for employees
Focused	15.	why everyone should have a hobby

SUGGESTED ANSWERS TO EXERCISE 5.27

Identify which of the models your outlines follow and read the others to see if you could have improved your thought processes. Each of these would require a good concluding statement to make the paragraph complete.

1. The following outlines were developed using examples of behaviours of superstitious people.

    CHOICE A—acceptable but a bit weak

    I. Belief in superstitions can cause people to react to situations in the most unusual ways.

    A. knock on wood
    B. throw salt over shoulder   } random order
    C. avoid walking under ladders
    D. walk around chair

    CHOICE B—improved flow of ideas

    I. Belief in superstitions can cause people to react to situations in the most unusual ways.

    A. knock on wood
    B. walk around chair   } These points were
    C. avoid walking under ladders   arranged in "good
    D. throw salt over shoulder   luck-bad luck" order.

    CHOICE C—to make the outline superior, add two points and change accordingly

    I. Their belief in superstitions can cause people to react to situations in the most unusual ways.

    A. **to change bad luck to good luck**
       1. knock on wood
       2. walk around chair

    B. **to ward off bad luck**
       1. avoid walking under ladders
       2. throw salt over shoulder

2. The following outline is developed by sequence. Since there is no alternative grouping, your outline should follow this pattern.

    I. For a teenager, one of the first steps into the adult world is learning how to drive.

    A. getting a beginner's licence

    B. sitting in the driver's seat

    C. being in traffic

    D. stopping at the first stoplight

    E. learning to park the car

    F. feelings of maturity when driving past friends

3. The following outlines were developed by points of contrast. The main-idea statement could be developed in either an XY XY XY pattern or an XXX YYY pattern. Which do you think is a more effective model for paragraph discussion?

CHOICE A—Note that the pattern follows the development stated in the main idea; that is, urban is mentioned first and rural is mentioned second. The points were arranged in ascending order of importance, XY XY XY.

I. In deciding where to set down roots, one needs to assess the differences between urban and rural living.

    A. close to neighbours

    B. space between neighbours

    C. likely to be "couch potatoes" once the working day is over

    D. outdoor living is the normal way of life

    E. family life is often weakened by constant activity and opportunities for individuals to act independently

    F. families tend to act as a unit that works and plays together

CHOICE B—Note that if you reserve your own personal preference for the last points of discussion, you persuade your reader to accept your beliefs as being more convincing. This outline could be improved by adding two major points for clarity, as demonstrated in Choice C.

I. In deciding where to set down roots, one needs to assess the differences between urban and rural living.

    A. close to neighbours

    B. likely to be "couch potatoes" once the working day is over

    C. family life is often weakened by constant activity and opportunities for individuals to act independently

    D. space between neighbours

    E. outdoor living is the normal way of life

    F. families tend to act as a unit that works and plays together

CHOICE C—Note that if your own preference is urban living, you would change the order in the main-idea sentence and discuss rural living first and city living second.

NOTE: Depending on the length of your written discussion, you may have to divide these differences into two separate paragraphs (see Unit Seven—Composition section)

I. In deciding where to set down roots, one needs to assess the differences between urban and rural living.

    A. **factors about city residents**
        1. close to neighbours
        2. likely to be "couch potatoes" once the working day is over
        3. family life is often weakened by constant activity and opportunities for individuals to act independently

    B. **views about country dwellers**
        1. space between neighbours
        2. outdoor living is the normal way of life
        3. families tend to act as a unit that works and plays together

4. The following outline is developed by an example procedure and suggestions for a person to quit smoking.

CHOICE A—acceptable but weak. If you followed this outline, your paragraph would tend to sound like a tedious list.

I. If you are serious about quitting smoking, you should follow what other successful people have done to rid themselves of this habit.

A. make a list of your reasons for quitting

B. tell others your intention

C. throw away your lighters and matches

D. put ashtrays away or throw them out

E. save and record your usual daily cigarette expenses

F. plan what you will do with your savings

G. replace your usual smoking times with another activity

H. exercise to relax

I. breathe deeply and relax

J. take lots of showers

K. eat carrots or celery and chew gum

CHOICE B—for a superior outline and composition, put related suggestions together under added subtopics that identify a specific procedure.

I. If you are serious about quitting smoking, you should follow what other successful people have done to rid themselves of this habit.

  A. **make a decision to quit**
    1. make a list of your reasons for quitting
    2. tell others of your intentions

  B. **eliminate any temptations to smoke**
    1. throw away your lighter and matches
    2. put ashtrays away or throw them out

  C. **replace your usual smoking times with another activity**
    1. exercise to relax
    2. breathe deeply and relax
    3. take lots of showers
    4. eat carrots or celery and chew gum

  D. **reward yourself for your efforts**
    1. save and keep track of your usual daily cigarette expenses
    2. plan what you will do with the savings

UNIT SIX: COMMUNICATING CORRECTLY

ANSWERS TO EXERCISE 6.1

1. deceive		14. pierce
2. veil		15. cashier
3. heir		16. conceited
4. receipt		17. grievous
5. grief		18. seize
6. leisure		19. counterfeit
7. sleigh		20. height

8. priest	21. What a *concieted* person she is!	conceited
9. believe	22. *Thier* receipts were not in order.	Their
10. eight	23. Our *liesure* time has greatly increased in the past eight years.	leisure
11. yield	24. My *nieghbour* came from a foreign country.	neighbour
12. neighbour	25. Looking down from such a *hieght* gave me a weird feeling.	height
13. weird		

ANSWERS TO EXERCISE 6.2

1. My high school *principal* was a person of *principles*.

2. Of *course*, I will need advice on which historic *sights* I should see on my trip to Singapore.

3. You may *proceed* to the next chapter only after you have *passed* the test for this section.

4. Officials appreciate those who demonstrate *decent* manners and follow the accepted *procedures* when they are *formally* introduced at public events.

5. The city *council* met with members of the *personnel* department and *discussed* the current staffing problems.

6. Oftentimes we can learn valuable *lessons* from examining the past.

7. Many small companies can be negatively *affected* by the bad business *practices* of one major company.

8. Climbers use a special *device* to lessen the dangers of coming down a steep descent.

9. The mayor, who was *formerly* a high school principal, was very *effective* in managing city business.

10. You must *accept* and *practise* all the company's *principles* if you hope *to* be promoted.

11. Once the rain had *lessened*, we knew that the worst part of the storm had *passed*.

12. If you have difficulties in a foreign country, the *consul* for your country will provide you with free *advice* and assistance.

13. Did you *hear* if our representative was fourth or *fifth* in the contest?

14. I am not sure *whether* this new medicine has the long-lasting *effects* I need *right* now; perhaps I should *choose* the brand that I formerly used.

15. I often end up with more *loose* change in my pocket *than* I *know* what to do with.

ANSWERS TO EXERCISE 6.3

1. She biked *(action)* to the station and then caught *(action)* the train.

2. Our team played *(action)* very well but it lost *(action)* the game.

3. Because Janice wrote *(action)* the best essay, she won *(action)* the contest.

4. Black coffee tastes *(non-action)* bitter; I put *(action)* sugar and cream in mine.

5. He became *(non-action)* the class president because most students believed *(action)* that he was *(non-action)* the best leader and they voted *(action)* for him.

ANSWERS TO EXERCISE 6.4

1. You <u>must have</u> <u>met</u> Franco before y<u>ou</u> <u>left</u> the party.

2. I <u>could have</u> <u>been</u> here earlier but I <u>woke</u> up late this morning.

3. I <u>may</u> <u>leave</u> before you <u>arrive</u> at the office because I <u>feel</u> <u>ill</u>.

4. I <u>think</u> Ann <u>might have</u> <u>gone</u> to the movies, but you <u>can</u> <u>ask</u> her best friend if she <u>knows</u> where Ann <u>has</u> <u>gone</u>.

5. If I <u>had</u> <u>known</u> you <u>were</u> <u>coming</u> here, I <u>would have</u> <u>prepared</u> something special.

ANSWERS TO EXERCISE 6.5

1. You <u>might have</u> <u>met</u> Juan before.

2. Why <u>do</u> you <u>bite</u> your nails?

3. With luck, I <u>will have</u> <u>finished</u> this project by the end of the month.

4. <u>Were</u> you <u>studying</u> in the library last night?

5. I <u>am</u> not <u>leaving</u> until four o'clock.

6. <u>May</u> I <u>go</u> home now?

7. Why <u>don't</u> you ever <u>listen</u> to instructions?

8. You <u>shouldn't</u> <u>have</u> <u>asked</u> her for money.

9. You <u>must have been</u> <u>working</u> very late last night.

10. Students <u>are</u> always <u>complaining</u> about their homework.

ANSWERS TO EXERCISE 6.6

1. bite	bit	bitten or bit	biting
2. forget	forgot	forgotten	forgetting
3. bring	brought	brought	bringing
4. drink	drank	drunk or drank	drinking
5. drown	drowned	drowned	drowning
6. sweep	swept	swept	sweeping
7. swear	swore	sworn	swearing
8. break	broke	broken	breaking
9. freeze	froze	frozen	freezing
10. choose	chose	chosen	choosing

ANSWERS TO EXERCISE 6.7

1. When I was young, I *drank* four glasses of milk a day.

2. Last week, we *made* our vacation plans, *chose* our destination, and *paid* for our airline tickets.

3. We had *begun* to worry about Rita because she was so late getting home from school.

4. It was reported in the paper that the police had *caught* the person who had *stolen* the car.

5. Last Christmas, we *bought* too many gifts and *spent* too much money.

6. What the secretary had *done* with the documents no one *knew*, but we all remembered that the manager had *brought* them to the office and had *given* them to her.

7. The student *said* that she had *forgotten* her report at home.

8. Yesterday, we *drove* to the site of the accident and *saw* where the bus had *run* off the road.

9. He *became* a teacher many years ago and has always *taught* at that school.

ANSWERS TO EXERCISE 6.8

1. Maria *had begun* to wonder if she would ever finish this course.
   began or

2. Last year Jake and Andy *had done* a lot to improve school spirit.
   did or

3. Have you ever *driven* on the super expressway?

4. *Have* you ever *eaten* in the cafeteria on the second floor?

5. I opened the door and two wasps *flew* in.

6. The train *had* just *gone* before I arrived at the station.

7. Barb *saw* that movie last Saturday.
   had seen or

8. Mr. West *has* often *spoken* to the students about their tardiness.

9. She *swore* that she wasn't guilty.

10. *Have* you *written* to your parents yet?

11. By mid-term, Sam knew he had *chosen* the wrong program.

12. I *saw* a full moon last night.

13. We *had* never *eaten* such a big meal!

14. Mika *brought* her lunch to school every day. (There is no such word as "brang"!)

15. Unfortunately, their mother *had forgotten* her cheque book at home.
    forgot or

SUGGESTED ANSWERS TO EXERCISE 6.9

1. The dog chased the red fox across the field.

2. *The city planning council* gave us approval to add an attached apartment to our suburban home. (Since this is a legal matter, "who" gave the approval is very important.)

3. After examining the tiny holes in the ceiling of our cottage, *we* discovered that a squirrel was the culprit who had resided in our summer home during the winter.

4. By placing butterfly appliqués over the holes, *I* cleverly and inexpensively repaired the ceiling. (The name of a person or a pronoun reference is necessary to identify the "doer" of the action.)

5. The students completed the assignments.

6. *The registrar* gave the student permission to delay payment of his tuition fees. (Because of the irregularity of this kind of action, someone must be accountable for the decision.)

7. *The teacher* has obviously made an error in calculating your grade for the mid-term test. (The "doer" of the action must be identified.)

8. In readiness for the tournament, the maintenance crew repaired the broken benches.

9. *The Federal Justice Department* will circulate information about the new divorce laws to all lawyers in the near future. (Someone must be clearly accountable for the proposed action.)

10. After a harried day of housework, shopping, and cranky kids, the *parents* put the children to bed early. (In the original version, it is not clear who had the "harried day"; therefore, the identity of the subject must be added.)

SUGGESTED ANSWERS TO EXERCISE 6.10

1. The chairperson informed us that the meeting would be postponed to next Monday.

2. *Correct*

3. The police suspect that the same group of thieves broke into several homes during the summer and took many valuable articles and pieces of jewellery. (Note how the active voice makes this information clearer and less wordy.)

4. *Correct*

5. By recognizing your most common errors and correcting them, you can improve your written work. (The introductory group of words describes the subject; therefore, "you" must be clearly placed at the beginning of the main sentence.)

6. *Correct* (It is not necessary to identify who erected the buildings.)

7. In the fall, students will submit recommendations to the student council for new and exciting activities for the upcoming school year. (For the students' sake, it must be very clear who will be making the recommendations!)

8. The professor gave the test answers to the students.

9. Tired and frustrated, the student finally completed her project at four o'clock in the morning. (The introductory group of words does not describe "the project"; it describes the student; therefore, that subject must be clearly placed at the beginning of the main part of the sentence.)

10. Unfortunately, our computer has made an error in your bank statement; we are investigating the matter and will correct your account as soon as possible. (Someone must be accountable for the error; computers are good scapegoats!)

ANSWERS TO EXERCISE 6.11

1. a) He *smokes* cigarettes even though he *knows* they *aren't* healthy for him.
    b) He *smoked* cigarettes even though he *knew* they *weren't* healthy for him.

2. a) Terry *says* that he *needs* more time to think about his answer.
    b) Terry *said* that he *needed* more time to think about his answer.

3. When I *stepped* off the curb yesterday, I *twisted* my ankle and *fell* on the pavement.

4. Mr. Marco *glared* at me for a while before he *reprimanded* me.

5. a) Marina always *consults* a dictionary when she *doesn't* know how to spell a word.
    b) Marina always *consulted* a dictionary when she *didn't* know how to spell a word.

6. a) Occasionally our family *prefers* to go out for Sunday brunch at a nice restaurant because the prices *are* usually reasonable and the food selection *is* excellent.
    b) Occasionally our family *preferred* to go out for Sunday brunch at a nice restaurant because the prices *were* usually reasonable and the food selection *was* excellent.

7. a) After the holiday weekend, traffic usually *is* very heavy; as a result, there are several accidents.
    b) After the holiday weekend, traffic usually *was* very heavy; as a result, there *were* several accidents.

8. Yesterday Joe *left* quickly and *drove* home.

9. After the teacher *had scolded* little Johnny, he *ran* home.

10. The roof *leaked* so he *repaired* it.

11. Last summer, we often *sat* around our camp fires and *sang* songs.

12. a) I *planned* to leave as soon as I *was* ready.
    b) I *plan* to leave as soon as I *am* ready.

13. a) As soon as the sun *shines,* the children *run* outside to play.
    b) As soon as the sun *shone,* the children *ran* outside to play.

14. a) Amina *found* that working after school *was* difficult, but she *made* the extra money because she *needed* it to continue her studies.
    b) Amina *finds* that working after school *is* difficult, but she *makes* the extra money because she *needs* it to continue her studies.

15. a) Rosa *was* nervous every time she *wrote* an exam; but as soon as she *read* the paper over and *jotted* down a few notes, she usually *gained* her confidence and *lost* her jitters.
    b) Rosa *is* nervous every time she *writes* an exam; but as soon as she *reads* the paper over and *jots* down a few notes, she usually *gains* her confidence and *loses* her jitters.

ANSWERS TO EXERCISE 6.12

1. I realized I *had been* wrong.

2. Miguel knew he *had met* Catrin somewhere before.

3. By the time the police arrived, the vandals *had disappeared.*

4. Johanna phoned home to find out if her parcel *had arrived.*

5. I answered the phone but the caller *had hung* up.

6. They drove past the place where the accident *had happened.*

7. When all the lights went out, we thought we *had blown* a fuse.

8. We heard on the radio that the rock concert *had been cancelled.*

9. Because Ricardo *had drunk* too much, his friend drove him home.

10. I was sure that he *had heard* that story before.

11. They *had driven* for miles before they finally found a gas station.

12. What she *had done* in the past was soon forgotten.

13. After Mike *had* carefully *considered* his answer, he wrote down his response to the question.

14. Robin left as soon as she *had completed* her work.

15. We *had* just *finished* dinner when we received the news.

ANSWERS TO EXERCISE 6.13

1. laid
2. lies
3. laid
4. lay or lies
5. lying
6. laid
7. laid
8. lain
9. laid
10. lying

ANSWERS TO EXERCISE 6.14

1. Our manager, who has just returned from a month-long vacation, plans to hire two new sales representatives.

2. Niagara Falls, a famous tourist attraction, was one of the places we planned to visit.

3. Sylvie would be surprised, as a matter of fact, to learn that her birthday present has been in her closet for a month.

4. For dinner we are having cheesecake, my favourite dessert.

5. Anyone who doesn't follow these instructions will probably make a mistake. (No commas, as this information is relevant to the meaning of the sentence.)

6. Shanthi's office, the one at the end of the hall, contains most of the books you are looking for.

7. Most students who plan their work carefully have no problems completing assignments on schedule. (No commas, as this information is relevant to the meaning of the sentence.)

8. Maggie and Kirise, who are bridge fanatics, will compete in the International Bridge Tournament.

9. We must, on the other hand, consider an alternative solution to that problem.

10. Carlo, who used to work in this department, is now a pilot for a wealthy business owner.

11. The old bank building, which had been built in 1910, was demolished this year as part of the city's renovation program.

12. This new plan, however, will not be implemented until the new year.

13. Police have the right to remove the licence plates from all vehicles that do not pass the safety check. (No commas, as the information is relevant to the meaning of the sentence.)

14. The winner of the lottery, we were surprised to learn, had also won a sizable amount of money just three months ago!

15. Students who concentrate on their studies usually get excellent grades. (No commas, as this information is relevant to the meaning of the sentence.)

ANSWERS TO EXERCISE 6.15

1. I was really impressed by that production of *Carmen*; however, I thought that some of the sets could have been improved.

2. Skiing can be a very dangerous sport; during our winter season, the hospitals report more incidents of broken bones and torn ligaments than at any other time of year.

3. Honestly, I just don't know how I am going to cope with this problem; I hope you can give me some advice.

4. In Canada, we travelled to Vancouver by train; travelling through the Prairie provinces and the Rocky Mountains was an unforgettable experience.

5. When you finish your assignment, you may leave; however, don't forget to proofread your work before submitting it to me for marking.

ANSWERS TO EXERCISE 6.16

1. When he was younger, he always made excuses for being late; but those excuses are just not acceptable today.

2. They had no immediate plans to sell their home; but if someone offered them a good price, I am sure they would not hesitate to move.

3. What you do with your time is your own business; but if your plans interfere with mine, then I will complain.

4. Her new job as marketing representative for the company involved her travelling twice a year to Tokyo, Japan; Seoul, Korea; Brisbane, Australia; and Hong Kong.

5. When financial cutbacks were announced, the manager quickly called a meeting of all the department heads; and together they explored various ways to readjust the budget for the coming year.

ANSWERS TO EXERCISE 6.17

1. She finished her dinner quickly; then she left the room without saying a word to anyone.

2. Many novels today, unfortunately, have boring story lines; after reading a few chapters, the average reader can recognize the same old plot because just the characters and the location have been changed.

3. When the rains came, the planned events for the day had to be cancelled; however, the committee rescheduled them for the following Sunday.

4. In my spare time, I like watching movies, especially the classics; listening to music; in the winter, skiing; and in the summer, playing tennis.

5. Some people welcome opportunities; others are afraid to risk the chance of change.

SUGGESTED ANSWERS TO EXERCISE 6.18

1. These two unrelated facts would destroy the unity of the paragraph. Therefore, do not include

—requires too much study time
—additional frustrations of learning math

Outline for a unified paragraph

I. If you want to have an enriching educational experience, study a foreign language.

    A. learn about another country
        1. history and geography
        2. culture and values
        3. people and traditions

    B. communicate with others of a different culture

    C. better understand your own language
        1. foreign words often basis for native language
        2. learn more about grammar and sentence structure

    D. expand your mental capacity

Therefore, learning another language has more educational value than just acquiring foreign language skills.

2. These two unrelated facts would destroy the unity of the paragraph. Therefore, do not include

—be humble
—wear conservative suits

Outline for a unified paragraph

I. One way to learn about being a famous sports announcer is to study and imitate the winning characteristics of popular ones.

    A. wear eye-catching clothes
        1. loud sports jackets
        2. unusual ties
        3. odd colour combinations

    B. cultivate a distinctive style of speaking
        1. monotone
        2. nasal whine

3. sports "lingo"
4. aggressive voice
C. have strong opinions
1. show favouritism
2. be argumentative

Therefore, if you break all the traditional rules of broadcasting, you may have just the right formula to become a well-known sportscaster.

SUGGESTED ANSWER TO EXERCISE 6.19

The following paragraph is now more coherent. By using the most appropriate transitional phrases and the sentence-refining techniques discussed in Unit Four, you can change the tone, style, and level of your writing. Also, with your thesaurus you can easily replace wordy expressions or simplistic language with more descriptive word choices.

When jobs are <u>scarce,</u> there is limited room for people to drift from one employer to another until they land in a position they like. Except in the case of <u>apprenticeship</u>—which is essentially a form of education in a working environment—on-the-job training alone is rarely <u>sufficient</u> for one to <u>secure</u> a well-paying job offering scope for personal growth. Employers are now demanding prior schooling. For example, child care workers, ambulance attendants, and retail clerks are all expected to have completed a course in a community college before they start work. In addition, even where on-the-job training is <u>acceptable,</u> employers tend to prefer the <u>applicant</u> with the better general education. For instance, recruits for most Canadian police forces and fire departments are required to have completed Grade Twelve. And so, employers quite logically assume that a person who has 12 years or more of schooling is a harder and more intelligent worker than one who has only 10 years or fewer.

SUGGESTED ANSWER TO EXERCISE 6.20

Many people who believe that dreams have hidden meanings consult dream books for interpretations. These books help them decode their night visions by attaching meanings to their nocturnal dramas and to the symbols involved in dreams. For example, a trip on a bus may mean that the dreamer is trying to fit in with a group or secretly wants to be accepted. A mountain may mean that the dreamer is exaggerating problems. However, because different books may provide different answers, there is no guarantee that these suggestions are trustworthy. Perhaps, then, dream interpretation is purely wishful thinking or a justification for an action that the dreamer wants to take.

If you had difficulty with this exercise, refer to the section on sentence refining in Unit Four.

UNIT SEVEN: WRITING MORE SKILLFULLY

ANSWERS TO EXERCISE 7.1

#						
1.	accept	accepted	accepting	acceptance	—	acceptation
2.	acquit	acquitted	acquitting	acquittance	—	—
3.	admit	admitted	admitting	admittance	—	admission
4.	allot	allotted	allotting	—	allotment	—
5.	audit	audited	auditing	—	—	audition
6.	benefit	benefited	benefiting	—	—	—
7.	begin	—	beginning	—	—	—
8.	budget	budgeted	budgeting	—	—	—
9.	cancel	cancelled	cancelling	—	—	cancellation
10.	canvass	canvassed	canvassing	(Note that *canvass*, meaning "go about asking for votes or orders," ends with two s's.)		
11.	commit	committed	committing	—	commitment	commission
12.	compel	compelled	compelling	—	—	compulsion

(Note the irregular *ion* form of *compel*.)

#						
13.	concur	concurred	concurring	concurrence	—	—
14.	control	controlled	controlling	—	—	—
15.	equip	equipped	equipping	—	equipment	—
16.	occur	occurred	occurring	occurrence	—	—
17.	omit	omitted	omitting	omittance	—	omission
18.	plan	planned	planning	—	—	—
19.	remit	remitted	remitting	remittance	—	remission
20.	run	—	running	—	—	—

ANSWERS TO EXERCISE 7.2

#						
1.	adjourn	adjourned	adjourning	—	adjournment	—
2.	confer	conferred	conferring	conference	conferment	conferable
3.	comfort	comforted	comforting	—	—	comfortable
4.	credit	credited	crediting	—	—	creditable
5.	debit	debited	debiting	—	—	—
6.	defer	deferred	deferring	deference	deferment	deferable
7.	develop	developed	developing	—	development	—
8.	deter	deterred	deterring	deterence	determent	deterable
9.	differ	differed	differing	difference	—	—
10.	govern	governed	governing	—	government	governable

11.	infer	inferred	inferring	inference	—	—
12.	offer	offered	offering	—	—	—
13.	prefer	preferred	preferring	preference	preferment	preferable
14.	refer	referred	referring	reference	—	referable
15.	transfer	transferred	transferring	transference	—	transferable

ANSWERS TO EXERCISE 7.3

(These answers are all in the subjective case, as they are the subjects in the sentences.)

1. My parents and *they* are friends.

2. The principal and *he* disagreed.

3. Jean, Monica, and *I* left early.

4. The school administrators and *we* are often frustrated by some students' lack of responsibility.

5. You and *I* should work well together.

6. My partner and *I* have both improved our tennis techniques over the summer.

7. Luis and *he* were leading in points.

8. Where Chandra and *he* went is not known.

9. Because *he* and Sam were late, they lost the game by default.

10. Victor, Laurie, Harry, and *we* all left the party at the same time.

ANSWERS TO EXERCISE 7.4

(These answers are all in the subjective case, as they all directly follow a form of the verb *to be*.)

1. It couldn't have been *we* who were wrong.

2. What would you have done if you had been *they?*

3. It must have been Rico and *he* who created this problem.

4. My best friends are Martti, Steve, and *he.*

5. That must be *they* now.

6. This year's recipients of the award were Bert and *I.*

7. I was surprised to learn that the culprits had been Dana and *she.*

8. How did you know it was *he* who called?

9. When I heard the conversation, I knew it must be *they* at the door.

10. If it had been *I* who had asked the professor for help, we would have solved this problem faster.

ANSWERS TO EXERCISE 7.5

1. The Bakers or *they* will drive to the meeting.
   (The subject is Bakers or they; *therefore, use the subjective pronoun.)*

2. The reporter snapped a picture of *her.*
   (The necessary pronoun is not the subject and does not directly follow a form of to be; *therefore, use the objective form—her.)*

3. Mrs. Maki said that you and *I* were not paying attention.
   (The subject is you and I; *therefore, use the subjective pronoun.)*

4. Among those at the party were Arjun and *she.*
(Arjun and she *directly follows a form of* to be; *therefore, use the subjective pronoun.*)

5. The college presented *him* with the award.
(*The necessary pronoun is not the subject and does not directly follow a form of* to be; *therefore, use the objective form*—him.)

6. I was suspicious of the man who sat beside Cathy and *me.*
(*The necessary pronoun is not the subject and does not directly follow a form of* to be; *therefore , use the objective form*—me.)

7. I sent *him* and *her* cards at Christmas time.
(*The necessary pronouns are not the subject and do not directly follow a form of* to be; *therefore, use the objective form*—him *and* her.)

8. They wrote *me* a letter.
(*The necessary pronoun is not the subject and does not directly follow a form of* to be; *therefore, use the objective form*—me.)

9. Neither *she* nor *I* like to walk home late at night.
(*The subject is* she nor I; *therefore, use the subjective pronoun.*)

10. Rod, Ira, and *I* waited for *them* after the meeting.
(*The subject is* I; *the other necessary pronoun is not the subject and does not directly follow a form of* to be; *therefore, use the objective form*—them.)

11. No one had the solution to the problem except André and *me.*
(*The pronoun is not the subject and does not follow a form of* to be; *therefore, use the objective form*—me.)

12. This agreement is just between you and *me.*
(*The pronoun is not the subject and does not follow a form of* to be; *therefore, use the objective form*—me.)

13. In a local contest, the Smiths and *they* both won trips to the Bahamas.
(*The subject is* the Smiths and they; *therefore, use the subjective pronoun.*)

14. Celine and *she* invested their money in a furniture store.
(*The subject is* Celine and she; *therefore, use the subjective pronoun.*)

15. The announced winners of this year's trophies were Sophia, Moira, Helen, and *I.*
(Sophia, Moira, Helen, and I *directly follows a form of* to be; *therefore, use the subjective pronoun.*)

ANSWERS TO EXERCISE 7.6

1. André plays tennis better than *I.* (… better than I can)
2. This outfit fits Maya better than *me.* (… better than it fits me)
3. Christine can decorate a cake better than *she.* (… better than she can)
4. His brother is more athletic than *he.* (… more athletic than he is.)
5. Is he as popular as *she?* (… as popular as she is)
6. No matter where you go, you will not meet a person as generous as *he.* (… as generous as he is)
7. No one was more surprised at the results than *she.* (… than she was)
8. The teacher gave Joan more marks than *me* for the very same question! (… more marks than the teacher gave me)
9. Because we ordered our tickets early in the season, we got better seats for the concert than *they.* (… than they did)
10. That company did not have a fair salary plan. They paid any relatives of management more per hour than *us.* (… than they paid us)

ANSWERS TO EXERCISE 7.7

1. Sven, Fritz, and *I* would represent our group at the meeting.

2. Choi and *I* went to the movies last night to see *The Titanic* with Leonardo DiCaprio.

3. *Correct*

4. Benazir arrived at the meeting earlier than *we*. (... earlier than we did)

5. The fastest runners in the race were *he* and Matthew.

6. *Correct*

7. He makes lasagna better than *I*. (... better than I do)

8. Paul and *he* met *us* associates in the bar.

9. They could probably do that job by *themselves*.

10. He'd probably rather go with you than *me*. (... than with me)

11. How did you know it was *I*?

12. She has more experience at typing than *I*. (... than I have)

13. You should return the key to Lee or *me*.

14. It might have been *she* who made the long distance phone call.

15. If it were *he*, why didn't you say so?

ANSWERS TO EXERCISE 7.8

1. *Who* do you think will answer the door?
   (*Do you think* he *will answer the door*)

2. *Whom* were you waving at?
   (*Were you waving at* him)

3. *Who* do you think will apply for that position?
   (*Do you think* he *will apply for that position*)

4. *Whom* is the parcel for?
   (*Is the parcel for* him)

5. *Whom* do you expect to do the dishes?
   (*Do you expect* him *to do the dishes*)

6. *Who* was there when you called?
   (He *was there when you called*)

7. *Who* do the police suspect broke into your house?
   (*Do the police suspect* he *broke into your house*)

8. *Who* is responsible for this mess?
   (He *is responsible for this mess*)

9. *Whom* would you consider a worthy candidate for the position?
   (*Would you consider* him *a worthy candidate for the position*)

10. *Who* could be phoning us at this time of night?
    (He *could be phoning us at this time of night*)

ANSWERS TO EXERCISE 7.9

1. The men *who* had been building the house went on strike.
   (... they *had been building the house*)

2. Do you know *who* she is?
   (... *she is* she — follows a form of *to be*)

3. This is the man *who* will be our new premier.
    (… he *will be our new premier*)

4. Guess *whom* I met today?
    (… *I met* him *today*)

5. *Whom* did she mention in her talk?
    (…*did she mention* him *in her talk*)

6. They asked me *whom* I had invited to the party.
    (… *I had invited* him *to the party.*)

7. The elderly woman *whom* they helped cross the street was very grateful.
    (… *they helped* her *cross the street*—to select the correct pronoun don't pay attention to number or gender.)

8. We will cooperate with the person *who* is in charge of the project.
    (… he *is in charge of the project*)

9. Mr. Rivera is a teacher *who* I know would be glad to help you with your assignment.
    (… *I know* he *would be glad to help you* …)

10. *Whom* did they choose to represent us on the negotiating committee?
    (… *did they choose* him *to represent us* …)

ANSWERS TO EXERCISE 7.10

1. Each student reviewed *his* own timetable.
                        or
    Each student reviewed *her* own timetable.

2. One of the robins built *its* nest in the eave of our porch.

3. Both Julie and Frieda added *their* contributions to the fund.

4. If anyone else wishes to go, tell *him* to notify the office.
                        or
    If anyone else wishes to go, tell *her* to notify the office.

5. Several of the boys have curled *their* hair.

6. Not one of the students turned in *his* paper late.
                        or
    Not one of the students turned in *her* paper late.

7. Neither Tom nor Dick has submitted *his* expense account on time.

8. Either the dean or the chairperson must give *his* permission.
                        or
    Either the dean or the chairperson must give *her* permission.

9. Each of the members must pay *his* dues by the end of September.
                        or
    Each of the members must pay *her* dues by the end of September.

10. Neither Betty nor Susan would tell what *she* had bought at the sale.

ANSWERS TO EXERCISE 7.11

1. *Besides* Barbara, who else is absent?

2. We had ten dollars *among* the five of us.

3. It seems *as if* I always have to cook dinner.

4. Did you buy the tickets *from* Cathy?

5. She reached *into* her purse for her wallet.

6. I got that idea *from* Emma!

7. It seems *as if* winter is never going to end.

8. The car crashed through the barrier and went *into* the ditch.

9. The book fell *off* the desk.

10. *Between* the two of us, we are sure to come up with the right answer.

ANSWERS TO EXERCISE 7.12

1. Why isn't our salary increase *retroactive to* last June?

2. Some types of jobs are often considered *inferior to* others.

3. Cooking in a microwave oven is certainly *different from* cooking in a conventional one.

4. I would like to see you *in regard to* the proposal you submitted.

5. I received that information *from* a very reliable source.

6. It seems *as if* I am never right!

7. After many years, I had the opportunity to tour my old high school again, but all the familiar rooms and places seemed *different from* the way I had remembered them to be.

8. Everyone became quiet when the tall, impressive-looking man stepped *into* the room.

9. *Correct*

10. Some people feel that being ignored is *preferable to* being seen as *different from* others.

ANSWERS TO EXERCISE 7.13

1. We had to listen to several customers' complaints.

2. My two brothers-in-law's boats were tied up at our dock.

3. The manager's decision was final.

4. Mrs. Davies' bookstore is closed on Saturday. (The extra s sound would be awkward; just add the apostrophe.)

5. The Curtises' home is in Academy Heights. (The home belonging to the Curtises—plural form of the family name.)

6. In the court case, many witnesses' testimonies supported Mr. Jones's alibi.

7. You will find both the women's and girls' fashions on the fifth floor of the department store.

8. Charles' European trip included visits to London, Paris, and Rome.

9. The company's new policies had been established by past practices, employees' recommend-

ations, and customers' suggestions.

10. Our country's economy is steadily improving in spite of the government's decline in popularity.

ANSWERS TO EXERCISE 7.14

1. Tuesday's meeting has been cancelled.

2. The capital city is just a day's journey from here.

3. There was two hours' delay in air traffic.

4. She took three weeks' vacation in Spain.

5. Where did you put last night's paper?

6. You should proceed without a moment's delay.

7. Yesterday's news is history.

8. A month's vacation sounds sufficient; and it usually is, until the last two days of your holidays.

9. The shiftless son inherited thousands of dollars' worth of stocks and bonds in his father's will.

10. Because of last night's snow storm, roads were closed and many residents' homes were with-

out electrical services.

ANSWERS TO EXERCISE 7.15

1. Anita and June's office is on the second floor. (one shared office)
2. Both Eaton's and Sears' department stores are having sales next week.
3. Kareem and Ahmed's problem would not be easy to resolve. (one common problem)
4. Did you see Sue's and Andrea's notebooks in this room?
5. Marilyn and Jason's home is on Mary Street. (one shared home)
6. The date of the spring break was determined on the basis of students' and teachers' opinion polls.
7. Both local residents' and campers' assistance was requested in the search for the missing child.

8. The bride and groom's honeymoon destination was Hawaii. (one honeymoon)

9. The ladies' and gentlemen's restrooms are on opposite sides of the mezzanine in the concert hall.

10. Todd and Dale's collie won a blue ribbon in the dog show. (one collie dog)

ANSWERS TO EXERCISE 7.16

1. *It's* said that the abacus, which has been used by the Chinese for hundreds of years, is the basis of all present-day computers; however, despite *its* effectiveness, it was not widely adopted in any country outside the Orient.

2. While *it's* recognized that the problem is in the abuse of alcohol and not in *its* use, alcoholism is one of the most subtle diseases that has ever confronted humankind.

3. *It's* now mandatory for everyone suspected of driving while under the influence of liquor to have a breathalizer test; and *it's* now possible to convict a person on the basis of the results.

4. *It's* the committee's responsibility to submit *its* report on time.

5. *It's* a long way to drive to the next town; therefore, have your car checked to ensure that *it's* in good repair.

ANSWERS TO EXERCISE 7.17

1. *I'm* bored because *there's* nothing to do.

2. *We're* not very well prepared for *our* test.

3. *Who's* responsible for that dent in the fender of our car?

4. *It's* a shame that *you're* leaving so soon.

5. *Don't their* parents know *they're there?*

6. Jon *doesn't* know *whose* books were left in our classroom.

7. As the saying goes, "Where *there's* smoke, *there's* usually fire!"

8. I *don't* know why *I'm* so tired; *I've* been sleeping all afternoon.

9. That company also submitted its proposal for the renovations, but *we've* not made a decision about whose offer *we'll* accept.

10. Is that Corvette parked in the driveway *hers* or *theirs?*

ANSWERS TO EXERCISE 7.18

1. The *Joneses'* car was stalled in *their* driveway.

2. *We're* planning to visit *Nancy's* and *Marilyn's* families in Toronto and Ottawa on *our* trip east this summer.

3. Whose sweater is this in *Cameron's* closet?

4. *There's* only one week left until Christmas and *we've* still not purchased *Tom's* and *Harry's* presents.

5. *We're* having *our* meeting in Mr. *Curtis's* office. (Add 's to Curtis as there is an extra s sound.)

SUGGESTED ANSWERS TO EXERCISE 7.19

1. Even in the case of what seems to be an emergency, *we* should be cautious about allowing *a stranger* to enter *our* homes. Because of the increase in crime rates, unfortunately, *we* cannot assume that *a person* making a simple request to use the telephone is *someone we* can trust!

In this selection, the writer corrected the errors by establishing that the pronoun focus would be first person plural; therefore, the references (*we, our*) had to be consistent throughout the paragraph. Also, the other reference words had to be consistent as well (*a stranger, a person, someone* ... all these must be similar in number).

Another acceptable reference would be second person (*you, your*); however, if any of the other pronoun cases had been used in this selection, the resulting message would lack clarity because of word repetition or confusing references:

Even in the case of what seems to be an emergency, *you* should be cautious about allowing *a stranger* to enter *your* home. Because of the increase in crime rates, unfortunately, *you* cannot assume that *a person* making a simple request to use the telephone is *someone you* can trust!

2. Procrastination is one of *my* worst faults. *My* tendency to put off things *I* dislike doing creates feelings of guilt and causes unnecessary worry. Those unwritten letters and unsavory tasks usually plague *my* mind; in fact, they may even cause *me* sleepless nights! I know that, if *I* spent as much time completing the things that needed to be done as I did thinking and worrying about them, there would be no problem of getting behind. As a result, I am attempting to overcome my bad habit by "not putting off until tomorrow what *I* should have done yesterday." I hope this revised motto helps!

The focus in the above paragraph is probably directed at the writer; therefore, the use of the first person singular throughout seems to be the most appropriate pronoun to use. However, the writer may wish to say that others in the same group also share this fault. If this is so, then all the pronouns would change to first person plural, as illustrated below:

Procrastination is one of *our* worst faults. *Our* tendency to put off things *we* dislike doing creates feelings of guilt and causes unnecessary worry. Those unwritten letters and unsavory tasks usually plague *our minds;* in fact, they may even cause *us* sleepless nights! *We* know that, if *we* spent as much time completing the things that needed to be done as *we* did thinking and worrying about them, there would be no problem of getting behind. As a result, *we are* attempting to overcome *our* bad habit by "not putting off until tomorrow what *we* should have done yesterday." *We* hope this revised motto helps!

Note that, in changing the focus to the first person plural, some other words had to be adjusted. For example, *minds* was pluralized to agree with the plural form of *our*. (It would not be feasible for *us* to have one mind!) Also, one verb had to be changed to agree with its plural subject.

The writer may wish to address this topic to many in a particular group. If this is so, then all pronouns would be changed to third person plural or to other words that would identify the members of the group. This reference change makes the topic an observable opinion of others and does not direct the comments to the writer. Note the changed focus in this revised copy:

Procrastination is one of *many people's* worst faults. *Their* tendency to put off things *they* dislike doing creates feelings of guilt and causes unnecessary worry. Those unwritten letters and unsavory tasks usually plague *their minds;* in fact, *these delayed duties* may even cause *them* sleepless nights! *These procrastinators* know that, if *they* spent as much time completing the things that needed to be done as *they* did thinking and worrying about these unfinished tasks, there would be no problem of getting behind. As a result, *many* are attempting to overcome *their bad habits* by "not putting off until tomorrow what *they* should have done yesterday." *They* hope this revised motto helps!

Note that, in changing the focus to third person plural, many adjustments had to be made. *These delayed duties* and *these procrastinators*, names to identify the specific tasks and members of the group, had to be used to avoid confusing the reader. If the plural word *they* had been used in either place, the pronoun could have referred to more than one group or thing.

If you chose the third person singular (*person, he, him, his,* or *she, her, hers*), then you became involved with the controversial gender problem. Unless the topic is directed at either a man or a woman, it is better to direct your comments to the anonymous group.

Unit Eight: Completing the Circuit

ANSWERS TO EXERCISE 8.1

1. mail*able*	8. predict*able*	15. aud*ible*
2. agree*able*	9. reason*able*	16. comprehens*ible*
3. perish*able*	10. understand*able*	17. horr*ible*
4. accept*able*	11. terr*ible*	18. plaus*ible*
5. profit*able*	12. cred*ible*	19. indel*ible*
6. adjust*able*	13. feas*ible*	20. ed*ible*
7. tax*able*	14. poss*ible*	

ANSWERS TO EXERCISE 8.2

1. amic*able*	5. indefatig*able*	9. leg*ible*
2. negli*gible*	6. intelli*gible*	10. for*cible*
3. invin*cible*	7. despic*able*	
4. redu*cible*	8. tan*gible*	

ANSWERS TO EXERCISE 8.3

1. compar*able*	5. receiv*able*	9. advis*able*
2. change*able*	6. marriage*able*	10. conceiv*able*
3. notice*able*	7. valu*able*	
4. us*able*	8. service*able*	

ANSWERS TO EXERCISE 8.4

1. It is *possible* that the *valuable* necklace was misplaced rather than stolen.
2. There was *tangible* evidence that this *despicable* practice had been carried on for years.
3. There was an *amicable* relationship between the two families.
4. He was *ineligible* for the printing course because his writing was *illegible*.
5. She is a *reasonable* woman who is also *indefatigable* in her efforts to keep her family a happy and healthy unit.
6. *Forcible* entry to the home was gained through the basement window.
7. The amount of his *taxable* income was *unbelievable*.
8. It is *advisable* to teach your children how to save before they reach a *marriageable* age.
9. Every *acceptable* solution to the problem was carefully assessed.
10. Because of the many exceptions, spelling rules are not always *applicable* to every situation; therefore, to make a *noticeable* improvement in your written work, double-check your spelling!

ANSWERS TO EXERCISE 8.5

1.	amplify	amplifies	amplified	amplifying	—	amplifiable	—	amplification
2.	apply	applies	applied	applying	—	applicable	—	application
3.	clarify	clarifies	clarified	clarifying	—	—	—	clarification
4.	certify	certifies	certified	certifying	—	certifiable	—	certification
5.	comply	complies	complied	complying	—	compliable	—	—
6.	deny	denies	denied	denying	—	deniable	denial	—
7.	electrify	electrifies	electrified	electrifying	—	—	—	electrification
8.	horrify	horrifies	horrified	horrifying	horrific	—	—	—
9.	justify	justifies	justified	justifying	—	justifiable	—	justification
10.	magnify	magnifies	magnified	magnifying	—	—	—	magnification
11.	multiply	multiplies	multiplied	multiplying	—	—	—	multiplication
12.	notify	notifies	notified	notifying	—	—	—	notification
13.	occupy	occupies	occupied	occupying	—	—	—	occupation
14.	ratify	ratifies	ratified	ratifying	—	—	—	ratification
15.	rely	relies	relied	relying	—	reliable	—	—
16.	reply	replies	replied	replying	—	—	—	—
17.	specify	specifies	specified	specifying	specific	—	—	specification
18.	supply	supplies	supplied	supplying	—	—	—	—
19.	terrify	terrifies	terrified	terrifying	terrific	—	—	—
20.	verify	verifies	verified	verifying	—	verifiable	—	verification

ANSWERS TO EXERCISE 8.6

1.	allay	allayed	allaying	allayer	—
2.	buy	—	buying	buyer	—
3.	convey	conveyed	conveying	conveyer conveyor	conveyance
4.	defray	defrayed	defraying	—	—
5.	delay	delayed	delaying	delayer	—
6.	lay	laid	laying	—	—
7.	obey	obeyed	obeying	obeyer	obeyance
8.	pay	paid	paying	payer	—
9.	pray	prayed	praying	prayer	—
10.	relay	relayed	relaying	relayer	—
11.	repay	repaid	repaying	—	—
12.	say	said	saying	sayer	—
13.	stay	stayed	staying	stayer	—
14.	stray	strayed	straying	strayer	—
15.	survey	surveyed	surveying	surveyor	—

ANSWERS TO EXERCISE 8.7

1. Aisha always *tries* to please her teachers by being polite and *complying* with their rules and regulations.

2. Were you notified about the *unpaid* balance of your account?

3. The supplier *said* that he had *tried* to obtain those materials as promised, but the continual strikes in the area were the main reason all his shipments had been delayed.

4. *Correct*

5. He *said* that his bill had been *paid*.

ANSWERS TO EXERCISE 8.8

1.	strong	stronger	strongest
2.	efficient	more efficient	most efficient
3.	friendly	friendlier	friendliest
4.	far	farther further	farthest furthest
5.	many	more	most
6.	fast	faster	fastest
7.	important	more important	most important
8.	kind	kinder	kindest
9.	ambitious	more ambitious	most ambitious
10.	fine	finer	finest

ANSWERS TO EXERCISE 8.9

1. Of the two types of pain relievers, I believe Tylenol is the *better* one for headaches.

2. Charles Atlas was at one time considered to be the *strongest* man in the world.

3. We received many submissions to the contest; however, the committee thought your ideas were *unique*. (cannot be compared)

4. Of the three apartments, we chose the one that was *closest* to the school.

5. Alex felt that he was the *luckiest* man in the world!

6. *Correct*

7. Among the three of us, Mom liked me *best*.

8. Being second means that you will have to try *harder* next time.

9. Since his illness, Mr. Spock says he is feeling *stronger* each day.

10. I have travelled by train just as frequently as I have by plane; but I have to admit that I like the train trip *better*.

ANSWERS TO EXERCISE 8.10

1. *Fewer* people are travelling today because they have *less* money to spend on luxuries.

2. Because there was *less* rain this summer, farmers had *fewer* vegetables to take to market.

3. There are *fewer* job opportunities today for anyone seeking a teaching position.

4. Because Tina was trying to maintain a full-time job and attend school at the same time, she had *less* time to devote to her studies.

5. Because there are *fewer* cars travelling on that particular highway, there are *fewer* accidents.

ANSWERS TO EXERCISE 8.11

1. To ensure that you make *fewer* errors on this test than you did on the last one, proofread your work *more carefully*.

2. Of all the lawyers who work in this office building, Clara dresses *most conservatively*.

3. Because my car operates *more efficiently* in the summer than it does in the winter, I have *fewer* car expenses during the months of May to September.

4. Although the new bank is *more conveniently* located to my workplace, I still prefer the other branch because the staff there is *friendlier*.

5. Raoul is one of the *healthiest* looking members of our team.

ANSWERS TO EXERCISE 8.12

1. We felt *bad* about the news. (no action—no *ly*)

2. The coffee tasted a little *strong*. (no action—no *ly*)

3. Things were looking *bad* for the our hometown baseball team. (no action—no *ly*)

4. Drive *slowly* as you approach the crosswalk. (action—add *ly*)

5. I felt my way *carefully* along the darkened hallway. (action—add *ly*)

6. The actor performed *poorly* because he was ill. (action—add *ly*)

7. Do those flowers smell *sweet* to you? (no action—no *ly*)

8. Eat your lunch *quickly* so we may leave. (action—add *ly*)

9. She tasted the hot beverage *cautiously*. (action—add *ly*)

10. The accused remained *silent* when questioned about the crime. (no action—no *ly*)

11. Wayne Gretzky *consistently* played *well* for his team. (action—adverbs *consistently, well*)

12. Celia is looking very *well* since her surgery. (no action—adjective *well* describing health)

13. I felt *good* about the interview I had last week. (no action—adjective *good*)

14. After Allan had eaten four hamburgers, he said he didn't feel very *well*. (no action—adjective *well* describing health)

15. She can play the piano really *well*. (action—adverb *well*)

ANSWERS TO EXERCISE 8.13

1. Helen is a *really* good friend of mine.

2. Preena has always had *really* good marks.

3. My school ring is made of *real* gold.

4. I was *really* disappointed to learn that our trip had been cancelled.

5. The *real* test was *really* difficult.

ANSWERS TO EXERCISE 8.14

1. Haven't you *ever* been to London?

2. I don't *ever* want to see you *any* more!

3. Because I was sitting at the back of the auditorium, I *could* hardly hear the speaker.

4. We don't get *any* satisfaction from that restaurant so we aren't going there *any* more.

5. Our committee had discussed that issue for two hours and still couldn't reach *any* decision.

6. The employee claimed that he had never received *any* notice about the changes in regulations.

7. The suspect said that she didn't know *anything* about the break-in.

8. I am not going *anywhere* tonight; I am staying home for a change.

9. I *could* scarcely see the road in the dense fog.

10. Some people never take *any* advice; they prefer to learn through life's experience.

ANSWERS TO EXERCISE 8.15

1. a) After the student completed his homework, he turned in his assignment.
   b) The student, after completing his homework, turned in his assignment.
   c) After completing his homework, the student turned in his assignment.

2. a) To achieve a better grade, you should do more studying before you write a test.
   b) You should do more studying before you write a test so you will achieve a better grade.
   c) If you want to achieve a better grade, do more studying before you write a test.

3. a) Not seeing the police car following, the driver drove down the street at an excessive rate of speed.
   b) The driver, not seeing the police car following, drove down the street at an excessive rate of speed.
   c) Because the driver did not see the police car following, he drove down the street at an excessive rate of speed.

4. a) After being late every day this week, the student received a severe scolding from the teacher.
   b) Because the student had been late every day this week, he received a severe scolding from the teacher.
   c) The student, after being late every day this week, received a severe scolding from the teacher.

5. a) Being a little tired today, I postponed my meeting until tomorrow.
   b) Because I was a little tired today, I postponed my meeting until tomorrow.

6. a) After Jawal graduated from high school, his parents bought him a car.
   b) After graduating from high school, Jawal received a car as a gift from his parents.

7. With our binoculars, we enjoy watching the birds building their nests.

8. a) After her canary had its bird bath, Angela fed it some lettuce.
   b) After having a bird bath, Angela's canary ate some lettuce.

9. a) Walking home, I saw several moving vans in front of the new house.
   b) As I was walking home, I saw several moving vans in front of the new house.
   c) I saw several moving vans in front of the new house when I was walking home.

10. a) To get to know the students better, the teacher memorized their names and faces during the first week of classes.
    b) Because the teacher wanted to get to know her students better, she memorized their names and faces during the first week of classes.
    c) During the first week of classes, the teacher memorized her students' names and faces so she could get to know them better.

ANSWERS TO EXERCISE 8.16

1. Turning on the light, I noticed that my book was on the chair.

2. Every Sunday I phone my sister who lives in Texas.

3. I always give Lara a kiss on her cheek before she goes to school.

4. As we all smiled, the photographer focused the camera and snapped our picture.

5. The members of the comedy team kept the audience laughing for nearly two hours.

6. We planned to serve steak and lobster to our guests who were arriving at seven for dinner.

7. Last night, a pedestrian wearing dark-coloured clothes was struck by a car.

8. a) At three o'clock, the lecturer will be speaking in the school auditorium about the dangers of drinking and driving.
   b) At three o'clock in the school auditorium, the lecturer will be speaking about the dangers of drinking and driving.

9. Only I was kept after class; everyone else was allowed to leave.

10. The bucket, which was fortunately empty, slipped out of my hands.

ANSWERS TO EXERCISE 8.17

1. She promised to *read a book* and *turn in her report* by Monday.

2. I often like to *go for a stroll* along the beach and *look for interesting shells.*

3. Arvo was wearing a black suit, a white shirt, a bow tie, and *brown shoes.*

4. Antonio found that the best way to get to the Queen Charlotte Islands was *to drive to Prince Rupert* and *to fly the rest of the way.*

5. Your letter of application should include relevant details about your education, *information about your past work experience,* and *the names of three references.*

6. Before we move into our summer cottage we have to remove all traces of "little critters," *wash the floors thoroughly,* and *clean all cupboards.*

7. You should proofread your written work for errors in *punctuation, grammar,* and *spelling.*

8. When Marga completes high school, she wants to *work for a year* and then *plan a trip to Europe* with the money she will have saved.

9. To keep proper balance in your life, make sure you allow equal time for *work, play,* and *relaxation.*

10. To get along in life, one needs *purpose, determination,* and *a good sense of humour.*

ANSWERS TO EXERCISE 8.18

1. Golf is a popular sport that appeals not only *to men* but *to women* too.

2. Any evening during the summer, you can find Farzin either *attending a ball game* or *watching one on television.*

3. You must either *find my book* or *buy me a new one.*

4. During my last term, I read not only *the required books for English* but also *several novels.*

5. We decided to cancel our plans for building a new home because both the *labour* and *material* costs are high.

6. Pierre accepted neither *the first job offer he received* nor *the second.*

7. The travellers were not only *tired* but *hungry as well.*

8. We had the choice of renting either *a fifth-floor* apartment or *the main floor of a house.*

9. Mrs. Hayashi's new home not only *is decorated with fine furniture in every room,* but also *has beautiful oil paintings on the walls.*

10. On the first day of classes, students were asked to bring both *their registration forms* and *their books* to every class.

ANSWERS TO EXERCISE 8.19

1. Students often earn extra money by *working in local hotels* or *clerking in stores.*

2. The aroma of freshly baked bread smelled so *delicious* that I had to stop and buy a loaf.

3. She has neither *cleaned her room* nor *washed the dishes.*

4. After I *had* studied for days, my exam did not seem so difficult.

5. I am *really* tired of seeing reruns on television.

6. Canadians are concerned not only *about national unity* but also *about retaining their cultural differences.*

7. If you take the time to collect and organize all your material, you won't have *any* problems writing an effective essay.

8. Your glass is more nearly full than mine.

9. *Fewer* people are attending the minor hockey league games than in previous years.

10. He was *honest, helpful*, and *well organized.*

ANSWERS TO EXERCISE 8.20

1. Do you subscribe to the newspaper <u>The Bulletin,</u> or do you just buy a copy on the weekends?

2. Did you read the article "Communications in the Future" in the latest edition of <u>Maclean's</u>?

3. Underline the most important parts of the chapter "Developing a Program" in the text <u>Introduction to Data Processing.</u>

4. L.M. Montgomery's books <u>Anne of Green Gables</u> and <u>Anne of Avonlea</u> have both been made into television serials.

5. There are many great songs on Leonard Cohen's album <u>The Future</u>, but "Closing Time" is a real classic.

ANSWERS TO EXERCISE 8.21

1. Use the word "and" sparingly in your compositions.

2. In business jargon, "downsizing" means reducing the number of employees in a firm.

3. If you want to make an effective presentation, do not use terms such as "gonna" and "youse"!

4. Computers have added many expressions to our everyday language: we ask for "feedback" instead of a response; we "interface" with each other instead of discussing; and we all get upset when the coffee machine is "down"!

5. Low-grade bonds, known as "junk bonds," are not usually very safe investments.

ANSWERS TO EXERCISE 8.22

1. Mark Twain once described golf as "a good walk spoiled."

2. My own personal motto is: "Practice makes perfect."

3. There are a number of sayings a person can use to get through difficult times. The ones I apply most are "First things first" and "One day at a time." Using these simple clichés seems to put my problems into perspective and also helps me to tackle them in manageable portions rather than all at one time.

4. A true friend can be defined as "one who knows you as you are, understands where you have been, accepts who you have become, and still invites you to grow."

5. In one of his articles, Mark Twain described his maturing years in the following way: "When I was a boy of fourteen, my father was so ignorant I could hardly stand to have the old man around. But when I got to be twenty-one, I was astonished at how much the old man had learned in seven years!"

ANSWERS TO EXERCISE 8.23

1. One of my favourite songs from <u>Fiddler on the Roof</u> is "If I Were a Rich Man."

2. The article, entitled "The Age of Communications" and published by the Royal Bank, points out the following fact: "Of the 550 million telephones in service today, three-quarters are confined to only eight of the world's 170-odd countries. The great bulk of the world's people live out their lives without what we Canadians regard as an indispensable communication device."

3. When questioned about her past, Mae West retorted, "I used to be Snow White but I drifted."

4. To say "I ain't got none" is a real reflection of one's command of the English language!

5. Although most employees work as team members, performance measures are written for individuals. The phrases "the client will ...," "the patient will ...," or "the student will ..." imply this directed focus and mean that each person will be evaluated individually in a group setting.

6. A few years ago, real estate agents noticed a "back-to-the-country" movement. More people seemed interested in relocating in some picturesque, quiet, rural area away from the "hustle and bustle" of the city.

7. Because of his film roles in such "chillers" as <u>The House of Wax</u> and <u>Fall of the House of Usher</u>, Vincent Price has become known as the "master of the macabre."

8. In the article "Walk Your Way to Good Health" in the magazine <u>Prevention</u>, researchers from Stanford University reported the following findings: "Brisk walking can lower blood pressure, help people lose weight without dieting, improve blood-fat levels, reduce the need for insulin in adult diabetics, relieve back pain and headaches, even improve mood and thinking skills."

9. One of the researchers also reported: "We found that men who walked nine or more miles a week had a risk of death 21 percent lower than those who walked less than three miles a week." Since this report has been made public, there has been more interest in establishing a "walk-a-mile-a-day" campaign.

10. Some advertisements "bug" us. However, in a recent survey about commercials people best remember, it was discovered that among the top contenders were eight of the most irritating ones. The researchers made the following conclusive comment: "Irritating commercials may be effective because they firmly establish a product name in your mind."

ANSWERS TO PRETESTS

UNIT ONE: DISCOVERING VOCABULARY SKILLS

ANSWERS TO PRETEST FOR "WORD CONSTRUCTION"

I. **1.** (c)   **2.** (c)   **3.** (a)   **4.** (b)   **5.** (a)

II. **6.** (b)   **7.** (c)   **8.** (a)   **9.** (b)   **10.** (c)

III. **11.** Because she appeared to have a form of *dermatitis*, she made an appointment to see a doctor.

  12. The courageous man was *fearless* even in the face of danger.

  13. The applicant was interviewed and hired by the *employer;* she was asked to start work at the beginning of the week.

  14. Colour *symbolism* differs from one culture to another; for example, in Japan white, not black, is the symbol of mourning.

  15. I suspected that John's *communication* skills were weak because he began the semester by making excuses for not completing his reading and writing assignments.

If you were successful in every section of the test (1 to 5, 6 to 10, 11 to 15), proceed to the Pretest for "Context Clues." If you had more than one error in any portion, review the appropriate vocabulary lessons.

ANSWERS TO PRETEST FOR "CONTEXT CLUES"

1. (c)   **3.** (b)   **5.** (b)   **7.** (b)   **9.** (a)

2. (c)   **4.** (a)   **6.** (d)   **8.** (c)   **10.** (c)

If you had eight or more answers correct, write the Unit One Post-Test. If you had fewer than eight answers correct, complete the lessons on context clues.

UNIT TWO: READING FOR COMPREHENSION

ANSWERS TO PRETEST FOR "MAIN IDEAS"

1. (c)   **3.** (a)   **5.** (b)   **7.** (b)   **9.** (a)

2. (d)   **4.** (c)   **6.** (d)   **8.** (c)   **10.** (d)

If you had eight or more answers correct, proceed to the Pretest for "Organizational Patterns in Reading." If you had fewer than eight answers correct, complete the lessons on main ideas.

ANSWERS TO PRETEST FOR "ORGANIZATIONAL PATTERNS IN READING"

I. **1.** The *life history* of the butterfly presents some very remarkable changes in this insect.
    Developed by (b) *sequence*

  2. Swimming in a pool is quite *different from* swimming in a lake.
    Developed by (c) *comparison or contrast*

  3. Morale, which is one of the most important elements in the working force, can be fostered *in many ways*.
    Developed by (a) *example or reason*

  4. Happiness is what *one* believes it to be.
    Developed by (a) *example or reason*

5. When you think about it, motivation is not much *different from* friendship.
   Developed by (c) *comparison*

6. Manners are simply modes of behaviour that have *developed throughout the centuries.*
   Developed by (b) *sequence*

II. 1. developed by (b) *sequence* or (c) *contrast.* (Either of these answers would be acceptable: clue words sequentially identify the centuries, but also suggest contrast with "opinions differ.")

2. developed by (a) *example or reason*

3. developed by (a) *example or reason*

4. developed by (b) *sequence*

If you had eight or more answers correct, proceed to the Pretest for "Outlining." If you had fewer than eight answers correct, complete the lessons on organizational patterns in reading.

ANSWERS TO PRETEST FOR "OUTLINING"

Your answer may be slightly different from the one given below; however, the format and content must be similar to be correct.

- Roman numerals identify each paragraph's main-idea statement.

- Capital letters identify major details of each paragraph.

- Arabic numbers identify minor details that support a major point.

    I. Collecting is not exclusive to human beings.

        A. pack rats, magpies stash away objects

        B. chimpanzees, whisky-jacks collect trash

   II. Psychologists have attributed people's urge to collect to many innate desires.

        A. Sigmund Freud says it is sublimation of sexual desire.
           1. not so with pack rats

        B. Other psychologists say it is lust for power.
           1. explains why the most powerful people in history have also been among greatest collectors

  III. A great many people collect a great many different things for a great many different reasons.

        A. We are all collectors.
           1. everyone collects trivial things
           2. some collect foodstuffs
           3. many are reluctant to part with useless junk
           4. homes contain a collection of objects that will never be used again.

  IV. It takes a superhuman effort to throw out everything that should be thrown out.

        A. Sophisticated collectors call this collecting—not accumulating.

        B. We are reluctant to part with useless items because they might come in handy someday.
           1. our own rubbish is part of our uniqueness.

If you had any errors, complete the lesson on outlining. If you successfully completed this Pretest, write the Unit Two Post-Test.

Unit Five: Putting the Basics Together

ANSWERS TO PRETEST FOR "SPELLING—PLURAL FORMS"

1. The owners of that complex are my two *brothers-in-law*.
2. The *Cortezes* are our next-door neighbours.
3. Two *attorneys* were hired by the defendants because they wanted their cases tried separately.
4. (*Mosquitoes or*) *Mosquitos* are the worst summer pests.
5. It seems to me that all the *Harrys* in this city answered our advertisement for an ambitious young salesperson.
6. We ordered several cargoes of *tomatoes* during the summer season.
7. We now have five *secretaries* in our main office.
8. John likes four *teaspoonfuls* of sugar in his coffee.
9. You should enclose any words of explanation in *parentheses*.
10. Omar arranged the cans neatly on the *shelves*.

If you had eight or more sentences correct, proceed to the Pretest for "Subject-Verb Agreement." If you had fewer than eight answers correct, complete the lessons on plural forms.

ANSWERS TO PRETEST FOR "SUBJECT-VERB AGREEMENT"

1. Neither of your answers *is* correct.
2. A stack of dirty dishes *was* left in the sink.
3. Either the vegetables or the meat *has* an odd smell.
4. One of those boys *has* to be guilty.
5. Professor Goodwin and her husband *are* leaving today for Ireland.
6. Spaghetti and meatballs *is* a good Italian meal.
7. Mr. Singh's new Honda *doesn't* use very much gasoline.
8. Physics, as well as mathematics, *requires* skill in logic.
9. There *doesn't* seem to be a solution to that problem.
10. *Are* parentheses required around that information?

If you had eight or more answers correct, proceed to the Pretest for "Basic Uses of the Comma." If you had fewer than eight answers correct, complete the lessons on subject-verb agreement.

ANSWERS TO PRETEST FOR "BASIC USES OF THE COMMA"

1. Do you plan to spend your vacation travelling, camping, or staying at home?
2. When you encounter problems, it is best to seek the advice of a professional counsellor or clergy.
3. The person of my dreams must have intelligence, a sense of humour, and the ability to listen.
4. Using the stairs in an office or apartment building would be an excellent way for workers to stay in shape, but not many people use this easy form of exercise in their daily lives because using the elevator is faster and more convenient for them during their busy schedules.
5. To win at any game of cards, you must practise and be able to remember each card that has been played.

6. *Correct*

7. *Correct*

8. *Correct*

9. Papers, books, magazines, etc., were scattered around the room.

10. Acting on the advice of Mr. Tanaka, I decided to invest in some stock.

If you had eight or more sentences correct, proceed to the next section, on "Outlining." If you had fewer than eight sentences correct, complete the lessons on basic uses of the comma.

UNIT SIX: COMMUNICATING CORRECTLY

ANSWERS TO PRETEST FOR "SPELLING—WORDS WITH EI OR IE AND CONFUSING WORDS"

1. Because my *niece* had been outstanding in her *field* of studies, she was chosen to *receive two science* awards.

2. I *hear* that the *personnel* department is planning to *proceed* with the hiring of two new *principals* for the vacant positions.

3. *There* was *dissent* among the *neighbourhood* groups about the *effects* of the new *procedure* to reduce the number of speeders in the suburban area. The construction of speed bumps was to start in the early spring. However, because those living in the small community would be *travelling* on these roads more often *than* the late-night speedsters, many people felt that the raised portions of the roads would be more damaging to *their* own vehicles.

4. I believe that the new legislation has been *passed,* and there will be workshops and self-paced *lesson* books in the near future for community members to learn about the new laws.

5. The city *council* members *discussed* the proposed *site* for the new casino. *There* was a great deal of debating, as many didn't *know whether* the downtown area would be preferable to the out-of-town location *formerly chosen* by the planning committee.

If you made two or fewer errors, go on to the Pretest for "Verbs." If you made more than two errors, complete the lessons on spelling in Unit Six.

ANSWERS TO PRETEST FOR "VERBS"

1. I have never *ridden* in a smoother riding car than Anton's new Cadillac.

2. *Correct*

3. Anna *wrote (or has written)* a book about her experiences in the Arctic.

4. During the past week I *saw (or have seen)* fifteen reruns on television!

5. He still *makes* mistakes even though he knows better. *OR* He still *made* mistakes even though he *knew* better.

6. *Lay* those books on my desk.

7. I *froze* my fingers trying to get that key into the lock.

8. Ahmed said that he *had given* (*or gave*) you those tickets last Saturday.

9. Ken ran quickly to the end of the dock and *jumped* into the water.

10. Everything Leta told me about the college I *had heard* before.

If you had eight or more sentences correct, proceed to the Pretest for "The Comma and the Semicolon." If you had fewer than eight sentences correct, complete the lessons on verbs.

ANSWERS TO PRETEST FOR "THE COMMA AND THE SEMICOLON"

1. The amount of time a lawyer must spend on your case, of course, determines his or her fee.
2. If you are going to Spain, take only the necessary items; leave all your heavy clothing at home.
3. After trying to contact the sales representative all morning, I left a message with his secretary; he would, she assured me, return my call before closing time.
4. *Correct*
5. Poor organizational ability, incidentally, is almost always revealed in your essays; poorly written essays, however, are not always the result of poor organization.
6. Our representative, Mr. Pierre Dionne, will call on you tomorrow.
7. Nicole, a very good friend of mine, wants me to go to Paris next spring; but I am hesitant about committing myself because of the devalued dollar.
8. Marina was thrilled with her birthday gift, a diamond dinner ring!
9. I hate to think of that embarrassing incident; I just wish everyone would forget it!
10. Javed spent his last loonie on a cup of coffee; as a result, he had to walk home.

If you had eight or more sentences correct, you have completed this section and are ready to write the Unit Six Post-Test. If you had fewer than eight sentences correct, complete the lessons on the comma and the semicolon.

UNIT SEVEN: WRITING MORE SKILLFULLY

ANSWERS TO PRETEST FOR "SPELLING—FINAL CONSONANTS"

1. What is your *preference*—tea or coffee?
2. We planned to attend the *conference* and discuss the *recurring* problem that faced us every year.
3. The *planning committee developed* the policy for *admissions*.
4. I am *beginning* to understand this work.
5. The employer *preferred* to check the applicants' *references*.
6. The two leaders *concurred* that both *governments* would have to set aside their *differences* and work together to control any future *development* of nuclear arms in order to reduce the danger of nuclear warfare that would destroy the world.
7. My request for new *equipment* was *referred* to the purchase officer who *controlled* all business expenses.
8. *Cancellations* for our banquet reservations will not be *accepted* on the day of the event; therefore, money has to be *budgeted* for people who may not honour their *commitments*.

If you had eighteen or more words spelled correctly, proceed to the Pretest for "Pronouns and Prepositions." If you had fewer than eighteen words spelled correctly, complete the lessons on spelling in Unit Seven.

ANSWERS TO PRETEST FOR "PRONOUNS AND PREPOSITIONS"

1. The group interviewed for the job included Bill, George, and *me*.
2. Our pay raises were *retroactive to* last January.
3. *Whom* did the college appoint as admissions officer?
4. Pauline has more artistic talent than *I*.
5. Each girl prepared *her* own report.

6. Either the architect or the engineer made an error in *his (or her)* calculations.

7. A bad job is *preferable to* no job at all.

8. Your opinions are quite different *from* hers.

9. The people who received notices were my cousin, my brother, and *I.*

10. Nobody works harder for her marks than *she.*

If you had eight or more sentences correct, proceed to the Pretest for "The Apostrophe and Its Uses." If you had fewer than eight sentences correct, complete the lessons on pronouns and prepositions.

ANSWERS TO PRETEST FOR "THE APOSTROPHE AND ITS USES"

1. My *brother-in-law's* office *doesn't* contain much furniture.

2. *You're* late for your appointment.

3. *Tomorrow's* meeting will have to be cancelled, as *we're* planning to be out of town.

4. In *everyone's* opinion, Banff is a *skiers'* paradise.

5. *It's* been two weeks since I ordered *Jim's* and Mario's jackets.

6. Several *students'* cars were parked in the *staff's* parking lot.

7. The *Walkers'* and the *Robinsons'* boats were tied up at their docks when the storm struck.

8. Several *dollars'* worth of merchandise was missing from the *supermarket's* shelves; but the police believed that, rather than one thief, many regular customers had shoplifted the goods during the day.

9. Because *Mr. Fernando's* firm is a proven and reliable one, you would be wise to transfer your *mother-in-law's* business to that company.

10. *They're* not interested in travelling to the Orient for two *weeks'* vacation.

If you made no more than two errors, you are ready to write the Unit Seven Post-Test. If you made more than two errors, complete the lessons on apostrophes.

UNIT EIGHT: COMPLETING THE CIRCUIT

ANSWERS TO PRETEST FOR "SPELLING—WORDS WITH *IBLE* OR *ABLE* AND THE FINAL *Y*"

1.	(receivable)	receivible	11.	applys	(applies)
2.	(credible)	credable	12.	(noticeable)	noticable
3.	changable	(changeable)	13.	(laid)	layed
4.	(negligible)	negligable	14.	multiplys	(multiplies)
5.	(valuable)	valueable	15.	(desirable)	desireable
6.	(despicable)	despicible	16.	(usable)	useable
7.	(delayed)	delaid	17.	(complying)	compling
8.	relys	(relies)	18.	(terrible)	terrable
9.	appling	(applying)	19.	predictible	(predictable)
10.	(said)	sayed	20.	possable	(possible)

If you made no more than two errors, proceed to the Pretest for "Modifiers and Parallel Structure." If you made more than two errors, complete the section on spelling in Unit Eight.

ANSWERS TO PRETEST FOR "MODIFIERS AND PARALLEL STRUCTURE"

1. a) Swimming in a pool is more fun than *swimming* in a lake.
    b) *To swim* in a pool is more fun than to swim in a lake.

2. Do you think he presented that information report *properly?*

3. Being an old-fashioned family, *we served a formal dinner* in the dining room every evening at precisely six o'clock.

4. I felt *really* bad about what I had said in my moment of anger.

5. She was responsible not only for designing the house but *for constructing* it too.

6. Some children get funnier as they grow older.

7. We saw the flight team of the Canadian Snowbirds flying overhead.

8. I am so pleased that, as I progress through this program, I have *fewer* grammatical errors in my written work.

9. The police officer charged the youth with resisting arrest and *assaulting* an officer.

10. When *one is* travelling in a strange city, a local map is an absolute necessity.

If you had eight or more sentences correct, proceed to the Pretest for "Underlining, Italics, and Quotation Marks." If you had fewer than eight sentences correct, complete the lessons on modifiers and parallel structure.

ANSWERS TO PRETEST FOR "UNDERLINING, ITALICS, AND QUOTATION MARKS"

1. For Christmas, Steffie bought her sister a gift subscription to <u>Châtelaine.</u>

2. Winston Churchill, famous for his brilliant words of wisdom, is the one who said: "Courage is what it takes to stand up and speak. Courage is also what it takes to sit down and listen!"

3. In the dictionary, the term "bibliophile" is defined as "a person who loves or collects books."

4. Joni Mitchell's album <u>Ladies of the Canyon</u> is still one of my favourites; I particularly like hearing the song "Big Yellow Taxi."

5. My assignment included reading an article entitled "Faith or Medicine" in the latest issue of <u>Maclean's.</u>

6. Try to avoid overusing the words "it" and "this" in your writing.

7. When I was young, the Beatles were the "grooviest" musical group going!

8. The "horse and buggy" style of management is becoming an obsolete method for motivating workers.

9. Potential car buyers can now purchase a book called <u>Lemon-Aid</u> to help them avoid buying a costly "lemon."

10. With the challenge of going where they are not supposed to go, many bright computer students use skill and luck to "hack" school computer systems and enter private protected files.

If you made no more than two errors, proceed to the Unit Eight Post-Test. If you made more than two errors, complete the lesson on "Underlining, Italics, and Quotation Marks."

GLOSSARY OF TERMS

UNIT ONE

prefix One or more letters (of Latin, Greek, or Old English origin) that can be attached to a word to give it a new meaning, e.g., *uni*cycle, *bi*cycle, *tri*cycle.

root word The basic component of a word (of Latin, Greek, or Old English origin); it can be situated at the beginning, middle, or end of a word depending on the prefixes or suffixes required to express the meaning of the word, e.g., *spec*tacle, in*spec*tion, retro*spect*.

suffix One or more letters (of Latin, Greek, or Old English origin) attached to the end of a word to change its meaning or function, e.g., mercy, merci*ful*, merci*less*.

context clues Clues given in a sentence or paragraph that further explain or clarify the meaning of an unknown or difficult word.

UNIT TWO

topic The subject or heading that describes, in a few words, what the passage is all about.

main ideas/main-idea statement The controlling or all-encompassing idea about a given paragraph or article that identifies the writer's central theme; all other ideas in the passage are related to and support this theme.

implied main idea The same as the main-idea statement, but not always stated in exact words. The main idea is strongly suggested or implied from all the information and/or details supplied in the passage.

major details The method used by the writer to support the main idea; the most commonly used patterns are reasons, examples, explanation, sequence of events, and points of comparison or contrast.

minor detail Elaboration or further explanation of a particular major detail.

Roman numerals A system of numbering used for formal outlines. Capital letters represent numbers; the common basic symbols are I, II, III, IV, V, VI, VII, VIII, IX, X.

UNIT THREE

underlining/highlighting Drawing a line under, or highlighting the words of, the most important ideas and details in a given passage to set the key message apart from the rest of the text. It is helpful to the student to make these identified portions link together meaningfully to create a readable summary.

marginal note Concise, clearly worded groups of words, written neatly in the margin either to define an unknown word, to title the adjacent content, to write the implied main idea, or to summarize/paraphrase a complicated portion.

Roman numerals See Unit Two.

UNIT FOUR

synonyms Words that have similar meanings, e.g., *topic, subject*.

antonyms Words that have opposite meanings, e.g., *good, bad*.

thesaurus A book that contains lists of synonyms and antonyms for most English words and expressions.

subject of the sentence The major topic that identifies who or what is being discussed in the sentence.

predicate The portion of the sentence that contains the action or gives information about the subject.

sentence A combination of a subject and a predicate that expresses a complete thought and gives a clear message to the reader.

sentence fragment A partial word group that does not convey a complete thought. Either the subject or the predicate is missing, or the message is incomplete.

run-on sentences Two or more sentences linked together without proper punctuation.

conjunctions Words that link words, groups of words, or sentences together in a meaningful way. There are two types of conjunctions, namely, coordinating conjunctions and subordinating conjunctions.

coordinating conjunctions The most commonly

used ones (*and*, *but*, *or*) join and relate two or more equal words, actions, word groups, or sentences for a specific purpose.

subordinating conjunctions   Words such as *when*, *because*, *even though* join and relate two sentences that do not have equal status. Subordinating conjunctions are used to relay an idea that is of lesser importance than the sentence it is joined to.

transitional words   Words or groups of words that help relate two ideas in a meaningful way; however, these words do not join two sentences. They are usually preceded by a semicolon to indicate a new, but related, thought.

summary   A condensed, clearly written paraphrased version (about two-thirds) of a written passage with the same focus as the original.

précis   A highly condensed version (about one-third) of a written passage with the same focus as the original.

abstract   A highly condensed summary of a study paper, review, report, or very detailed experimental study. Regardless of the length of the study paper, an abstract is only a single paragraph of approximately 75 to 100 words. It presents a very brief overview of the study paper that would follow.

Roman numerals   See Unit Two.

UNIT FIVE

noun   A word that names a person, place, thing, or idea. Use *the* in front of a word to test whether it is a noun, e.g., *the* fire, *the* park, *the* paper, *the* thought.

verb   The most essential part of any sentence. Located in the predicate, this word or word group expresses the action or state of being of the subject. It also indicates the time period of the sentence.

homonyms   Words that sound the same but have different meanings and spellings, e.g., *patience*, *patients*.

simple subject   A most important word that names the person, place, thing, or idea that is the main topic of the sentence. The simple subject will never be the last word in a phrase of words: "*One* of the boys will be the winner." (*One* is the simple subject; *boys* is the last word in the phrase *of the boys*, so this word does not qualify to be the subject.)

compound sentence   Two or more complete sentences joined by *and*, *but*, or *or*.

comma   A punctuation mark (,) that separates items within a sentence; it does not, however, act as an end punctuation mark.

main-idea statement   See Unit Two.

major detail   See Unit Two.

minor detail   See Unit Two.

concluding sentence   A statement that gives advice, a result, a prediction, or a summary about the information discussed in the paragraph. This statement can be interchanged with the main idea.

Roman numerals   See Unit Two.

UNIT SIX

verb   See Unit Five.

participle   Part of a verb. Although this word contains the root verb, it needs a helper verb or verbs to make its meaning complete, e.g., participle—*writing*; complete verb—*is writing* or *has been writing*, depending on the time expression required. The correct forms for each root verb are listed in the dictionary. With a helper, this word forms a verb phrase; used alone it is only description, e.g., the *travelling* salesperson, the *steaming* kettle.

verb tense   A single verb or a verb group (phrase) that expresses various times or actions in the sentence, e.g., *went*, *has been going*.

active voice   A term applied to the verb in a sentence that has been worded in a direct way; that is, the subject is performing the action of the verb; e.g., *My mother baked* a cake yesterday.

passive voice   A term applied to the verb in a sentence in which the subject is the receiver of the action; the actual doer of the action is placed in a phrase after the verb or is dropped altogether; e.g., *The cake was baked* by my mother yesterday. *The cake was baked* yesterday.

semicolon   A punctuation mark (;) used between two related sentences, in a compound sentence if commas have been used in other parts of the sentence, or to separate major items in a series that already contains commas.

topic   See Unit Two.

main-idea statement   See Unit Two.

unity   A paragraph that contains a main idea, supporting details, and a concluding sentence. The information follows one pattern of development and focuses on one point of view.

coherence   Sentences in a paragraph that are linked together with effective transitional words and refined sentence patterns to create a good flow of ideas for the reader. You need to apply your knowledge of editing and transitional expressions as well as subordinating and coordinating conjunctions to create well-refined sentences.

concluding sentence   See Unit Five.

Roman numerals   See Unit Two.

UNIT SEVEN

suffix   See Unit One.

consonants   All the letters in the alphabet except *a*, *e*, *i*, *o*, *u*. The latter are vowels.

pronoun   A word that takes the place of the noun.

subjective pronoun   A word used to replace a noun that is functioning as the subject of a sentence or is following a form of the verb *to be*, e.g., *I*, *you*, *he*, *she*, *we*, *they*.

objective pronoun   A word used to replace a noun that follows the action word in the sentence. Any pronoun that is not functioning in the subject role is an objective pronoun, e.g., *me, him, her, us, them*.

reflexive pronoun   Any pronoun with the suffix -*self* or -*selves* added, e.g., *myself, himself, ourselves, themselves*.

preposition   A word used to link a noun or a pronoun to other words in a sentence to create a clear message; e.g., the milk *on* the table, the driver *of* the car, the dust *under* the furniture, a letter *from* her.

apostrophe   A punctuation mark (') used to indicate ownership (e.g., the *cat's* paw, *John's* car, many *students'* problems) or used to indicate that letters have been omitted, e.g., *we're* (we are), *he'll* (he will), *can't* (can not).

contraction   A shortened form of two words to make one word; an apostrophe is used in place of the missing letters, e.g., *there's* (there is), *doesn't* (does not).

thesis statement   A sentence that introduces the topic of your piece of writing and, in a two-paragraph composition, also introduces the two aspects or points of view you are planning to discuss. This statement is followed by the main-idea statement of the first paragraph (see Unit Two).

transitional expressions   Suitable linking words that are used within and between paragraphs and/or sentences to relate ideas to one another to create a cohesive and meaningful flow of information.

conclusion/concluding statement   See Unit Five; however, for the composition in Unit Seven, your concluding statement must address the ideas from both paragraphs and be interchangeable with your thesis statement.

Roman numerals   See Unit Two.

Fog Index   A mathematical formula for self-testing the appropriateness of the level of written paragraphs/articles/essays for the intended audience. Although this method can help direct the writer to any needed revisions, it cannot be used as the only factor in assessment because it presupposes that the information is accurate and also correct in grammar, spelling, and punctuation.

UNIT EIGHT

adjective   A word that describes a noun (see Unit Five). This descriptive word can precede the noun it describes or follow any form of the verb *to be*; e.g., The *happy* child is laughing. The child is *happy*.

adverb   A word that describes action words, adjectives, or other adverbs. This word responds to the questions how?, where?, when?, why?, how much?, under what conditions?, and to what extent?, and can be found anywhere in the sentence; e.g., We moved *quickly*. We moved *forward*. *Suddenly* we heard a sound.

positive form   The basic form of an adjective or adverb; e.g., *strong, quickly*.

comparative form   The form used to compare two adjectives or adverbs, e.g., *stronger, more quickly*.

superlative form   The form used to compare more than two adjectives or adverbs, e.g., *strongest, most quickly*.

power adverbs   A term used in this text to help you correctly use adverbs describing other adjectives or adverbs, e.g., *very* strong, *too* quickly.

double negatives   The grammatical error of using two negative words with one verb; e.g., I don't have *no* money.

modifiers   All words or word groups that describe nouns, pronouns, action words, or other descriptive words.

dangling modifier   A descriptive group of words with no reference word to indicate who or what is being described; the resulting sentence can be unclear or ambiguous.

misplaced modifier   Words or word groups that are not correctly placed in the sentence; as a result, the sentence can be confusing or misinterpreted.

parallel structure   Two or more words or word groups of equal status that are correctly joined together with coordinate conjunctions (see Unit Four).

underlining   Titles of complete works must be underlined or italicized in an essay or published work.

quotation marks   A set of punctuation marks (" ") used to enclose titles identifying portions of a larger work, any words or phrases that have special significance, or quotations from printed sources.

expository essay   A written discussion (in complete sentences) of three or more paragraphs that gives information on or offers an explanation about a specific topic.

thesis statement   See Unit Seven; however, in an essay, this statement must encompass all points of view in the essay.

introduction   The purpose of an introduction is to create interest, provide necessary background information, set the mood, or provide the focus for the reader. The introductory paragraph or paragraphs usually conclude with the thesis statement.

conclusion to an expository essay   See Unit Five; however, for a multi-paragraph composition, the conclusion may be one or more sentences that encompass the whole theme of the essay. If the writer uses one sentence to conclude, it should be attached to the last paragraph. If the writer uses more than one sentence, then this portion would be placed in a separate concluding paragraph. This sentence or sentences should be interchangeable with the thesis statement.

Roman numerals   See Unit Two.

NOTES

UNIT ONE
1 "Rediscovering the City," Royal Bank Letter, June 1979, vol. 60, no. 6.

UNIT TWO
1 "Mysteries of Motivation," Royal Bank Letter, January 1980, vol. 61, no. 1.
2 "Writing a Report," Royal Bank Letter, February 1976, vol. 57, no. 2.
3 "On Criticism," Royal Bank of Canada Letter, November 1976, vol. 57, no. 11.
4 Ibid.
5 "On Reading Profitably," Royal Bank of Canada Letter, September 1977, vol. 58, no. 9.
6 "God Bless Americans," Royal Bank of Canada Letter, August 1979, vol. 60, no. 8.
7 "On Straight Thinking," Royal Bank of Canada Letter, March 1976, vol. 57, no. 3.
8 Nila Banton Smith, Be a Better Reader, Book 4 (Englewood Cliffs, N.J.: Prentice Hall, 1971).
9 "When You Are on Your Own," Royal Bank of Canada Letter, April 1977, vol. 58, no. 4.
10 "To Become a Manager," Royal Bank of Canada Letter, January 1971, vol. 52, no. 1.
11 "What Use History," Royal Bank of Canada Letter, March 1977, vol. 58, no. 3.
12 Ibid.
13 "The March of Standards," Royal Bank of Canada Letter, February 1980, vol. 61, no. 2.
14 "The State of Courtesy," Royal Bank of Canada Letter, March/April 1981, vol. 62, no. 2.
15 "The Urge to Collect," Royal Bank of Canada Letter, May 1980, vol. 61, no. 5.
16 Ibid.
17 "Doing Your Own Thing," Royal Bank of Canada Letter, May 1980, vol. 61, no. 5.
18 "The Practical Writer," Royal Bank of Canada Letter, January/February 1981, vol. 62, no. 1.
19 "Mysteries of Motivation."
20 "About Building Morale," Royal Bank of Canada Letter, July 1977, vol. 58, no. 7.
21 "Mysteries of Motivation."
22 "The State of Courtesy."
23 "The Search for Happiness," Royal Bank of Canada Letter, December 1976, vol. 57, no. 12.
24 "On Straight Thinking."
25 Adapted from "On Straight Thinking."
26 "Writing a Report," Royal Bank of Canada Letter, February 1976, vol. 57, no. 2.
27 "The March of Standards."
28 "The Practical Writer."
29 "On Reading Profitably."
30 "The State of Courtesy."
31 "The Road to Safe Driving."
32 "Canada in the Air," Royal Bank of Canada Letter, March 1980, vol. 61. no. 3.
33 "Dealing with Danger," Royal Bank of Canada Letter, July 1980, vol. 61, no. 3.
34 "The Urge to Collect."
35 "Writing a Report."
36 "Let's Preserve Family Life," Royal Bank of Canada Letter, October 1977, vol. 58, no. 10.
37 "The Practical Writer."
38 "The Urge to Collect."
39 "The Practical Writer."
40 "E-mail not replacing letters yet," Associated Press, November 10, 1998.
41 "Anne Frank hiding place restored for documentary," Toronto Star, February 19, 1993.
42 "Coke set to tap into bottled water," Guardian, November 10, 1998.
43 Irwin G. Sarason and Barbara R. Sarason, Abnormal Psychology, 9th ed. (Englewood Cliffs, N.J.: Prentice Hall).
44 F.A. Starke et al, An Introduction to Canadian Business, 4th ed. (Toronto: Allyn & Bacon).
45 Ibid., 118.

UNIT THREE
1 Adapted from "The Urge to Collect."
2 "What Use Is Education?" Royal Bank of Canada Letter, April 1976, vol. 57, no. 4.
3 "The Practical Writer."
4 "On Reading Profitably."
5 Ibid.
6 Ibid.
7 "Mysteries of Motivation."
8 Ibid.
9 "What Use Is Education?"
10 "'Green' house will power itself and recycle waste," Chronicle Journal, Thunder Bay, Ont., February 12, 1993.
11 "Pepsi turning blue to lure markets," Reuter, April 4, 1996.
12 "On Reading Profitably."

UNIT FOUR
1 Roget's Thesaurus, Harper Paperback Edition. Copyright 1946 by Harper & Row, Inc. Reprint 1991 by HarperCollins Publishers, p. 420.
2 Ibid., 165. Reprinted by permission of the publisher.
3 Ibid., 166. Reprinted by permission of the publisher.
4 The Random House Thesaurus, First Ballantine Books Edition, 472. Reprinted by permission of the publisher.
5 "Let's Preserve Family Life."
6 Ibid.
7 "The State of Courtesy."
8 "Mysteries of Motivation."
9 "The State of Courtesy."
10 "Writing a Report."
11 "Dealing with Danger."
12 "Rediscovering the City."
13 "Doing Your Own Thing."
14 "Smart cards a tough sell in U.S., proponents concede," Associated Press, November 10, 1998.
15 "Developing nations hostile to greenhouse gas proposal," Associated Press, November 4, 1998.
16 "Group re-creates atomic bomb horror of Hiroshima," Daily Yomiuri, Tokyo, Japan, January 12, 1999.
17 William R. Aveson and John H. Kunkel, "Socialization," in Introduction to Sociology: A Canadian Focus, 6th ed., ed. James J. Teevan (Scarborough, Ont.: Prentice Hall Canada).

UNIT FIVE
1 The Random House Dictionary, Ballantine Edition. Copyright 1980, 1978 by Random House Inc., p. 736.

UNIT SIX
1 "Writing a Report."
2 Ibid.

UNIT SEVEN
1 Adapted from The Techniques of Clear Thinking, rev. ed. (New York: McGraw-Hill, 1973), and used with permission of the copyright owner.

INDEX

USING THE INTERNET AS A RESOURCE

The Internet is a valuable tool for any student because it offers easy access to so much useful information. Many research resources on the Web are reliable and pose no problem (newspaper articles, for example). However, trying to find a good Web site can sometimes be frustrating and time consuming. Almost anyone can develop a Web site and they do so for a variety of reasons. Some Web sites may have impressive-looking home pages but limited information. Others may offer a few free excerpts of textbooks or lessons for you to preview, but their main purpose is to advertise a book or course for purchase. Some may serve only as links to other Web sites, requiring extra time and patience as you search through them. Then there are the sites that contain pages of explanations but few examples and no interactive exercises or features. And, of course, you must beware of the sites with inaccurate information or random quizzes of little value. Clearly, finding the right source of information on the Internet can be a difficult.

If you want to use the Internet in connection with this text, the following information on some recommended sites and the paths to reach them should prove helpful.

FOR UNITS TWO, THREE, FOUR

News articles—for reading, summarizing, evaluating, and collaborative exercises.

> Go to **Yahoo** ➜   Scroll down to and choose
>   **Current News**

FOR UNIT THREE

Royal Bank letters—interesting topics and well-written materials for practice in previewing techniques, research reading, marking textbooks, making marginal notes, listening, and note-taking, as well as for general information.

Go to **Yahoo** ➜   Type in the Search box : **Royal Bank Letter Archives**

(The site will contain a long list of banking services available.)

Scroll down to and choose

hhtp:/www.royalbank.com/

(Options will be listed on the left side of the Web page.)

Choose **Library** ➜   then choose

Royal Bank Letter

This site contains eight or more current letters for you to choose from as well as the Archives option, which will give you access to selections from the past three years.

FOR UNITS FOUR, FIVE, SIX, SEVEN, EIGHT

Grammar, composition, writing essays—for additional explanations and exercises, refer to the following ranked sources. Included is a synopsis of what each site contains as well as comments on how well they suit the content of this text.

Go to **Yahoo** ➜   Scroll down to and choose

References

Scroll down to and choose

English Language Usage

Scroll down and choose from the following:

1. **Darling's Guide to Grammar and Writing by Dr. Charles Darling**—This Web site is by far the best for most points in grammar, punctuation, and composition writing. It offers good explanations, examples, and related interactive quizzes on most points in grammar and punctuation.

    For composition topics, scroll down to the end of this home page to the topic "Principles of Composition." This site also is the best one for additional information, examples, and exercises on the various points of writing.

2. **11 Rules of Grammar**—This Web site is limited to eleven rules, nearly all of them focused on punctuation. It also is a link to other Web sites, none of which are recommended at this time.

3. **Elements of Style by William Strunk, Jr.**—This Web site contains a lot of information about grammar and writing but no interactive quizzes.

Many, many other sites are listed in this particular directory, but only the ones listed above effectively relate to this text at this time.